A Dictionary of
Ships of the
Royal Navy
of the
Second World War

John Young

A Dictionary of
Ships of the
Royal Navy
of the
Second World War

Patrick Stephens, Cambridge **PSL**

First published in 1975

ISBN 0 85059 185 6

Text set in Helvetica Medium by
Blackfriars Press Limited, Leicester,
and printed by The Garden City Press,
Letchworth, on 80 gsm Antique Wove.
Illustrations printed by Stevenage
Printing Limited, Stevenage. Bound by
Hunter & Foulis Limited, Edinburgh.
Published by Patrick Stephens
Limited, Bar Hill, Cambridge,
CB3 8EL.

Preface

Between September 3, 1939 and August 15, 1945, several thousand vessels served in the Royal Navy. This book provides an easy reference guide for anyone who wishes to know something of those ships and what happened to them when their World War 2 service life was over. To keep the layout simple, the details are necessarily very brief. The book covers those warships built, or specifically bought, for the Royal Navy. It also contains regular warships leased to, or otherwise acquired by, the Royal Navy, but it does not include a host of merchant ships of all sizes temporarily requisitioned for the duration of hostilities. They all performed useful service and many fought gallantly in famous actions, but it would have been wrong to include some, and not all, of them. To have done the latter would have doubled the size of the book.

Warships ordered and launched during the war but not completed until after August 15, 1945 have also been omitted. However, included are those warships ordered and built as part of a Royal Navy class, but which were transferred on completion or commissioning into a Commonwealth or foreign navy for the duration of the war or longer.

It should be remembered that a warship's armament and displacement often varies considerably during her life. The high speed of her trials is probably never attained in service, while her complement may well expand to man new equipment or to administer a fleet or squadron. Even her basic dimensions may be altered by radical reconstruction. It is therefore quite easy for different details and statistics to be quoted by different official records.

My sincere thanks are extended to a great many people and organisations who so kindly answered my enquiries. Without the particular help of Craig J. M. Carter (Editor of the magazine *Sea Breezes),* Lloyd's Register of Shipping and the Naval Historical Branch of the Ministry of Defence, there would have been many gaps in this record. And I should also like to extend my thanks to Martin Brice for his work on the final manuscript.

However, the fate of some of these ships remains a mystery and I shall be only too grateful to hear from readers who can throw light on any unanswered questions.

JOHN YOUNG
Liverpool, March 1975

Contents

Illustrations

All the pictures in this book have been supplied by Wright & Logan, Albert Road Junction, Southsea, Portsmouth, PO5 2SE, England.

Bibliography

British Fleet and Escort Destroyers, Vols I-II by H. T. Lenton (Macdonald)

British Submarines by H. T. Lenton (Macdonald)

Chronology of the War at Sea, Vols I-II by J. Rohwer and G. Hummelchen (Ian Allan)

Empire Ships of World War II by W. H. Mitchell and L. A. Sawyer (David & Charles)

Janes Fighting Ships (various editions)

Journal of Commerce (various editions)

Lloyd's Register of Shipping (various issues)

Marine News (World Ship Society publication)

Oceans, Forts and Parks by W. H. Mitchell and L. A. Sawyer (David & Charles)

Ships of the Royal Navy, Vols I-II by J. J. Colledge (David & Charles)

Sea Breezes Magazine (Journal of Commerce)

Fleet list

Ships are arranged under type
and class.

Battleships and Battlecruisers

HOOD CLASS BATTLECRUISER
Hood

KING GEORGE V CLASS BATTLESHIPS
Anson
Duke of York
Howe
King George V
Prince of Wales

NELSON CLASS BATTLESHIPS
Nelson
Rodney

QUEEN ELIZABETH CLASS BATTLESHIPS
Barham
Malaya
Queen Elizabeth
Valiant
Warspite

REPULSE CLASS BATTLECRUISERS
Renown
Repulse

ROYAL SOVEREIGN CLASS BATTLESHIPS
Ramillies
Resolution
Revenge
Royal Oak
Royal Sovereign

Aircraft Carriers

ARCHER CLASS
Archer
Avenger
Biter
Dasher

ATTACKER CLASS
Attacker
Battler
Chaser
Fencer
Hunter
Pursuer

Stalker
Striker

COLOSSUS CLASS
Colossus
Glory
Ocean
Venerable
Vengeance

COURAGEOUS CLASS
Courageous
Glorious

ILLUSTRIOUS CLASS
Formidable
Illustrious
Indomitable
Victorious

IMPLACABLE CLASS
Implacable
Indefatigable

SMITER CLASS
Ameer
Arbiter
Atheling
Begum
Emperor
Empress
Khedive
Nabob
Patroller
Premier
Puncher
Queen
Rajah
Ranee
Ravager
Reaper
Ruler
Searcher
Shah
Slinger
Smiter
Speaker
Thane
Tracker
Trouncer
Trumpeter

OTHER AIRCRAFT CARRIERS
Activity
Argus
Ark Royal
Audacity
Campania
Eagle
Furious
Hermes
Nairana
Pretoria Castle
Vindex

Aircraft Maintenance Ships
Perseus
Pioneer
Unicorn

Cruisers

ARETHUSA CLASS
Arethusa
Aurora
Galatea
Penelope

CALEDON CLASS
Caledon
Calypso
Caradoc

CARLISLE CLASS
Cairo
Calcutta
Capetown
Carlisle
Colombo

CERES CLASS
Cardiff
Ceres
Coventry
Curacoa
Curlew

D CLASS
Danae
Dauntless
Delhi
Despatch
Diomede

Dragon
Dunedin
Durban

DIDO CLASS
Argonaut
Bonaventure
Charybdis
Cleopatra
Dido
Euryalus
Hermione
Naiad
Phoebe
Scylla
Sirius

IMPROVED DIDO CLASS
Bellona
Black Prince
Diadem
Royalist
Spartan

E CLASS
Emerald
Enterprise

FIJI CLASS
Bermuda
Fiji
Gambia
Jamaica
Kenya
Mauritius
Nigeria
Trinidad

HAWKINS CLASS
Effingham
Frobisher
Hawkins

KENT CLASS
Berwick
Cornwall
Cumberland
Kent
Suffolk

LEANDER CLASS
Achilles
Ajax
Leander

Neptune
Orion

LONDON CLASS
Devonshire
London
Shropshire
Sussex

NORFOLK CLASS
Dorsetshire
Norfolk

SOUTHAMPTON CLASS
Birmingham
Glasgow
Gloucester
Liverpool
Manchester
Newcastle
Sheffield
Southampton

IMPROVED SOUTHAMPTON CLASS
Belfast
Edinburgh

SWIFTSURE CLASS
Superb
Swiftsure

UGANDA CLASS
Ceylon
Newfoundland
Uganda

OTHER CRUISERS
Exeter
York

Destroyers
A TYPE
Amazon
Ambuscade

A CLASS
Acasta
Achates
Acheron
Active
Antelope
Anthony
Ardent

Arrow
Codrington

BATTLE CLASS
Armada
Barfleur
Camperdown
Hogue
Trafalgar

B CLASS
Basilisk
Beagle
Blanche
Boadicea
Boreas
Brazen
Brilliant
Bulldog
Keith

Ca CLASS
Caesar
Cambrian
Caprice
Carron
Carysfort
Cassandra
Cavalier
Cavendish

Co CLASS
Comet

D CLASS
Dainty
Daring
Decoy
Defender
Delight
Diamond
Diana
Duchess
Duncan

E CLASS
Echo
Eclipse
Electra
Encounter
Escapade
Escort
Esk
Exmouth
Express

F CLASS
Fame
Faulknor
Fearless
Firedrake
Foresight
Forester
Fortune
Foxhound
Fury

G CLASS
Gallant
Garland
Gipsy
Glowworm
Grafton
Grenade
Grenville
Greyhound
Griffin

H CLASS
Hardy
Hasty
Havock
Hereward
Hero
Hostile
Hotspur
Hunter
Hyperion

HAVANT CLASS
(Building in UK for
Brazil, taken over by
RN)
Harvester
Havant
Havelock
Hesperus
Highlander
Hurricane

HUNT CLASS —
ATHERSTONE TYPE
Atherstone
Berkeley
Cattistock
Cleveland
Cotswold
Cottesmore
Eglinton

Exmoor
Fernie
Garth
Hambledon
Holderness
Mendip
Meynell
Pytchley
Quantock
Quorn
Southdown
Tynedale
Whaddon

HUNT CLASS —
BLANKNEY TYPE
Avon Vale
Badsworth
Beaufort
Bedale
Bicester
Blackmore
Blankney
Blencathra
Bramham
Brocklesby
Calpe
Chiddingfold
Cowdray
Croome
Dulverton
Eridge
Exmoor
Farndale
Grove
Heythrop
Hursley
Hurworth
Lamerton
Lauderdale
Ledbury
Liddesdale
Middleton
Oakley (1)
Oakley (2)
Puckeridge
Silverton
Southwold
Tetcott
Wheatland
Wilton

Zetland

HUNT CLASS —
ALBRIGHTON TYPE
Airedale
Albrighton
Aldenham
Belvoir
Blean
Bleasdale
Bolebroke
Border
Catterick
Derwent
Easton
Eggesford
Eskdale
Glaisdale
Goathland
Haldon
Hatherleigh
Haydon
Holcombe
Limbourne
Melbreak
Modbury
Penylan
Rockwood
Stevenstone
Talybont
Tanatside
Wensleydale

HUNT CLASS —
BRECON TYPE
Brecon
Brissenden

I CLASS
Icarus
Ilex
Imogen
Imperial
Impulsive
Inglefield
Intrepid
Isis
Ivanhoe
Building for Turkey —
taken over by RN
Inconstant
Ithuriel

J CLASS
Jackal
Jaguar
Janus
Javelin
Jersey
Jervis
Juno
Jupiter

K CLASS
Kandahar
Kashmir
Kelly
Kelvin
Khartoum
Kimberley
Kingston
Kipling

L CLASS
Gurkha
Laforey
Lance
Legion
Lightning
Lively
Lookout
Loyal

M CLASS
Mahratta
Marne
Martin
Matchless
Meteor
Milne
Musketeer
Myrmidon

N CLASS
Napier
Nepal
Nerissa
Nestor
Nizam
Noble
Nonpareil
Norman

O CLASS
Obdurate
Obedient
Offa

Onslaught
Onslow
Opportune
Oribi
Orwell

P CLASS
Pakenham
Paladin
Panther
Partridge
Pathfinder
Penn
Petard
Porcupine

Q CLASS
Quadrant
Quail
Quality
Queenborough
Quentin
Quiberon
Quickmatch
Quilliam

ADMIRALTY R CLASS
Skate

R CLASS
Racehorse
Raider
Rapid
Redoubt
Relentless
Rocket
Roebuck
Rotherham

ADMIRALTY S CLASS
Sabre
Saladin
Sardonyx
Scimitar
Scout
Shikari
Stronghold
Sturdy
Tenedos
Thanet
Thracian

S CLASS
Saumarez
Savage

Scorpion
Scourge
Serapis
Shark
Success
Swift

SCOTT CLASS
Bruce
Campbell
Douglas
Mackay
Malcolm
Montrose

SHAKESPEARE
CLASS
Broke
Keppel
Wallace

TOWN CLASS
Annapolis
Bath
Belmont
Beverley
Bradford
Brighton
Broadwater
Broadway
Burnham
Burwell
Buxton
Caldwell
Cameron
Campbeltown
Castleton
Charlestown
Chelsea
Chesterfield
Churchill
Clare
Columbia
Georgetown
Hamilton
Lancaster
Leamington
Leeds
Lewes
Lincoln
Ludlow
Mansfield
Montgomery

Newark
Newmarket
Newport
Niagara
Ramsey
Reading
Richmond
Ripley
Rockingham
Roxburgh
St Albans
St Clair
St Croix
St Francis
St Mary's
Salisbury
Sherwood
Stanley
Wells

TRIBAL CLASS
Afridi
Ashanti
Bedouin
Cossack
Eskimo
Gurkha
Maori
Mashona
Matabele
Mohawk
Nubian
Punjabi
Sikh
Somali
Tartar
Zulu

T CLASS
Teazer
Tenacious
Termagant
Terpsichore
Troubridge
Tumult
Tuscan
Tyrian

U CLASS
Grenville
Ulster
Ulysses
Undaunted

Undine
Urania
Urchin
Ursa

ADMIRALTY V CLASS
Valentine
Valorous
Vanessa
Vanity
Vanoc
Vanquisher
Vega
Velox
Venetia
Verdun
Versatile
Vesper
Vidette
Vimiera
Vimy
Vivacious
Vivien
Vortigern

THORNYCROFT V CLASS
Viceroy
Viscount

V CLASS
Hardy
Valentine
Venus
Verulam
Vigilant
Virago
Vixen
Volage

ADMIRALTY W CLASS
Wakeful
Walker
Walpole
Warwick
Watchman
Wessex
Westcott
Westminster
Whirlwind
Whitley
Winchelsea
Winchester
Windsor

Wolfhound
Wrestler
Wryneck

THORNYCROFT W CLASS
Wolsey
Woolston

ADMIRALTY MODIFIED W CLASS
Vansittart
Venomous
Verity
Veteran
Volunteer
Wanderer
Whitehall
Whitshed
Wild Swan
Witherington
Wivern
Wolverine
Worcester
Wren

THORNYCROFT MODIFIED W CLASS
Wishart
Witch

W CLASS
Kempenfelt
Wager
Wakeful
Wessex
Whelp
Whirlwind
Wizard
Wrangler

Z CLASS
Myngs
Zambesi
Zealous
Zebra
Zenith
Zephyr
Zest
Zodiac

Submarines
A CLASS
Amphion

Astute

H CLASS
H-28
H-31
H-32
H-33
H-34
H-43
H-44
H-49
H-50

L CLASS
L-23
L-26
L-27

O CLASS
Oberon
Odin
Olympus
Orpheus
Osiris
Oswald
Otus
Otway
Oxley

P CLASS
Pandora
Parthian
Perseus
Phoenix
Proteus

PORPOISE CLASS
Cachalot
Grampus
Narwhal
Porpoise
Rorqual
Seal

EX-UNITED STATES NAVY R CLASS
P-511
P-512
P-514

R CLASS
Rainbow
Regent
Regulus
Rover

RIVER CLASS
Clyde
Severn
Thames

EX-UNITED STATES NAVY S CLASS
P-551
P-552
P-553
P-554
P-555
P-556

S CLASS
P-222
Safari
Saga
Sahib
Salmon
Sanguine
Saracen
Satyr
Sceptre
Scorcher
Scotsman
Scythian
Sea Devil
Seadog
Seahorse
Sealion
Sea Nymph
Sea Rover
Sea Scout
Seawolf
Selene
Seraph
Shakespeare
Shalimar
Shark
Sibyl
Sickle
Sidon
Simoon
Sirdar
Sleuth
Snapper
Solent
Spark
Spearfish
Spearhead
Spirit

Spiteful
Splendid
Sportsman
Springer
Spur
Starfish
Statesman
Sterlet
Stoic
Stonehenge
Storm
Stratagem
Strongbow
Stubborn
Sturdy
Sturgeon
Stygian
Subtle
Sunfish
Supreme
Surf
Swordfish
Syrtis

T CLASS
P-311
Taciturn
Tactician
Taku
Talent (1)
Talent (2)
Talisman
Tally-Ho
Tantalus
Tantivy
Tapir
Tarn
Tarpon
Taurus
Telemachus
Tempest
Templar
Terrapin
Tetrarch
Thistle
Thorn
Thorough
Thrasher
Thule
Thunderbolt
Tigris

Tiptoe
Tireless
Token
Torbay
Totem
Tradewind
Traveller
Trenchant
Trespasser
Triad
Tribune
Trident
Triton
Triumph
Trooper
Truant
Truculent
Trump
Truncheon
Trusty
Tudor
Tuna
Turbulent
Turpin

U CLASS
P-32
P-33
P-36
P-38
P-39
P-47
P-48
P-52
Ultimatum
Ultor
Umbra
Umpire
Una
Unbeaten
Unbending
Unbroken
Undaunted
Undine
Union
Unique
Unison
United
Unity
Universal
Unrivalled

Unruffled
Unruly
Unseen
Unshaken
Unsparing
Unswerving
Untamed
Untiring
Upholder
Upright
Uproar
Upstart
Urchin
Uredd
Urge
Ursula
Usk
Usurper
Uther
Utmost
Vandal
Varangian
Varne
Vox

V CLASS
Upshot
Urtica
Vagabond
Vampire
Variance
Varne
Veldt
Vengeful
Venturer
Vigorous
Viking
Vineyard
Virtue
Virulent
Visigoth
Vivid
Volatile
Voracious
Vortex
Votary
Vox
Vulpine

BUILDING IN UK FOR
TURKEY — TAKEN

OVER BY RN
P-611
P-612
P-614
P-615

CAPTURED GERMAN
SUBMARINE
Graph

CAPTURED ITALIAN
SUBMARINES
P-711
P-712
P-714

Escorts

ABERDEEN CLASS
SLOOPS
Aberdeen
Fleetwood

BAY CLASS
FRIGATES
Bigbury Bay
Cardigan Bay
St Austell Bay
St Brides Bay
Veryan Bay
Whitesand Bay
Widemouth Bay

BITTERN CLASS
SLOOPS
Bittern
Enchantress
Stork

BLACK SWAN CLASS
SLOOPS
Black Swan
Erne
Flamingo
Ibis
Whimbrel
Wild Goose
Woodcock
Woodpecker
Wren

MODIFIED BLACK
SWAN CLASS
SLOOPS
Alacrity
Amethyst

Chanticleer
Crane
Cygnet
Hart
Hind
Kite
Lapwing
Lark
Magpie
Mermaid
Opossum
Peacock
Pheasant
Redpole
Starling

BRIDGEWATER
CLASS SLOOPS
Bridgewater
Sandwich

CAPTAIN CLASS
FRIGATES
Ex-USN Evarts class
Bayntun
Bazely
Berry
Blackwood
Burges
Capel
Cooke
Dacres
Domett
Drury
Foley
Gardiner
Garlies
Goodall
Goodson
Gore
Gould
Grindall
Hoste
Inglis
Inman
Keats
Kempthorne
Kingsmill
Lawford
Lawson
Loring
Louis

Manners
Moorsom
Mounsey
Pasley
Ex-USN Buckley class
Affleck
Aylmer
Balfour
Bentinck
Bentley
Bickerton
Bligh
Braithwaite
Bullen
Byard
Byron
Calder
Conn
Cosby
Cotton
Cranstoun
Cubitt
Curzon
Dakins
Deane
Duckworth
Duff
Ekins
Essington
Fitzroy
Halsted
Hargood
Holmes
Hotham
Narborough
Redmill
Retalick
Riou
Rowley
Rupert
Rutherford
Seymour
Spragge
Stayner
Stockham
Thornbrough
Torrington
Trollope
Tyler
Waldegrave
Whitaker

CASTLE CLASS
CORVETTES
Allington Castle
Alnwick Castle
Amberley Castle
Bamborough Castle
Berkeley Castle
Caistor Castle
Carisbrooke Castle
Denbigh Castle
Dumbarton Castle
Farnham Castle
Flint Castle
Hadleigh Castle
Hedingham Castle
Hurst Castle
Kenilworth Castle
Knaresborough Castle
Lancaster Castle
Launceston Castle
Leeds Castle
Morpeth Castle
Oakham Castle
Oxford Castle
Pevensey Castle
Portchester Castle
Rushen Castle
Shrewsbury Castle
Tintagel Castle

COLONY CLASS
FRIGATES
Anguilla
Antigua
Ascension
Bahamas
Barbados
Caicos
Cayman
Dominica
Labuan
Montserrat
Nyasaland
Papua
Perim
Pitcairn
St Helena
Sarawak
Seychelles
Somaliland
Tobago

Tortola
Zanzibar
FALMOUTH CLASS
SLOOPS
Dundee
Falmouth
Milford
Weston
FLOWER CLASS
SLOOPS
Cornflower
Foxglove
Laburnum
Lupin
Rosemary
FLOWER CLASS
CORVETTES
Abelia
Acanthus
Aconite
Alisma
Alyssum
Amaranthus
Anchusa
Anemone
Arabis
Arbutus
Armeria
Arrowhead
Asphodel
Aster
Aubrietia
Auricula
Azalea
Balsam
Begonia
Bellwort
Bergamot
Bittersweet
Bluebell
Borage
Bryony
Burdock
Buttercup
Calendula
Camellia
Campanula
Campion
Candytuft
Carnation

Celandine
Chrysanthemum
Clarkia
Clematis
Clover
Coltsfoot
Columbine
Convolvulus
Coreopsis
Coriander
Cowslip
Crocus
Cyclamen
Dahlia
Delphinium
Dianella
Dianthus
Eglantine
Erica
Eyebright
Fennel
Fleur de Lys
Freesia
Fritillary
Gardenia
Genista
Gentian
Geranium
Gladiolus
Gloxinia
Godetia (1)
Godetia (2)
Heartsease
Heather
Heliotrope
Hepatica
Hibiscus
Hollyhock
Honeysuckle
Hyacinth
Hyderabad
Hydrangea
Jasmine
Jonquil
Kingcup
La Malouine
Larkspur
Lavender
Lobelia
Loosestrife
Lotus (1)

Lotus (2)
Mallow
Marguerite
Marigold
Mayflower
Meadowsweet
Mignonette
Mimosa
Monkshood
Montbretia
Myosotis
Narcissus
Nasturtium
Nigella
Orchis
Oxlip
Pennywort
Pentstemon
Peony
Periwinkle
Petunia
Picotee
Pimpernel
Pink
Polyanthus
Poppy
Potentilla
Primrose
Primula
Ranunculus
Rhododendron
Rockrose
Rose
Salvia
Samphire
Saxifrage
Snapdragon
Snowberry
Snowdrop
Snowflake
Spikenard
Spiraea
Starwort
Stonecrop
Sundew
Sunflower
Sweetbriar
Tamarisk
Thyme
Trillium
Tulip

Verbena
Veronica
Vervain
Vetch
Violet
Wallflower
Windflower
Woodruff
Zinnia

MODIFIED FLOWER
CLASS CORVETTES
Arabis
Arbutus
Betony
Buddleia
Bugloss
Bulrush
Burnet
Candytuft
Ceanothus
Charlock
Comfrey
Cornel
Dittany
Flax
Honesty
Linaria
Mandrake
Milfoil
Musk
Nepeta
Privet
Rosebay
Smilax
Statice
Willowherb

GRIMSBY CLASS
SLOOPS
Deptford
Grimsby
Leith
Londonderry
Lowestoft
Wellington

GUILLEMOT CLASS
SLOOPS
Guillemot
Pintail
Shearwater

HASTINGS CLASS
SLOOPS
Folkestone
Hastings
Penzance
Scarborough

KIL CLASS ESCORTS
Kilbirnie
Kilbride
Kilchattan
Kilchrenan
Kildary
Kildwick
Kilham
Kilkenzie
Kilkhampton
Kilmalcolm
Kilmarnock
Kilmartin
Kilmelford
Kilmington
Kilmore

KINGFISHER CLASS
SLOOPS
Kingfisher
Kittiwake
Mallard
Puffin
Sheldrake
Widgeon

LOCH CLASS
FRIGATES
Loch Achanalt
Loch Achray
Loch Alvie
Loch Ard
Loch Arkaig
Loch Boisdale
Loch Craggie
Loch Cree
Loch Dunvegan
Loch Eck
Loch Fada
Loch Fyne
Loch Glendhu
Loch Gorm
Loch Insh
Loch Katrine
Loch Killin
Loch Killisport

Loch Lomond
Loch More
Loch Morlich
Loch Quoich
Loch Ruthven
Loch Scavaig
Loch Shin
Loch Tarbert
Loch Tralaig

LULWORTH CLASS
ESCORTS
Banff
Culver
Fishguard
Gorleston
Hartland
Landguard
Lulworth
Sennen
Totland
Walney

PC CLASS SLOOP
PC-74

PELICAN CLASS
SLOOPS
Auckland
Egret
Pelican

RIVER CLASS
FRIGATES
Aire
Annan
Avon
Awe
Ballinderry
Bann
Barle
Braid
Cam
Chelmer
Cuckmere
Dart
Derg
Deveron
Dovey
Ettrick
Evenlode
Exe
Fal

Findhorn
Frome
Halladale
Helford
Helmsdale
Inver
Itchen
Jed
Kale
Lagan
Lochy
Lossie
Meon
Monnow
Mourne
Moyola
Nadder
Nene
Ness
Nith
Odzani
Parret
Plym
Ribble (1)
Ribble (2)
Rother
Shiel
Spey
Strule
Swale
Taff
Tavy
Tay
Tees
Teme
Test
Teviot
Torridge
Towy
Trent
Tweed
Usk
Waveney
Wear
Windrush
Wye

SHOREHAM CLASS
SLOOPS
Bideford
Fowey

Rochester
Shoreham

24 CLASS SLOOP
Herald

Minesweepers

ALGERINE CLASS
Acute
Alarm
Albacore
Algerine
Antares
Arcturus
Aries
Bramble
Brave
Cadmus
Chameleon
Cheerful
Circe
Clinton
Cockatrice
Coquette
Courier
Espiegle
Fancy
Fantome
Felicity
Fly
Flying Fish
Friendship
Golden Fleece
Gozo
Hare
Hound
Hydra
Jaseur
Jewel
Laertes
Larne
Lennox
Liberty
Lightfoot
Lioness
Loyalty
Lysander
Maenad
Magicienne
Mameluke
Mandate

Mariner
Marmion
Marvel
Mary Rose
Melita
Michael
Minstrel
Moon
Mutine
Myrmidon
Mystic
Octavia
Onyx
Orcadia
Orestes
Pelorus
Persian
Pickle
Pincher
Plucky
Pluto
Postillion
Prompt
Providence
Rattlesnake
Ready
Recruit
Regulus
Rifleman
Rinaldo
Romola
Rosario
Rowena
Seabear
Serene
Skipjack
Spanker
Squirrel
Stormcloud
Sylvia
Tanganyika
Thisbe
Truelove
Vestal
Waterwitch
Wave
Welcome
Welfare

BANGOR CLASS
Ardrossan

Bangor
Bayfield
Beaumaris
Blackpool
Blyth
Bootle
Boston
Bridlington
Bridport
Brixham
Bude
Canso
Caraquet
Clacton
Clydebank
Cromarty
Cromer
Dornoch
Dunbar
Eastbourne
Felixstowe
Fort York
Fraserburgh
Greenock
Guysborough
Hartlepool
Harwich
Hythe
Ilfracombe
Ingonish
Llandudno
Lyme Regis (1)
Lyme Regis (2)
Middlesbrough
Newhaven
Padstow
Parrsborough
Peterhead
Polruan
Poole
Qualicum
Rhyl
Romney
Rothesay
Rye
Seaham
Shippigan
Sidmouth
Stornoway
Tadoussac
Tenby

Tilbury
Wedgeport
Whitehaven
Worthing

CATHERINE CLASS
Catherine
Cato
Chamois
Chance
Combatant
Cynthia
Elfreda
Fairy
Florizel
Foam
Frolic
Gazelle
Gorgon
Grecian
Jasper
Magic
Pique
Pylades
Steadfast
Strenuous
Tattoo
Tourmaline

HALCYON CLASS
Bramble
Britomart
Franklin
Gleaner
Gossamer
Halcyon
Harrier
Hazard
Hebe
Hussar
Jason
Leda
Niger
Salamander
Scott
Seagull
Sharpshooter
Skipjack
Speedwell
Speedy
Sphinx

HUNT CLASS
Aberdare
Abingdon
Albury
Alresford
Bagshot
Derby
Dundalk
Dunoon
Elgin
Fareham
Fermoy
Fitzroy
Flinders
Harrow
Huntley
Kellett
Lydd
Pangbourne
Ross
Saltash
Saltburn
Selkirk
Stoke
Sutton
Tedworth
Widnes

MINE DESTRUCTOR VESSELS
Borde
Bushwood
Corbrae
Corburn
Corfield
Cybele
Cyrus
Queenworth
Springdale
Springtide

Monitors

ABERCROMBIE CLASS
Abercrombie
Roberts

EREBUS CLASS
Erebus
Terror

Minelayers

MANXMAN CLASS
Abdiel
Apollo
Ariadne
Latona
Manxman
Welshman

OTHER MINELAYERS
Adventure

BIRD CLASS
CONTROLLED
MINELAYERS
Blackbird
Corncrake
Dabchick
Redshank
Stonechat
Whitethroat

LINNET CLASS
COASTAL
MINELAYERS
Linnet
Redstart
Ringdove

OTHER COASTAL
MINELAYERS
Medusa
Melpomene
Miner I
Miner II
Miner III
Miner IV
Miner V
Miner VI
Miner VII
Miner VIII
Minerva
Plover

River Gunboats

INSECT CLASS
Aphis
Cicala
Cockchafer
Cricket
Gnat
Ladybird
Mantis

Moth
Scarab
Tarantula

LOCUST CLASS
Dragonfly
Grasshopper
Locust
Mosquito

PETEREL CLASS
Gannet
Peterel

TERN CLASS
Seamew
Tern

OTHER RIVER
GUNBOATS
Falcon
Robin
Sandpiper
Scorpion

Landing Ships

LANDING SHIPS
DOCK (LSD)
Eastway
Highway
Northway
Oceanway

LANDING SHIPS,
GANTRY
Derwentdale
Dewdale
Ennerdale

EMPIRE CLASS
LANDING SHIPS,
INFANTRY
Cicero
Donovan
Empire Broadsword
Empire Javelin
Empire Rapier
Empire Spearhead
Galtee More
Rocksand
Sainfoin
Sansovino
Sefton
Silvio
Sir Hugo

LANDING SHIP,
INFANTRY
Lamont

LANDING SHIPS,
TANK (LST)
LST 3001
LST 3006
LST 3007
LST 3008
LST 3009
LST 3010
LST 3011
LST 3012
LST 3014
LST 3016
LST 3017
LST 3019
LST 3020
LST 3021
LST 3022
LST 3024
LST 3025
LST 3026
LST 3028
LST 3031
LST 3033
LST 3035
LST 3036
LST 3037
LST 3038
LST 3041
LST 3043
LST 3501
LST 3502
LST 3503
LST 3504
LST 3506
LST 3507
LST 3508
LST 3512
LST 3514
LST 3515
LST 3516

Trawlers

AXE CLASS
Dee
Garry
Kennet
Liffey

BASSET CLASS
Basset
Mastiff

BERBERIS CLASS
Alder
Beech
Berberis
Cedar
Cypress
Hawthorn
Holly
Hornbeam
Larch
Laurel
Lilac
Magnolia
Maple
Myrtle
Oak
Redwood
Sycamore
Syringa
Willow

DANCE CLASS
Cotillion
Coverley
Fandango
Foxtrot
Gavotte
Hornpipe
Mazurka
Minuet
Morris Dance
Pirouette
Polka
Quadrille
Rumba
Saltarelo
Sarabande
Sword Dance
Tango
Tarantella
Valse
Veleta

FISH CLASS
Bonito
Bream
Grayling
Grilse
Herring

Mullet
Pollack
Whiting

GEM CLASS
Agate
Amber
Amethyst
Beryl
Coral
Cornelian
Jade
Jasper
Moonstone
Pearl
Ruby
Sapphire
Topaze
Tourmaline
Turquoise

HILLS CLASS
Birdlip
Bredon
Butser
Duncton
Dunkery
Inkpen
Portsdown
Yes Tor

ISLES CLASS
Ailsa Craig
Annet
Anticosti
Arran
Baffin
Balta
Bardsey
Benbecula
Bern
Biggal
Bressay
Brora
Bruray
Bryher
Burra
Bute
Cailiff
Caldy
Calvay
Campobello
Canna

Cava
Coll
Colsay
Copinsay
Crowlin
Cumbrae
Damsay
Dochet
Earraid
Eday
Egilsay
Ensay
Eriskay
Fara
Farne
Fetlar
Fiaray
Filla
Flatholm
Flint
Flotta
Foula
Foulness
Fuday
Gairsay
Ganilly
Gateshead
Gillstone
Gorregan
Graemsay
Grain
Grassholm
Gruinard
Gulland
Gweal
Hannaray
Harris
Hascosay
Hayling
Hellisay
Hermetray
Herschell
Hildasay
Hoxa
Hoy
Hunda
Imersay
Inchcolm
Inchkeith
Inchmarnock
Ironbound

Islay
Jura
Kerrera
Killegray
Kintyre
Kittern
Lindisfarne
Lingay
Liscomb
Longa
Lundy
Magdalen
Manitoulin
Mewstone
Minalto
Mincarlo
Miscou
Mousa
Mull
Neave
Orfasy
Oronsay
Orsay
Oxna
Pladda
Porcher
Prospect
Ronaldsay
Ronay
Rosevean
Rousay
Ruskholm
Rysa
St Agnes
St Kilda
Sanda
Sandray
Scalpay
Scaravay
Scarba
Shapinsay
Sheppey
Shiant
Shillay
Skokholm
Skomer
Skye
Sluna
Staffa
Steepholm
Stroma

Stronsay
Sursay
Switha
Tahay
Texada
Tiree
Tocogay
Trodday
Trondra
Ulva
Unst
Vaceasay
Vallay
Vatersay
Wallasea
Westray
Whalsay
Wiay

LAKE CLASS
Buttermere
Ellesmere
Thirlmere
Ullswater
Wastwater
Windermere

MERSEY CLASS
Blackwater
Boyne
Cherwell
Colne
Doon
Eden
Excellent
Foyle
James Ludford
Moy
Ouse
Stour

MILITARY CLASS
Bombardier
Coldstreamer
Fusilier
Grenadier
Guardsman
Home Guard
Lancer
Royal Marine
Sapper

PROFESSOR CLASS
Probe

Proctor
Prodigal
Product
Professor
Promise
Prong
Proof
Property
Prophet
Protest
Prowess

**ROUND TABLE
CLASS**
Sir Agravaine
Sir Galahad
Sir Gareth
Sir Geraint
Sir Kay
Sir Lamorack
Sir Lancelot
Sir Tristram

**SHAKESPEARIAN
CLASS**
Celia
Coriolanus
Fluellen
Hamlet
Horatio
Juliet
Laertes
Macbeth
Ophelia
Othello
Romeo
Rosalind

STRATH CLASS
Strathcoe

TREE CLASS
Acacia
Almond
Ash
Bay
Birch
Blackthorn
Chestnut
Deodar
Elm
Fir
Hazel

Hickory
Juniper
Mangrove
Olive
Pine
Rowan
Walnut
Whitethorn
Wistaria

OTHER TRAWLERS
Guava
Tamarisk

Anti-Aircraft Ships

Pozarica
Tynwald

Fighter Direction Ships

Boxer
Bruizer
Palomares
Thruster

Auxiliary & Support Ships

Aircraft Component Repair Ships

Cuillin Sound
Deer Sound
Holm Sound

Aircraft Depot & Repair Ships

Assistance
Diligence

Aircraft Transports

Athene
Engadine

Ammunition Ships

Bedenham
Kinterbury
Throsk

Armament Carriers

Chattenden
Isleford
John Evelyn

Boom Defence Vessels

BAR CLASS
Barbain
Barbarian
Barbecue
Barberry
Barbette (1)
Barbette (2)
Barbican
Barbour
Barbourne
Barbrake
Barbridge
Barbrook
Barcarole
Barcastle
Barcliff
Barclose
Barcock
Barcombe
Barcote
Barcroft
Barcross
Bardell
Bardolf
Barfair
Barfield
Barflake
Barfoam
Barfoil
Barfoot
Barford
Barfoss
Barfount
Barglow
Barhill
Barholm

Barilla
Baritone
Barking
Barkis
Barlake
Barlane
Barleycorn
Barlight
Barlow
Barmill
Barmond
Barmouth
Barnaby
Barnard
Barndale
Barneath
Barnehurst
Barnstone
Barnwell
Baron
Baronia
Barova
Barrage
Barranca
Barrhead
Barricade
Barrier
Barrington
Barrymore
Barsing
Barsound
Barspear
Barstoke
Barthorpe
Bartizan
Barwind

BAYONET CLASS
Bayonet
Bownet
Burgonet
Dragonet
Falconet
Magnet
Martinet
Planet
Plantagenet
Signet
Sonnet

PREFECT CLASS
Precept

Precise
Prefect
Pretext
Preventer

Boom Working Vessels

Barnet
Coronet
Dunnet
Fastnet
Jennet
Punnet
Quannet
Rennet

Cable Vessels

BULL CLASS
Bullfinch
Bullfrog
Bullhead
St Margarets

OTHER CABLE VESSELS
Kilmun
Lasso

Catapult Trials & Maintenance Ship

Pegasus

Depot Ships

Adamant
Alecto
Blenheim
Bonaventure
Cochrane
Cyclops
Derby Haven
Dunluce Castle
Edinburgh Castle
Forth
Greenwich
Hecla
Lucia
Maidstone
Marshal Ney
Medway
Montclare

Philoctetes
Ranpura
Sandhurst
Titania
Tyne
Vulcan
Wayland
Westernland
Wolfe
Woolwich

Gunnery Training Ships

Iron Duke
Marshal Soult

Hospital Ship

Maine

Mooring Vessels

ADMIRALTY TYPE
Moorburn
Moorcock
Mooress
Moorfield
Moorfire
Moorfly
Moorgrass
Moorgrieve
Moorhen
Moormyrtle
Moorpout
Moorsman

MOOR CLASS
Moor
Moordale
Moorfowl
Moorhill
Moorlake
Moorstone

OTHER MOORING VESSELS
Moorland

Netlayers

Guardian
Protector

Oilers

ABBEYDALE CLASS
Abbeydale
Aldersdale
Arndale
Bishopdale
Boardale
Broomdale

BELGOL CLASS
Belgol
Celerol
Fortol
Francol
Montenol
Prestol
Rapidol
Serbol
Slavol

DALE CLASS
Cairndale
Cedardale
Darkdale
Denbydale
Dingledale
Eaglesdale
Easedale
Echodale

ELMOL CLASS
Birchol
Boxol
Distol
Ebonol
Elderol
Elmol
Hickorol
Kimmerol
Larchol
Limol
Philol
Scotol
Viscol

LEAF CLASS
Appleleaf
Brambleleaf
Cherryleaf
Orangeleaf
Pearleaf
Plumleaf

RANGER CLASS
Black Ranger
Blue Ranger
Brown Ranger
Gold Ranger
Gray Ranger
Green Ranger

WAR CLASS
War Afridi
War Bahadur
War Bharata
War Brahmin
War Diwan
War Hindoo
War Krishna
War Mehtar
War Nawab
War Nizam
War Pathan
War Pindari
War Sepoy
War Sirdar
War Sudra

OTHER OILERS
British Lady
Dinsdale
Empire Salvage
Lucigen
Mixol
Olcades
Oleander
Oligarch
Olna (1)
Olna (2)
Olwen
Olynthus
Ruthenia
Scottish American
Thermol

Petrol Carriers
Airsprite
Nasprite
Petrella
Petrobus

Repair Ships
Alaunia
Albatross
Artifex

Ausonia
Beachy Head
Beauly Firth
Berry Head
Buchan Ness
Dodman Point
Dullisk Cove
Duncansby Head
Dungeness
Flamborough Head
Hartland Point
Mullion Cove
Mull of Galloway
Resource
Solway Firth
Vindictive

Royal Yacht
Victoria and Albert

Salvage Ships
KIN CLASS COASTAL
SALVAGE SHIPS
Dispenser
Help
Kinbrace
Kingarth
Kinloss
Lifeline
Succour
Swin
Uplifter
KING SALVOR CLASS
King Salvor
Ocean Salvor
Prince Salvor
Salvage Duke
Salventure
Salvestor
Salvictor
Sea Salvor

EX-USN SALVAGE
SHIPS
American Salvor
Boston Salvor
Caledonian Salvor
Cambrian Salvor
Lincoln Salvor
Southampton Salvor

OTHER SALVAGE
SHIPS
Salveda

Store Ships
Bacchus
Durham Castle
Fort Charlotte
Fort Dunvegan
Fort Rosalie
Fort Sandusky
Reliant
Robert Dundas
Robert Middleton

Survey Ships
Challenger
Endeavour

Target Ship
Centurion

Training Ship
Caledonia

Tugs
ASSURANCE CLASS
Adept
Adherent
Allegiance
Antic
Assiduous
Assurance
Charon
Dexterous
Earner
Frisky
Griper
Hengist
Horsa
Jaunty
Prosperous
Prudent
Restive
Saucy
Sesame
Stormking
Tenacity
BAT CLASS
Advantage

Aimwell
Aspirant
Athlete
Bold
Cheerly
Destiny
Eminent
Emphatic
Favourite
Flare
Flaunt
Integrity
Lariat
Masterful
Mindful
Oriana
Patroclus
Vagrant
Weazel

BRIGAND CLASS
Bandit
Brigand
Buccaneer
Freebooter
Marauder

BUSTLER CLASS
Bustler
Growler
Hesperia
Mediator
Reward
Samsonia
Turmoil
Warden

ENVOY CLASS
Enchanter
Encore
Enforcer
Enigma
Enticer
Envoy

JUSTICE CLASS
Director
Emulous
Freedom
Justice

NIMBLE CLASS
Nimble

ROLLICKER CLASS
Resolve
Respond
Retort
Rollicker
Roysterer

SAINT CLASS
St Abbs
St Blazey
St Breock
St Clears
St Cyrus
St Day
St Dogmael
St Fagan
St Issey
St Just
St Martin
St Mellons
St Monance
St Omar

Water Carriers

Petronel
Spa
Spabeck
Spabrook

FRESH CLASS
COASTAL WATER
CARRIERS
Freshbrook
Freshburn
Freshener
Freshet
Freshford
Freshlake
Freshmere
Freshpond
Freshpool
Freshtarn
Freshwater
Freshwell

Wreck Disposal Ship

Rampant

Alphabetical list

Ship's name; class (cls) and type; displacement tonnage; overall length x breadth; speed in knots; complement; main armament; builder's name, where built, year completed; year returned (rtnd) or sold, new owners/managers, new name (rnd); where and year broken up (b/up).

In the case of submarines, the displacement tonnage and the speed are for above/below the surface.

Abbeydale: Abbeydale cls oiler; 17, 210; 481½ x 62; 11½; 40; --; Swan Hunter & Wigham Richardson, Wallsend, 1937; b/up Barrow 1960.

Abdiel: Manxman cls minelayer; 4000; 418 x 39; 40; 246; 160 mines, six 4.7-in; J. S. White & Co, Cowes, 1940; mined at Taranto, Sept 9, 1943.

Abelia: Flower cls corvette; 925; 205 x 33; 16; 85; one 4-in; Harland & Wolff, Belfast, 1941; 1948 A/S Kosmos, Norway, converted to whale catcher rnd *Kraft,* rnd *Arne Skontorp* 1954; b/up Grimstad 1966.

Abercrombie: Abercrombie cls monitor; 7850; 373⅓ x 89¾; 12; 350; two 15-in; Vickers-Armstrongs, Tyne, 1943; b/up Barrow 1954.

Aberdare: Hunt cls minesweeper; 800; 231 x 28½; 16; 74; one 4-in, one 3-in; Ailsa SB Co, Troon, 1918; sold Liege shipbreakers 1947.

Aberdeen: Aberdeen cls sloop; 990; 266 x 36; 16½; 100; four 4-in; HM Dockyard, Devonport, 1936; b/up Hayle 1949.

Abingdon: Hunt cls minesweeper; 800; 231 x 28½; 16; 74; one 4-in. one 3-in; Ailsa SB Co, Troon, 1918; sunk by German aircraft at Malta, Apr 5, 1942, wreck reported b/up 1950.

Acacia: Tree cls trawler; 530; 164 x 27½; 11½; 35; one 12-pdr; Ardrossan Dockyard Ltd, Ardrossan, 1940; 1948, Scottish Home Dept as fisheries patrol ship, rnd *Vaila;* struck rocks on Iuvard Island, Lewis, Jan 6, 1957, foundered.

Acanthus: Flower cls corvette; 925; 205 x 33; 16; 85; one 4-in; Ailsa SB Co, Troon, 1941; transferred 1942 to Royal Norwegian Navy, rnd *Andenes,* returned RN 1946; 1956, Union Whaling Co, Durban, converted to whale catcher, rnd *Colin Frye;* 1957, Taiyo Gyogyo KK, Japan, rnd *Toshi Maru No 2;* b/up Japan 1971.

Acasta: A cls destroyer; 1350; 323 x 32¼; 35; 138; four 4.7-in, eight 21-in tt; John Brown & Co, Clydebank, 1930; sunk in action with German battlecruisers *Scharnhorst* and *Gneisenau* near Narvik, June 8, 1940.

Achates: A cls destroyer; 1350; 323 x 32¼; 35; 138; four 4.7-in, eight 21-in tt; John Brown & Co, Clydebank, 1930; sunk in action with German cruiser *Admiral Hipper* in Barentz Sea, Dec 31, 1942.

Acheron: A cls destroyer; 1350; 323 x 32¼; 35; 138; four 4.7-in, eight 21-in tt; J. I. Thornycroft & Co, Southampton, 1931: mined off Isle of Wight, Dec 17, 1940.

Achilles: Leander cls cruiser; 7030; 554½ x 55¼; 32½; 680; eight 6-in, four 4-in, eight 21-in tt; Cammell Laird, Birkenhead, 1933; transferred 1936 to Royal New Zealand Navy, rtnd RN 1943; 1948 Indian Navy, rnd *Delhi;*

Aconite: Flower cls corvette; 925; 205 x 33; 16; 85; one 4-in; Ailsa SB Co, Troon, 1941; transferred 1941 to French Navy, rnd *Aconit,* returned RN 1947; 1947, United Whaling Co, Durban, converted to whale catcher, rnd *Terje II;* 1960, South Georgia Co (C. Salvesen), Leith, rnd *Southern Terrier;* b/up Bruges 1967.

Active: A cls destroyer; 1350; 323 x 32¼; 35; 138; four 4.7-in, eight 21-in tt; Hawthorn Leslie, Hebburn, 1930; b/up Troon 1947.

Activity: escort carrier; 11,800; 512 x 66½; 18; 700; 15 aircraft, two 4-in; Caledon SB & E Co, Dundee, 1942; ex cargo ship *Telemachus,* (Blue Funnel Line, Liverpool), purchased by RN on stocks, rnd *Empire Activity,* then rnd *Activity;* 1946, Glen Line, London, converted to cargo liner, rnd *Breconshire;* b/up Kobe 1967.

Acute: Algerine cls minesweeper; 950; 235 x 35½; 16½; 104; one 4-in; Harland & Wolff, Belfast, 1942; ex-*Alert,* 1942; sunk off Malta as torpedo target, 1964.

Adamant: submarine depot ship; 12,500; 658 x 70½; 17; 520; eight 4.5-in; Harland & Wolff, Belfast, 1942; b/up Inverkeithing 1970.

Adept: Assurance cls tug; 1045; 157 x 35; 13; 31; one 3-in; Cochrane & Sons, Selby, 1941; wrecked on Hebrides, Mar 17, 1942.

Adherent: Assurance cls tug; 1045; 157 x 35; 13; 31; one 3-in; Cochrane & Sons, Selby, 1941; foundered North Atlantic, Jan 14, 1944.

Advantage: BAT cls tug; 783; 143 x 33; 14; 34; one 3-in; Levingston SB Co, Orange, 1943; ex USN, transferred Lease/Lend to RN 1943, rtnd USN

1946; 1946, China Merchants SN Co, Shanghai, rnd *Ming 309;* b/up 1965.

Adventure: minelayer; 7260; 520 x 59; 27¾; 400; 340 mines, four 4.7in; HM Dockyard, Devonport, 1927; 1943, refitted as repair ship; b/up Briton Ferry 1947.

Affleck: Captain cls frigate; 1400; 306 x 36¾; 23½; 220; three 3-in; Bethlehem-Hingham Shipyard, 1943; ex-USN Buckley cls destroyer-escort *Oswald, DE-71;* transferred Lease/Lend to RN 1943; damaged by torpedo from U-boat, Dec 27, 1944; towed Feb, 1949, Barrow to Antwerp; 1954, converted and in service as floating power station at Santa Cruz de Teneriffe, rnd *Nostra Senora de la Luz;*

Afridi: Tribal cls destroyer; 1870; 377 x 36½; 36½; 219; eight 4.7-in, four 21-in tt; Vickers-Armstrongs, Tyne, 1938; sunk by German aircraft off Namsos, May 3, 1940.

Agate: Gem cls trawler; 627; 157 x 26; 12; 18; one 4-in; Smith's Dock Co, Middlesbrough, 1934; ex *Mavis Rose* (Boston Deep Sea Fishing & Ice Co, Fleetwood) bought by RN 1935; wrecked off Cromer, Aug 6, 1941.

Ailsa Craig: Isles cls trawler; 560; 164 x 27½; 12; 40; one 12-pdr; Cook, Welton & Gemmell, Beverley, 1944; 1946, Skibs A/S Veas Rederi, Norway, converted to tanker, rnd *Veslemoy;* 1952 A/S Chr Christensen, Norway, rnd *Toran;* sunk in ice off Langesund Fjord, Feb 19, 1955.

Aimwell: BAT cls tug; 783; 143 x 33; 14; 34; one 3-in; Defoe SB, Bay City, 1942; ex-USN, transferred Lease/Lend to RN 1943, rtnd USN 1946; 1948, Moller Line, rnd *Patricia Moller;* 1952, Alpha Shipping Co, Hong Kong, rnd *Golden Cape;* 1971, Luzon Stevedoring Corp, Philippines, rnd *Hawkeye.*

Aire: River cls frigate; 1370; 301½ x 36½; 19; 140; two 4-in; Fleming & Ferguson, Paisley, 1943; wrecked Bombay Reef, near Singapore, Dec 23, 1946.

Airedale: Hunt cls destroyer — Albrighton type; 1050; 280 x 31½; 27; 168; four 4-in, two 21-in tt; John Brown & Co, Clydebank, 1942;

bombed and sunk by German aircraft in central Mediterranean, June 15, 1942.

Airsprite: petrol carrier; 1600; 214 x 33¼; 11; 23; --; Blythswood SB & E Co, Scotstoun, 1943; b/up Belgium 1965.

Ajax: Leander cls cruiser; 6985; 554½ x 55¾; 32½; 680; eight 6-in, eight 4-in, eight 21-in tt; Vickers-Armstrongs, Barrow, 1935; b/up Newport 1949.

Alacrity: Modified Black Swan cls sloop; 1430; 299½ x 38; 20; 192; six 4-in; Wm Denny & Bros, Dumbarton, 1945; b/up Dalmuir 1956.

Alarm: Algerine cls minesweeper; 950; 235 x 35½; 16½; 104; one 4-in; Harland & Wolff, Belfast, 1942; irreparably damaged by aircraft at Bone, Jan 1943, and b/up.

Alaunia: heavy repair ship; 14,030 grt; 538 x 65; 15½; 592; twenty 20-mm; John Brown & Co, Clydebank, 1925; ex passenger ship (Cunard Line, Liverpool) acquired by RN 1944 and converted; b/up Blyth, 1957.

Albacore: Algerine cls minesweeper; 950; 235 x 35½; 16½; 104; one 4-in; Harland & Wolff, Belfast, 1942; b/up Port Glasgow 1963.

Albatross: repair ship; 4,800; 443¾ x 58; 21; 450; four 4.7-in; Cockatoo Docks & Engineering Co, Sydney, 1928; ex Royal Australian Navy seaplane carrier, transferred to RN 1938, and converted to repair ship 1941; 1947, South Western SN Co, for conversion to passenger liner, to be renamed *Pride of Torquay,* instead used as storage hulk; 1948, China Hellenic Lines, Hong Kong, converted to emigrant carrier, rnd *Hellenic Prince;* b/up Hong Kong 1954.

Albrighton: Hunt cls destroyer — Albrighton type; 1050; 280 x 31½; 27; 168; four 4-in, two 21-in tt; John Brown & Co, Clydebank, 1942; transferred 1959 to West German Navy, rnd *Raule;* b/up 1969.

Albury: Hunt cls minesweeper; 800; 231 x 28½; 16; 74; one 4-in, one 3-in; Ailsa SB Co, Troon, 1919; sold Liege shipbreakers 1947.

Aldenham: Hunt cls destroyer — Albrighton type; 1050; 280 x 31½; 27; 168; four 4-in, two 21-in tt; Cammell Laird, Birkenhead, 1942; mined in north-east Adriatic, Dec 14, 1944.

Alder: Berberis cls trawler; 346 grt; 140 x 24; 11; 18; one 12-pdr; Cochrane & Sons, Selby, 1929; ex-*Lord Davidson* (Pickering & Haldane's Steam Trawling Co, Hull) bought RN 1939; wrecked east coast Scotland, Oct 22, 1941.

Aldersdale: Abbeydale cls oiler; 17,231; 481½ x 62; 11½; 40; --; Cammell Laird, Birkenhead, 1937; damaged by German aircraft on passage Iceland to North Russia, July 5, 1942, and sunk by *U-457*, July 7, 1942.

Alecto: submarine depot ship; 935; 212 x 32½; 14; 76; --; Cammell Laird, Birkenhead, 1911; b/up Faslane 1949.

Algerine: Algerine cls minesweeper; 950; 235 x 35½; 16½; 104; one 4-in; Harland & Wolff, Belfast 1942; torpedoed and sunk off Bougie by Italian submarine *Ascianghi,* Nov 15, 1942.

Alisma: Flower cls corvette; 925; 205 x 33; 16; 85; one 4-in; Harland & Wolff, Belfast, 1941; 1948, Cia Maritima Mensabe SA, Panama, converted to cargo ship, rnd *Laconia;* 1950, K Samartzopoulos, Greece, rnd *Constantinos S;* 1952, D. Efthimiou, Greece, rnd *Parnon;* lost Tyrrhenian Sea, July 16, 1954.

Allegiance: Assurance cls tug; 1045; 157 x 35; 13; 31; one 3-in; Cochrane & Sons, Selby, 1943; 1949, on charter, rnd *Allegiance 2;* 1955, on charter, rnd *Kowloondocks;* foundered in typhoon in China Sea, 100 miles from Hong Kong, Sept 1, 1962.

Allington Castle: Castle cls corvette; 1010; 252 x 36¾; 16½; 120; one 4-in; Fleming & Ferguson, Paisley, 1944; ex-*Amaryllis,* 1943; b/up Sunderland 1958.

Almond: Tree cls trawler; 530; 164 x 27½; 11½; 35; one 12-pdr; Ardrossan Dockyard Ltd, Ardrossan, 1940; mined off Falmouth, Feb 2, 1941.

Alnwick Castle: Castle cls corvette; 1010; 252 x 36¾; 16½; 120; one 4-in; Geo Brown & Co, Greenock, 1944; b/up Gateshead 1958.

Alresford: Hunt cls minesweeper; 800; 231 x 28½; 16; 74; one 4-in, one 3-in; Ailsa SB Co, Troon, 1919; sold Liege

shipbreakers 1947.

Alyssum: Flower cls corvette; 925; 205 x 33; 16; 85; one 4-in; Geo Brown & Co, Greenock, 1941; transferred 1941 to French Navy, rnd *Alysse;* torpedoed and sunk by *U-654* in Western Atlantic, Feb 8, 1942.

Amaranthus: Flower cls corvette; 925; 205 x 33; 16; 85; one 4-in; Fleming & Ferguson, Paisley, 1941; 1946, Wheelock Marden & Co, Hong Kong, converted to cargo ship, no name change; b/up Hong Kong 1953.

Amazon: A type destroyer; 1350; 323 x 31½; 37; 138; four 4.7-in, six 21-in tt; J. I. Thornycroft & Co, Southampton, 1926; b/up Troon 1949.

Amber: Gem cls trawler; 700; 161 x 26½; 12; 18; one 4-in; Cochrane & Sons, Selby, 1934; ex-*Cape Barfleur* (Hudson Steam Fishing Co, Hull), bought RN 1939; 1946, Eton Steam Fishing Co, Hull, rnd *Etonian;* 1950, Boyd Line, Hull, rnd *Arctic Crusader;* 1952, Eton Steam Fishing Co, Hull, rnd *Etonian;* 1955, J. Marr & Sons, Hull, rnd *Glenella;* b/up Gateshead 1957.

Amberley Castle: Castle cls corvette; 1010; 252 x 36¾; 16½; 120; one 4-in; S. P. Austin & Son, Sunderland, 1944; transferred 1960 to Air Ministry, converted to weather ship, rnd *Weather Adviser;*

Ambuscade: A type destroyer; 1173; 322 x 31; 37; 138; four 4.7-in, six 21-in tt; Yarrow & Co, Scotstoun, 1927; b/up Troon 1947.

Ameer: Smiter cls escort carrier; 11,420; 496 x 69½; 16; 650; 20 aircraft, two 5-in; Seattle-Tacoma SB Corp, Tacoma, 1943; ex-USN *Baffins Bay, BCVE-35,* trs Lease/Lend to RN, 1943; rtnd USN 1946; 1946, Seas Shipping Co, New York, converted cargo ship, rnd *Robin Kirk;* 1957, Moore-McCormack Lines, no name change; b/up Kaohsiung 1969.

American Salvor: salvage vessel; 800; 183¼ x 37; 12; 35; one 3-in; Barbour Boat Works, New Bern, 1943; ex-USN, transferred Lease/Lend to RN 1943, rtnd USN 1946; 1947, Greek Government, rnd *Aptotos;* b/up Greece 1954.

Amethyst: Gem cls trawler; 627; 157 x 26; 11; 18; one 4-in; Smith's Dock Co,

Middlesbrough, 1934; ex-*Phyllis Rosalie* (Boston Deep Sea Fishing & Ice Co, Fleetwood) bought RN 1935; mined Thames Estuary, Nov 24, 1940.
Amethyst: Modified Black Swan cls sloop; 1430; 299½ x 38; 20; 192; six 4-in; Alex Stephen & Sons, Linthouse, 1943; b/up Plymouth 1957.
Amphion: A cls submarine; 1120/1620; 281⅔ x 22¼; 19/8; 60; ten 21-in tt, one 4-in; Vickers-Armstrongs, Barrow, 1945; ex-*Anchorite;* b/up Inverkeithing 1971.
Anchusa: Flower cls corvette; 925; 205 x 33; 16; 85; one 4-in; Harland & Wolff, Belfast, 1941; 1946, Compania Maritima Mensabe, Panama, for conversion, rnd *Macedonia;* 1949, Indian Ocean Trading Co, Port Louis, converted to trawler, rnd *Silverlord;* 1954, G. O'Brien Davis, Port Louis, rnd *Sir Edgar;* foundered at Port Louis during cyclone Jan 18-19, 1960, raised and b/up.
Anemone: Flower cls corvette; 925; 205 x 33; 16; 85; one 4-in; Blyth SB & DD Co, Blyth, 1940; 1949, Hvalfangerslsk Pelagos A/S, Norway, converted to whale catcher, rnd *Pelikan;* 1964, A/S Ostfold, Norway, rnd *Ostfold;* b/up Norway 1964.
Anguilla: Colony cls frigate; 1430; 304 x 37½; 18; 120; three 3-in; Walsh-Kaiser Co, Providence, 1943; ex-USN *PF-72,* transferred Lease/Lend to RN rnd *Hallowell,* rnd *Anguilla,* 1943, returned USN 1946; sold for commercial use 1949 (nothing more known).
Annan: River cls frigate; 1370; 301½ x 36½; 19; 140; two 4-in; Hall Russell, Aberdeen, 1944; transferred 1945 to Danish Navy, rnd *Niels Ebbesen;* sold Odense shipbreakers 1963.
Annapolis: Towns cls destroyer; 1060; 314⅓ x 30½; 30; 122; one 4-in, three 21-in tt; Union Iron Works, San Francisco, 1919; ex-USN *Mackenzie,* transferred 1940 to Royal Canadian Navy; b/up US 1945.
Annet: Isles cls trawler; 560; 164 x 27½; 12; 40; one 12-pdr; Cook, Welton & Gemmell, Beverley, 1943; transferred 1957 to Scottish Home Dept as fisheries patrol ship, rnd *Ulva;* b/up Ardrossan 1971-72.

Anson: King George V cls battleship; 35,000; 745 x 103; 28; 1900; ten 14-in, sixteen 5.25-in; Swan Hunter & Wigham Richardson, Wallsend, 1942; ex-*Jellicoe;* b/up Faslane 1957.
Antares: Algerine cls minesweeper; 950; 235 x 35½; 16½; 104; one 4-in; Toronto Shipyards, Toronto, 1942; ex-USN, transferred Lease/Lend to RN 1942, rtnd USN 1946; sold 1947.
Antelope: A cls destroyer; 1350; 323 x 32¼; 35; 138; four 4.7-in, eight 21-in tt; Hawthorn Leslie, Hebburn, 1930; b/up Blyth 1946.
Anthony: A cls destroyer; 1350; 323 x 32¼; 35; 138; four 4.7-in, eight 21-in tt; Scotts SB & E Co, Greenock, 1930; b/up Troon 1948.
Antic: Assurance cls tug; 1045; 157 x 35; 13; 31; one 3-in; Cochrane & Sons, Selby, 1943; ex-*Ant,* 1943; b/up Blyth 1969.
Anticosti: Isles cls trawler; 560; 164 x 27½; 12; 40; one 12-pdr; Collingwood Shipyards, Collingwood, 1942; 1946, L. Myreboe, Norway, rnd *Guloy;* 1948, Fastighets A/B, Sweden, rnd *Barbro;* 1953, Bellavia & De Nadai, Ethiopia, rnd *Giuseppina;* 1970, IRTA (International Refrigerated Transport Asmara) Share Co, Ethiopia, no name change.
Antigua: Colony cls frigate; 1430; 304 x 37½; 18; 120; three 3-in; Walsh-Kaiser, Providence, 1943; ex-USN *PF-73,* transferred Lease/Lend to RN rnd *Hammond,* rnd *Antigua* 1943, returned USN 1946; b/up Chester, Pa, 1947.
Aphis: Insect cls river gunboat; 625; 237½ x 36; 14; 65; two 6-in, one 3-in; Ailsa SB Co, Troon, 1916; sold 1947 at Singapore and broken up.
Apollo: Manxman cls minelayer; 4000; 418 x 39; 40; 246; 160 mines, four 4-in; Hawthorn Leslie, Hebburn, 1944; b/up Blyth 1962.
Appleleaf: Leaf cls oiler; 12,370; 425 x 54½; 14; 26; --; Workman Clark & Co, Belfast, 1917; ex-*Texol,* 1917; b/up Troon 1947.
Arabis: Flower cls corvette; 925; 205 x 33; 16; 85; one 4-in; Harland & Wolff, Belfast, 1940; transferred US Navy, rnd *Saucy,* returned RN 1945, rnd *Snapdragon;* 1947, Cia de Vapores

"Albatros" SA, Panama, converted to cargo ship, rnd *Katina;* 1950, Fareed Awad, Syria, rnd *Tewfik;* b/up Italy 1964.

Arabis: Modified Flower cls corvette; 980; 208¼ x 33; 16; 109; one 4-in; Geo Brown & Co, Greenock, 1944; transferred RNZN 1944; rtnd 1948; b/up Grays 1951.

Arbiter: Smiter cls escort carrier; 11,420; 496 x 69½; 16; 650; 20 aircraft, two 5-in; Seattle-Tacoma SB Corp, Tacoma, 1944; ex-USN *St Simon, BCVE-51,* transferred Lease/Lend to RN 1944, returned USN 1946; 1947, Cia Argentina de Nav Dodero SA (later ELMA), Argentina, converted to cargo liner, rnd *Coracero;* 1965, Philippine President Lines, Philippines, rnd *President Macapagal,* rnd *Lucky Two,* 1971, same owners; b/up Kaohsiung 1972.

Arbutus: Flower cls corvette; 925; 205 x 33; 16; 85; one 4-in; Blyth SB & DD Co, Blyth, 1940; torpedoed and sunk by *U-136* in North Atlantic, Feb 5, 1942.

Arbutus: Modified Flower cls corvette; 980; 208¼ x 33; 16; 109; one 4-in; Geo Brown & Co, Greenock, 1944; transferred RNZN 1944, rtnd 1948; b/up Dunston 1951.

Archer: Archer cls escort carrier; 12,300; 492 x 69½; 16½; 520; 20 aircraft, one 4-in; Sun SB & DD Corp, Chester, 1941; ex cargo liner *Mormacland,* ex-USN, *BAVG-1,* transferred Lease/Lend to RN 1941; transferred 1945 to Ministry of War Transport, London, and rnd *Empire Lagan;* rtnd USN 1946; 1947, Sven Salen, Sweden, converted to passenger liner, rnd *Anna Salen;* 1955, Hellenic Mediterranean Lines, Greece, rnd *Tasmania;* 1961, China Union Lines, Taiwan, rnd *Union Reliance;* badly damaged in collision in Houston Ship Canal with tanker *Berean,* followed by fire, Nov 7, 1961; b/up New Orleans 1962.

Arcturus: Algerine cls minesweeper; 950; 235 x 35½; 16½; 104; one 4-in; Redfern Construction Co, Toronto, 1942; ex-USN, transferred Lease/Lend to RN 1942, rtnd USN 1946; transferred 1947 to Greek Navy, rnd

Pirpolitis.

Ardent: A cls destroyer; 1350; 323 x 32¼; 35; 138; four 4.7-in, eight 21-in tt; Scotts SB & E Co, Greenock, 1930; sunk in action with German battle-cruisers *Scharnhorst* and *Gneisenau* near Narvik, June 8, 1940.

Ardrossan: Bangor cls minesweeper; 656; 174 x 28½; 16; 60; one 3-in; Blyth SB & DD Co, Blyth, 1941; b/up Thornaby-on-Tees 1948.

Arethusa: Arethusa cls cruiser; 5220; 506 x 51; 32¼; 450; six 6-in, eight 4-in, six 21-in tt; HM Dockyard, Chatham, 1935; b/up Newport, 1950.

Argonaut: Dido cls cruiser; 5450; 512 x 50½; 33; 620; ten 5.25-in, six 21-in tt; Cammell Laird, Birkenhead, 1942; b/up Newport 1955.

Argus: aircraft carrier; 14,450; 565 x 75; 20; 373; 20 aircraft, six 4-in; Wm Beardmore, Dalmuir, 1918; laid down 1914 as liner *Conte Rosso* for Italian owners, purchased by Admiralty 1916, completed as aircraft carrier; b/up Inverkeithing 1946.

Ariadne: Manxman cls minelayer; 4000; 418 x 39; 40; 246; 160 mines, six 4.7-in; Alex Stephen & Sons, Linthouse, 1943; b/up Dalmuir 1965.

Aries: Algerine cls minesweeper; 950; 235 x 35½; 16½; 104; one 4-in; Toronto Shipyard, Toronto, 1942; ex-USN, transferred Lease/Lend to RN 1942, rtnd USN 1946; transferred 1947 to Greek Navy, rnd *Armatolos.*

Ark Royal: aircraft carrier; 22,000; 800 x 96; 30¾; 1646; 60 aircraft, sixteen 4.5-in; Cammell Laird, Birkenhead, 1938; torpedoed in Mediterranean near Gibraltar by *U-81,* Nov 13, 1941, and sank in tow the following day.

Armada: Battle cls destroyer; 2325; 379 x 40¼; 36; 308; four 4.5-in, eight 21-in tt; Hawthorn Leslie, Hebburn, 1945; b/up Inverkeithing 1965.

Armeria: Flower cls corvette; 925; 205 x 33; 16; 85; one 4-in; Harland & Wolff, Belfast, 1941; 1948, Cia Faralon de Navegacion, Panama, converted to cargo ship, rnd *Deppie;* 1950, Scotto, Ambrosino, Pugliese Fils & Co, Algeria, rnd *Canastel;* 1952, Salvo & Fontaine, Chile, rnd *Rio Blanco;* 1955, H. Ossa, Chile, rnd *Lilian;* b/up Chile 1961.

Arndale: Abbeydale cls oiler; 17,210; 481½ x 62; 11½; 40; --; Swan Hunter & Wigham Richardson, Wallsend, 1937; b/up Belgium 1960.

Arran: Isles cls trawler; 560; 164 x 27½; 12; 40; one 12-pdr; Cook, Welton & Gemmell, Beverley, 1941; 1946, NV Verre Visscherij Maats, Holland, rnd *Assan Reis;* 1952, Schlienz-Hagemann Hochsee & Gefrierfischi, West Germany, rnd *Prof Henking;* 1956, R. Kienass, West Germany, rnd *Berta Kienass;* lost, North Sea, February 1962.

Arrow: A cls destroyer; 1350; 323 x 32¼; 35; 138; four 4.7-in, eight 21-in tt; Vickers-Armstrongs, Barrow, 1930; irreparably damaged by explosion of ammunition ship at Algiers, Aug 4, 1943, b/up 1947.

Arrowhead: Flower cls corvette; 925; 205 x 33; 16; 85; one 4-in; Marine Industries, Sorel, 1940; transferred 1941 to Royal Canadian Navy, rtnd RN 1945; 1948, South Georgia Co (C. Salvesen), Leith, converted to whale catcher, rnd *Southern Larkspur;* b/up Odense 1959.

Artifex: heavy repair ship; 13,984 grt; 538 x 65; 15½; 592; twenty 20-mm; Swan Hunter & Wigham Richardson, Wallsend, 1924; ex-passenger liner *Aurania* (Cunard Line, Liverpool), acquired by RN 1942, converted and renamed; b/up Italy 1961.

Ascension: Colony cls frigate; 1430; 304 x 37½; 18; 120; three 3-in; Walsh-Kaiser Co, Providence, 1943; ex-USN *PF-74,* transferred Lease/Lend to RN rnd *Hargood,* rnd *Ascension,* 1943, rtnd USN 1946; sold 1947, b/up Newburgh, NY.

Ash: Tree cls trawler; 530; 164 x 27½; 11½; 35; one 12-pdr; Cochrane & Sons, Selby, 1940; mined Thames Estuary, June 5, 1941.

Ashanti: Tribal cls destroyer; 1870; 377 x 36½; 36½; 190; eight 4.7-in, four 21-in tt; Wm Denny & Bros, Dumbarton, 1938; b/up Troon 1949.

Asphodel: Flower cls corvette; 925; 205 x 33; 16; 85; one 4-in; Geo Brown & Co, Greenock, 1940; torpedoed and sunk by *U-575* off Cape Finisterre, Mar 9. 1944.

Aspirant: BAT cls tug; 783; 143 x 33;

14; 34; one 3-in; Levingston SB, Orange, 1943; ex-USN, transferred Lease/Lend to RN 1943; rtnd USN 1946; 1947, Office d'Exploitation des Transports Coloniaux, Belgium, rnd *Vivi.*

Assiduous: Assurance cls tug; 1045; 157 x 35; 13; 31; one 3-in; Cochrane & Sons, Selby, 1943; 1961, J. D. Irving, Canada, rnd *Irving Tamarack;* b/up Canada 1968.

Assistance: aircraft depot and repair ship; 11,500; 441½ x 57; 12½; 489; one 5-in; Bethlehem-Fairfield, Baltimore, 1944; ex-USN, transferred Lease/Lend to RN 1944, rtnd USN 1946; sold Cleveland shipbreakers 1974.

Assurance: Assurance cls tug; 1045; 157 x 35; 13; 31; one 3-in; Cochrane & Sons, Selby, 1940; wrecked in Lough Foyle, Oct 18, 1941.

Aster: Flower cls corvette; 925; 205 x 33; 16; 85; one 4-in; Harland & Wolff, Belfast, 1941; b/up Bo'ness 1946.

Astute: A cls submarine; 1120/1620; 281⅔ x 22¼; 19/8; 60; ten 21-in tt, one 4-in; Vickers-Armstrongs, Barrow, 1945; b/up Dunston 1970.

Atheling: Smiter cls escort carrier; 11,420; 496 x 69½; 16; 650; 20 aircraft, two 5-in; Seattle-Tacoma SB Corp, Tacoma, 1943; ex-USN *Glacier, BCVE-33,* transferred Lease/Lend to RN 1943, rtnd USN 1946; 1950. Achille Lauro, Italy, converted to passenger ship, rnd *Roma;* b/up Vado 1967.

Athene: aircraft transport; 10,700; 487¾ x 63; 17; --; 40 aircraft, two 4-in; Greenock Dockyard Co, Greenock, 1941; 1946, Clan Line, London, converted to cargo liner, rnd *Clan Brodie;* b/up Hong Kong 1963.

Atherstone: Hunt cls destroyer — Atherstone type; 1000; 280 x 29; 27½; 146; four 4-in; Cammell Laird, Birkenhead, 1940; b/up Port Glasgow 1957.

Athlete: BAT cls tug; 783; 143 x 33; 14; 34; one 3-in; Levingston SB, Orange, 1943; ex-USN, transferred Lease/Lend to RN 1943; mined at Leghorn July 17, 1945.

Attacker: Attacker cls escort carrier; 10,200; 496 x 69½; 16; 650; 15-20 aircraft; Western Pipe & Steel Co, San

Francisco 1942; ex cargo ship *Steel Artisan,* ex-USN *Barnes, BAVG-7,* transferred Lease/Lend to RN 1942, rtnd USN 1946; 1950, Soc. Italiana Transporti Maritimi SpA, Italy, converted to passenger ship, rnd *Castel Forte;* 1958, Fairline Shipping Co, Monrovia, rnd *Fairsky;*

Aubrietia: Flower cls corvette; 925; 205 x 33; 16; 85; one 4-in; Geo Brown & Co, Greenock, 1940; 1948, A/S Kosmos, Norway, converted to whale catcher, rnd *Arnfinn Bergan;* b/up Grimstad 1966.

Auckland: Pelican cls sloop; 1250; 293 x 37½; 19¼; 188; eight 4-in; Wm Denny & Bros, Dumbarton, 1938; bombed and sunk by German/Italian aircraft off Bardia, June 24, 1941.

Audacity: escort carrier; 6000; 467 x 56; 16; --; 6 aircraft; Bremer Vulkan, Bremen, 1940; ex-passenger liner *Hannover,* (Norddeutscher Lloyd, Germany), captured Feb 1940, rnd *Empire Audacity,* converted and rnd; torpedoed and sunk by *U-751* near Portugal, Dec 21, 1941.

Auricula: Flower cls corvette; 925; 205 x 33; 16; 85; one 4-in; Geo Brown & Co, Greenock, 1941; mined in Courrier Bay, Madagascar, May 5, 1942, and foundered the next day.

Aurora: Arethusa cls cruiser; 5270; 506 x 51; 32¼; 450; six 6-in, eight 4-in, six 21-in tt; HM Dockyard, Portsmouth, 1937; transferred to Nationalist China May 1948, rnd *Chungking;* taken over by Republican forces, Feb 1949, rnd *Victory;* sunk by Nationalist aircraft off Hulutao, Mar 1949; salved and used as hulk, believed rnd *Pei Ching,* 1951 (nothing more known).

Ausonia: heavy repair ship; 20,760; 538 x 65; 15½; 600; twenty 20-mm; Armstrong Whitworth & Co, Newcastle, 1922; ex-passenger liner (Cunard Line, Liverpool) acquired by RN 1939, and converted; b/up Castellon 1965.

Avenger: Archer cls escort carrier; 12,150; 492 x 69½; 16½; 520; 20 aircraft, one 4-in; Sun SB & DD Co, Chester, 1941; ex-cargo ship *Rio Hudson,* ex-USN *BAVG-2,* transferred Lease/Lend to RN 1941; torpedoed and sunk by *U-155* near Gibraltar, Nov 15, 1942.

Avon: River cls frigate; 1370; 301½ x 36½; 19; 140; two 4-in; C. Hill & Sons, Bristol, 1943; transferred 1948 to Portuguese Navy, rnd *Nuno Tristao;* for disposal and breaking-up 1971.

Avon Vale: Hunt cls destroyer — Blankney type; 1050; 280 x 31½; 27; 168; six 4-in; John Brown & Co, Clydebank, 1940; b/up Sunderland 1958.

Awe: River cls frigate; 1370; 301½ x 36½; 19; 140; two 4-in; Fleming & Ferguson, Paisley, 1944; transferred 1948 to Portuguese Navy, rnd *Diogo Gomez;* for disposal and breaking-up 1969.

Aylmer: Captain cls frigate; 1400; 306 x 36¾; 23½; 220; three 3-in; Bethlehem-Hingham Shipyard, 1943; ex-USN Buckley cls destroyer-escort *Harmon, DE-72,* transferred Lease/Lend to RN 1943, rtnd USN 1945, b/up.

Azalea: Flower cls corvette; 925; 205 x 33; 16; 85; one 4-in; Cook, Welton & Gemmell, Beverley, 1941; 1946, Soc Anon Maritime et Commerciale, Switzerland, converted to cargo ship, rnd *Norte;* sunk in collision off Cape Santa Marta, Jan 19, 1955.

Bacchus: store ship; 5150; 337 x 49; 12; 44; --; Caledon SB & E Co, Dundee, 1936; 1962, Chip Hwa Shipping & Trading Co, Singapore, rnd *Pulau Bali;* b/up Singapore 1964.

Badsworth: Hunt cls destroyer — Blankney type; 1050; 280 x 31½; 27; 168; six 4-in; Cammell Laird, Birkenhead, 1941; transferred 1946 to Royal Norwegian Navy, rnd *Arendal;* sold Arendal shipbreakers 1962.

Baffin: Isles cls trawler; 560; 164 x 27½; 12; 40; one 12-pdr; Collingwood Shipyards, Collingwood, 1942; transferred RCN 1942; rtnd 1945; 1947, Harbour Specialities, London, no name change; 1952, F. Osterwisr & Co, West Germany, converted to cargo ship, rnd *Niedermehnen;* 1965, H. Petersen, West Germany, rnd *Kellenhusen;* 1969, H. Thiessen, West Germany, rnd *Kairos;* 1971, G.

Karlovits & F. Papadopoulou, Greece, rnd *Theoxenia;*
Bagshot: Hunt cls minesweeper; 800; 231 x 28½; 16; 74; one 4-in, one 3-in; Ardrossan Dockyard Ltd, Ardrossan, 1918; converted to depot ship, rnd *Medway II*, 1945; 1947, Greek shipbreakers, mined off Corfu in tow to breakers at Trieste, Sept 1, 1951.
Bahamas: Colony cls frigate; 1430; 304 x 37½; 18; 120; three 3-in; Walsh-Kaiser Co, Providence, 1943; ex-USN *PF-75,* transferred Lease/Lend to RN, rnd *Hotham,* rnd *Bahamas,* 1943, rtnd USN 1946; sold Quincy shipbreakers 1947.
Balfour: Captain cls frigate; 1400; 306 x 36¾; 23½; 220; three 3-in; Bethlehem-Hingham Shipyard, 1943; ex-USN Buckley cls destroyer-escort *McAnn DE-73,* transferred Lease/Lend to RN 1943, rtnd USN 1945; b/up.
Ballinderry: River cls frigate; 1370; 301½ x 36½; 19; 140; two 4-in; Blyth SB & DD Co, Blyth, 1943; b/up Barrow 1961.
Balsam: Flower cls corvette; 925; 205 x 33; 16; 85; one 4-in; Geo Brown & Co, Greenock, 1942; ex-*Chelmer* 1941; b/up Newport, 1947.
Balta: Isles cls trawler; 560; 164 x 27½; 12; 40; one 12-pdr; Cook, Welton & Gemmell, Beverley, 1941; 1949, Tai Chong Cheang SS Co, China, converted to cargo ship, rnd *Ching Hai;*
Bamborough Castle; Castle cls corvette; 1010; 252 x 36¾; 16½; 120; one 4-in; J. Lewis & Sons, Aberdeen, 1944; b/up Llanelly 1959.
Bandit: Brigand cls tug; 840; 174 x 32; 15½; 43; one 3-in; Fleming & Ferguson, Paisley, 1938; rnd *Briton,* 1947; b/up Antwerp 1960.
Banff: Lulworth cls escort; 1546; 250 x 42; 16; 200; one 5-in, two 3-in; Gen. Eng & DD Co, Oakland, 1930; ex-US Coast Guard cutter *Saranac,* transferred Lease/Lend to RN 1941, rtnd USCG 1946, rnd *Sebec,* rnd *Tampa,* 1947; sold Baltimore shipbreakers 1959.
Bangor: Bangor cls minesweeper; 590; 162 x 28; 16; 60; one 3-in; Harland & Wolff, Govan, 1940; transferred 1946 to Royal Norwegian Navy, rnd

Glomma; sold Bergen shipbreakers 1962.
Bann: River cls frigate; 1370; 301½ x 36½; 19; 140; two 4-in; C. Hill & Sons, Bristol, 1943; transferred 1945 to Indian Navy, rnd *Tir;* converted to training ship 1948;
Barbados: Colony cls frigate; 1430; 304 x 37½; 18; 120; three 3-in; Walsh-Kaiser Co, Providence, 1943; ex-USN *PF-76,* transferred Lease/Lend to RN, rnd *Halsted,* rnd *Barbados* 1943, rtnd USN 1946; sold Chester, Pa, shipbreakers 1947.
Barbain; Bar cls boom defence vessel; 730; 173¾ x 32; 11¾; 32; one 3-in; Blyth SB & DD Co, Blyth, 1940;
Barbarian: Bar cls boom defence vessel; 730; 173¾ x 32; 11¾; 32; one 3-in; Blyth SB & DD Co, Blyth, 1938; transferred 1946 to Turkish Navy, rnd *AG-1.*
Barbecue: Bar cls boom defence vessel; 730; 173¾ x 32; 11¾; 32; one 3-in; Ardrossan Dockyard Ltd, Ardrossan, 1945; 1970, S.A. Codemar, Panama; (nothing more known).
Barberry: Bar cls boom defence vessel; 730; 173¾ x 32; 11¾; 32; one 3-in; Ferguson Bros, Port Glasgow, 1943; sold Portsmouth shipbreakers 1958.
Barbette: Bar cls boom defence vessel; 730; 173¾ x 32; 11¾; 32; one 3-in; Blyth SB & DD Co, Blyth, 1938; transferred 1941 to Turkish Navy, rnd *AG-2;*
Barbette: Bar cls boom defence vessel; 730; 173¾ x 32; 11¾; 32; one 3-in; Wm Simons & Co, Renfrew, 1943; 1964, Fair Chance (Marine) Co, rnd *Fair Barbette;* b/up Belgium 1965.
Barbican: Bar cls boom defence vessel; 730; 173¾ x 32; 11¾; 32; one 3-in; Blyth SB & DD Co, Blyth, 1938; b/up Inverkeithing 1968.
Barbour: Bar cls boom defence vessel; 730; 173¾ x 32; 11¾; 32; one 3-in; Blyth SB & DD Co, Blyth, 1941; b/up Bo'ness 1952.
Barbourne: Bar cls boom defence vessel; 730; 173¾ x 32; 11¾; 32; one 3-in; Wm Simons & Co, Renfrew, 1942; b/up Briton Ferry 1964.
Barbrake: Bar cls boom defence

vessel; 730; 173¾ x 32; 11¾; 32; one
3-in; Wm Simons & Co, Renfrew, 1942;
transferred 1951 to South African
Navy, rnd *Fleur;* sunk as gunnery
target, Oct 5, 1965.

Barbridge: Bar cls boom defence
vessel; 730; 173¾ x 32; 11¾; 32; one
3-in; Lobnitz & Co, Renfrew, 1940;
b/up Inverkeithing 1964.

Barbrook: Bar cls boom defence
vessel; 730; 173¾ x 32; 11¾; 32; one
3-in; Blyth SB & DD Co, Blyth, 1938;
sold Portsmouth shipbreakers 1958.

Barcarole: Bar cls boom defence
vessel; 730; 173¾ x 32; 11¾; 32; one
3-in; Ardrossan Dockyard Ltd,
Ardrossan, 1945; b/up North
Queensferry 1967.

Barcastle: Bar cls boom defence
vessel; 730; 173¾ x 32; 11¾; 32; one
3-in; Blyth SB & DD Co, Blyth, 1938;
sold Portsmouth shipbreakers 1962.

Barcliff: Bar cls boom defence vessel;
730; 173¾ x 32; 11¾; 32; one 3-in;
Lobnitz & Co, Renfrew, 1940,
ex-*Barwick,* 1940; b/up Belgium 1967.

Barclose: Bar cls boom defence
vessel; 730; 173¾ x 32; 11¾; 32; one
3-in; Blyth SB & DD Co, Blyth, 1941;
b/up Dalmuir 1962.

Barcock: Bar cls boom defence
vessel; 730; 17¾ x 32; 11¾; 32; one
3-in; Blyth SB & DD Co, Blyth, 1942;
transferred 1946 to Belgian Navy, no
name change, rtnd RN 1949; 1962, H.
G. Pounds, Portsmouth, no name
change; 1963 Denak Denizcilik ve
Ticaret AS, Turkey, rnd *Denak 1;* 1968,
Celal Yildiran, Turkey, rnd *Talas,*
converted to cargo ship 1970;

Barcombe: Bar cls boom defence
vessel; 730; 173¾ x 32; 11¾; 32; one
3-in; Goole SB & Repairing Co, Goole,
1938; wrecked Scotland, Aug 1957.

Barcote: Bar cls boom defence vessel;
730; 173¾ x 32; 11¾; 32; one 3-in;
Blyth SB & DD Co, Blyth, 1940; b/up
Holland 1963.

Barcroft: Bar cls boom defence
vessel; 730; 173¾ x 32; 11¾; 32;
one 3-in; Goole SB & Repairing Co,
Goole, 1938; 1962, H. G. Pounds,
Portsmouth, no name change; 1965,
Meeching Engineering (Marine),
Newhaven, no name change; b/up
Belgium 1965.

Barcross: Bar cls boom defence
vessel; 730; 173¾ x 32; 11¾; 32; one
3-in; Blyth SB & DD Co, Blyth, 1942;
transferred 1951 to South African
Navy, rnd *Somerset;*

Bardell: Bar cls boom defence vessel;
730; 173¾ x 32; 11¾; 32; one 3-in;
Blyth SB & DD Co, Blyth, 1942; sold
March 1950 at Freetown, purchaser
not known.

Bardolf: Bar cls boom defence vessel;
730; 173¾ x 32; 11¾; 32; one 3-in;
Blyth SB & DD Co, Blyth, 1942; b/up
Hendrik Ido Ambacht 1964.

Bardsey: Isles cls trawler; 560; 164 x
27½; 12; 40; one 12-pdr; Fleming &
Ferguson, Paisley, 1943; 1959, Malta
Drydocks, Malta, as tank cleaning
vessel, no name change; b/up 1971.

Barfair: Bar cls boom defence vessel;
730; 173¾ x 32; 11¾; 32; one 3-in; J.
Lewis & Sons, Aberdeen, 1938;
transferred 1946 to Turkey, rnd *AG-3;*

Barfield: Bar cls boom defence vessel;
730; 173¾ x 32; 11¾; 32; one 3-in; J.
Lewis & Sons, Aberdeen, 1938; b/up
Belgium 1971.

Barflake: Bar cls boom defence
vessel; 730; 173¾ x 32; 11¾; 32; one
3-in; Philip & Son, Dartmouth, 1942;
mined off Naples Nov 22, 1943.

Barfleur: Battle cls destroyer; 2325;
379 x 40¼; 36; 308; four 4.5-in, eight
21-in tt; Swan Hunter & Wigham
Richardson, Wallsend, 1944; b/up
Dalmuir 1966.

Barfoam: Bar cls boom defence
vessel; 730; 173¾ x 32; 11¾; 32; one
3-in; Wm Simons & Co, Renfrew, 1941;
sold Singapore shipbreakers 1967.

Barfoil: Bar cls boom defence vessel;
730; 173¾ x 32; 11¾; 32; one 3-in;
Philip & Son, Dartmouth, 1942;

Barfoot: Bar cls boom defence vessel;
730; 173¾ x 32; 11¾; 32; one 3-in; J.
Lewis & Sons, Aberdeen, 1942;

Barford: Bar cls boom defence vessel;
730; 173¾ x 32; 11¾; 32; one 3-in; Wm
Simons & Co, Renfrew, 1942; sold at
Singapore 1958.

Barfoss: Bar cls boom defence vessel;
730; 173¾ x 32; 11¾; 32; one 3-in; Wm
Simons & Co, Renfrew, 1942; b/up
Belgium 1968.

Barfount: Bar cls boom defence
vessel; 730; 173¾ x 32; 11¾; 32; one

3-in; Wm Simons & Co, Renfrew, 1942;
b/up Hendrik Ido Ambacht 1964.
Barglow: Bar cls boom defence
vessel; 730; 173¾ x 32; 11¾; 32; one
3-in; J. Lewis & Sons, Aberdeen, 1943;
1970, S. A. Codemar, Panama;
(nothing more known).
Barham: Queen Elizabeth cls
battleship; 31,100; 643 x 104; 24; 1184;
eight 15-in, twelve 6-in, eight 4-in, two
21-in tt; John Brown & Co, Clydebank,
1915; torpedoed and sunk by *U-331* in
eastern Mediterranean Nov 25, 1941.
Barhill: Bar cls boom defence vessel;
730; 173¾ x 32; 11¾; 32; one 3-in;
Ferguson Bros, Port Glasgow, 1943;
1970, S. A. Codemar, Panama;
(nothing more known).
Barholm: Bar cls boom defence
vessel; 730; 173¾ x 32; 11¾; 32; one
3-in; Ardrossan Dockyard Ltd,
Ardrossan, 1943; b/up Spezia 1962.
Barilla: Bar cls boom defence vessel;
730; 173¾ x 32; 11¾; 32; one 3-in; J.
Lewis & Sons, Aberdeen, 1943; sold
Portsmouth shipbreakers 1958.
Baritone: Bar cls boom defence
vessel; 730; 173¾ x 32; 11¾; 32; one
3-in; Philip & Son, Dartmouth, 1945;
sold Portsmouth shipbreakers 1958.
Barking: Bar cls boom defence vessel;
730; 173¾ x 32; 11¾; 32; one 3-in;
Lobnitz & Co, Renfrew, 1941; lost,
aground Mill Bay, Mar 20, 1964, on
way to shipbreakers at Briton Ferry;
wreck b/up 1974.
Barkis: Bar cls boom defence vessel;
730; 173¾ x 32; 11¾; 32; one 3-in;
Ferguson Bros, Port Glasgow, 1945;
b/up Inverkeithing 1964.
Barlake: Bar cls boom defence vessel;
730; 173¾ x 32; 11¾; 32; one 3-in;
Blyth SB & DD Co, Blyth, 1940; sold
Antwerp shipbreakers 1964.
Barlane: Bar cls boom defence vessel;
730; 173¾ x 32; 11¾; 32; one 3-in;
Lobnitz & Co, Renfrew, 1938; sold
Antwerp shipbreakers 1958.
Barle: River cls frigate; 1370; 301½ x
36½; 19; 140; two 4-in; Canadian
Vickers, Montreal, 1943; ex-USN
PG-103, transferred Lease/Lend to RN
1943, rtnd USN 1946; sold 1947.
Barleycorn: Bar cls boom defence
vessel; 730; 173¾ x 32; 11¾; 32; one
3-in; J. Lewis & Sons, Aberdeen, 1943;

b/up Inverkeithing 1964.
Barlight: Bar cls boom defence vessel;
730; 173¾ x 32; 11¾; 32; one 3-in;
Lobnitz & Co, Renfrew, 1939; scuttled
Hong Kong, Dec 19, 1941; salved by
Japanese and commissioned as *No
101;* acquired by China 1945, nothing
more known.
Barlow: Bar cls boom defence vessel;
730; 173¾ x 32; 11¾; 32; one 3-in; Wm
Simons & Co, Renfrew, 1938; sold
Antwerp shipbreakers 1958.
Barmill: Bar cls boom defence vessel;
730; 173¾ x 32; 11¾; 32; one 3-in;
Blyth SB & DD Co, Blyth, 1941; sold
Antwerp shipbreakers 1958.
Barmond: Bar cls boom defence
vessel; 730; 173¾ x 32; 11¾; 32; one
3-in; Wm Simons & Co, Renfrew, 1943;
b/up Bilbao 1974.
Barmouth: Bar cls boom defence
vessel; 730; 173¾ x 32; 11¾; 32; one
3-in; Wm Simons & Co, Renfrew, 1938;
1964, Risdon Beazley, Southampton,
rnd *Topmast 19;* b/up Belgium 1966.
Barnaby: Bar cls boom defence
vessel; 730; 173¾ x 32; 11¾; 32; one
3-in; Wm Simons & Co, Renfrew, 1943;
b/up St Davids on Forth 1965.
Barnard: Bar cls boom defence
vessel; 730; 173¾ x 32; 11¾; 32; one
3-in; J. Lewis & Sons, Aberdeen, 1942;
b/up Briton Ferry 1970.
Barndale: Bar cls boom defence
vessel; 730; 173¾ x 32; 11¾; 32; one
3-in; Lobnitz & Co, Renfrew, 1940;
1970, S. A. Codemar, Panama;
(nothing more known).
Barneath: Bar cls boom defence
vessel; 730; 173¾ x 32; 11¾; 32; one
3-in; J. Lewis & Sons, Aberdeen, 1942;
1958, Nundy (Marine Metals), no name
change; 1972, Scapa Salvage Co, no
name change;
Barnehurst: Bar cls boom defence
vessel; 730; 173¾ x 32; 11¾; 32; one
3-in; Blyth SB & DD Co, Blyth, 1939;
b/up Port Glasgow 1964.
Barnet: boom working vessel; 423;
148 x 23¾; 11; 15; one 3-in; Cochrane
& Sons, Selby, 1919; ex-Mersey cls
trawler *John Mann,* 1919, ex-*Earl Haig*
(Hellyer Bros, Hull) acquired by RN
1934 and rnd; sold 1945.
Barnstone: Bar cls boom defence
vessel; 730; 173¾ x 32; 11¾; 32; one

3-in; Blyth SB & DD Co, Blyth, 1940;
b/up Boom 1969.

Barnwell: Bar cls boom defence
vessel; 730; 173¾ x 32; 11¾; 32; one
3-in; Lobnitz & Co, Renfrew, 1940; sold
at Singapore 1958.

Baron: Bar cls boom defence vessel;
730; 173¾ x 32; 11¾; 32; one 3-in;
Philip & Son, Dartmouth, 1944; 1958,
Colombo Port Commission.

Baronia: Bar cls boom defence vessel;
730; 173¾ x 32; 11¾; 32; one 3-in; C.
Hill & Sons, Bristol, 1941; sold at
Singapore 1959.

Barova: Bar cls boom defence vessel;
730; 173¾ x 32; 11¾; 32; one 3-in; C.
Hill & Sons, Bristol, 1941; b/up
Holland 1964.

Barrage: Bar cls boom defence
vessel; 730; 173¾ x 32; 11¾; 32; one
3-in; Hall Russell & Co, Aberdeen,
1938; b/up Briton Ferry 1970.

Barranca: Bar cls boom defence
vessel; 730; 173¾ x 32; 11¾; 32; one
3-in; Hall Russell & Co, Aberdeen,
1938; b/up Port Glasgow 1964.

Barrhead: Bar cls boom defence
vessel; 730; 173¾ x 32; 11¾; 32; one
3-in; Wm Simons & Co, Renfrew, 1940;
b/up Faslane 1964.

Barricade: Bar cls boom defence
vessel; 730; 173¾ x 32; 11¾; 32; one
3-in; C. Hill & Sons, Bristol, 1938;
ex-*Ebgate*, 1937; b/up Bo'ness 1952.

Barrier: Bar cls boom defence vessel;
730; 173¾ x 32; 11¾; 32; one 3-in; C.
Hill & Sons, Bristol, 1938; ex-*Bargate*,
1937; sold Holland shipbreakers 1963.

Barrington: Bar cls boom defence
vessel; 730; 173¾ x 32; 11¾; 32; one
3-in; Wm Simons & Co, Renfrew, 1941;
b/up Boom about 1970.

Barrymore: Bar cls boom defence
vessel; 730; 173¾ x 32; 11¾; 32; one
3-in; Wm Simons & Co, Renfrew, 1942;
wrecked October 1949.

Barsing: Bar cls boom defence vessel;
730; 173¾ x 32; 11¾; 32; one 3-in; Wm
Simons & Co, Renfrew, 1941: 1962,
Land & Marine Contractors,
Bromborough, converted to
pipe-laying ship, rnd *L.M. Sea Piper;*
1970, SUM Ltd, Havant, rnd *Salvager;*
1971, Ship Trail Ltd, Portsmouth, no
name change; aground west coast of
Africa July 18, 1971.

Barsound: Bar cls boom defence
vessel; 730; 173¾ x 32; 11¾; 32; one
3-in; Wm Simons & Co, Renfrew, 1941;
b/up Holland 1964.

Barspear: Bar cls boom defence
vessel; 730; 173¾ x 32; 11¾; 32; one
3-in; Ferguson Bros, Port Glasgow,
1943; b/up Spezia 1962.

Barstoke: Bar cls boom defence
vessel; 730; 173¾ x 32; 11¾; 32; one
3-in; Wm Simons & Co, Renfrew, 1941;
on loan 1946 to Rangoon Port
Authority, rtnd RN 1959; sold at
Singapore 1960.

Barthorpe: Bar cls boom defence
vessel; 730; 173¾ x 32; 11¾; 32; one
3-in; Lobnitz & Co, Renfrew, 1940;
b/up Holland 1963.

Bartizan: Bar cls boom defence
vessel; 730; 173¾ x 32; 11¾; 32; one
3-in; Ardrossan Dockyard Ltd,
Ardrossan, 1943; b/up Jurong 1967.

Barwind: Bar cls boom defence
vessel; 730; 173¾ x 32; 11¾; 32; one
3-in; Ferguson Bros, Port Glasgow,
1942; b/up Briton Ferry 1964.

Basilisk: B cls destroyer; 1360; 323 x
32¼; 35; 138; four 4.7-in, eight 21-in tt;
John Brown & Co, Clydebank, 1931;
sunk by German aircraft off Dunkirk,
June 1, 1940.

Basset: Basset cls trawler; 461; 160½
x 27½; 12; 33; one 4-in; H. Robb, Leith,
1936; 1948, Radcliffe Channel Islands
SS Co, Alderney, converted to
cargo ship, rnd *Radford;* b/up UK
1953.

Bath: Town cls destroyer; 1060; 314⅓
x 30½; 30; 122; three 4-in, six 21-in tt;
Newport News SB & DD Co, Newport
News, 1919: ex-USN *Hopewell,*
transferred to RN, 1940; torpedoed
and sunk by U-boat in North Atlantic,
Aug 19, 1941.

Battler: Attacker cls escort carrier;
10,200; 496 x 69½; 16; 650; 15-20
aircraft; Ingalls SB Co, Pascagoula,
1942; ex-cargo liner *Mormacmail,*
ex-USN *Altamaha, BAVG-6,*
transferred Lease/Lend to RN, 1942,
rtnd USN 1946; b/up Baltimore 1946.

Bay: Tree cls trawler; 530; 164 x 27½;
11½; 35; one 12-pdr; Cochrane &
Sons, Selby, 1940; 1947, Norwegian
owners, no name change; 1952 Tristan
da Cunha Development Co, South

Africa, converted to cargo ship, rnd *Tristania;* 1973, Marine & Industrial Cleaning, South Africa;

Bayfield: Bangor cls minesweeper; 672; 180 x 28½; 16; 60; one 3-in; Port Arthur SB Co, Port Arthur, 1941; transferred RCN 1941; rtnd 1945; b/up Gateshead 1948.

Bayntun: Captain cls frigate; 1140; 289½ x 35; 21; 200; three 3-in; Navy Yard, Boston, 1943; ex-USN Evarts cls destroyer-escort *BDE-1,* transferred Lease/Lend to RN 1943, rtnd USN 1945; b/up.

Bayonet: Bayonet cls boom defence vessel; 530; 159¾ x 30½; 11½; 32; one 3-in; Blyth SB & DD Co, Blyth, 1939; ex-*Barnehurst,*1938; mined in Firth of Forth, Dec 21, 1939.

Bazely: Captain cls frigate; 1140; 289½ x 35; 21; 200; three 3-in; Navy Yard, Boston, 1943; ex-USN Evarts cls destroyer-escort *BDE-2,* transferred Lease/Lend to RN 1943, rtnd USN 1945; b/up.

Beachy Head: escort repair ship; 8580; 441½ x 57; 11; 440; sixteen 20-mm; Burrard DD Co, Vancouver, 1945; transferred 1947 to Royal Netherlands Navy, rnd *Vulkaan,* rtnd RN 1950, rnd *Beachy Head;* transferred 1952 to Royal Canadian Navy, rnd *Cape Scott;*

Beagle: B cls destroyer; 1360; 323 x 32¼; 35; 138; four 4.7-in, eight 21-in tt; John Brown & Co, Clydebank, 1931; b/up Rosyth 1946.

Beaufort: Hunt cls destroyer — Blankney type; 1050; 280 x 31½; 27; 168; six 4-in; Cammell Laird, Birkenhead, 1941; transferred 1954 to Royal Norwegian Navy, rnd *Haugesund;* sold Sarpsborg shipbreakers 1966.

Beauly Firth: repair ship; 8650 grt; 447¾ x 56¼; 11; --; twelve 20-mm; J. Readhead & Sons, South Shields, 1945; 1948, Stanhope SS Co, London, converted to cargo ship, rnd *Stanfirth;* 1961, Cia Nav y de Comercio Degedo, Panama, rnd *Akamas;* 1968, Akamas Shipping Co, Cyprus, rnd *Skepsis;* b/up Shanghai 1968.

Beaumaris: Bangor cls minesweeper; 656; 174 x 28½; 16; 60; one 3-in; Ailsa SB Co, Troon, 1941; b/up Milford

Haven 1948.

Bedale: Hunt cls destroyer — Blankney type; 1050; 280 x 31½; 27; 168; six 4-in; Hawthorn Leslie, Hebburn, 1941; transferred 1942 to Polish Navy, rnd *Slazak,* rtnd RN 1945, rnd *Bedale;* transferred 1953 to Indian Navy, rnd *Godavari;*

Bedenham: ammunition ship; 1191 grt; 230 x 37½; 10; --; --; Ailsa SB Co, Troon, 1938; blew up at Gibraltar, Apr 27, 1951, remains b/up Dunston 1952.

Bedouin: Tribal cls destroyer; 1870; 377 x 36½; 36½; 190; eight 4.7-in, four 21-in tt; Wm Denny & Bros, Dumbarton, 1939; damaged in action with Italian surface force in Mediterranean, torpedoed and sunk by Italian aircraft when under tow, June 15, 1942.

Beech: Berberis cls trawler; 346 grt; 140 x 24; 11; 18; one 12-pdr; Cochrane & Sons, Selby, 1929; ex-*Lord Dawson* (Pickering & Haldane's Steam Trawling Co, Hull) bought RN 1939; sunk in air attack at Scrabster, June 22, 1941.

Begonia: Flower cls corvette; 925; 205 x 33; 16; 85; one 4-in; Cook Welton & Gemmell, Beverley, 1941; transferred 1942 to US Navy, rnd *Impulse,* rtnd RN 1946, rnd *Begonia;* 1946, Wheelock Marden, Hong Kong, converted to cargo ship, rnd *Begonlock;* 1949, Adrilleros Luzurinaga SA, Spain, rnd *Fundiciones Molinas;* 1951, Astilleros Luzurinaga SA Spain, rnd *Astiluzu;* 1955, Naviera Compostela SA, Spain, rnd *Rio Mero;* wrecked on passage Canary Islands to Valencia, Jan 21, 1970.

Begum: Smiter cls escort carrier; 11,420; 496 x 69½; 16; 650; 20 aircraft, two 5-in; Seattle-Tacoma SB Corp, Tacoma, 1943; ex-*Balinas, BCVE-36* transferred Lease/Lend to RN 1943, rtnd USN 1946; 1947, Stoom Maats "Nederland", Holland, converted to cargo liner, rnd *Raki;* 1966, Zui Kong SS Co, Liberia, rnd *I-Yung;* b/up Kaohsiung 1974.

Belfast: Improved Southampton cls cruiser; 10,260; 613½ x 63¼; 32; 847; twelve 6-in, twelve 4-in, six 21-in tt; Harland & Wolff, Belfast, 1939; museum ship on River Thames, 1971.

Belgol: Belgol cls oiler; 5620; 335 x 41½; 14; 39; --; Irvine SB & DD Co, West Hartlepool 1917; b/up 5770; 512 x 50½; 33; 620; eight 5.25-in,

Bellona: Improved Dido cls cruiser; 5770; 512 x 50½; 33; 620; eight 5.25-in, six 21-in tt; Fairfield SB & E Co, Govan, 1943; transferred Royal New Zealand Navy 1948, rtnd RN 1956; b/up Briton Ferry 1959.

Bellwort: Flower cls corvette; 925; 205 x 33; 16; 85; one 4-in; Geo Brown & Co, Greenock, 1941; 1946, Eire government, rnd Cliona; b/up 1970-71.

Belmont: Town cls destroyer; 1190; 314½ x 30½; 30; 122; three 4-in, six 21-in tt; Newport News SB & DD Co, Newport News, 1919; ex-USN Satterlee, transferred 1940 to RN; torpedoed and sunk by U-82 in west Atlantic, Jan 31, 1942.

Belvoir: Hunt cls destroyer — Albrighton type; 1050; 280 x 31½; 27; 168; four 4-in, two 21-in tt; Cammell Laird, Birkenhead, 1942; b/up Bo'ness 1957.

Benbecula: Isles cls trawler; 560; 164 x 27½; 12; 40; one 12-pdr; Cook, Welton & Gemmell, Beverley, 1942; 1946, HM Customs & Excise, London, rnd Vigilant; 1962, Lloyd's Albert Yard & Motor Packet Services, Southampton, converted to accommodation ship; nothing more known.

Bentinck: Captain cls frigate; 1400; 306 x 36¾; 23½; 220; three 3-in; Bethlehem-Hingham Shipyard, 1943; ex-USN Buckley cls destroyer-escort Bull, DE-52, transferred Lease/Lend to RN 1943, rtnd USN 1946; b/up.

Bentley: Captain cls frigate; 1400; 306 x 36¾; 23½; 220; three 3-in; Bethlehem-Hingham Shipyard, 1943; ex-USN Buckley cls destroyer-escort Ebert, DE-74, transferred Lease/Lend to RN 1943, rtnd USN 1945; b/up.

Berberis: Berberis cls trawler; 540; 140 x 24; 11; 18; one 12-pdr; Cochrane & Sons, Selby, 1928; ex-Lord Hewart (Pickering & Haldane's Steam Trawling Co, Hull) bought RN 1939; 1947, NV Vissch Maats "Peten", Holland, rnd Bergen; b/up Holland 1957.

Bergamot: Flower cls corvette; 925; 205 x 33; 16; 85; one 4-in; Harland & Wolff, Belfast, 1941; 1947, Greek government, rnd Syros; 1951, Kavounides Shipping Co, Greece, converted to cargo ship, rnd Delphini, rnd Delfini 1955, rnd Ekaterini 1955;

Berkeley: Hunt cls destroyer — Atherstone type; 1000; 280 x 29; 27½; 146; four 4-in; Cammell Laird, Birkenhead, 1940; disabled by German aircraft during Dieppe raid, Aug 19, 1942, sunk by RN.

Berkeley Castle: Castle cls corvette; 1010; 252 x 36¾; 16½; 120; one 4-in; Barclay Curle & Co, Glasgow, 1943; b/up Grays 1956.

Bermuda: Fiji cls cruiser; 8525; 555½ x 62; 33; 980; twelve 6-in, eight 4-in, six 21-in tt; John Brown & Co, Clydebank, 1942; b/up Briton Ferry 1965.

Bern: Isles cls trawler; 560; 164 x 27½; 12; 40; one 12-pdr; Cook Welton & Gemmell, Beverley, 1942;

Berry: Captain cls frigate; 1140; 289½ x 35; 21; 200; three 3-in; Navy Yard, Boston, 1943; ex-USN Evarts cls destroyer-escort BDE-3, transferred Lease/Lend to RN 1943, rtnd USN 1946; b/up.

Berry Head: escort repair ship; 8580; 441½ x 57; 11; 440; sixteen 20-mm; Burrard DD, Vancouver, 1945;

Berwick: Kent cls cruiser; 10,900; 630 x 68⅓; 31½; 679; eight 8-in, eight 4-in; Fairfield SB & E Co, Govan, 1928; b/up Blyth 1948.

Beryl: Gem cls trawler; 615; 154½ x 25½; 12; 18; one 4-in; Cook Welton & Gemmell, Beverley, 1934; ex-Lady Adelaide (Jutland Amalgamated Trawlers, Hull) bought RN 1939; 1946, Iago Steam Trawling Co, London, rnd Red Knight; b/up Barrow 1962.

Betony: Modified Flower cls corvette; 980; 208¼ x 33; 16; 109; one 4-in; Alex Hall & Co, Aberdeen, 1943; transferred 1945 to Indian Navy, rnd Sind, rtnd RN 1946, rnd Betony; transferred 1947 to Siam (Thailand) Navy, rnd Prase; lost Korean War, Jan 13, 1951.

Beverley: Town cls destroyer; 1190; 314½ x 30½; 30; 122; one 4-in, three 21-in tt; Newport News SB & DD Co, Newport News, 1920; ex-USN Branch, transferred 1940 to RN; torpedoed and sunk by *U-188* in western Atlantic, Apr 11, 1943.

Bicester: Hunt cls destroyer — Blankney type; 1050; 280 x 31½; 27; 168; six 4-in; Hawthorn Leslie, Hebburn, 1942; b/up Grays 1956.

Bickerton: Captain cls frigate; 1400; 306 x 36¾; 23½; 220; three 3-in; Bethlehem-Hingham Shipyard, 1943; ex-USN Buckley cls destroyer-escort *Eisele, DE-75,* transferred Lease/Lend to RN 1943; torpedoed by *U-354* off North Cape, sunk by RN, Aug 22, 1944.

Bideford: Shoreham cls sloop; 1105; 266 x 34; 16; 100; two 4-in; HM Dockyard Devonport, 1931; b/up Milford Haven 1949.

Bigbury Bay: Bay cls frigate; 1580; 307½ x 38½; 19½; 157; four 4-in; Hall Russell & Co, Aberdeen, 1945; ex-*Loch Carloway* 1944; transferred 1959 to Portuguese Navy, rnd *Pacheo Pereira;* for disposal and breaking up 1970.

Biggal: Isles cls trawler; 560; 164 x 27½; 12; 40; one 12-pdr; Ferguson Bros, Port Glasgow, 1945; 1946, (owners not known), rnd *Frankfurt-Main;* pre-1949, NV Ostendsche Reederij, Belgium, rnd *Winston Spencer Churchill;* b/up Hamburg 1961.

Birch: Tree cls trawler; 530; 164 x 27½; 11½; 35; one 12-pdr; Cook Welton & Gemmell, Beverley, 1940; sold 1952, buyers not known, no name change; 1955, St Andrew's Steam Fishing Co, Hull, rnd *Magnolia;* b/up Holland 1962.

Birchol: Elmol cls oiler; 2410; 220 x 34⅔; 9½; 19; --; Barclay Curle & Co, Glasgow, 1917; stranded in Hebrides, Nov 29, 1939, and b/up.

Birdlip: Hills cls trawler; 750; 181¼ x 28; 11; 35; one 12-pdr; Cook Welton & Gemmell, Beverley, 1941; torpedoed by *U-547* off West Africa, June 13, 1944.

Birmingham: Southampton cls cruiser; 9100; 591½ x 61⅔; 32; 830; twelve 6-in, eight 4-in, six 21-in tt; HM Dockyard, Devonport, 1937; b/up Inverkeithing 1960.

Bishopdale: Abbeydale cls oiler; 17,357; 481½ x 62; 11½; 40; --; Lithgows Ltd, Port Glasgow, 1937; b/up Bilbao 1970.

Biter: Archer cls escort carrier; 12,150; 492 x 69½; 16½; 520; 20 aircraft, one 4-in; Sun SB & DD Co, Chester, 1942; ex cargo ship *Rio Parana;* ex USN, *BAVG-3,* transferred Lease/Lend to RN 1942, rtnd USN 1945; transferred to French Navy, 1945, rnd *Dixmude,* converted to barracks ship 1960; rtnd USN 1966; sunk as target.

Bittern: Bittern cls sloop; 1190; 282 x 37; 18¾; 125; four 4-in; J. S. White & Co, Cowes, 1937; sunk by German aircraft at Namsos, Apr 30, 1940.

Bittersweet: Flower cls corvette; 925; 205 x 33; 16; 85; one 4-in; Marine Industries, Sorel, 1940; transferred 1941 to Royal Canadian Navy, rtnd RN 1945; b/up Rosyth 1947.

Blackbird: Bird cls controlled minelayer; 560; 164 x 27½; 12; 40; one 4-in; Cook Welton & Gemmell, Beverley, 1943; ex-Isles cls trawler *Sheppey,* 1942; 1949, Gwent & Co, Aberdeen, converted to trawler, rnd *Goodmar;* 1953, G. J. Livanos, Greece, rnd *Iason;* foundered March 1955.

Blackmore: Hunt cls destroyer — Blankney type; 1050; 280 x 31½; 27; 168; six 4-in; Alex Stephen & Sons, Linthouse, 1942; transferred 1953 to Danish Navy, rnd *Esbern Snare;* sold Ystad shipbreakers 1966.

Blackpool: Bangor cls minesweeper; 590; 162 x 28; 16; 60; one 3-in; Harland & Wolff, Govan, 1940; transferred 1946 to Royal Norwegian Navy, rnd *Tana;* sold Bergen shipbreakers 1962.

Black Prince: Improved Dido cls cruiser; 5770; 512 x 50½; 33; 620; eight 5.25-in, six 21-in tt; Harland & Wolff, Belfast, 1943; transferred 1948 to Royal New Zealand Navy; b/up Japan 1962.

Black Ranger: Ranger cls oiler; 3417 grt; 365¾ x 47; 14; 47; --; Harland & Wolff, Govan, 1941; 1973, J. S. Latsis, Greece, rnd *Petrola XIV;*

Black Swan: Black Swan cls sloop; 1350; 299½ x 38; 19¼; 180; six 4-in; Yarrow & Co, Scotstoun, 1940; b/up Troon 1956.

Blackthorn: Tree cls trawler; 530; 164 x 27½; 11½; 35; one 12-pdr; Cook

Welton & Gemmell, Beverley, 1940;
1949, Vosper Ltd, Cosham, rnd
Maythorn; 1955, A/S Bergens
Fiskeriselskap, Norway, rnd *Klan;*
1963, Olav Ostervold Partrederi,
Norway, rnd *Jan Ove;* b/up Norway
1971.
Blackwater: Mersey cls trawler; 551;
148 x 22¾; 11; 20; two 3-in; Cochrane
& Sons, Selby, 1918; ex-*William
Inwood,* 1920; 1946, P. Jacobsen & H.
Jansen, Norway, rnd *Spleis;* lost Feb
12, 1956.
Blackwood: Captain cls frigate; 1140;
289½ x 35; 21; 200; three 3-in; Navy
Yard, Boston, 1943; ex-USN Evarts cls
destroyer-escort *BDE-4,* transferred
Lease/Lend to RN, 1943; torpedoed
and sunk by *U-764* off Portland, June
15, 1944.
Blanche: B cls destroyer; 1360; 323 x
32¼; 35; 138; four 4.7-in, eight 21-in tt;
Hawthorn Leslie, Hebburn, 1931;
mined in Thames estuary, Nov 13,
1939.
Blankney: Hunt cls destroyer —
Blankney type; 1050; 280 x 31½; 27;
168; six 4-in; John Brown & Co,
Clydebank, 1941; b/up Blyth 1959.
Blean: Hunt cls destroyer —
Albrighton type; 1050; 280 x 31½; 27;
168; four 4-in, two 21-in tt; Hawthorn
Leslie, Hebburn, 1942; torpedoed and
sunk by *U-443* off Oran, Dec 11, 1942.
Bleasdale: Hunt cls destroyer —
Albrighton type; 1050; 280 x 31½; 27;
168; four 4-in, two 21-in tt;
Vickers-Armstrongs, Tyne, 1941; b/up
Blyth 1956.
Blencathra: Hunt cls destroyer —
Blankney type; 1000; 280 x 29; 27½;
146; four 4-in; Cammell Laird,
Birkenhead, 1940; b/up Barrow 1957.
Blenheim: destroyer depot ship;
11,400 grt; 507¼ x 63¼; 14; 674;
four 4-in; Scotts SB & E Co, Greenock,
1920; ex-cargo liner *Achilles* (Ocean
SS Co, Liverpool) bought RN 1940 and
converted; b/up Barrow 1948.
Bligh: Captain cls frigate; 1400; 306 x
36¾; 23½; 220; three 3-in;
Bethlehem-Hingham Shipyard, 1943;
ex-USN Buckley cls destroyer-escort
Liddle, DE-76, transferred Lease/Lend
to RN 1943, rtnd USN 1945; b/up.
Bluebell: Flower cls corvette; 925; 205

x 33; 16; 85; one 4-in; Fleming &
Ferguson, Paisley, 1940; torpedoed
and sunk by *U-711* in Barentz Sea, Feb
17, 1945.
Blue Ranger: Ranger cls oiler; 3417
grt; 365¾ x 47; 14; 47; --; Harland &
Wolff, Govan, 1941; 1972, Crew
Tankershipping Co, Greece, rnd
Korytsa;
Blyth: Bangor cls minesweeper; 672 ;
180 x 28½; 16; 60; one 3-in; Blyth SB &
DD Co, Blyth, 1940; 1949, Radcliffe
Channel Islands Shipping Co,
Alderney, converted to
passenger-cargo ship, rnd
Radbourne; b/up Briton Ferry 1952.
Boadicea: B cls destroyer; 1360; 323 x
32¼; 35; 138; four 4.7-in, eight 21-in tt;
Hawthorn Leslie, Hebburn, 1931; sunk
by German aircraft off Portland, June
13, 1944.
Boardale: Abbeydale cls oiler; 17,338;
481½ x 62; 11½; 40; --; Harland & Wolff,
Govan, 1937; sunk after grounding
Assund Fjord, Apr 30, 1940.
Bold: BAT cls tug; 783; 143 x 33; 14; 34;
one 3-in; Defoe SB, Bay City, 1942;
ex-USN, transferred Lease/Lend to RN
1942, rtnd USN 1946; sold 1948.
Bolebroke: Hunt cls destroyer —
Albrighton type; 1050; 280 x 31½; 27;
168; four 4-in, two 21-in tt; Swan
Hunter & Wigham Richardson,
Wallsend, 1942; transferred 1942 to
Royal Hellenic Navy, rnd *Pindos,* rtnd
RN 1959; b/up Greece 1960.
Bombardier: Military cls trawler; 750;
193 x 30; 11; 40; one 4-in; Cook Welton
& Gemmell, Beverley, 1943; 1946,
Northern Fishing Co, Hull, rnd
Norman; wrecked south-east
Greenland, Oct 4, 1952.
Bonaventure: Dido cls cruiser; 5450;
512 x 50½; 33; 620; eight 5.25-in, six
21-in tt; Scotts SB & E Co, Greenock,
1940; torpedoed and sunk by Italian
submarine *Ambra* in Mediterranean,
Mar 31, 1941.
Bonaventure: midget submarine
depot ship; 10,423; 487¾ x 63; 10; --;
two 4-in; Greenock Dockyard Co,
Greenock, 1943; 1948, Clan Line,
London, converted to cargo ship, rnd
Clan Davidson; b/up Hong Kong 1962.
Bonito: Fish cls trawler; 670; 162 x
25¼; 11; 35; one 4-in; Cochrane &

Sons, Selby, 1942; 1946, Consolidated Fisheries, Grimsby, rnd *Blaefell;* 1956, B. Gelcer & Co, South Africa, rnd *Benjamin Gelcer;* scuttled off South Africa, February 1967.

Bootle: Bangor cls minesweeper; 656; 174 x 28½; 16; 60; one 3-in; Ailsa SB Co, Troon, 1942; b/up Charlestown 1949.

Borage: Flower cls corvette; 925; 205 x 33; 16; 85; one 4-in; Geo Brown & Co, Greenock, 1942; 1946, Eire Government, rnd *Macha;* b/up 1970-71.

Borde: mine destructor vessel; 2014 grt; 280¼ x 38; --; --; two 12-pdr; J. Crown & Sons, Sunderland, 1921; ex-cargo ship (Stephenson Clarke, London), bought RN 1939, converted 1942 to repair ship; b/up Milford Haven 1945.

Border: Hunt cls destroyer — Albrighton type; 1050; 280 x 31½; 27; 168; four 4-in, two 21-in tt; Swan Hunter & Wigham Richardson, Wallsend, 1942; transferred 1942 to Royal Hellenic Navy, rnd *Adrias;* irreparably damaged by mine, east of Kalymnos, Oct 22, 1943, b/up Gateshead 1945.

Boreas: B cls destroyer; 1360; 323 x 32¼; 35; 138; four 4.7-in, eight 21-in tt; Palmers SB & Iron Co, Hebburn, 1931; transferred 1944 to Royal Hellenic Navy rnd *Salamis,* rtnd RN 1951; b/up Rosyth 1952.

Boston: Bangor cls minesweeper; 656; 174 x 28½; 16; 60; one 3-in; Ailsa SB Co, Troon, 1941; b/up Charlestown 1949.

Boston Salvor: salvage vessel; 800; 183¼ x 37; 12; 35; one 3-in; Barbour Boat Works, New Bern, 1943; ex-USN, transferred Lease/Lend to RN, 1944; wrecked by flying bomb at Antwerp, Mar 16, 1945.

Bownet: Bayonet cls boom defence vessel; 530; 159¾ x 30½; 11½; 32; one 3-in; Blyth SB & DD Co, Blyth, 1939; sold Portsmouth shipbreakers 1958.

Boxer: fighter direction ship; 5,970; 400 x 49; 17; 500; eight 20-mm; Harland & Wolff, Belfast, 1943; b/up Barrow 1958.

Boxol: Elmol cls oiler; 2410; 220 x 34⅔; 9½; 19; --; Barclay Curle & Co, Glasgow, 1917; 1948, Oscar Shipping Co, London, rnd *Portnall;* 1951, Admiralty, rnd *Boxol;* b/up Llanelly 1959.

Boyne: Mersey cls trawler; 551; 148 x 22¾; 11; 20; two 3-in; Cochrane & Sons, Selby, 1918; ex-*William Jones,* 1920; 1946 P/f Vagaklettur, Denmark, rnd *Nypuberg;* b/up Germany 1957.

Bradford: Town cls destroyer; 1190; 314½ x 30½; 30; 122; one 4-in, three 21-in tt; Bethlehem SB Corp, Squantum, 1919; ex-USN *McLanahan,* transferred 1940 to RN; b/up Troon 1946.

Braid: River cls frigate; 1370; 301½ x 36½; 19; 140; two 4-in; Wm Simons & Co, Renfrew, 1944; transferred 1944 to French Navy, rnd *L'Aventure;* in reserve at L'Ecole Navale, 1961.

Braithwaite: Captain cls frigate; 1400; 306 x 36¾; 23½; 220; three 3-in; Bethlehem-Hingham Shipyard, 1943; ex-USN Buckley cls destroyer-escort *Straub, DE-77,* transferred Lease/Lend to RN 1943, rtnd USN 1945; b/up.

Bramble: Halcyon cls minesweeper; 875; 245 x 33½; 17; 80; two 4-in; HM Dockyard, Devonport, 1938; sunk by German surface force in Barentz Sea, Dec 31, 1942.

Bramble: Algerine cls minesweeper; 950; 235 x 35½; 16½; 104; one 4-in; Lobnitz & Co, Renfrew, 1945; b/up Gateshead 1961.

Brambleleaf: Leaf cls oiler; 12,370; 425 x 54½; 14; 26; --; Russell & Co, Port Glasgow, 1917; ex-*Rumol,* 1917; torpedoed in eastern Mediterranean and beached Alexandria, June 1942; b/up Spezia 1953.

Bramham: Hunt cls destroyer — Blankney type; 1050; 280 x 31½; 27; 168; six 4-in; Alex Stephen & Sons, Linthouse, 1942; transferred 1942 to Royal Hellenc Navy, rnd *Themistoklis,* rtnd RN 1959; b/up Greece 1960.

Brave: Algerine cls minesweeper; 950; 235 x 35½; 16½; 104; one 4-in; Blyth SB & DD Co, Blyth, 1943; rnd *Satellite* 1954 (Tyne RNVR training ship); b/up Dunston 1958.

Brazen: B cls destroyer; 1360; 323 x 32¼; 35; 138; four 4.7-in, eight 21-in tt; Palmers SB & Iron Co, Hebburn 1931; damaged by German aircraft, sunk off

Dover in tow, July 20, 1940.

Bream: Fish cls trawler; 670; 162 x 25¼; 11; 35; one 4-in; Cochrane & Sons, Selby, 1943; 1946, Consolidated Fisheries, Grimsby, rnd *Valafell;* b/up UK 1961.

Brecon: Hunt cls destroyer — Brecon type; 1175; 296 x 33⅓; 27; 170; six 4-in, three 21-in tt; J. I. Thornycroft & Co, Southampton, 1943; b/up Faslane 1962.

Bredon: Hills cls trawler; 750; 181¼ x 28; 11; 35; one 12-pdr; Cook Welton & Gemmell, Beverley, 1942; sunk by U-boat in North Atlantic Feb 8, 1943.

Bressay: Isles cls trawler; 560; 164 x 27½; 12; 40; one 12-pdr; Cook Welton & Gemmell, Beverley, 1942; sold 1946, buyers not known.

Bridgewater: Bridgewater cls sloop; 1045; 266 x 34; 16; 100; two 4-in; Hawthorn Leslie, Hebburn, 1928; b/up Milford Haven 1947.

Bridlington: Bangor cls minesweeper; 590; 162 x 28; 16; 60; one 3-in; Wm Denny & Bros, Dumbarton, 1940; transferred 1946 to Royal Air Force, no name change; b/up Plymouth 1958.

Bridport: Bangor cls minesweeper; 590; 162 x 28; 16; 60; one 3-in; Wm Denny & Bros, Dumbarton, 1940; transferred 1946 to Royal Air Force, rnd *Cawley;* b/up Plymouth 1958.

Brigand: Brigand cls tug; 840; 174 x 32; 15½; 43; one 3-in; Fleming & Ferguson, Paisley, 1937; sold Spezia shipbreakers 1960.

Brighton: Town cls destroyer; 1060; 314⅓ x 30½; 30; 122; one 4-in, three 21-in tt; Bethlehem SB, Fore River, 1919; ex-USN *Cowell,* transferred to RN 1940; transferred 1944 to Russia, rnd *Zharki,* rtnd RN 1949; b/up Bo'ness 1949.

Brilliant: B cls destroyer; 1360; 323 x 32¼; 35; 138; four 4.7-in, eight 21-in tt; Swan Hunter & Wigham Richardson, Wallsend, 1931; b/up Troon 1948.

Brissenden: Hunt cls destroyer — Brecon type; 1175; 296 x 33½; 27; 170; six 4-in, three 21-in tt; J. I. Thornycroft & Co, Southampton, 1943; b/up Dalmuir 1965.

British Lady: oiler; 6098 grt; 412 x 54¾; --; --; --; Sir J. L. Thompson & Sons, Sunderland, 1923; ex-tanker, same name (British Tanker Co, London) bought RN 1939; b/up Dunston 1947.

Britomart: Halcyon cls minesweeper; 875; 245 x 33½; 17; 80; two 4-in; HM Dockyard, Devonport, 1938; bombed in error by Allied aircraft off Normandy, Aug 27, 1944.

Brixham: Bangor cls minesweeper; 656; 174 x 28½; 16; 60; one 3-in; Blyth SB & DD Co, Blyth, 1942; b/up Dunston 1948.

Broadwater: Town cls destroyer; 1190; 314½ x 30½; 30; 122; three 4-in, six 21-in tt; Newport News SB & DD Co, Newport News, 1920; ex-USN *Mason,* transferred to RN 1940; torpedoed and sunk by *U-101* in North-West Approaches, Oct 18, 1941.

Broadway: Town cls destroyer; 1190; 314½ x 30½; 30; 122; one 4-in, three 21-in tt; Newport News SB & DD Co, Newport News, 1920; ex-USN *Hunt,* transferred to RN 1940; b/up Charlestown 1948.

Brocklesby: Hunt cls destroyer — Blankney type; 1000; 280 x 29; 27½; 146; four 4-in; Cammell Laird, Birkenhead, 1940; b/up Faslane 1968.

Broke: Shakespeare cls destroyer; 1480; 329 x 31; 31; 183; two 4.7-in; six 21-in tt; J. I. Thornycroft, Southampton/HM Dockyard, Pembroke, 1924; ex-*Rooke* 1921; damaged by shore batteries at Algiers, foundered in tow, Nov 8, 1942.

Broomdale: Abbeydale cls oiler; 17,338; 481½ x 62; 11½; 40; --; Harland & Wolff, Govan, 1938; b/up Bruges 1960.

Brora: Isles cls trawler; 560; 164 x 27½; 12; 40; one 12-pdr; Cook Welton & Gemmell, Beverley, 1941; wrecked in Hebrides, Sept 6, 1941.

Brown Ranger: Ranger cls oiler; 3417 grt; 365¾ x 47; 14; 47; --; Harland & Wolff, Govan, 1941;

Bruce: Scott cls destroyer; 1530; 332½ x 31¾; 31; 183; --; Cammell Laird, Birkenhead, 1918; expended as target off Isle of Wight, November, 1939.

Bruizer: fighter direction ship; 5970; 400 x 49; 17; 500; eight 20-mm; Harland & Wolff, Belfast, 1943; 1948, Soc Anon des Enterprises Chimiques et Electriques, Belgium, converted to merchant ship, rnd *Nilla;* 1950, Cia

Naviera Estrella de Plata SA, Panama, lengthened and converted to passenger ship, rnd *Silver Star;* 1957, Compania de Navegacion Fluvial Argentina, Argentine, rnd *Ciudad de Santa Fe;* b/up Argentina 1968.

Bruray: Isles cls trawler: 560; 164 x 27½; 12; 40; one 12-pdr; Cook Welton & Gemmell, Beverley, 1942; transferred 1943 to Portuguese Navy, rnd *P-1,* rnd *San Miguel,* 1946; b/up Lisbon 1957.

Bryher: Isles cls trawler; 560; 164 x 27½; 12; 40; one 12-pdr; Cook Welton & Gemmell, Beverley, 1943; sold 1947 to unknown Norwegian owners.

Bryony: Flower cls corvette; 925; 205 x 33; 16; 85; one 4-in; Harland & Wolff, Belfast, 1941; 1947, Den norske Stat, Norway, converted to weather ship, rnd *Polarfront II;*

Buccaneer: Brigand cls tug; 840; 174 x 32; 15½; 43; one 3-in; Fleming & Ferguson, Paisley, 1937; sank after collision with destroyer *Saintes,* Aug 25/26, 1946.

Buchan Ness: landing craft repair ship; 8580; 441½ x 57; 11; 440; sixteen 20-mm; West Coast Shipbuilders, Vancouver, 1945; b/up Faslane 1959.

Buddleia: Modified Flower cls corvette; 980; 208¼ x 33; 16; 109; one 4-in; Alex Hall, Aberdeen, 1943; transferred 1944 to Royal Canadian Navy, rnd *Giffard;* b/up Canada 1952.

Bude: Bangor cls minesweeper; 672; 180 x 28½; 16; 60; one 3-in; Lobnitz & Co, Renfrew, 1941; transferred 1946 to Egyptian Navy, rnd *Nasr;*

Bugloss: Modified Flower cls corvette; 980; 208¼ x 33; 16; 109; one 4-in; John Crown & Sons, Sunderland, 1943; transferred 1945 to Indian Navy, rnd *Assam;*

Bulldog: B cls destroyer; 1360; 323 x 32¼; 35; 138; four 4.7-in, eight 21-in tt; Swan Hunter & Wigham Richardson, Wallsend, 1931; b/up Rosyth 1946.

Bullen: Captain cls frigate; 1400; 306 x 36¾; 23½; 220; three 3-in; Bethlehem-Hingham Shipyard, 1943; ex-USN Buckley cls destroyer-escort *DE-78,* transferred Lease/Lend to RN 1943; torpedoed by *U-775* off Cape Wrath, Dec 6, 1944.

Bullfinch: Bull cls cable ship; 2600; 252 x 36½; 12; 46; one 4-in; Swan Hunter & Wigham Richardson, Wallsend, 1940;

Bullfrog: Bull cls cable ship; 2600; 252 x 36½; 12; 46; one 4-in; Swan Hunter & Wigham Richardson, Wallsend, 1944; 1947, Cable & Wireless, London, rnd *Retriever,* rnd *Retriever III,* 1960; 1961, Commercial Cable Co, London, rnd *Cable Restorer;* 1972, South Atlantic Cable Co, Capetown, no name change;

Bullhead: Bull cls cable ship; 2600; 252 x 36½; 12; 46; one 4-in; Swan Hunter & Wigham Richardson, Wallsend, 1945; 1947, Cable & Wireless, London, rnd *Electra;* 1959, Commercial Cable Co, London, rnd *Cable Guardian;* b/up Inverkeithing 1964.

Bulrush: Modified Flower cls corvette; 980; 208¼ x 33; 16; 109; one 4-in; John Crown & Sons, Sunderland, 1944; transferred 1944 to Royal Canadian Navy, rnd *Mimico;* 1950, Balleneros Ltd SA, Uruguay, converted to whale catcher rnd *Olympic Victor;* 1956, Kyokuyo Hogei KK, Japan, rnd *Otori Maru No 12,* rnd *Kyo Maru No 25,*1962;

Burdock: Flower cls corvette; 925; 205 x 33; 16; 85; one 4-in; John Crown & Sons, Sunderland, 1941; b/up Hayle 1947.

Burges: Captain cls frigate; 1140; 289½ x 35; 21; 200; three 3-in; Navy Yard, Boston, 1943; ex-USN Evarts cls destroyer-escort *BDE-12,* transferred Lease/Lend to RN 1943, rtnd USN 1946; b/up.

Burgonet: Bayonet cls boom defence vessel; 530; 159¾ x 30½; 11½; 32; one 3-in; Blyth SB & DD Co, Blyth, 1939; sold Italian buyers 1959.

Burnet: Modified Flower cls corvette; 980; 208¼ x 33; 16; 109; one 4-in; Ferguson Bros, Port Glasgow, 1943; transferred 1945 to Indian Navy, rnd *Gondwana,* rtnd RN 1945, rnd *Burnet;* transferred 1947 to Royal Siamese Navy, rnd *Bangpakong;*

Burnham: Town cls destroyer; 1190; 314½ x 30½; 30; 122; one 4-in, three 21-in tt; Bethlehem SB, Quincy, 1919; ex-USN *Aulick,* transferred to RN 1940; b/up Pembroke Dock 1948.

Burra: Isles cls trawler; 560; 164 x

27½; 12; 40; one 12-pdr; Goole SB & Repairing Co, Goole, 1941; transferred 1946 to Italian Navy, rnd *RD-301;* used as target, mid-1960s.

Burwell: Town cls destroyer; 1190; 314½ x 30½; 30; 122; one 4-in, three 21-in tt; Bethlehem SB, Squantum, 1919; ex-USN *Laub,* transferred to RN 1940; b/up Milford Haven 1948.

Bushwood: mine destructor vessel; 2314 grt; 293½ x 41½; --; --; --; S. P. Austin & Son, Sunderland, 1930; ex-cargo ship, same name (W. France Fenwick, London) bought RN 1940; converted to degaussing vessel, 1942; 1946, General Investment Co, Hong Kong, converted to cargo ship, no name change; b/up Hong Kong 1951.

Bustler: Bustler cls tug; 1800; 205 x 38½; 15; 42; one 3-in; H. Robb, Leith, 1942; 1973, Brodopas, Yugoslavia, rnd *Mocni;*

Bute: Isles cls trawler; 560; 164 x 27½; 12; 40; one 12-pdr; Goole SB & Repairing Co, Goole, 1941; sold 1946, buyers not known.

Butser: Hills cls trawler; 750; 181¼ x 28; 11; 35; one 12-pdr; Cook Welton & Gemmell, Beverley, 1941; 1946, Devon Fishing Co, Hull, rnd *Balthazar;* 1952, Loyal Steam Fishing Co, Grimsby, rnd *Royal Marine;* damaged by fire, July 25, 1963, b/up Troon 1963.

Buttercup: Flower cls corvette; 925; 205 x 33; 16; 85; one 4-in; Harland & Wolff, Belfast, 1942; transferred 1942 to Royal Norwegian Navy, rnd *Nordkyn;* 1956, Thor Dahl, Norway, converted to whale catcher, rnd *Thoris;* b/up Norway 1970.

Buttermere: Lake cls trawler; 560; 147½ x 26½; 12½; 36; one 12-pdr; Smith's Dock Co, Middlesbrough, 1939; ex-whale catcher *Kos XXV,* (A. Jahre, Norway) bought RN 1939, rnd; 1948, A/S Thor Dahl, Norway, converted to whale catcher, rnd *Tiern;* 1959, Nor'-West Whaling Co, Australia, rnd *Robert Moore;* about 1965, J. Franetovich, Australia, converted to tug, no name change; dismantled and scuttled.

Buxton: Town cls destroyer; 1190; 314½ x 30½; 30; 122; one 4-in, three 21-in tt; Bethlehem SB, Squantum, 1919; ex-USN *Edwards,* transferred

RN 1940; transferred to Royal Canadian Navy, 1942; b/up US 1945.

Byard: Captain cls frigate; 1400; 306 x 36¾; 23½; 220; three 3-in; Bethlehem-Hingham Shipyard, 1943; ex-USN Buckley cls destroyer-escort *Donaldson, DE-55,* transferred Lease/Lend to RN 1943, rtnd USN 1945; b/up.

Byron: Captain cls frigate; 1400; 306 x 36¾; 23½; 220; three 3-in; Bethlehem-Hingham Shipyard, 1943; ex-USN Buckley cls destroyer-escort *DE-79,* transferred Lease/Lend to RN 1943, rtnd USN 1945; b/up.

Cachalot: Porpoise cls minelaying submarine; 1520/2117; 293 x 25½; 15¾/8¾; 55; 50 mines, six 21-in tt, one 4-in; Scotts SB & E Co, Greenock, 1938; sank after being rammed by Italian torpedo boat *Papa* off Benghazi, July 30, 1941.

Cadmus: Algerine cls minesweeper; 950; 235 x 35½; 16½; 104; one 4-in; Harland & Wolff, Belfast, 1942; transferred 1950 to Belgian Navy, rnd *Georges Lecointe;* b/up Burght 1960.

Caesar: CA cls destroyer; 1730; 362¾ x 35¾; 36; 222; four 4.5-in, eight 21-in tt; John Brown & Co, Clydebank, 1944; ex-*Ranger* 1944; b/up Blyth 1967.

Caicos: Colony cls frigate; 1430; 304 x 37½; 18; 120; three 3-in; Walsh-Kaiser Co, Providence, 1943; ex USN *PF-77,* transferred Lease/Lend to RN rnd *Hannam* rnd *Caicos* 1943, rtnd USN 1946; transferred 1946 to Argentine Navy, rnd *Santissima Trinidad,* converted to survey ship, rnd *Comodoro Augusto Lassere,* 1963; withdrawn from service 1970.

Cailiff: Isles cls trawler; 560; 164 x 27½; 12; 40; one 12-pdr; Collingwood Shipyards, Collingwood, 1942; 1947, A/S Heinsa, Norway, rnd *Borgenes;*

Cairndale: Dale cls oiler; 17,000; 483 x 59½; 11½; 40; --; Harland & Wolff, Belfast, 1939; ex-tanker *Erato* (Shell Tanker Co, London) bought on stocks RN 1939; sunk by Italian submarine *Guglielmo Marconi* west of Gibraltar, May 30, 1941.

Cairo: Carlisle cls cruiser; 4200; 451½

x 43½; 29; 400; eight 4-in; Cammell
Laird, Birkenhead, 1919; damaged by
torpedo from Italian submarine *Axum*
in Mediterranean on Aug 12, 1942, and
sunk by RN.

Caistor Castle: Castle cls corvette;
1010; 252 x 36¾; 16½; 120; one 4-in; J.
Lewis & Sons, Aberdeen, 1944; b/up
Troon 1956.

Calcutta: Carlisle cls cruiser; 4200;
451½ x 43½; 29; 400; eight 4-in;
Vickers Ltd, Barrow, 1919; bombed
and sunk by aircraft north of
Alexandria, June 1, 1941.

Calder: Captain cls frigate; 1400; 306
x 36¾; 23½; 220; three 3-in;
Bethlehem-Hingham Shipyard, 1943;
ex-USN Buckley cls destroyer-escort
Formoe, DE-58, transferred
Lease/Lend to RN 1943, rtnd USN
1946; b/up.

Caldwell: Town cls destroyer; 1090;
314⅓ x 30½; 30; 122; three 4-in, six
21-in tt; Bath Iron Works, Bath, 1919;
ex-USN *Hale,* transferred RN 1940;
b/up Granton 1945.

Caldy: Isles cls trawler; 560; 164 x
27½; 12; 40; one 12-pdr; J. Lewis &
Sons, Aberdeen, 1943;

Caledon: Caledon cls cruiser; 4120;
450 x 42; 29; 437; five 6-in, two 3-in,
eight 21-in tt; Cammell Laird,
Birkenhead, 1917; b/up Dover 1948.

Caledonia: training ship; 56,599 grt;
956 x 100; --; --; --; Blohm & Voss,
Hamburg 1922; ex-*Bismarck* 1922;
ex-passenger liner *Majestic* (Cunard
White Star Line, Liverpool) bought by
Admiralty from T. W. Ward & Sons,
shipbreakers, 1936; irreparably
damaged by fire Sep 29, 1939, b/up
Inverkeithing 1943.

Caledonian Salvor: salvage vessel;
1360; 213 x 39; 16½; 35; one 3-in;
Basalt Rock Co, California, 1943;
ex-USN transferred Lease/Lend to RN
1943, transferred 1943 to
Commonwealth Marine Salvage
Board, Sydney NSW; rtnd USN 1946;
1948 Royal Australian Navy; 1958,
Island Tug & Barge Ltd, Canada, rnd
Sudbury II;

Calendula: Flower cls corvette; 925;
205 x 33; 16; 85; one 4-in; Harland &
Wolff, Belfast, 1940; transferred to US
Navy, rnd *Ready,* 1942, rtnd RN 1946,

rnd *Calendula;* 1948, Zubi Shipping
Co, London, converted to cargo ship,
rnd *Villa Cisneros;* 1949, Bens
Industrias Pesqueras Africanas SA,
Spain, rnd *Villa Bens;* 1963, Spanish
government, no name change
(nothing more known).

Calpe: Hunt cls destroyer — Blankney
type; 1050; 280 x 31½; 27; 168; six
4-in; Swan Hunter & Wigham
Richardson, Wallsend, 1941;
transferred 1952 to Danish Navy, rnd
Rolf Krake; sold Ystad shipbreakers
1966.

Calvay: Isles cls trawler; 560; 164 x
27½; 12; 40; one 12-pdr; Cook Welton
& Gemmell, Beverley, 1944; 1948,
Humber Pilots Steam Cutter Co, Hull,
converted to pilot cutter, rnd *Wm
Fenton;*

Calypso: Caledon cls cruiser; 4120;
450 x 42; 29; 437; five 6-in, two 3-in,
eight 21-in tt; Hawthorn Leslie,
Hebburn, 1917; sunk by Italian
submarine *Bagnolini* in
Mediterranean, June 12, 1940.

Cam: River cls frigate; 1370; 301½ x
36½; 19; 140; two 4-in; Geo Brown &
Co, Greenock, 1944; irreparably
damaged by mine, 1944, b/up Tyne
1945.

Cambrian: CA cls destroyer; 1710;
362¾ x 35¾; 36; 186; four 4.5-in, eight
21-in tt; Scotts SB & E Co, Greenock,
1944; ex-*Spitfire,* 1943; b/up Briton
Ferry 1971.

Cambrian Salvor: salvage vessel;
1360; 213 x 39; 16½; 35; one 3-in;
Basalt Rock Co, California, 1943;
ex-USN, transferred Lease/Lend to RN
1943, transferred 1943 to
Commonwealth Marine Salvage
Board, Sydney NSW; rtnd USN 1946;
1948, Royal Australian Navy; 1958,
Island Tug & Barge Ltd, Canada, no
name change; 1962, L. Smit & Co's
Internationale Sleepdienst, Holland,
rnd *Caribische Zee;* 1964, Collins
Submarine Pipelines, London, rnd
Collinsea; 1971, Establishment Collins
International, Kuwait, rnd *Francois C.;*

Camellia: Flower cls corvette; 925;
205 x 33; 16; 85; one 4-in; Harland &
Wolff, Belfast, 1940; 1948, Ned Mij
voor de Walvisvaart, Holland,
converted to whale catcher, rnd *Hetty*

W. Vinke; b/up Cape Town 1965.

Cameron: Town cls destroyer; 1190; 314½ x 30½; 30; 122; three 4-in, six 21-in tt; Bethlehem SB, Quincy, 1919; ex-USN *Welles,* transferred to RN 1940; damaged by German aircraft at Portsmouth, Dec 15, 1940, b/up Falmouth 1944.

Campania: escort carrier; 12,450; 540 x 70; 17; 700; 20 aircraft, two 4-in; Harland & Wolff, Belfast, 1944; ex-cargo liner (Shaw Savill Line, London) bought RN on stocks; b/up Blyth 1955.

Campanula: Flower cls corvette; 925; 205 x 33; 16; 85; one 4-in; Fleming & Ferguson, Paisley, 1940; b/up Tyne 1947.

Campbell: Scott cls destroyer; 1530; 332½ x 31¾; 31; 183; three 4.7-in, one 4-in; Cammell Laird, Birkenhead, 1919; b/up Rosyth 1948.

Campbeltown: Town cls destroyer; 1090; 314⅓ x 30½; 30; 122; one 4-in, three 21-in tt; Bath Iron Works, Bath, 1919; ex-USN *Buchanan,* transferred to RN 1940; expended in destroying lock gates at St Nazaire, Mar 28, 1942; wreck b/up St Nazaire 1946.

Camperdown: Battle cls destroyer; 2315; 379 x 40¼; 36; 247; four 4.5-in, eight 21-in tt; Fairfield SB & E Co, Govan, 1945; b/up Faslane 1970.

Campion: Flower cls corvette; 925; 205 x 33; 16; 85; one 4-in; J. Crown & Sons, Sunderland, 1941; b/up Newport 1947.

Campobello: Isles cls trawler; 560; 164 x 27½; 12; 40; one 12-pdr; Collingwood Shipyards, Collingwood, 1942; lost in North Atlantic, March 1943.

Candytuft: Flower cls corvette; 925; 205 x 33; 16; 85; one 4-in; Grangemouth Dockyard Co, Grangemouth, 1940; transferred 1942 to US Navy rnd *Tenacity,* rtnd RN 1946 rnd *Candytuft;* 1946, Wheelock Marden, Hong Kong, no name change; 1947, China owners (nothing more known).

Candytuft: Modified Flower cls corvette; 980; 208¼ x 33; 16; 109; one 4-in; A. & J. Inglis, Glasgow, 1944; transferred 1944 to Royal Canadian Navy, rnd *Longbranch;* 1947; Rexton Kent, Canada, converted, rnd *Rexton*

Kent II, rnd *Rexton Kent,* 1948; scuttled off Canada 1966.

Canna: Isles cls trawler; 560; 164 x 27½; 12; 40; one 12-pdr; Cochrane & Sons, Selby, 1941; lost in explosion at Lagos, Dec 5, 1942.

Canso: Bangor cls minesweeper; 672; 180 x 28½; 16; 60; one 3-in; North Vancouver Ship Repairs, North Vancouver, 1941; b/up Sunderland 1948.

Capel: Captain cls frigate; 1140; 289½ x 35; 21; 200; three 3-in; Navy Yard, Boston, 1943; ex-USN Evarts cls destroyer-escort *Wintle, DE-266,* transferred Lease/Lend to RN 1943; torpedoed by *U-486* in English Channel, Dec 26, 1944.

Capetown: Carlisle cls cruiser; 4200; 451½ x 43½; 29; 437; five 6-in, two 3-in, eight 21-in tt; Cammell Laird, Birkenhead/HM Dockyard, Pembroke, 1922; b/up Preston 1946.

Caprice: CA cls destroyer; 1710; 362¾ x 35¾; 36; 186; four 4.5-in, eight 21-in tt; Yarrow & Co, Scotstoun, 1944; ex-*Swallow,* 1943;

Caradoc: Caledon cls cruiser; 4120; 450 x 42; 29; 437; five 6-in, two 3-in, eight 21-in tt; Scotts SB & E Co, Greenock, 1917; b/up Briton Ferry 1946.

Caraquet: Bangor cls minesweeper; 672; 180 x 28½; 16; 60; one 3-in; North Vancouver Ship Repairs, North Vancouver, 1941; transferred RCN 1941; rtnd 1945; transferred 1946 to Portuguese Navy, rnd *Almirante Lacerda;*

Cardiff: Ceres cls cruiser; 4190; 450 x 43½; 29; 437; five 6-in, two 3-in, eight 21-in tt; Fairfield SB & E Co, Govan, 1917; b/up Troon 1946.

Cardigan Bay: Bay cls frigate; 1580; 307½ x 38½; 19½; 157; four 4-in; H. Robb, Leith, 1945; ex-*Loch Laxford,* 1944; b/up Troon 1962.

Carisbrooke Castle: Castle cls corvette; 1010; 252 x 36¾; 16½; 120; one 4-in; Caledon SB & E Co, Dundee, 1943; b/up Faslane 1958.

Carlisle: Carlisle cls cruiser; 4200; 451½ x 43½; 29; 400; eight 4-in; Fairfield SB & E Co, Govan, 1918; damaged by German aircraft off Strait of Scarpanto, Oct 9, 1943, used as accommodation ship at Alexandria; b/up Alexandria 1948.

Carnation: Flower cls corvette; 925; 205 x 33; 16; 85; one 4-in; Grangemouth Dockyard Co, Grangemouth, 1940; transferred 1943 to Royal Netherlands Navy, rnd *Friso,* rtnd RN 1945, rnd *Carnation;* 1949, South Georgia Co (C. Salvesen), Leith, converted to whale catcher, rnd *Southern Laurel;* b/up Stavanger 1966.

Carron: CA cls destroyer; 1710; 362¾ x 35¾; 36; 186; four 4.5-in, eight 21-in tt; Scotts SB & E Co, Greenock, 1944; ex-*Strenuous,* 1943; b/up Inverkeithing 1967.

Carysfort: CA cls destroyer; 1710; 362¾ x 35¾; 36; 186; four 4.5-in, eight 21-in tt; J. S. White & Co, Cowes, 1945; ex-*Pique,* 1943; b/up 1970.

Cassandra: CA cls destroyer; 1710; 362¾ x 35¾; 36; 186; four 4.5-in, eight 21-in tt; Yarrow & Co, Scotstoun, 1944; ex-*Tourmaline,* 1943; b/up Inverkeithing 1967.

Castleton: Town cls destroyer; 1090; 314⅓ x 30½; 30; 122; one 4-in, three 21-in tt; Bath Iron Works, Bath, 1919; ex-USN *Aaron Ward,* transferred 1940 to RN; b/up Bo'ness 1948.

Catherine: Catherine cls minesweeper; 890; 221 x 32; 18; 109; one 3-in; Associated Shipbuilders, Seattle, 1943; ex-USN Auk cls minesweeper *BAM-9,* transferred Lease/Lend to RN 1943, rtnd USN 1946; transferred 1947 to Turkish Navy, rnd *Erdemli,* withdrawn from service 1963.

Cato: Catherine cls minesweeper; 890; 221 x 32; 18; 109; one 3-in; Associated Shipbuilders, Seattle, 1943; ex-USN Auk cls minesweeper *BAM-10* transferred Lease/Lend to RN 1943; sunk off Normandy by human torpedo, July 6, 1944.

Catterick: Hunt cls destroyer — Albrighton type; 1050; 280 x 31½; 27; 168; four 4-in, two 21-in tt; Vickers-Armstrongs, Barrow, 1942; transferred 1946 to Royal Hellenic Navy, rnd *Hastings;* b/up Piraeus 1963.

Cattistock: Hunt cls destroyer — Atherstone type; 1000; 280 x 29; 27½;

146; four 4-in; Yarrow & Co, Scotstoun 1940; b/up Newport 1957.

Cava: Isles cls trawler; 560; 164 x 27½; 12; 40; one 12-pdr; Fleming & Ferguson, Paisley, 1941; 1947, 'Venturi' Salvataggi, Ricuperi & Imprese Marittime, Italy, converted to tug, rnd *Lucia Venturi;*

Cavalier: CA cls destroyer; 1710; 362¾ x 35¾; 36; 186; four 4.5-in, eight 21-in tt; J. S. White & Co, Cowes, 1944; ex-*Pellew,* 1943; for disposal; preservation as museum ship proposed, 1974.

Cavendish: CA cls destroyer; 1730; 362¾ x 35¾; 36; 222; four 4.5-in, eight 21-in tt; John Brown & Co, Clydebank, 1944; ex-*Sibyl,* 1943; b/up Blyth 1967.

Cayman: Colony cls frigate; 1430; 304 x 37½; 18; 120; three 3-in; Walsh-Kaiser Co, Providence, 1944; ex-USN *PF-78,* transferred Lease/Lend to RN rnd *Harland,* rnd *Cayman,* 1944, rtnd USN 1946; sold New York shipbreakers 1947.

Ceanothus: Modified Flower cls corvette; 980; 208¼ x 33; 16; 109; one 4-in; Ferguson Bros, Port Glasgow, 1943; transferred 1944 to Royal Canadian Navy, rnd *Forest Hill;* sold Hamilton, Ont, shipbreakers 1945.

Cedar: Berberis cls trawler; 649; 154½ x 25½; 11½; 18; one 12-pdr; Cook Welton & Gemmell, Beverley, 1933; ex-*Arab* (Hellyer Bros, Hull) bought RN 1935; 1946, Iago Steam Trawler Co, London, rnd *Red Gauntlet;* wrecked Aug, 1947.

Cedardale: Dale cls oiler; 17,000; 483 x 59½; 11½; 40; --; Blythswood SB Co, Glasgow, 1939; bought from Shell Tanker Co, 1939; b/up Hong Kong 1961.

Celandine: Flower cls corvette; 925; 205 x 33; 16; 85; one 4-in; Grangemouth Dockyard Co, Grangemouth, 1941; b/up Portaferry 1948.

Celerol: Belgol cls oiler; 5620; 335 x 41½; 14; 39; --; Short Bros, Sunderland, 1917; b/up Rosyth 1958.

Celia: Shakespearian cls trawler; 545; 164 x 27¾; 12; 35; one 12-pdr; Cochrane & Sons, Selby, 1940; 1946, Armand Vella, France, converted to cargo ship, no name change; 1958, J.

Prat, France, rnd *Vanda;* 1961, Ong
Kin Hock, Malaya, rnd *Kuala Kangsar;*
sunk at Singapore, Mar 19, 1969.

Centurion: target ship; 25,500; 597½ x
89; 16; 250; --; HM Dockyard,
Devonport, 1913; former King George
V cls battleship, converted 1926-27 to
wireless controlled target; became
dummy battleship *Anson,* 1941;
expended as part of breakwater
forming temporary harbour,
Arromanches June 1944.

Ceres: Ceres cls cruiser; 4190; 450 x
43½; 29; 437; five 6-in, two 3-in, eight
21-in tt; John Brown & Co, Clydebank,
1917; b/up Blyth 1946.

Ceylon: Uganda cls cruiser; 8875;
555½ x 62; 31½; 950; nine 6-in, eight
4-in, six 21-in tt; Alex Stephen & Sons,
Linthouse, 1943; transferred 1960 to
Peru, rnd *Coronel Bolognesi;*

Challenger: survey ship; 1140; 220 x
36; 12½; 84; --; HM Dockyard,
Chatham, 1931; b/up Dover 1945.

Chameleon: Algerine cls
minesweeper; 950; 235 x 35½; 16½;
104; one 4-in; Harland & Wolff, Belfast,
1944; b/up Silloth 1966.

Chamois: Catherine cls minesweeper;
890; 221 x 32; 18; 109; one 3-in;
Associated Shipbuilders, Seattle,
1943; ex-USN Auk cls minesweeper
BAM-12 transferred Lease/Lend to RN
1943; damaged by mine off Normandy,
July 21, 1944; 1948, sold for
conversion to passenger ship, to be
renamed *Morning Star,* work stopped;
1949, South Western Steam
Navigation Co, Totnes, for parts (see
Strenuous).

Chance: Catherine cls minesweeper;
890; 221 x 32; 18; 109; one 3-in; Gulf
SB Corp, Houston, 1943; ex-USN Auk
cls minesweeper *BAM-13* transferred
Lease/Lend to RN 1943, rtnd USN,
1946; transferred 1947 to Turkish
Navy, rnd *Edremit;* withdrawn from
service 1965.

Chanticleer: Modified Black Swan cls
sloop; 1430; 299½ x 38; 20; 192; six
4-in; Wm Denny & Bros, Dumbarton,
1942; damaged by torpedo from
U-238, Nov 18, 1943, towed to Azores,
became base ship *Lusitania,* rnd
Lusitania II, rnd *Hesperides;*
b/up Lisbon 1946.

Charlestown: Town cls destroyer;
1060; 314⅓ x 30½; 30; 122; one 4-in,
three 21-in tt; Newport News SB & DD
Co, Newport News, 1919; ex-USN
Abbot, transferred 1940 to RN; b/up
Sunderland 1947.

Charlock: Modified Flower cls
corvette; 980; 208¼ x 33; 16; 109; one
4-in; Ferguson Bros, Port Glasgow,
1944; transferred 1946 to Indian Navy,
rnd *Mahratta;*

Charon: Assurance cls tug; 1045; 157
x 35; 13; 31; one 3-in; Cochrane &
Sons, Selby, 1942; 1947, rnd *Alligator;*
1958, H. G. Pounds, Portsmouth, no
name change; 1958, J. D. Irving,
Canada, rnd *Irving Birch,* rnd *Irving
Forty,* 1967; sold Sussex NB
shipbreakers 1972.

Charybdis: Dido cls cruiser; 5450; 512
x 50½; 33; 620; eight 4.5-in, six 21-in
tt; Cammell Laird, Birkenhead, 1941;
torpedoed and sunk by German
torpedo boats off North France, Oct
23, 1943.

Chaser: Attacker cls escort carrier;
10,200; 496 x 69½; 16; 650; 15-20
aircraft; Ingalls SB Corp, Pascagoula,
1943; ex-cargo liner *Mormacgulf,*
ex-USN *Breton, BAVG-10,* transferred
Lease/Lend to RN 1943, rtnd USN
1946; 1948, Vereenig de
Nederlandsche Scheep Maats
Holland, converted to cargo ship, rnd
Aagtekerk; 1967, Chinese Maritime
Trust, Taiwan, rnd *E. Yung;* damaged
by fire at Kaohsiung Dec 3, 1972, b/up
Kaohsiung 1973.

Chattenden: armament carrier; 663;
137 x 24½; 8; --; --; Richards
Ironworks, Lowestoft, 1944; converted
to dumb derrick lighter, 1961; sold
Portsmouth shipbreakers 1967.

Cheerful: Algerine cls minesweeper;
950; 235 x 35½; 16½; 104; one 4-in;
Harland & Wolff, Belfast, 1944; b/up
Sheerness 1963.

Cheerly: BAT cls tug; 783; 143 x 33;
14; 34; one 3-in; Levingston SB,
Orange, 1944; ex-USN, transferred
Lease/Lend to RN 1944, rtnd USN
1946; sold 1946.

Chelmer: River cls frigate; 1370; 301½
x 36½; 19; 140; two 4-in; Geo Brown &
Co, Greenock, 1943; b/up
Charlestown 1957.

Chelsea: Town cls destroyer; 1090; 314⅓ x 30½; 30; 122; one 4-in, three 21-in tt; Bath Iron Works, Bath, 1919; ex-USN *Crowninshield,* transferred 1940 to RN; transferred 1944 to Soviet Union, rnd *Derzki,* rtnd RN 1949; b/up Bo'ness 1949.

Cherryleaf: Leaf cls oiler; 12,370; 425 x 54½; 14; 26; --; Sir Raylton Dixon & Co, Middlesbrough, 1917; ex-*Persol,* 1917; 1946, British Oil Shipping Co, London, rnd *Alan Clore;* b/up Dalmuir 1950.

Cherwell: Mersey cls trawler; 551; 148 x 22¾; 11; 20; two 3-in; Cochrane & Sons, Selby, 1918; ex-*James Jones,* 1920; sold UK company 1946.

Chesterfield: Town cls destroyer, 1190; 314½ x 30½; 30; 122; one 4-in, three 21-in tt; Newport News SB & DD Co, Newport News, 1920; ex-USN *Welborn C. Wood,* transferred to RN 1940; b/up Dunston 1947.

Chestnut: Tree cls trawler; 530; 164 x 27½; 11½; 35; one 12-pdr; Goole SB & Repairing Co, Goole, 1940; mined off North Foreland, Nov 30, 1940.

Chiddingfold: Hunt cls destroyer — Blankney type; 1050; 280 x 31½; 27; 168; six 4-in; Scotts SB & E Co, Greenock, 1941; transferred 1953 to India, rnd *Ganga;*

Chrysanthemum: Flower cls corvette; 925; 205 x 33; 16; 85; one 4-in; Harland & Wolff, Belfast, 1942; transferred 1942 to French Navy, rnd *Commandant Drogou,* rtnd RN 1946; 1948, United Whaling Co, Durban, converted to whale catcher, rnd *Terje 10;* 1959, Portuguese Navy, converted to survey ship, rnd *Carvalho Araujo;*

Churchill: Town cls destroyer; 1190; 314½ x 30½; 30; 122; one 4-in, three 21-in tt; Newport News SB & DD Co, Newport News, 1920; ex-USN *Herndon,* transferred 1940 to RN; transferred 1944 to Soviet Union, rnd *Deiatelnyi;* torpedoed and sunk by U-boat in Arctic, Jan 16, 1945.

Cicala: Insect cls river gunboat; 625; 237½ x 36; 14; 65; two 6-in, one 3-in; Barclay Curle & Co, Glasgow, 1916; sunk by Japanese aircraft at Hong Kong, Dec 21, 1941.

Cicero: Empire cls infantry landing ship; 11,650; 418 x 60; 14; 898; one 4-in; Consolidated Steel Corp, Wilmington, 1944; launched as *Cape St Vincent* (US Maritime Commission, Washington); transferred Lease/Lend to Ministry of War Transport, London, 1944, rnd *Empire Arquebus,* transferred 1944 to RN, rnd; rtnd MoWT rnd *Empire Arquebus,* 1945; rtnd USMC 1946; 1946, Soc Misr de Navegation Maritime SAE, Egypt, converted to passenger-cargo liner, rnd *Al Sudan;*

Circe: Algerine cls minesweeper; 950; 235 x 35½; 16½; 104; one 4-in; Harland & Wolff, Belfast, 1942; b/up Dalmuir 1967.

Clacton: Bangor cls minesweeper; 656; 174 x 28½; 16; 60; one 3-in; Ailsa SB Co, Troon, 1942; mined off east Corsica, Dec 31, 1943.

Clare: Town cls destroyer; 1190; 314½ x 31¾; 30; 122; one 4-in, three 21-in tt; Newport News SB & DD Co, Newport News, 1920; ex-USN *Abel P. Upshur,* transferred 1940 to RN; b/up Troon 1947.

Clarkia: Flower cls corvette; 925; 205 x 33; 16; 85; one 4-in; Harland & Wolff, Belfast, 1940; b/up Hayle 1947.

Clematis: Flower cls corvette; 925; 205 x 33; 16; 85; one 4-in; C. Hill & Sons, Bristol, 1940; b/up Charlestown 1949.

Cleopatra: Dido cls cruiser; 5450; 512 x 50½; 33; 620; ten 5.25-in, six 21-in tt; Hawthorn Leslie, Hebburn, 1941; b/up Newport 1958.

Cleveland: Hunt cls destroyer — Atherstone type; 1000; 280 x 29; 27½; 146; four 4-in; Yarrow & Co, Scotstoun, 1940; wrecked on Rhossili Sands on way to Llanelly for b/up, June 28, 1957, wreck blown up, December 1959.

Clinton: Algerine cls minesweeper; 950; 235 x 35½; 16½; 104; one 4-in; Toronto Shipyards, Toronto, 1943; ex-USN, transferred Lease/Lend to RN 1943, rtnd USN 1946; sold 1947.

Clover: Flower cls corvette; 925; 205 x 33; 16; 85; one 4-in; Fleming & Ferguson, Paisley, 1941; 1947, Wheelock Marden, Hong Kong, converted to cargo ship, rnd *Cloverlock;* 1952, Chinese Navy, rnd *Kai Feng;* (nothing more known).

Clyde: River cls submarine; 1850/2710; 345 x 28¼; 22½/10; 60; six 21-in tt, one 4-in; Vickers-Armstrongs, Barrow, 1935; b/up Durban 1946.

Clydebank: Bangor cls minesweeper; 672; 180 x 28½; 16; 60; one 3-in; Lobnitz & Co, Renfrew, 1942; transferred 1942 to Indian Navy, rnd *Orissa;* reported b/up 1949.

Cochrane: depot ship; 6480; 387¾ x 47½; 14½; 238; two 3-in; Sir Raylton Dixon & Co, Middlesbrough, 1903; ex-passenger liner *Ambrose* (Booth SS Co, Liverpool) bought RN and converted 1915, rnd 1938; b/up Inverkeithing 1946.

Cockatrice: Algerine cls minesweeper; 950; 235 x 35½; 16½; 104; one 4-in; Fleming & Ferguson, Paisley, 1943; b/up Inverkeithing 1963.

Cockchafer: Insect cls river gunboat; 625; 237½ x 36; 14; 65; two 6-in, one 3-in; Barclay Curle & Co, Glasgow, 1916; b/up Singapore 1949(?).

Codrington: A cls destroyer; 1540; 343 x 33¾; 35; 185; five 4.7-in, eight 21-in tt; Swan Hunter & Wigham Richardson, Wallsend 1930; damaged by German aircraft in Dover Harbour July 27, 1940; b/up 1947.

Coldstreamer: Military cls trawler; 750; 193 x 30; 11; 40; one 4-in; Cook Welton & Gemmell, Beverley, 1943; 1946 (owners not known) rnd *Eskimo;* 1953, J. Ostensio & Co, Norway, converted to cargo ship, rnd *Zero;* 1963, People's Republic of China, no name change;

Coll: Isles cls trawler; 560; 164 x 27½; 12; 40; one 12-pdr; Ardrossan Dockyard Ltd, Ardrossan, 1942;

Colne: Mersey cls trawler; 551; 148 x 22¾; 11; 20; two 3-in; Lobnitz & Co, Renfrew, 1918; ex-*Isaac Chant,* 1920; 1946, T. H. Scales, Edinburgh, rnd *Heather Island;* 1947, Oddson & Co, Hull, rnd *Saudanes;* 1949, Heather Fishing Co, Edinburgh, rnd *Heather Island;* b/up 1951.

Colombo: Carlisle cls cruiser; 4290; 451½ x 43½; 29; 400; eight 4-in; Fairfield SB & E Co, Govan, 1919; b/up Newport 1948.

Colossus: Colossus cls aircraft carrier; 13,190; 694½ x 112½; 25; 1350; 39-44 aircraft;

Vickers-Armstrongs, Tyne 1944; transferred 1945 to France rnd *Arromanches,* bought outright, 1951;

Colsay: Isles cls trawler; 560; 164 x 27½; 12; 40; one 12-pdr; Cook Welton & Gemmell, Beverley, 1944; sunk by human torpedo off Ostend, Nov 2, 1944.

Coltsfoot: Flower cls corvette; 925; 205 x 33; 16; 85; one 4-in; Alex Hall & Co, Aberdeen, 1941; 1947, Compania Divisa de Vapores SA, Panama, converted, rnd *Alexandra;* 1953, Foustanos Bros, Greece, rnd *Hermopolis;* lost, aground near Syra, Nov 21, 1954.

Columbia: Town cls destroyer; 1060; 314⅓ x 30½; 30; 122; three 4-in, six 21-in tt; Newport News SB & DD Co, Newport News; 1919; ex-USN *Haraden;* transferred 1940 to Royal Canadian Navy; sold Canadian shipbreakers 1945.

Columbine: Flower cls corvette; 925; 205 x 33; 16; 85; one 4-in; C. Hill & Sons, Bristol, 1940; 1949, A/S Kosmos, Norway, converted to whale catcher, rnd *Leif Welding;* b/up Grimstad 1966.

Combatant: Catherine cls minesweeper; 890; 221 x 32; 18; 109; one 3-in; Associated Shipbuilders, Seattle, 1943; ex-USN Auk cls minesweeper *BAM-14* transferred Lease/Lend to RN 1943, rtnd USN 1946; 1947, Greece, nothing more known.

Comet: CO cls destroyer; 1710; 362¾ x 35¾; 36; 186; four 4.5-in, four 21-in tt; Yarrow & Co, Scotstoun, 1945; b/up Troon 1962.

Comfrey: Modified Flower cls corvette; 980; 208¼ x 33; 16; 109; one 4-in; Collingwood Shipyards, Collingwood, 1943; transferred 1943 to USN, rnd *Action;* 1947, Rederi Tuxen & Hagerman, Denmark, converted to cargo ship, rnd *Arne Presthus;* 1967, Orri Navigation Co, Saudi Arabia, rnd *Star of Mariam;* 1971, Fontana Shipping Co, Cyprus, rnd *Star of Beirut;* 1972, Orri Nav Lines, Jeddah, rnd *Star of Riwiah;* lost, aground near Ashrafi Lighthouse, Gulf of Suez, Apr 6, 1972.

Conn: Captain cls frigate; 1400; 306 x

36¾; 23½; 220; three 3-in;
Bethlehem-Hingham Shipyard, 1943;
ex-USN Buckley cls destroyer-escort
DE-80, transferred Lease/Lend to RN,
1943, rtnd USN 1945; b/up.

Convolvulus: Flower cls corvette; 925;
205 x 33; 16; 85; one 4-in; C. Hill &
Sons, Bristol, 1941; b/up Newport
1947.

Cooke: Captain cls frigate; 1140;
289½ x 35; 21; 200; three 3-in; Navy
Yard, Boston, 1943; ex-USN Evarts cls
destroyer-escort *Dempsey, DE-267,*
transferred Lease/Lend, to RN 1943,
rtnd USN 1946, b/up.

Copinsay: Isles cls trawler; 560; 164 x
27½; 12; 40; one 12-pdr; Cochrane &
Sons, Selby, 1941; transferred 1946 to
War Dept, converted to cargo ship;
1956, E. Abbot & Ph. Georgiades,
Greece, rnd *Ion;* sank after collision
north of Crete, Dec 31, 1958.

Coquette: Algerine cls minesweeper;
950; 235 x 35½; 16½; 104; one 4-in;
Redfern Construction Co, Toronto,
1944; ex-*Bowmanville* (RCN) 1943;
b/up Charlestown 1958.

Coral: Gem cls trawler; 700; 158 x
26½; 12; 18; one 4-in; Cochrane &
Sons, Selby, 1935; ex-*Cape Duner*
(Hudson Steam Fishing Co, Hull)
bought RN 1939; bombed at Malta,
April 1942, wreck b/up 1943.

Corbrae: mine destructor vessel; 1788
grt; 265 x 39½; --; --; eight 20-mm;
Burntisland SB Co, Burntisland, 1935;
ex-cargo ship (Wm Cory & Son,
London,) bought RN 1940; converted
to repair ship, 1944; 1947, Kinburn
Shipping Co, London, converted
cargo ship, rnd *Kinburn;* 1949,
Williamstown Shpg Co, London, rnd
Kentbrook; 1951, Ouse SS Co. Goole.
rnd *Whitfleet;* b/up Dunston 1960.

Corburn: mine destructor vessel; 1786
grt; 265 x 39½; --; --; --; Burntisland SB
Co, Burntisland, 1936; ex-cargo ship
(Wm Cory & Son, London) bought RN
1940; mined off Le Havre, May 21,
1940.

Coreopsis: Flower cls corvette; 925;
205 x 33; 16; 85; one 4-in; A. & J. Inglis,
Glasgow, 1940; transferred 1943 to
Royal Hellenic Navy, rnd *Kriezis,* rtnd
RN 1952; b/up Sunderland 1952.

Corfield: mine destructor vessel; 1791

grt; 265 x 39½; --; --; --; Burntisland SB
Co, Burntisland, 1937; ex-cargo ship
(Wm Cory & Son, London) bought RN
1940; mined off River Humber, Sept 8,
1941.

Coriander: Flower cls corvette; 925;
205 x 33; 16; 85; one 4-in; Hall Russell,
Aberdeen, 1941; ex-*Iris,* 1940;
transferred 1942 to French Navy, rnd
Commandant Detroyat; b/up Troon
1948.

Coriolanus: Shakespearian cls
trawler; 545; 164 x 27¾; 12; 35; one
12-pdr; Cochrane & Sons, Selby, 1941;
mined in Adriatic, May 5, 1945.

Corncrake: Bird cls controlled
minelayer; 670; 162 x 25¼; 11; 35; one
4-in; Cochrane & Sons, Selby, 1942;
ex-Fish cls trawler *Mackerel,* 1942;
foundered in North Atlantic, Jan 25,
1943.

Cornel: Modified Flower cls corvette;
980; 208¼ x 33; 16; 109; one 4-in;
Collingwood Shipyards, Collingwood,
1942; transferred 1943 to USN, rnd
Alacrity; 1948 (owner not known),
converted to cargo ship, rnd *Rio
Marina;* 1951, Navigazione Toscana
SpA, Italy, rnd *Portoferraio;* b/up Italy
1971.

Cornelian: Gem cls trawler; 568; 152 x
25½; 12; 18; one 4-in; Cochrane &
Sons, Selby, 1933; ex-*Cape Warwick*
(Hudson Steam Fishing Co, Hull)
bought RN 1935; 1947, Consolidated
Fisheries, Grimsby, rnd *Lincoln City;*
b/up Belgium 1963.

Cornflower: Flower cls sloop; 1175;
267¾ x 33½; 16½; 98; two 4-in; Barclay
Curle & Co, Glasgow, 1916; sold 1940
(owners not known) rnd *Tai Hing;* 1940,
bought by RN, rnd *Cornflower;* sunk by
Japanese aircraft, Hong Kong, Dec 15,
1941.

Cornwall: Kent cls cruiser; 10,900; 630
x 68⅓; 31½; 679; eight 8-in, eight 4-in;
HM Dockyard, Devonport, 1928; sunk
by Japanese aircraft near Ceylon, Apr
5, 1942.

Coronet: boom working vessel; 429;
134 x 22½; 10½; 18; one 3-in; Bow
MacLachlan & Co, Paisley, 1918;
ex-Castle cls trawler *Robert
Cloughton,* converted and renamed
1933; b/up Northam 1953.

Cosby: Captain cls frigate; 1400; 306 x

36¾; 23½; 220; three 3-in;
Bethlehem-Hingham Shipyard, 1943;
ex-USN Buckley cls destroyer-escort
DE-94, transferred Lease/Lend to RN
1943, rnd *Reeves*, rnd *Cosby*, rtnd USN
1946, b/up.

Cossack: Tribal cls destroyer; 1870;
377 x 36½; 36½; 219; eight 4.7-in, four
21-in tt; Vickers-Armstrongs, Tyne,
1938; torpedoed by *U-563* in North
Atlantic, Oct 23, 1941, foundered west
of Gibraltar, Oct 27, 1941.

Cotillion: Dance cls trawler; 530; 160½
x 27½; 11½; 35; one 4-in; Ardrossan
Dockyard Ltd, Ardrossan, 1941; sold
1947, buyers not known.

Cotswold: Hunt cls destroyer —
Atherstone type; 1000; 280 x 29; 27½;
146; four 4-in; Yarrow & Co,
Scotstoun, 1940; b/up Grays 1957.

Cottesmore: Hunt cls destroyer —
Atherstone type; 1000; 280 x 29; 27½;
146; four 4-in; Yarrow & Co,
Scotstoun, 1940; transferred 1950 to
Egyptian Navy, rnd *Ibraham El Awal*,
rnd *Mohamed Ali El Kebir* 1951, rnd
Port Said;

Cotton: Captain cls frigate; 1400; 306
x 36¾; 23½; 220; three 3-in;
Bethlehem-Hingham Shipyard, 1943;
ex-USN Buckley cls destroyer-escort
DE-81, transferred Lease/Lend to RN
1943, rtnd USN 1945, b/up.

Courageous: Courageous cls aircraft
carrier; 22,500; 786¼ x 100; 30; 1216;
48 aircraft, sixteen 4.7-in; Armstrong
Whitworth & Co, Newcastle, 1916;
completed as light battle cruiser,
converted to aircraft carrier HM
Dockyard Devonport, 1924-28;
torpedoed and sunk by *U-29* west of
Ireland, Sept 17, 1939.

Courier: Algerine cls minesweeper;
950; 235 x 35½; 16½; 104; one 4-in;
Redfern Construction Co, Toronto,
1944; ex-*Arnprior* (RCN) 1943; b/up
Llanelly 1959.

Coventry: Ceres cls cruiser; 4200; 450
x 43½; 29; 400; ten 4-in; Swan Hunter
& Wigham Richardson, Wallsend,
1918; sunk by German and Italian
aircraft off Tobruk, Sept 14, 1942.

Coverley: Dance cls trawler; 530;
160½ x 27½; 11½; 35; one 4-in;
Ardrossan Dockyard Ltd, Ardrossan,
1941; 1947 (owner not known) rnd

Jannikke; 1948, A/S Narvik Damps,
Norway, converted to cargo ship, rnd
Ofotfjord;

Cowdray: Hunt cls destroyer —
Blankney type; 1050; 280 x 31½; 27;
168; six 4-in; Scotts SB & E Co,
Greenock, 1941; b/up Gateshead
1959.

Cowslip: Flower cls corvette; 925; 205
x 33; 16; 85; one 4-in; Harland & Wolff,
Belfast, 1941; b/up Troon 1949.

Crane: Modified Black Swan cls
sloop; 1430; 299½ x 38; 20; 192; six
4-in; Wm Denny & Bros, Dumbarton,
1943; b/up Queenborough 1965.

Cranstoun: Captain cls frigate; 1400;
306 x 36¾; 23½; 220; three 3-in;
Bethlehem-Hingham Shipyard, 1943;
ex-USN Buckley cls destroyer-escort
DE-82, transferred Lease/Lend to RN
1943, rtnd USN 1945, b/up.

Cricket: Insect cls river gunboat; 625;
237½ x 36; 14; 65; two 6-in, one 3-in;
Barclay Curle & Co, Glasgow, 1915;
irreparably damaged by aircraft off
Mersa Matruh, June 1941, b/up
Alexandria 1942.

Crocus: Flower cls corvette; 925; 205
x 33; 16; 85; one 4-in; A. & J. Inglis,
Glasgow, 1940; 1947, Wheelock
Marden, Hong Kong, converted to
merchant ship, rnd *Annlock;* b/up
Hong Kong 1952.

Cromarty: Bangor cls minesweeper;
656; 174 x 28½; 16; 60; one 3-in; Blyth
SB & DD Co, Blyth, 1941; mined in
Strait of Bonifacio, Oct 23, 1943.

Cromer: Bangor cls minesweeper;
672; 180 x 28½; 16; 60; one 3-in;
Lobnitz & Co, Renfrew, 1941; mined
off Libya, Nov 9, 1942.

Croome: Hunt cls destroyer —
Blankney type; 1050; 280 x 31½; 27;
168; six 4-in; Alex Stephen & Sons,
Linthouse, 1941; b/up Briton Ferry
1957.

Crowlin: Isles cls trawler; 560; 164 x
27½; 12; 40; one 12-pdr; Cook Welton
& Gemmell, Beverley, 1944; 1946,
Express-Service A/S, Norway,
converted to cargo ship, no name
change; 1955, Govert Grindhaug,
Norway, rnd *Thermo;* 1961, Navigation
Maritime Bulgare, Bulgaria, rnd
Chernomorez; 1964, Red Sea
Development Corp, Ethiopia, rnd

Axum;
Cubitt: Captain cls frigate; 1400; 306 x
36¾; 23½; 220; three 3-in;
Bethlehem-Hingham Shipyard, 1943;
ex-USN Buckley cls destroyer-escort
DE-83, transferred Lease/Lend to RN
1943, rtnd USN 1946, b/up.
Cuckmere: River cls frigate; 1370;
301½ x 36½; 19; 140; two 4-in;
Canadian Vickers, Montreal, 1943;
ex-USN *PG-104,* transferred
Lease/Lend to RN 1943, rtnd USN
1946; sold 1948.
Cuillin Sound: aircraft component
repair ship; 10,000; 447¾ x 56; 11; --;
twelve 20-mm; W. Gray & Co, West
Hartlepool, 1945; 1948, Clunies
Shipping Co, Greenock, converted to
cargo ship, rnd *James Clunies;* lost,
aground off Punta Mogotas, Apr 21,
1949.
Culver: Lulworth cls escort; 1546; 250 x
42; 16; 200; one 5-in, two 3-in;
Bethlehem SB Corp, Quincy, 1928;
ex-US Coast Guard cutter *Mendota,*
transferred Lease/Lend to RN 1941;
torpedoed and sunk by *U-105* in east
Atlantic, Jan 31, 1942.
Cumberland: Kent cls cruiser; 10,800;
630 x 68⅓; 31½; 679; eight 8-in, eight
4-in; Vickers-Armstrongs, Barrow,
1928; b/up Newport, 1959.
Cumbrae: Isles cls trawler; 560; 164 x
27½; 12; 40; one 12-pdr; Cochrane &
Sons, Selby, 1941; transferred 1946 to
Italian Navy, rnd *RD-302;* used as
target, mid-1960s.
Curacoa: Ceres cls cruiser; 4290; 450
x 43½; 29; 437; eight 4-in; HM
Dockyard, Pembroke, 1918; lost in
collision with liner *Queen Mary* off
Bloody Foreland, Oct 2, 1942.
Curlew: Ceres cls cruiser; 4200; 450 x
43½; 29; 400; ten 4-in; Vickers Ltd,
Barrow, 1917; sunk by German aircraft
off Skaanland, May 26, 1940.
Curzon: Captain cls frigate; 1400; 306
x 36¾; 23½; 220; three 3-in;
Bethlehem-Hingham Shipyard, 1943;
ex-USN Buckley cls destroyer-escort
DE-84, transferred Lease/Lend to RN
1943, rtnd USN 1946, b/up.
Cybele: experimental mine destructor
vessel; 4000; --; --; --; --; Wm Denny &
Bros, Dumbarton, 1944; listed as
Algerine cls minesweeper for security

reasons; b/up Troon 1946.
Cyclamen: Flower cls corvette; 925;
205 x 33; 16; 85; one 4-in; J. Lewis &
Sons, Aberdeen, 1940; 1948, South
Georgia Co (C. Salvesen) Leith,
converted to whale catcher, rnd
Southern Briar; lost, aground Jutland
Dec 18, 1966, after breaking tow on
way to shipbreakers at Ghent.
Cyclops: depot ship; 11,300; 477 x 55;
11¾; 266; six 4-in; Sir J. Laing & Co,
Sunderland, 1905; ex-passenger
cargo liner *Indrabarah,* purchased on
stocks and converted to repair ship;
converted to depot ship 1922; b/up
Newport, 1947.
Cygnet: Modified Black Swan cls
sloop; 1430; 299½ x 38; 20; 192; six
4-in; Cammell Laird, Birkenhead,
1942; b/up Rosyth 1956.
Cynthia: Catherine cls minesweeper;
890; 221 x 32; 18; 109; one 3-in;
Associated Shipbuilders, Seattle,
1943; ex-USN Auk cls minesweeper
BAM-15 transferred Lease/Lend to RN
1943, rtnd USN 1946; sold 1947.
Cypress: Berberis cls trawler; 347;
140 x 24½; 11; 18; one 12-pdr;
Cochrane & Sons, Selby, 1930;
ex-*Cape Finisterre* (Hudson Steam
Fishing Co, Hull) bought RN 1935;
1946, P/F Mullin, Denmark, rnd
Vardberg; b/up Denmark 1959.
Cyrus: experimental mine destructor
vessel; 4000; --; --; --; --; Swan Hunter &
Wigham Richardson, Wallsend 1944;
listed as Algerine cls minesweeper for
security reasons; wrecked Seine Bay,
Dec 5, 1944.

Dabchick: Bird cls controlled
minelayer; 560; 164 x 27½; 12; 40; one
4-in; Cook Welton & Gemmell,
Beverley, 1943; ex-Isles cls trawler,
converted while building; transferred
1954 to Royal Malay Navy, rnd *Penyu;*
sold 1959.
Dacres: Captain cls frigate; 1140;
289½ x 35; 21; 200; three 3-in; Navy
Yard, Boston, 1943; ex-USN Evarts cls
destroyer-escort *Duffy, DE-268,*
transferred Lease/Lend to RN 1943,
rtnd USN 1946, b/up.
Dahlia: Flower cls corvette; 925; 205 x

33; 16; 85; one 4-in; J. Lewis & Sons, Aberdeen, 1941; b/up Milford Haven 1948.

Dainty: D cls destroyer; 1375; 329 x 33; 35½; 145; four 4.7-in, eight 21-in tt; Fairfield SB & E Co, Govan, 1933; sunk by German and Italian aircraft in Tobruk Harbour, Feb 24, 1941.

Dakins: Captain cls frigate; 1400; 306 x 36¾; 23½; 220; three 3-in; Bethlehem-Hingham Shipyard, 1943; ex-USN Buckley cls destroyer-escort *DE-85,* transferred Lease/Lend to RN 1943; damaged by mine off Belgian coast, Dec 25, 1944, b/up Holland 1947.

Damsay: Isles cls trawler; 560; 164 x 27½; 12; 40; one 12-pdr; Geo Brown & Co, Greenock, 1942; b/up Troon 1960.

Danae: D cls cruiser; 4850; 472½ x 46½; 29; 469; five 6-in, twelve 21-in tt; Armstrong Whitworth & Co, Newcastle, 1918; transferred 1944 to Poland, rnd *Conrad,* rtnd RN 1946; b/up Barrow 1948.

Daring: D cls destroyer; 1375; 329 x 33; 35½; 145; four 4.7-in, eight 21-in tt; J. I. Thornycroft & Co, Southampton, 1932; sunk by *U-23* in North Sea, Feb 18, 1940.

Darkdale: Dale cls oiler; 17,000; 483 x 59½; 11½; 40; --; Blythswood SB Co, Glasgow, 1941; ex-*Empire Oil;* sunk by *U-68* off St Helena, Oct 22, 1941.

Dart: River cls frigate; 1370; 301½ x 36½; 19; 140; two 4-in; Blyth SB & DD Co, Blyth, 1943; b/up Newport 1956.

Dasher: Archer cls escort carrier; 12,150; 492 x 69½; 16½; 520; 20 aircraft, one 4-in; Sun SB & DD Co, Chester, 1942; ex-cargo ship *Rio de Janeiro,* ex-USN *BAVG-5* converted, transferred Lease/Lend to RN 1942; destroyed through internal explosion in Firth of Clyde, Mar 27, 1943.

Dauntless: D cls cruiser; 4850; 472½ x 46½; 29; 469; six 6-in, three 4-in, twelve 21-in tt; Palmers SB & Iron Co, Hebburn, 1918; b/up Inverkeithing 1946.

Deane: Captain cls frigate; 1400; 306 x 36¾; 23½; 220; three 3-in; Bethlehem-Hingham Shipyard, 1943; ex-USN Buckley cls destroyer-escort *DE-86,* transferred Lease/Lend to RN 1943, rtnd USN 1946, b/up.

Decoy: D cls destroyer; 1375; 329 x 33; 35½; 145; four 4.7-in, eight 21-in tt; J. I. Thornycroft & Co, Southampton, 1933; transferred 1943 to Royal Canadian Navy, rnd *Kootenay;* sold Hamilton, Ont, shipbreakers 1945.

Dee: Axe cls trawler; 393; 139 x 23½; 10½; 18; one 3-in; Smith's Dock Co, Middlesbrough, 1916; ex-Russian trawler *T-16,* acquired by RN 1918, rnd *Battleaxe,* rnd 1920; 1946, J. L. Eltvik & Others, Norway, rnd *Safir;* 1947, Skibs A/S Vilnes, Norway, rnd *Vilfjell;* 1948, A/S Opotens Damps, Norway, rnd *Tranoy;* as *Tran* (owners not known) capsized and sank off Egeroy, Nov 19, 1954.

Deer Sound: aircraft component repair ship; 6294 grt; 488 x 59½; --; --; two 4-in; J. L. Thompson & Sons, Sunderland, 1939; ex-cargo liner *Port Quebec,* 1939, taken over by RN and fitted out as minelayer; bought RN, converted to repair ship, rnd, 1943; 1947, Port Line, London, converted to cargo ship, rnd *Port Quebec;* b/up Taiwan 1968.

Defender: D cls destroyer; 1375; 329 x 33; 35½; 145; four 4.7-in, eight 21-in tt; Vickers-Armstrongs, Barrow, 1932; bombed by Italian aircraft off Bardia, July 11, 1941, sunk in tow the next day.

Delhi: D cls cruiser; 4850; 472½ x 46½; 29; 469; six 6-in, twelve 21-in tt; Armstrong Whitworth & Co, Newcastle, 1919; b/up Newport 1948.

Delight: D cls destroyer; 1375; 329 x 33; 35½; 145; four 4.7-in, eight 21-in tt; Fairfield SB & E Co, Govan, 1933; sunk by German aircraft off Portland, July 29, 1940.

Delphinium: Flower cls corvette; 925; 205 x 33; 16; 85; one 4-in; H. Robb, Leith, 1940; b/up Pembroke Dock 1949.

Denbigh Castle: Castle cls corvette; 1010; 252 x 36¾; 16½; 120; one 4-in; J. Lewis & Sons, Aberdeen, 1944; damaged by *U-992,* aground Kola Inlet, Feb 13, 1945.

Denbydale: Dale cls oiler; 17,000; 483 x 59½; 11½; 40; --; Blythswood SB Co, Glasgow, 1941; severely damaged by explosives placed by Italian frogmen at Gibraltar, Sept 20, 1942, became fuel and accommodation hulk; b/up

Blyth 1955.
Deodar: Tree cls trawler; 530; 164 x
27½; 11½; 35; one 12-pdr; Goole SB &
Repairing Co, Goole, 1940; 1947,
(owner not known) rnd *Mollex VI;*
1955, H. & W. Felter, West Germany,
rnd *Werner Felter;* 1962, W. v. Essen
U. W. Jacoby, West Germany, rnd
Clipper; lost on voyage, Klaipeda to
Raahe, Nov 26, 1965.
Deptford: Grimsby cls sloop; 990; 266
x 36; 16½; 100; two 4.7-in, one 3-in;
HM Dockyard, Chatham, 1935; b/up
Milford Haven 1948.
Derby: Hunt cls minesweeper; 800;
231 x 28½; 16; 74; one 4-in, one 3-in;
Clyde SB & E Co, Port Glasgow, 1918;
1945, C. McGrail & Co, Gibraltar; b/up
Spain 1946.
Derby Haven: coastal forces depot
ship; 1580; 307 x 38½; 19½; 120; two
4-in; Swan Hunter & Wigham
Richardson, Wallsend, 1945; ex-*Loch
Assynt,* 1944; transferred 1949 to !ran
Navy, converted to frigate rnd *Babr;*
paid off 1969, laid up Persian Gulf, to
be scrapped shortly.
Derg: River cls frigate; 1370; 301½ x
36½; 19; 140; two 4-in; H. Robb, Leith,
1943; rnd *Wessex,* then *Cambria,* 1951
(RNVR drillship); b/up Newport 1960.
Derwent: Hunt cls destroyer —
Albrighton type; 1050; 280 x 31½; 27;
168; four 4-in, two 21-in tt;
Vickers-Armstrongs, Barrow, 1942;
irreparably damaged by torpedo from
German aircraft at Tripoli, Mar 19,
1943; b/up Falmouth 1947.
Derwentdale: landing ship, gantry;
17,000; 483 x 59½; 11½; 65; one
4.7-in; fifteen landing craft (LCM);
Harland & Wolff, Govan, 1941;
converted to oiler, 1946; 1959, Kent
Line, Canada, rnd *Irvingdale 1;* b/up
Ferrol 1966.
Despatch: D cls cruiser; 4850; 472½ x
47; 29; 469; six 6-in, three 4-in, twelve
21-in tt; Fairfield SB & E Co/HM
Dockyard, Chatham, 1922; b/up Troon
1946.
Destiny: BAT cls tug; 783; 143 x 33;
14; 34; one 3-in; Defoe SB, Bay City,
1942; ex-USN, transferred Lease/Lend
to RN 1942, rtnd USN 1946; 1947,
Mollers Towages, Hong Kong, rnd
Frosty Moller, rnd *Christine Moller,*

1950; 1951, NV "Holland" Maatsothet
Urtvoeren van Scheeps &
Bergingswerken, Holland, rnd
Oceanus; 1953, L. Smit & Co's Intern,
Sleepdienst, Holland, rnd *Gele Zee;*
1964, L. Matsas & Sons, Greece, rnd
Atlas/
Deveron: River cls frigate; 1370; 301½
x 36½; 19; 140; two 4-in; Smith's Dock
Co, Middlesbrough, 1943; transferred
1945 to Indian Navy, rnd *Dhanush;*
transferred 1948 to Royal Pakistan
Navy, rnd *Zulfiquar,* converted to
survey ship;
Devonshire: London cls cruiser; 9850;
633 x 66; 32¼; 850; eight 8-in, eight
4-in, eight 21-in tt; HM Dockyard,
Devonport, 1929; b/up Newport 1954.
Dewdale: landing ship, gantry; 17,000;
483 x 59½; 11½; 65; one 4.7-in; fifteen
landing craft (LCM); Cammell Laird,
Birkenhead, 1941; converted to oiler,
1946-47; b/up Belgium 1959.
Dexterous: Assurance cls tug; 1045;
157 x 35; 13; 31; one 3-in; Cochrane &
Sons, Selby, 1942; 1957, BP Tanker
Co, London, rnd *Zurmand;* 1965,
Tsavliris (Salvage & Towage), Greece,
rnd *Nisos Ikaria;* b/up Greece 1971.
Diadem: Improved Dido cls cruiser;
5770; 512 x 50½; 33; 620; eight
5.25-in, six 21-in tt; Hawthorn Leslie,
Hebburn, 1944; transferred 1956 to
Pakistan Navy, rnd *Babur;*
Diamond: D cls destroyer; 1375; 329 x
33; 35½; 145; four 4.7-in, eight 21-in tt;
Vickers-Armstrongs, Barrow, 1932;
sunk by German and Italian aircraft,
Gulf of Nauplia, Apr 27, 1941.
Diana: D cls destroyer; 1375; 329 x 33;
35½; 145; four 4.7-in, eight 21-in tt;
Palmers SB & Iron Co, Hebburn, 1932;
transferred 1940 to Royal Canadian
Navy, rnd *Margaree;* lost in collision in
North Atlantic, Oct 22, 1940.
Dianella: Flower cls corvette; 925; 205
x 33; 16; 85; one 4-in; J. Lewis & Sons,
Aberdeen, 1941; ex-*Daffodil,* 1940;
b/up Portaferry 1948.
Dianthus: Flower cls corvette; 925;
205 x 33; 16; 85; one 4-in; H. Robb,
Leith, 1941; 1949, A/S Odd, Norway,
converted to whale catcher rnd
Thorslep; b/up Norway 1970.
Dido: Dido cls cruiser; 5450; 512 x
50½; 33; 620; ten 5.25-in, six 21-in tt;

Cammell Laird, Birkenhead, 1940; b/up Barrow 1957.

Diligence: aircraft depot and repair ship; 11,500; 441½ x 57; 12½; 489; one 5-in; Bethlehem-Fairfield, Baltimore, 1944; ex-USN, transferred Lease/Lend to RN, 1944, rtnd USN 1946, same name; b/up Kaohsiung 1973.

Dingledale: Dale cls oiler; 17,000; 483 x 59½; 11½; 40; --; Harland & Wolff, Govan, 1941; 1959, Cie d'Armament Maritimi SA, Djibouti, rnd *Royaumont* oil storage hulk; b/up Santander 1967.

Dinsdale: oiler; 8200 grt; 483 x 59½; 11½; 40; --; Harland & Wolff, Belfast, 1942; sunk by U-boat in South Atlantic, May 31, 1942.

Diomede: D cls cruiser; 4850; 472½ x 47; 29; 469; six 6-in, three 4-in, twelve 21-in tt; Vickers Ltd, Barrow/HM Dockyard, Portsmouth, 1922; b/up Dalmuir 1946.

Director: Justice cls tug; 1360; 165 x 34; 12; 32; one 3-in; Camden SB, New York, 1943; ex-USN, transferred Lease/Lend to RN 1943, rtnd USN 1946; sold 1947.

Dispenser: Kin cls coastal salvage vessel; 950; 179½ x 35¾; 9; 34; two 20-mm; Smith's Dock Co, Middlesbrough, 1943;

Distol: Elmol cls oiler; 2410; 220 x 34⅔; 9½; 19; --; Wm Dobson & Co, Newcastle, 1916; 1946, Kuwait Oil Co, London, rnd *Akhawi;* b/up Bombay 1954.

Dittany: Modified Flower cls corvette; 980; 208¼ x 33; 16; 109; one 4-in; Collingwood Shipyards, Collingwood, 1942; was to be US Navy, not transferred; 1950, Balleneros Ltd SA, Uruguay, converted to whale catcher, rnd *Olympic Cruiser;* 1956, Kyokuyo Hogei KK, Japan, rnd *Otori Maru No 2;* b/up Japan 1966.

Dochet: Isles cls trawler; 560; 164 x 27½; 12; 40; one 12-pdr; G. T. Davie, Lauzon, 1942; transferred 1946 to West German Navy, rnd *Catherine,* rnd *Eider;*

Dodman Point: landing craft repair ship; 8580; 441½ x 57; 11; 440; sixteen 20-mm; Burrard DD Co, Vancouver, 1945; b/up Spezia 1963.

Domett: Captain cls frigate; 1140;

289½ x 35; 21; 200; three 3-in; Navy Yard, Boston, 1943; ex-USN Evarts cls destroyer-escort *Eisner, DE-269,* transferred Lease/Lend to RN 1943, rtnd USN 1946, b/up.

Dominica: Colony cls frigate; 1430; 304 x 37½; 18; 120; three 3-in; Walsh-Kaiser Co, Providence, 1944; ex-USN *PF-79,* transferred Lease/Lend to RN rnd *Harman;* rnd *Dominica,* 1944, rtnd USN 1946; sold Chester, Pa, shipbreakers 1947.

Donovan: Empire cls infantry landing ship; 11,650; 418 x 60; 14; 898; one 4-in; Consolidated Steel Corp, Wilmington, 1943; launched as *Cape Berkeley* (US Maritime Commission, Washington) transferred Lease/Lend to Ministry of War Transport, London 1943, rnd *Empire Battleaxe,* transferred RN, rnd, 1944; rtnd MoWT 1946 rnd *Empire Battleaxe,* rtnd USMC 1946 rnd *Cape Berkeley;* 1948, was to be sold to China and renamed *Hai Ou* but not transferred; 1948, rnd *Empire Battleaxe;* sold New York shipbreakers 1965.

Doon: Mersey cls trawler; 551; 148 x 22¾; 11; 20; two 3-in; Cochrane & Sons, Selby, 1918; ex-*Fraser Eaves,* 1920; 1947, East Fisheries, South Africa, rnd *Donesse;* sunk as target off South Africa, Spring 1955.

Dornoch: Bangor cls minesweeper; 656; 174 x 28½; 16; 60; one 3-in; Ailsa SB Co, Troon, 1942; b/up Thornaby-on-Tees 1948.

Dorsetshire: Norfolk cls cruiser; 9900; 630 x 66; 32¼; 820; eight 8-in, eight 4-in, eight 21-in tt; HM Dockyard, Portsmouth, 1930; sunk by Japanese aircraft near Ceylon, Apr 5, 1942.

Douglas: Scott cls destroyer; 1530; 332½ x 31¾; 31; 183; three 4.7-in, three 21-in tt; Cammell Laird, Birkenhead, 1918; b/up Inverkeithing 1945.

Dovey: River cls frigate; 1370; 301½ x 36½; 19; 140; two 4-in; Fleming & Ferguson, Paisley, 1944; ex-*Lambourne,* 1942; b/up Preston 1955.

Dragon: D cls cruiser; 4850; 472½ x 46½; 29; 469; six 6-in, three 4-in, twelve 21-in tt; Scotts SB & E Co,

Greenock, 1918; transferred 1943 to
Poland; sunk as part of artificial
breakwater at Normandy, June, 1944.

Dragonet: Bayonet cls boom defence
vessel; 530; 135 x 30½; 11½; 32; one
3-in; Blyth SB & DD Co, Blyth, 1939;
1961, Foundation Maritime, Canada,
converted to salvage ship, rnd
Foundation Venture; 1973, Marine
Industries, Canada, rnd *Mil Venture*
1974;

Dragonfly: Locust cls river gunboat;
585; 197 x 33; 17; 74; two 4-in, one
3.7-in howitzer; J. I. Thornycroft & Co,
Southampton, 1939; sunk by Japanese
aircraft off Singapore, Feb 14, 1942.

Drury: Captain cls frigate; 1140; 289½
x 35; 21; 200; three 3-in; Navy Yard,
Philadelphia, 1943; ex-USN Evarts cls
destroyer-escort *BDE-46,* transferred
Lease/Lend to RN 1943, rnd
Cockburn, rnd *Drury* 1943, rtnd USN
1945, b/up.

Duchess: D cls destroyer; 1375; 329 x
33; 35½; 145; four 4.7-in, eight 21-in tt;
Palmers SB & Iron Co, Hebburn, 1933;
lost in collision with battleship
Barham in Western Approaches, Dec
12, 1939.

Duckworth: Captain cls frigate; 1400;
306 x 36¾; 23½; 220; three 3-in;
Bethlehem-Hingham Shipyard, 1943;
ex-USN Buckley cls destroyer-escort
Gary, DE-61, transferred Lease/Lend
to RN 1943, rtnd USN 1945, b/up.

Duff: Captain cls frigate; 1400; 306 x
36¾; 23½; 220; three 3-in;
Bethlehem-Hingham Shipyard, 1943;
ex-USN Buckley cls destroyer-escort
Lamons, DE-64, transferred
Lease/Lend to RN 1943; irreparably
damaged by mine off Dutch coast, Nov
30, 1944, rtnd USN 1945, b/up Holland
1947.

Duke of York: King George V cls
battleship; 35,000; 745 x 103; 28; 1900;
ten 14-in, sixteen 5.25-in; J. Brown &
Co, Clydebank, 1941; ex-*Anson,* 1938;
b/up Faslane 1958.

Dullisk Cove: repair ship; 8402 grt;
447¾ x 56¼; 11; --; twelve 20-mm;
Short Bros, Sunderland, 1945; 1947,
Kefalonian SS Co, London, converted
to cargo ship, rnd *Kefalonia;* 1951,
Dept of Shpg & Transport, Australia,
rnd *Tyalla;* 1957, Cambay Prince SS

Co, Hong Kong, rnd *Wear Breeze;*
b/up Japan 1962.

Dulverton: Hunt cls destroyer —
Blankney type; 1050; 280 x 31½; 27;
168; six 4-in; Alex Stephen & Sons
Linthouse, 1941; sunk by German
aircraft in Aegean, Nov 13, 1943.

Dumbarton Castle: Castle cls
corvette; 1010; 252 x 36¾; 16½; 120;
one 4-in; Caledon SB & E Co, Dundee,
1943; b/up Gateshead 1961.

Dunbar: Bangor cls minesweeper;
656; 174 x 28½; 16; 60; one 3-in; Blyth
SB & DD Co, Blyth, 1941; b/up
Southampton 1948.

Duncan: D cls destroyer; 1400; 329 x
33; 35½; 165; four 4.7-in, eight 21-in tt;
HM Dockyard, Portsmouth, 1933; b/up
Barrow 1945.

Duncansby Head: escort repair ship;
8580; 441½ x 57; 11; 440; --; Burrard
DD Co, Vancouver, 1945; at Rosyth
1962 with *Girdle Ness,* both forming
HMS *Cochrane;* b/up Spain 1969.

Duncton: Hills cls trawler; 750; 181¼ x
28; 11; 35; one 12-pdr; Cook Welton &
Gemmell, Beverley, 1942; 1945,
Marine Steam Fishing Co, Hull, rnd
Colwyn Bay; b/up Holland 1964.

Dundalk: Hunt cls minesweeper; 800;
231 x 28½; 16; 74; one 4-in, one 3-in;
Clyde SB & E Co, Port Glasgow, 1919;
mined off Harwich Oct 16, 1940.

Dundee: Falmouth cls sloop; 1060;
266 x 34; 16; 100; two 4-in; HM
Dockyard, Chatham, 1933; torpedoed
and sunk by *U-48* in Western
Approaches, Sept 15, 1940.

Dunedin: D cls cruiser; 4850; 472½ x
46½; 29; 469; six 6-in, three 4-in,
twelve 21-in tt; Armstrong Whitworth &
Co, Newcastle, 1919; torpedoed and
sunk by *U-124* in South Atlantic, Nov
24, 1941.

Dungeness: landing craft repair ship;
8580; 441½ x 57; 11; 440; sixteen
20-mm; West Coast Shipbuilders,
Vancouver, 1945; 1947, W. R.
Carpenter & Co, Australia, converted
to cargo ship, rnd *Levuka;* 1948,
British Phosphate Commissioners,
Australia, rnd *Triadic;*

Dunkery: Hills cls trawler; 750; 181¼ x
28; 11; 35; one 12-pdr; Cook Welton &
Gemmell, Beverley, 1942; 1946,
Charleson-Smith Trawlers, Hull, rnd

Stella Capella; b/up Blyth 1963.
Dunluce Castle: depot ship; 8130
grt; 490 x 56½; 14; --; --; Harland &
Wolff, Belfast, 1904; ex-passenger
liner (Union-Castle SS Co, London)
sold 1939 to shipbreakers, purchased
by RN and converted 1939; b/up
Inverkeithing 1945.
Dunnet: boom working vessel; 385;
140 x 26½; 10; 15; one 3-in; Lytham SB
& E Co, Lytham, 1936; 1947, London
Marine Salvors, London, rnd
Kingsmoor; b/up Preston 1951.
Dunoon: Hunt cls minesweeper; 800;
231 x 28½; 16; 74; one 4-in, one 3-in;
Clyde SB & E Co, Port Glasgow, 1919;
mined off Smiths Knoll,• Apr 30, 1940.
Durban: D cls cruiser; 4850; 472½ x
46½; 29; 469; six 6-in, three 4-in,
twelve 21-in tt; Scotts SB & E Co,
Greenock/HM Dockyard, Devonport,
1921; sunk as part of artificial
breakwater at Normandy, June 1944.
Durham Castle: store ship; 8240 grt;
475¼ x 56½; --; --; --; Fairfield Co,
Glasgow, 1904; ex-passenger liner
(Union-Castle SS Co, London) bought
RN 1939; mined off Cromarty, Jan 26,
1940.

Eagle: aircraft carrier; 22,600; 667 x
105; 24; 748; 21 aircraft, nine 6-in, four
4-in; laid down by Armstrong
Whitworth, Newcastle, as Chilean
battleship *Almirante Cochrane* 1913,
hull taken over 1917, converted HM
Dockyard, Portsmouth to aircraft
carrier, completed 1923; torpedoed
and sunk by *U-73* in Mediterranean,
Aug 11, 1942.
Eaglesdale: Dale cls oiler; 17,000; 483
x 59½; 11½; 40; --; Furness SB Co,
Haverton Hill, 1942; launched as
Empire Metal; 1959, Soc Misr de Nav
Mar SAE, Egypt, no name change;
b/up Hamburg 1959.
Earner: Assurance cls tug; 1045; 157 x
35; 13; 31; one 3-in; Cochrane & Sons,
Selby, 1943; 1965, Tsavliris (Salvage &
Towage) Greece, rnd *Nisos Rodos;*
b/up Greece 1972.
Earraid: Isles cls trawler; 560; 164 x
27½; 12; 40; one 12-pdr; J. Crown &
Sons, Sunderland, 1942; ex-*Gruna,*

1941; sold Dumbarton owners 1951,
nothing more known.
Easedale: Dale cls oiler; 17,000; 483 x
59½; 11½; 40; --; Furness SB Co,
Haverton Hill, 1942; 1960, sold Belgian
owners as storage hulk.
Eastbourne: Bangor cls minesweeper;
672; 180 x 28½; 16; 60; one 3-in;
Lobnitz & Co, Renfrew, 1941; b/up
Dunston 1948.
Easton: Hunt cls destroyer —
Albrighton type; 1050; 280 x 31½; 27;
168; four 4-in, two 21-in tt; J. S. White
& Co, Cowes, 1942; b/up Rosyth 1953.
Eastway: landing ship, dock; 7930;
457¾ x 72; 15; 260; one 4-in; Newport
News SB & DD Co, Newport News,
1943; ex-USN *Battleaxe, LSD-9,*
transferred Lease/Lend to RN 1943,
rnd, rtnd USN 1946; transferred 1947
to Royal Hellenic Navy, rnd *Hyperion,*
rnd *Nafkratoussa;* withdrawn from
service 1971.
Ebonol: Elmol cls oiler; 2410; 220 x
34⅔; 9½; 19; --; Clyde SB & E Co, Port
Glasgow, 1917; scuttled at Hong Kong
Dec 20, 1941, raised by Japanese,
refitted, rnd, *Enoshima Maru,* retaken
1945 rnd *Ebonol;* 1948, Chin Ah Co,
Singapore no name change; mined
Hong Kong, May 24, 1950.
Echo: E cls destroyer; 1405; 329 x
33¼; 35½; 145; four 4.7-in, eight 21-in
tt; Wm Denny & Bros, Dumbarton,
1934; transferred 1942 to Royal
Hellenic Navy, rnd *Navarinon,* rtnd RN
1956; b/up Dunston 1956.
Echodale: Dale cls oiler; 17,000; 483 x
59½; 11½; 40; --; Hawthorn Leslie,
Hebburn, 1941; b/up Spezia 1961.
Eclipse: E cls destroyer; 1405; 329 x
33¼; 35½; 145; four 4.7-in, eight 21-in
tt; Wm Denny & Bros, Dumbarton,
1934; mined east of Kalymnos, Oct 24,
1943.
Eday: Isles cls trawler; 560; 164 x 27½;
12; 40; one 12-pdr; Cochrane & Sons,
Selby, 1941; transferred 1944 to Royal
Norwegian Navy, rnd *Tromoy,* rtnd RN
1944, rnd *Eday;* 1948, A/S Fjeldoy,
Norway, converted to cargo ship, rnd
Fjellberg; 1952, Keller Shipping,
Switzerland, rnd *Sempach;* sunk after
explosion near Nemours, Apr 27, 1953.
Eden: Mersey cls trawler; 551; 148 x
22¾; 11; 20; two 3-in; Cochrane &

Sons, Selby, 1918; ex-*Thomas Johns,* 1920; ex-*Eden* 1921, ex-*Immortelle* (South African Navy) 1934; b/up UK 1947.

Edinburgh: Improved Southampton cls cruiser; 10,260; 613½ x 63¼; 32; 847; twelve 6-in, twelve 4-in, six 21-in tt; Swan Hunter & Wigham Richardson, Wallsend, 1939; torpedoed by *U-456* and destroyers *Z-24* and *Z-25* in Barentz Sea, sunk by RN two days later, May 2, 1942.

Edinburgh Castle: depot ship; 13,329 grt; 570¼ x 64½; --; --; --; Harland & Wolff, Belfast, 1910; ex-passenger liner (Union-Castle SS Co, London) bought RN 1939; scuttled by gunfire off Freetown, Sept 25, 1945.

Effingham: Hawkins cls cruiser; 9550; 605 x 65; 30½; 749; nine 6-in, eight 4-in, four 21-in tt; HM Dockyard, Portsmouth, 1925; wrecked in Norwegian campaign and destroyed by RN, May 21, 1940.

Eggesford: Hunt cls destroyer — Albrighton type; 1050; 280 x 31½; 27; 168; four 4-in, two 21-in tt; J. S. White & Co, Cowes, 1943; transferred 1958 to West German Navy, rnd *Brommy;* b/up 1969.

Egilsay: Isles cls trawler; 560; 164 x 27½; 12; 40; one 12-pdr; Cook Welton & Gemmell, Beverley, 1942; transferred 1946 to Italian Navy, rnd *RD-306;* sold mid-1960s.

Eglantine: Flower cls corvette; 925; 205 x 33; 16; 85; one 4-in; Harland & Wolff, Belfast, 1941; transferred 1941 to Royal Norwegian Navy, rnd *Soroy;* 1956, Thor Dahl, Norway, converted to whale catcher, rnd *Thorglimt;* b/up Norway 1970.

Eglinton: Hunt cls destroyer — Atherstone type; 1000; 280 x 29; 27½; 146; four 4-in; Vickers-Armstrongs, Tyne, 1940; b/up Blyth 1956.

Egret: Pelican cls sloop; 1250; 293 x 37½; 19¼; 188; eight 4-in; J. S. White & Co, Cowes, 1938; sunk by German aircraft, Bay of Biscay, Aug 27, 1943.

Ekins: Captain cls frigate; 1400; 306 x 36¾; 23½; 220; three 3-in; Bethlehem-Hingham Shipyard, 1943; ex-USN Buckley cls destroyer-escort *DE-87,* transferred Lease/Lend to RN 1943; irreparably damaged by mine in

North Sea, Apr 16, 1945, b/up Holland 1947.

Elderol: Elmol cls oiler; 2410; 220 x 34⅔; 9½; 19; --; Swan Hunter & Wigham Richardson, Wallsend, 1917; b/up Llanelly 1959.

Electra: E cls destroyer; 1405; 329 x 33¼; 35½; 145; four 4.7-in, eight 21-in tt; Hawthorn Leslie, Hebburn, 1934; sunk by Japanese surface force, Java Sea, Feb 27, 1942.

Elfreda: Catherine cls minesweeper; 890; 221 x 32; 18; 109; one 3-in; Associated Shipbuilders, Seattle, 1943; ex-USN Auk cls minesweeper *BAM-16* transferred Lease/Lend to RN 1943, rtnd USN 1946; transferred 1947 to Turkish Navy, rnd *Cesme;*

Elgin: Hunt cls minesweeper; 800; 231 x 28½; 16; 74; one 4-in, one 3-in; Wm Simons & Co, Renfrew, 1919; b/up Gateshead 1945.

Ellesmere: Lake cls trawler; 560; 147½ x 26½; 12½; 36; one 12-pdr; Smith's Dock Co, Middlesbrough, 1939; ex-whale catcher *Kos XXIV* (A. Jahre, Norway) bought RN 1939; sunk by U-boat in English Channel, Feb 24, 1945.

Elm: Tree cls trawler; 530; 164 x 27½; 11½; 35; one 12-pdr; A. & J. Inglis, Glasgow, 1940; 1946, Tyne pilot cutter, rnd *Helm;* 1948, Portuguese Government, rnd *Magul* (nothing more known).

Elmol: Elmol cls oiler; 2410; 220 x 34⅔; 9½; 19; --; Swan Hunter & Wigham Richardson, Wallsend, 1917; 1959, Enid Shipping Co, Edinburgh, no name change; 1961, Hammond Lane Foundry, Dublin, for b/up; 1961, A. G. Weser, Bremen, converted to oil sludge carrier, rnd *AGW VII;*

Emerald: E cls cruiser; 7550; 570 x 54½; 32; 572; seven 6-in, three 4-in, sixteen 21-in tt; Armstrong Whitworth & Co, Newcastle/HM Dockyard, Chatham, 1926; b/up Troon 1948.

Eminent: BAT cls tug; 783; 143 x 33; 14; 34; one 3-in; Defoe SB, Bay City, 1942; ex-USN transferred Lease/Lend to RN 1942, rtnd USN 1946; 1946, China Merchants SN Co, Shanghai, rnd *Ming 305;*

Emperor: Smiter cls escort carrier; 11,420; 496 x 69½; 16; 650; 20 aircraft,

two 5-in; Seattle-Tacoma SB Corp,
Tacoma, 1943; ex-USN *Pybus,
BCVE-34* transferred Lease/Lend to
RN 1943, rtnd USN 1946; b/up US
1946.

Emphatic: BAT cls tug; 783; 143 x 33;
14; 34; one 3-in; Levingston SB,
Orange, 1944; ex-USN, transferred
Lease/Lend to RN 1944, rtnd USN
1946, rnd *ATR-96;* transferred 1948 to
Philippine Navy, rnd *Ifugao;*

Empire Broadsword: Empire class
infantry landing ship; 11,650; 418 x 60;
14; 898; one 4-in; Consolidated Steel
Corp, Wilmington, 1943; launched as
Cape Marshall (US Maritime
Commission, Washington) transferred
Lease/Lend to Ministry of War
Transport, London; mined off
Normandy July 2, 1944.

Empire Javelin: Empire cls infantry
landing ship; 11,650; 418 x 60; 14; 898;
one 4-in; Consolidated Steel Corp,
Wilmington, 1944; launched as *Cape
Lobos* (US Maritime Commission,
Washington) transferred Lease/Lend
to Ministry of War Transport, London;
lost, English Channel, Dec 28, 1944.

Empire Rapier: Empire cls infantry
landing ship; 11,650; 418 x 60; 14; 898;
one 4-in; Consolidated Steel Corp,
Wilmington, 1943; launched as *Cape
Turner* (US Maritime Commission,
Washington) transferred Lease/Lend
to Ministry of War Transport, London,
rnd *Empire Rapier* 1943, transferred to
RN, no name change, 1945; rtnd
MoWT, 1946, rtnd USMC, rnd *Cape
Turner,* 1948; sold New York
shipbreakers 1965.

Empire Salvage: oiler; 10,476 grt; 496
x 73; 12½; --; --; Rotterdam DD Co,
Rotterdam, 1940; ex-*Papendrecht*
(Van Ommeren, Holland)
commandeered by Germany, rnd
Lotharingen; captured RN, rnd; rtnd
Van Ommeren, rnd *Papendrecht,*
1946; b/up Japan 1964.

Empire Spearhead: Empire cls
infantry landing ship; 11,650; 418 x 60;
14; 898; one 4-in; Consolidated Steel
Corp, Wilmington, 1944; launched as
Cape Girardeau (US Maritime
Commission, Washington),
transferred Lease/Lend to Ministry of
War Transport, London, rnd *Empire*

Spearhead 1944, transferred to RN
1945 no name change; rtnd MoWT
1946, rtnd USMC rnd *Cape Girardeau*
1946; 1948, was to be sold to China,
rnd *Hai Mei* not sold; rnd *Empire
Spearhead,* 1950; b/up Baltimore
1965.

Empress: Smiter cls escort carrier;
11,420; 496 x 69½; 16; 650; 20 aircraft,
two 5-in; Seattle-Tacoma SB Corp,
Tacoma, 1943; ex-USN *Carnegie,
BCVE-38,* transferred Lease/Lend to
RN 1943, rtnd USN 1946; b/up US
1949.

Emulous: Justice cls tug; 1360; 165 x
34; 12; 32; one 3-in; Camden SB, New
Jersey, 1943; ex-USN transferred
Lease/Lend to RN 1944, rtnd USN
1946; sold 1948.

Enchanter: Envoy cls tug; 1332; 174½
x 34½; 13; 33; one 3-in; Cochrane &
Sons, Selby, 1945; 1947, United
Towing, Co, Hull, rnd *Englishman;*
1962, Suprema Cia Nav SA, Panama,
rnd *Cintra;* 1968, Tsavliris (Salvage &
Towage) Greece, rnd *Nisos Skiathos;*
1972, Papageorgiou Salvage &
Towage Co, Greece, no name change;
b/up Perama 1972.

Enchantress: Bittern cls sloop; 1085;
282 x 37; 18¾; 125; two 4.7-in, one
3-in; John Brown & Co, Clydebank,
1935; ex-*Bittern,* 1934; former
Admiralty yacht; 1946, Three Star
Shipping Co, London, converted to
excursion vessel, rnd *Lady
Enchantress;* b/up Dunston 1952.

Encore: Envoy cls tug; 1332; 174½ x
34½; 13; 33; one 3-in; Cochrane &
Sons, Selby, 1945; 1968, Selco
(Panama) Pte, rnd *Salvaliant;* b/up
Singapore 1972.

Encounter: E cls destroyer; 1405; 329
x 33¼; 35½; 145; four 4.7-in, eight
21-in tt; Hawthorn Leslie, Hebburn,
1934; sunk by Japanese surface force
in Java Sea, Mar 1, 1942.

Endeavour: survey ship; 1280; 241¼ x
34; 13; 139; --; Fairfield SB & E Co,
Govan, 1912; 1946, Mr Panoyoti C.
Pateras, Alexandria; nothing more
known.

Enforcer: Envoy cls tug; 1332; 174½ x
34½; 13; 33; one 3-in; Cochrane &
Sons, Selby, 1944; b/up St David's on
Forth 1963.

Engadine: aircraft transport; 10,700; 487¾ x 63; 17; --; 40 aircraft; two 4-in; Wm Denny & Bros, Dumbarton, 1941; 1946, Clan Line, London, converted to cargo ship, rnd *Clan Buchanan;* b/up Carthagena 1962.

Enigma: Envoy cls tug; 1332; 174½ x 34½; 13; 33; one 3-in; Cochrane & Sons, Selby, 1944; 1964, N. E. Vernicos Shipping Co, Greece, rnd *Vernicos;* b/up Greece 1972.

Ennerdale: landing ship, gantry; 17,000; 483 x 59½; 11½; 65; one 4.7-in; fifteen landing craft (LCM); Swan Hunter & Wigham Richardson, Wallsend, 1941; converted to oiler, 1946-47; b/up Faslane 1959.

Ensay: Isles cls trawler; 560; 164 x 27½; 12; 40; one 12-pdr; Cook Welton & Gemmell, Beverley, 1942; transferred 1946 to Italian Navy, rnd *RD-314;* used as target, mid-1960s.

Enterprise: E cls cruiser; 7580; 570 x 54½; 32; 572; seven 6-in, three 4-in, sixteen 21-in tt; John Brown & Co, Clydebank/HM Dockyard, Devonport, 1926; b/up Newport 1946.

Enticer: Envoy cls tug; 1332; 174½ x 34½; 13; 33; one 3-in; Cochrane & Sons, Selby, 1944; lost in heavy weather about 300 miles south-west of Hong Kong, Dec 21, 1946.

Envoy: Envoy cls tug; 1332; 174½ x 34½; 13; 33; one 3-in; Cochrane & Sons, Selby, 1944; 1965, L. Matsas & Sons, Greece, rnd *Matsas,* rnd *Georgios L. Matsas* 1969; b/up Greece 1973.

Erebus: Erebus cls monitor; 7200; 405 x 88; 12; 315; two 15-in; Harland & Wolff, Govan, 1916; b/up Inverkeithing 1946.

Erica: Flower cls corvette; 925; 205 x 33; 16; 85; one 4-in; Harland & Wolff, Belfast, 1940; mined off Benghazi, Feb 9, 1943.

Eridge: Hunt cls destroyer — Blankney type; 1050; 280 x 31½; 27; 168; six 4-in; Swan Hunter & Wigham Richardson, Wallsend, 1941; irreparably damaged by torpedo from E-boat in Mediterranean, Aug 29, 1942; used as accommodation ship at Alexandria; b/up Alexandria 1947.

Eriskay: Isles cls trawler; 560; 164 x 27½; 12; 40; one 12-pdr; Fleming &

Ferguson, Paisley, 1942; transferred 1943 to Portuguese Navy, rnd *P-8,* rtnd RN 1945; foundered off Sao Jorge, Azores, Nov 12, 1945.

Erne: Black Swan cls sloop; 1350; 299½ x 38; 19¼; 180; six 4-in; Furness SB Co, Haverton Hill, 1941; rnd *Wessex* (RNVR drillship) 1952; b/up Antwerp 1965.

Escapade: E cls destroyer; 1405; 329 x 33¼; 35½; 145; four 4.7-in, eight 21-in tt; Scotts SB & E Co, Greenock, 1934; b/up Newport 1947.

Escort: E cls destroyer; 1405; 329 x 33¼; 35½; 145; four 4.7-in, eight 21-in tt; Scotts SB & E Co, Greenock, 1934; torpedoed by Italian submarine *Guglielmo Marconi* in western Mediterranean, July 8, 1940, foundered in tow, July 11, 1940.

Esk: E cls destroyer; 1405; 329 x 33¼; 35½; 145; four 4.7-in, eight 21-in tt; Swan Hunter & Wigham Richardson, Wallsend, 1934; mined in North Sea, north-west of Texel, Aug 31, 1940.

Eskdale: Hunt cls destroyer — Albrighton type; 1050; 280 x 31½; 27; 168; four 4-in, two 21-in tt; Cammell Laird, Birkenhead, 1942; transferred 1942 to Royal Norwegian Navy, no name change; torpedoed and sunk by E-boat off the Lizard, Apr 14, 1943.

Eskimo: Tribal cls destroyer; 1870; 377 x 36½; 36½; 190; eight 4.7-in, four 21-in tt; Vickers-Armstrongs, Tyne, 1938; b/up Troon 1949.

Espiegle: Algerine cls minesweeper; 950; 235 x 35½; 16½; 104; one 4-in; Harland & Wolff, Belfast, 1942; b/up Dalmuir 1967.

Essington: Captain cls frigate; 1400; 306 x 36¾; 23½; 220; three 3-in; Bethlehem-Hingham Shipyard, 1943; ex-USN Buckley cls destroyer-escort *DE-67,* transferred Lease/Lend to RN, 1943, rtnd USN 1945, b/up.

Ettrick: River cls frigate; 1370; 301½ x 36½; 19; 140; two 4-in; J. Crown & Sons, Sunderland, 1943; b/up Grays 1953.

Euryalus: Dido cls cruiser; 5450; 512 x 50½; 33; 620; ten 5.25-in, six 21-in tt; HM Dockyard, Chatham, 1940; b/up Blyth 1959.

Evenlode: River cls frigate; 1370; 301½ x 36½; 19; 140; two 4-in;

Canadian Vickers, Montreal, 1943; ex-USN *PG-105*, transferred Lease/Lend to RN 1943, rtnd USN 1946; sold 1946.

Excellent: Mersey cls trawler; 551; 148 x 22¾; 11; 20; two 3-in; Cochrane & Sons, Selby, 1918; ex-*Andrew Jewer*, 1920; ex-*Nith*, 1922; 1946, Yolland Bros, Milford Haven, rnd *Malvern;* b/up 1954.

Exe: River cls frigate; 1370; 301½ x 36½; 19; 140; two 4-in; Fleming & Ferguson, Paisley, 1942; b/up Preston 1956.

Exeter: cruiser; 8390; 575 x 58; 32; 630; six 8-in, four 4-in, six 21-in tt; HM Dockyard, Devonport, 1931; sunk in Battle of Java Sea by Japanese forces, Mar 1, 1942.

Exmoor: Hunt cls destroyer — Atherstone type; 1000; 280 x 29; 27½; 146; four 4-in; Vickers-Armstrongs, Tyne, 1940; sunk by German E-boat off Lowestoft, Feb 25, 1941.

Exmoor: Hunt cls destroyer — Blankney type; 1050; 280 x 31½; 27; 168; six 4-in; Swan Hunter & Wigham Richardson, Wallsend, 1941; ex-*Burton*, 1941; transferred 1953 to Danish Navy, rnd *Valdemar Sejr;* sold Ystad shipbreakers 1966.

Exmouth: E cls destroyer; 1475; 343 x 33¾; 36; 175; five 4.7-in, eight 21-in tt; HM Dockyard, Portsmouth, 1934; mined in North Sea, Jan 21, 1940.

Express: E cls destroyer; 1405; 329 x 33¼; 35½; 145; four 4.7-in, eight 21-in tt; Swan Hunter & Wigham Richardson, Wallsend, 1934; transferred 1943 to Royal Canadian Navy, rnd *Gatineau;* b/up Victoria BC 1946.

Eyebright: Flower cls corvette; 925; 205 x 33; 16; 85; one 4-in; Canadian Vickers, Montreal, 1940; transferred 1941 to Royal Canadian Navy, rtnd RN 1945; 1950, Nederlandsche Maats voor de Walvischvaart NV, Holland, converted to whale catcher, rnd *Albert W. Vinke;* b/up South Africa 1965.

Fairy: Catherine cls minesweeper; 890; 221 x 32; 18; 109; one 3-in; Associated Shipbuilders, Seattle,

1943; ex-USN Auk cls minesweeper *BAM-25*, transferred Lease/Lend to RN 1943, rtnd USN 1946; sold 1947.

Fal: River cls frigate; 1370; 301½ x 36½; 19; 140; two 4-in; Smith's Dock Co, Middlesbrough, 1943; transferred 1947 to Burma, rnd *Mayu;*

Falcon: river gunboat; 372; 150 x 28⅔; 15; 55; one 3.7-in howitzer; Yarrow & Co, Scotstoun, 1931; presented to Nationalist China, Feb 1942, rnd *Lung Huan*, rnd *Ying Teh*, rnd *Nan Chiang;* taken over by Republicans, 1947, (nothing more known).

Falconet: Bayonet cls boom defence vessel; 530; 135 x 30½; 11½; 32; one 3-in; Blyth SB & DD Co, Blyth, 1939; ex-*Barnham*, 1938; sold Portsmouth shipbreakers 1958.

Falmouth: Falmouth cls sloop; 1060; 266 x 34; 16; 100; two 4-in; HM Dockyard, Devonport, 1932; rnd *Calliope* (RNVR drillship) 1952; b/up Blyth 1968.

Fame: F cls destroyer; 1405; 329 x 33¼; 35½; 145; four 4.7-in, eight 21-in tt; Vickers-Armstrongs, Barrow, 1935; transferred 1949 to Dominican Republic, rnd *Generalisimo*, rnd *Sanchez* 1962; withdrawn from service 1968.

Fancy: Algerine cls minesweeper; 950; 235 x 35½; 16½; 104; one 4-in; Blyth SB & DD Co, Blyth, 1943; transferred 1951 to Belgium, rnd *A. F. Dufour*, training hulk in Congo rnd *N'Zadi*, 1959; sunk Congo, 1960.

Fandango: Dance cls trawler; 530; 160½ x 27½; 35; one 4-in; Cochrane & Sons, Selby, 1940; 1946, Skibs A/S Argo, Norway, converted to cargo ship, no name change; 1966, A/S Samfrost, Norway, rnd *Samfrost;* damaged by fire off Kvitsoy, July 23, 1972, b/up.

Fantome: Algerine cls minesweeper; 950; 235 x 35½; 16½; 104; one 4-in; Harland & Wolff, Belfast, 1942; irreparably damaged by mine in Mediterranean, May 20, 1943, b/up Milford Haven 1947.

Fara: Isles cls trawler; 560; 164 x 27½; 12; 40; one 12-pdr; Cochrane & Sons Selby, 1941; sold 1946, buyers not known.

Fareham: Hunt cls minesweeper; 800

231 x 28½; 16; 74; one 4-in, one 3-in;
Dunlop Bremner & Co, Port Glasgow,
1918; b/up Hayle 1951.

Farndale: Hunt cls destroyer —
Blankney type; 1050; 280 x 31½; 27;
168; six 4-in; Swan Hunter & Wigham
Richardson, Wallsend, 1941; b/up
Blyth 1962.

Farne: Isles cls trawler; 560; 164 x
27½; 12; 40; one 12-pdr; Cook Welton
& Gemmell, Beverley, 1943; 1946,
Rederi A/S Ranvik, Norway, no name
change; lost December 1948.

Farnham Castle: Castle cls corvette;
1010; 252 x 36¾; 16½; 120; one 4-in; J.
Crown & Sons, Sunderland, 1944;
b/up Gateshead 1960.

Fastnet: boom working vessel; 444;
138½ x 23¾; 11; 15; --; Goole SB &
Repairing Co, Goole, 1919; ex-Mersey
cls trawler *Benjamin Hawkins;*
ex-*Frobisher* (Goole SB & Repairing
Co, Goole) acquired by RN, 1933,
transferred 1942 to Royal Netherlands
Navy; abandoned at Batavia, April,
1942.

Faulknor: F cls destroyer; 1475; 343 x
33¾; 36; 175; five 4.7-in, eight 21-in tt;
Yarrow & Co, Scotstoun, 1935; b/up
Milford Haven 1946.

Favourite: BAT cls tug; 783; 143 x 33;
14; 34; one 3-in; Levingston SB,
Orange, 1942; ex-USN, transferred
Lease/Lend to RN 1942, rtnd USN
1946; 1946, Moran Towing Corp, US,
rnd *Susan A. Moran,* rnd *Eugene F.
Moran;* 1947, Cia Colonial de
Navegacao, Portugal, rnd *Monsanto;*

Fearless: F cls destroyer; 1405; 329 x
33¼; 35½; 145; four 4.7-in, eight 21-in
tt; Cammell Laird, Birkenhead, 1934;
badly damaged by Italian aircraft in
Mediterranean, July 23, 1941, sunk by
RN.

Felicity: Algerine cls minesweeper;
950; 235 x 35½; 16½; 104; one 4-in;
Redfern Construction Co, Toronto,
1944; ex-*Coppercliff* (RCN) 1943;
1947, South Georgia Co (C. Salvesen)
Leith, converted to fish freezer ship,
rnd *Fairfree;* b/up Charlestown 1957.

Felixstowe: Bangor cls minesweeper;
672; 180 x 28½; 16; 60; one 3-in;
Lobnitz & Co, Renfrew, 1941; mined
off Sardinia, Dec 18, 1943.

Fencer: Attacker cls escort carrier;

10,200; 496 x 69½; 16; 650; 15-20
aircraft; Western Pipe & Steel Co, San
Francisco, 1942; ex-USN *Croatan,
BAVG-14,* transferred Lease/Lend to
RN 1942, rtnd USN 1946; 1950, Achille
Lauro, Italy, converted to passenger
liner, rnd *Sydney,* rnd *Roma* 1967;
1971, Sovereign Cruise Ships, Cyprus,
rnd *Galaxy Queen;* 1972, G. Kotzovilis,
Greece, rnd *Lady Dina,* rnd *Caribia 2,*
1973.

Fennel: Flower cls corvette; 925; 205 x
33; 16; 85; one 4-in; Marine Industries,
Sorel, 1940; transferred 1941 to Royal
Canadian Navy, rtnd RN 1945; 1948,
A/S Kosmos, Norway, converted to
whale catcher, rnd *Milliam Kihl;* b/up
Grimstad 1966.

Fermoy: Hunt cls minesweeper; 800;
231 x 28½; 16; 74; one 4-in, one 3-in;
Dundee SB Co, Dundee, 1919;
irreparably damaged in air attack, May
4, 1941.

Fernie: Hunt cls destroyer —
Atherstone type; 1000; 280 x 29; 27½;
146; four 4-in; John Brown & Co,
Clydebank, 1940; b/up Port Glasgow
1956.

Fetlar: Isles cls trawler; 560; 164 x
27½; 12; 40; one 12-pdr; Cochrane &
Sons, Selby, 1941; b/up Antwerp 1960.

Fiaray: Isles cls trawler; 560; 164 x
27½; 12; 40; one 12-pdr; Goole SB &
Repairing Co, Goole, 1942; 1946, Cie
Cherifienne d'Armemente, Morocco,
converted to cargo ship, rnd *Atlas;*
1955, Gabriele Zunini, Italy, rnd *Aris;*

Fiji: Fiji cls cruiser; 8525; 555½ x 62;
33; 980; twelve 6-in, eight 4-in, six
21-in tt; John Brown & Co, Clydebank,
1940; destroyed by German and Italian
aircraft off Crete, May 22, 1941.

Filla: Isles cls trawler; 560; 164 x 27½;
12; 40; one 12-pdr; J. Crown & Sons,
Sunderland, 1942; transferred 1946 to
Italian Navy, rnd *RD-305;* sold
mid-1960s.

Findhorn: River cls frigate; 1370;
301½ x 36½; 19; 140; two 4-in;
Canadian Vickers, Montreal, 1943;
ex-USN *PG-106,* transferred
Lease/Lend to RN 1943, rtnd USN
1946; sold 1947.

Fir: Tree cls trawler; 530; 164 x 27½;
11½; 35; one 12-pdr; A. & J. Inglis,
Glasgow, 1940; 1946, sold Norwegian

shipowners, nothing more known.
Firedrake: F cls destroyer; 1405; 329 x
33¼; 35½; 145; four 4.7-in, eight
21-in tt; Vickers-Armstrongs, Tyne
1935; torpedoed and sunk by *U-211* in
west Atlantic, Dec 17, 1942.
Fishguard: Lulworth cls escort; 1546;
250 x 42; 16; 200; one 5-in, two 3-in;
Bethlehem SB Corp, Quincy, 1927;
ex-US Coast Guard cutter *Tahoe,*
transferred Lease/Lend to RN 1941,
rtnd USCG 1946; sold New York
shipbreakers 1947.
Fitzroy: Hunt cls minesweeper: 800;
231 x 28½; 16; 74; one 4-in, one 3-in;
Lobnitz & Co, Renfrew, 1919;
ex-*Pinner* 1919; former survey ship;
mined in North Sea, May 27, 1942.
Fitzroy: Captain cls frigate; 1400; 306
x 36¾; 23½; 220; three 3-in;
Bethlehem-Hingham Shipyard, 1943;
ex-USN Buckley cls destroyer-escort
DE-88, transferred Lease/Lend to RN
1943, rtnd USN 1946, b/up.
Flamborough Head: escort repair
ship; 8580; 441½ x 57, 11; 440; --;
Burrard DD Co, Vancouver, 1945;
transferred 1951 to Royal Canadian
Navy, rnd *Cape Breton* 1953;
Flamingo: Black Swan cls sloop;
1350; 299½ x 38; 19¼; 180; six 4-in;
Yarrow & Co, Scotstoun, 1939;
transferred 1958 to West German
Navy, rnd *Graf Spee;* b/up 1965.
Flare: BAT cls tug; 783; 143 x 33; 14;
34; one 3-in; Levingston SB, Orange,
1943; ex-USN, transferred Lease/Lend
to RN 1943, rtnd USN 1946; 1946,
China Merchants SN Co, Shanghai,
rnd *Ming 301;* b/up 1960.
Flatholm: Isles cls trawler; 560; 164 x
27½; 12; 40; one 12-pdr; Cook Welton
& Gemmell, Beverley, 1943; b/up
Antwerp 1960.
Flaunt: BAT cls tug; 783; 143 x 33; 14;
34; one 3-in; Levingston SB, Orange,
1943, ex-USN, transferred Lease/Lend
to RN 1943, rtnd USN 1946; 1946,
China Merchants SN Co, Shanghai,
rnd *Ming 102,* rnd *Ming 302* 1951;
Flax: Modified Flower cls corvette;
980; 208¼ x 33; 16; 109; one 4-in;
Kingston SB Co, Kingston, 1942;
transferred 1942 to USN, rnd *Brisk,*
rtnd RN 1946; 1947, Rederi Tuxen &
Hageman, Denmark, converted to

cargo ship, rnd *Brisk;* 1951,
International Trading Corp, Liberia,
rnd *Ariana;* 1955, Three Bays Corp,
Liberia, rnd *Arvida Bay;* 1963, D.
Stephen, Honduras, rnd *Zaida;*
Fleetwood: Aberdeen cls sloop; 990;
266 x 36; 16½; 100; four 4-in; HM
Dockyard, Devonport, 1936; b/up
Gateshead 1959.
Fleur de Lys: Flower cls corvette; 925;
205 x 33; 16; 85; one 4-in; Smith's
Dock Co, Middlesbrough, 1940; ex-*La
Dieppoise,* 1940; sunk by *U-206* off
Gibraltar, Oct 14, 1941.
Flinders: Hunt cls minesweeper; 800;
231 x 28½; 16; 74; one 4-in, one 3-in;
Lobnitz & Co, Renfrew, 1919;
ex-*Radley,* 1919; former survey ship;
b/up Hayle 1946.
Flint: Isles cls trawler; 560; 164 x 27½;
12; 40; one 12-pdr; G. T. Davie,
Lauzon, 1942; transferred 1947 to
West German Navy, rnd *Caroline,* rnd
Trave; withdrawn from service 1971.
Flint Castle: Castle cls corvette; 1010;
252 x 36¾; 16½; 120; one 4-in; H.
Robb, Leith, 1943; b/up Faslane 1958.
Florizel: Catherine cls minesweeper;
890; 221 x 32; 18; 109; one 3-in;
Associated Shipbuilders, Seattle,
1943; ex-USN Auk cls minesweeper
BAM-26 transferred Lease/Lend to RN
1943, rtnd USN 1946; 1949, Greek
Navy rnd *Lasithi;* 1952, A. Halkoussis &
Co, Greece, converted to cargo ship,
rnd *Aida;* b/up Italy 1967.
Flotta: Isles cls trawler; 560; 164 x
27½; 12; 40; one 12-pdr; Cochrane &
Sons, Selby, 1941; grounded off
Buchan Ness, Oct 29, 1941, and
foundered Nov 6, 1941.
Fluellen: Shakespearian cls trawler;
545; 164 x 27¾; 12; 35; one 12-pdr;
Cochrane & Sons, Selby, 1941;
transferred 1947 to Scottish Home
Dept as fisheries research trawler, rnd
Scotia, rnd *Scarba* 1972; b/up Dalmuir
1973.
Fly: Algerine cls minesweeper; 950;
235 x 35½; 16½; 104; one 4-in; Lobnitz
& Co, Renfrew, 1942; transferred 1949
to Iran, rnd *Palang;* withdrawn from
service, to be scrapped shortly.
Flying Fish: Algerine cls
minesweeper; 950; 235 x 35½; 16½;
104; one 4-in; Redfern Construction

Co, Toronto, 1944; ex-*Tillsonburg*
(RCN) 1943; transferred 1949 to
Ceylon, rnd *Vijaya;* now used for
training purposes at Trincomalee.
Foam: Catherine cls minesweeper;
890; 221 x 32; 18; 109; one 3-in;
Associated Shipbuilders, Seattle, 1943;
ex-USN Auk cls minesweeper *BAM-27*
transferred Lease/Lend to RN 1943,
rtnd USN 1946; sold 1947.
Foley: Captain cls frigate; 1140; 289½
x 35; 21; 200; three 3-in; Navy Yard,
Boston, 1943; ex-USN Evarts cls
destroyer-escort *Gillette, DE-270,*
transferred Lease/Lend to RN 1943,
rtnd USN 1945, b/up.
Folkestone: Hastings cls sloop; 1045;
266 x 34; 16; 100; two 4-in; Swan
Hunter & Wigham Richardson,
Wallsend, 1930; b/up Milford Haven
1947.
Foresight: F cls destroyer; 1405; 329 x
33¼; 35½; 145; four 4.7-in, eight 21-in
tt; Cammell Laird, Birkenhead, 1935;
torpedoed by Italian aircraft in
Mediterranean, Aug 12, 1942, sank
next day in tow.
Forester: F cls destroyer; 1405; 329 x
33¼; 35½; 145; four 4.7-in, eight 21-in
tt; J. S. White & Co, Cowes, 1935; b/up
Rosyth 1947.
Formidable: Illustrious cls aircraft
carrier; 23,000; 753 x 95; 31; 1600; 54
aircraft, sixteen 4.5-in; Harland &
Wolff, Belfast, 1940; b/up
Inverkeithing 1953.
Fort Charlotte: store ship; 14,000;
441½ x 57; 11; 94; --; North Van
Shiprepairers, Vancouver 1944;
ex-*Buffalo Park,* 1944; b/up Singapore
1968.
Fort Dunvegan: store ship; 14,000;
441½ x 57; 11; 94; --; Burrard DD Co,
Vancouver, 1944; b/up Taiwan 1968.
Forth: submarine depot ship; 8900;
531 x 75; 17; 502; eight 4.5-in; J.
Brown & Co, Clydebank, 1939;
modified 1962-66 for nuclear
submarines; rnd *Defiance* 1972:
Fortol: Belgol cls oiler; 5620; 335 x
41½; 14; 39; --; A. McMillan & Son,
Dumbarton, 1917; b/up Rosyth 1958.
Fort Rosalie: store ship; 14,000;
441½ x 57; 11; 94; --; United
Shipyards, Montreal, 1945; b/up
Castellon 1973.

Fort Sandusky: store ship; 14,000;
441½ x 57; 11; 94; --; United
Shipyards, Montreal, 1945; b/up
Castellon 1973.
Fortune: F cls destroyer; 1405; 329 x
33¼; 35½; 145; four 4.7-in, eight 21-in
tt; J. Brown & Co, Clydebank, 1935;
transferred 1943 to Royal Canadian
Navy, rnd *Saskatchewan;* sold
Hamilton, Ont, shipbreakers 1946.
Fort York: Bangor cls minesweeper;
672; 180 x 28½; 16; 60; one 3-in;
Dufferin SB Co, Toronto, 1941;
ex-*Mingan,* 1941; converted to fleet
tug, 1946; transferred 1950 to
Portuguese Navy, converted to survey
ship, rnd *Comandante Almeida
Carvalho;* converted to corvette, rnd
Cacheu; for disposal and breaking-up
1973.
Foula: Isles cls trawler; 560; 164 x
27½; 12; 40; one 12-pdr; Cochrane &
Sons, Selby, 1941; transferred 1946 to
Italian Navy, rnd *RD-313;* used as
target, mid-1960s.
Foulness: Isles cls trawler; 560; 164 x
27½; 12; 40; one 12-pdr; J. Lewis &
Sons, Aberdeen, 1942; believed sold
1973;
Fowey: Shoreham cls sloop; 1105; 266
x 34; 16; 100; two 4-in; HM Dockyard,
Devonport, 1931; 1947, Wheelock
Marden, Hong Kong, converted to
merchant ship, rnd *Fowlock;* b/up
Mombasa 1949.
Foxglove: Flower cls sloop; 1165;
262½ x 33; 16; 104; two 4-in; Barclay
Curle & Co, Glasgow, 1915; b/up
Troon 1946.
Foxhound: F cls destroyer; 1405; 329 x
33¼; 35½; 145; four 4.7-in, eight 21-in
tt; John Brown & Co, Clydebank, 1935;
transferred 1943 to Royal Canadian
Navy, rnd *Qu'Appelle;* b/up Montreal
1948.
Foxtrot: Dance cls trawler; 530; 160½
x 27½; 11½; 35; one 4-in; Cochrane &
Sons, Selby, 1940; transferred 1947 to
Royal Army Service Corps; b/up
Barrow 1951.
Foyle: Mersey cls trawler; 551; 148 x
22¾; 11; 20; two 3-in; Goole SB &
Repairing Co, Goole, 1918; ex-*John
Edmund,* 1920; ex-*Foyle, 1921;*
ex-*Sonneblom* (South African Navy),
1934; 1947, Oddson & Co, Hull, rnd

Cramond Island, rnd *Brimnes,* 1949; 1950, A. R. Milne, Aberdeen, rnd *Hetty Milne;* b/up Belgium 1954.

Francol: Belgol cls oiler; 5620; 335 x 41½; 14; 39; --; Earle's SB & E Co, Hull, 1918; sunk by Japanese surface force, south of Java, Mar 3, 1942.

Franklin: Halcyon cls minesweeper; 835; 245 x 33½; 17; 80; one 4-in; Ailsa SB Co, Troon, 1938; completed as survey ship, converted 1939; b/up Dunston 1956.

Fraserburgh: Bangor cls minesweeper; 672; 180 x 28½; 16; 60; one 3-in; Lobnitz & Co, Renfrew, 1941; b/up Thornaby-on-Tees 1948.

Freebooter: Brigand cls tug; 840; 174 x 32; 15½; 43; one 3-in; Fleming & Ferguson, Paisley, 1941; sold Genoa shipbreakers 1959.

Freedom: Justice cls tug; 1360; 165 x 34; 12; 32; one 3-in; Camden SB, New Jersey, 1943; ex-USN, transferred Lease/Lend to RN 1944, rtnd USN 1946; sold 1948.

Freesia: Flower cls corvette; 925; 205 x 33; 16; 85; one 4-in; Harland & Wolff, Belfast, 1940; 1946, Wheelock Marden, Hong Kong, rnd *Freelock;* broke from tow April 1, 1947, drifted ashore at San Jorge.

Freshbrook: Fresh cls coastal water carrier; 594; 126¼ x 24½; 9½; 12; --; Lytham SB, Lytham, 1943; 1963, Park Stanton & Co, London, no name change; b/up Holland 1963.

Freshburn: Fresh cls coastal water carrier; 594; 126¼ x 24½; 9½; 12; --; Lytham SB, Lytham, 1944;

Freshener: Fresh cls coastal water carrier; 594; 126¼ x 24½; 9½; 12; --; Lytham SB, Lytham, 1942; target ship at Gibraltar.

Freshet: Fresh cls coastal water carrier; 594; 126¼ x 24½; 9½; 12; --; Lytham SB, Lytham, 1940; sold 1963, buyers not known.

Freshford: Fresh cls coastal water carrier; 594; 126¼ x 24½; 9½; 12; --; Lytham SB, Lytham, 1944; sold Antwerp shipbreakers 1967.

Freshlake: Fresh cls coastal water carrier; 594; 126¼ x 24½; 9½; 12; --; Lytham SB, Lytham, 1942;

Freshmere: Fresh cls coastal water carrier; 594; 126¼ x 24½; 9½; 12; --;

Lytham SB, Lytham, 1943;

Freshpond: Fresh cls coastal water carrier; 594; 126¼ x 24½; 9½; 12; --; Lytham SB, Lytham, 1945;

Freshpool: Fresh cls coastal water carrier; 594; 126¼ x 24½; 9½; 12; --; Lytham SB, Lytham, 1943;

Freshtarn: Fresh cls coastal water carrier; 594; 126¼ x 24½; 9½; 12; --; Lytham SB, Lytham, 1944; sold 1969, buyers not known.

Freshwater: Fresh cls coastal water carrier; 594; 126¼ x 24½; 9½; 12; --; Lytham SB, Lytham, 1940; 1968, Ferro & Co, Portugal, rnd *Porto Grande;*

Freshwell: Fresh cls coastal water carrier; 594; 126¼ x 24½; 9½; 12; --; Lytham SB, Lytham, 1943; b/up Passage West 1968.

Friendship: Algerine cls minesweeper; 950; 235 x 35½; 16½; 104; one 4-in; Toronto Shipyards, Toronto, 1943; ex-USN, transferred Lease/Lend to RN 1943, rtnd USN 1946; sold 1947.

Frisky: Assurance cls tug; 1045; 157 x 35; 13; 31; one 3-in; Cochrane & Sons, Selby, 1941; 1948, Kuwait Oil Co, London, rnd *Hasan;* 1961, N. E. Vernicos Shipping Co, Greece, rnd *Vernicos Marina;* b/up Piraeus 1973.

Fritillary: Flower cls corvette; 925; 205 x 33; 16; 85; one 4-in; Harland & Wolff, Belfast, 1941; 1947, Cia Maritima Mensabe SA, Panama, converted to cargo ship, rnd *Andria;* 1949, Air, Steamer & General Agencies, Bombay, rnd *V. O. Chidambaram;* b/up India 1955.

Frobisher: Hawkins cls cruiser; 9860; 605 x 65; 30½; 749; five 7.5-in, five 4-in, four 21-in tt; HM Dockyard, Devonport, 1924; b/up Newport 1949.

Frolic: Catherine cls minesweeper; 890; 221 x 32; 18; 109; one 3-in; General Engineering & DD Co, Alameda, 1943; ex-USN Auk cls minesweeper *BAM-28* transferred Lease/Lend to RN 1943, rtnd USN 1946; transferred 1947 to Turkey, rnd *Candarli;*

Frome: River cls frigate; 1370; 301½ x 36½; 19; 140; two 4-in; Blyth SB & DD Co, Blyth, 1944; transferred 1944 to French Navy, rnd *L'Escarmouche,* rnd *L'Ailette,* 1956; condemned 1961 rnd

Q-307, b/up Brest.

Fuday: Isles cls trawler; 560; 164 x 27½; 12; 40; one 12-pdr; Cook Welton & Gemmell, Beverley, 1944; 1946, NV Verre Visscherij Maats, Holland, rnd *Simon de Danser;* 1952, Schlienz-Hagemann Hochsee & Gefrierfisch, West Germany, rnd *Prof Heincke;* 1953, F. Wilberg ULP Paes Leme, Brazil, rnd *Carola;* 1958, Empresa de Nav.e Pesca Vieira, Brazil, rnd *Orion 1;*

Furious: aircraft carrier; 22,450; 786¼ x 89¾; 31; 1200; 33 aircraft, twelve 4-in; Armstrong Whitworth & Co, Newcastle, launched as light battlecruiser, 1916, completed 1917, rebuilt 1917-18; b/up Dalmuir 1948.

Fury: F cls destroyer; 1405; 329 x 33¼; 35½; 145; four 4.7-in, eight 21-in tt; J. S. White & Co, Cowes, 1935; damaged by mine off Normandy, June 21 1944, constructive total loss, b/up Briton Ferry 1944.

Fusilier: Military cls trawler; 750; 193 x 30; 11; 40; one 4-in; Cook Welton & Gemmell, Beverley, 1943; 1946, Standard Steam Fishing Co, Grimsby, rnd *Serron;* b/up Grays 1965.

Gairsay: Isles cls trawler; 560; 164 x 27½; 12; 40; one 12-pdr; Ardrossan Dockyard Ltd, Ardrossan, 1942; sunk off Normandy, Aug 3, 1944.

Galatea: Arethusa cls cruiser; 5220; 506 x 51; 32¼; 450; six 6-in, four 4-in, six 21-in tt; Scotts SB & E Co, Greenock, 1935; torpedoed and sunk by *U-557* off Alexandria, Dec 15, 1941.

Gallant: G cls destroyer; 1335; 323 x 33; 35½; 145; four 4.7-in, eight 21-in tt; A. Stephen & Sons, Linthouse, 1936; mined south of Pantelleria Jan 10, 1941, towed to and beached at Malta; damaged in air attack while under repair, Apr 5, 1942; sunk as blockship at St Paul's Island, September 1943.

Galtee More: Empire cls infantry landing ship; 11,600; 418 x 60; 14; 898; one 4-in; Consolidated Steel Corp, Wilmington, 1943; launched as *Cape St Roque* (US Maritime Commission, Washington) transferred Lease/Lend to Ministry of War Transport, London, 1943, rnd *Empire Mace,* transferred 1945 to RN, rnd; trs MoWT, rnd *Empire Mace* 1946, rtnd USMC 1946, rnd *Cape St Roque;* 1947, Soc Misr de Navegation Maritime SAE, Egypt, converted to passenger-cargo ship, rnd *Misr;*

Gambia: Fiji cls cruiser; 8525; 555½ x 62; 33; 980; twelve 6-in, eight 4-in, six 21-in tt; Swan Hunter & Wigham Richardson, Wallsend, 1942; RNZN 1943, rtnd RN 1948; b/up Inverkeithing 1968.

Ganilly; Isles cls trawler; 560; 164 x 27½; 12; 40; one 12-pdr; Cook Welton & Gemmell, Beverley, 1943; mined off Normandy, July 5, 1944.

Gannet: Peterel cls river gunboat; 310; 184⅔ x 29; 16; 55; two 3-in; Yarrow & Co, Scotstoun, 1927; presented to Nationalist China, Feb 1942, rnd *Ying Shan;* taken over by Republicans, 1947 (nothing more known).

Gardenia: Flower cls corvette; 925; 205 x 33; 16; 85; one 4-in; Wm Simons & Co, Renfrew, 1940; lost in collision with trawler *Fluellen* off Oran, Nov 9, 1942.

Gardiner: Captain cls frigate; 1140; 289½ x 35; 21; 200; three 3-in; Navy Yard Boston, 1943; ex-USN Evarts cls destroyer-escort *O'Toole, DE-274,* transferred Lease/Lend to RN 1943, rtnd USN 1946, b/up.

Garland: G cls destroyer; 1335; 323 x 33; 35½; 145; four 4.7-in, eight 21-in tt; Fairfield SB & E Co, Govan, 1936; transferred 1940 to Polish Navy, no name change, rtnd RN 1946; transferred 1947 to Royal Netherlands Navy, rnd *Marnix;* sold Antwerp shipbreakers 1964.

Garlies: Captain cls frigate; 1140; 289½ x 35; 21; 200; three 3-in; Navy Yard, Boston, 1943; ex-USN Evarts cls destroyer-escort *Fleming, DE-271,* transferred Lease/Lend to RN 1943, rtnd USN 1945; b/up US 1947.

Garry: Axe cls trawler; 417; 139 x 23½; 10½; 18; one 3-in; Smith's Dock Co, Middlesbrough 1916; ex-Russian *T-13,* acquired by RN, 1918 rnd *Goldaxe,* rnd 1920; 1946, Brodrene Lothe A/S, Norway, no name change; 1948, G. Seberg, Norway, converted to cargo

ship, no name change; 1953, J.
Seberg, Norway, no name change;
Garth: Hunt cls destroyer —
Atherstone type; 1000; 280 x 29; 27½;
146; four 4-in; J. Brown & Co,
Clydebank, 1940; b/up Barrow 1958.
Gateshead: Isles cls trawler; 560; 164
x 27½; 12; 40; one 12-pdr; G. T. Davie,
Lauzon, 1942; b/up Holland 1959.
Gavotte: Dance cls trawler; 530; 160½
x 27½; 11½; 35; one 4-in; Cook Welton
& Gemmell, Beverley, 1940;
transferred 1946 to Italian Navy, rnd
RD-312; used as target mid-1960s.
Gazelle: Catherine cls minesweeper;
890; 221 x 32; 18; 109; one 3-in;
Savannah Machinery & Foundry Co,
Savannah, 1943; ex-USN Auk cls
minesweeper *BAM-17,* transferred
Lease/Lend to RN 1943, rtnd USN 1946;
sold 1947.
Genista: Flower cls corvette; 925; 205
x 33; 16; 85; one 4-in; Harland & Wolff,
Belfast, 1941; transferred 1947 to Air
Ministry, converted to weather ship,
rnd *Weather Recorder;* b/up Belgium
1961.
Gentian: Flower cls corvette; 925; 205
x 33; 16; 85; one 4-in; Harland & Wolff,
Belfast, 1940; b/up Purfleet 1947.
Georgetown: Town cls destroyer;
1060; 314⅓ x 30½; 30; 122; one 4-in,
three 21-in tt; Bethlehem SB, Fore
River, 1919; ex-USN *Maddox,*
transferred 1940 to RN; transferred
1944 to Soviet Union, rnd *Zhostki,* rtnd
RN 1952; b/up Inverkeithing 1952.
Geranium: Flower cls corvette; 925;
205 x 33; 16; 85; one 4-in; Wm Simons
& Co, Renfrew, 1940; transferred 1947
to Danish Navy, rnd *Thetis;* sold
Odense shipbreakers 1963.
Gillstone: Isles cls trawler; 560; 164 x
27½; 12; 40; one 12-pdr; Cochrane &
Sons, Selby, 1943; 1947, D/S A/S
Anglo, Norway, rnd *Argo,* converted to
cargo ship 1952; 1961, Freedom Line,
Panama, rnd *Freedom First;* 1964,
Hudson Shipping Corp, US, rnd
Glenrock; 1969, Seaway Lines, US,
rnd *Sea Enterprise;* 1970, Linea
Panama Imperial Reefers SA, Panama,
rnd *Almirante;*
Gipsy: G cls destroyer; 1335; 323 x 33;
35½; 145; four 4.7-in, eight 21-in tt;
Fairfield SB & E Co, Govan, 1936;

mined off Harwich, Nov 21, 1939.
Gladiolus: Flower cls corvette; 925;
205 x 33; 16; 85; one 4-in; Smith's
Dock Co, Middlesbrough, 1940;
torpedoed and sunk by U-boat in
Western Approaches, Oct 16, 1941.
Glaisdale: Hunt cls destroyer —
Albrighton type; 1050; 280 x 31½; 27;
168; four 4-in, two 21-in tt; Cammell
Laird, Birkenhead, 1942; transferred
1942 to Royal Norwegian Navy, rnd
Narvik 1946; b/up Masnedo 1961.
Glasgow: Southampton cls cruiser;
9100; 591½ x 61⅔; 32; 830; twelve
6-in, eight 4-in, six 21-in tt; Scotts SB &
E Co, Greenock, 1937; b/up Blyth
1958.
Gleaner: Halcyon cls minesweeper;
835; 245 x 33½; 17; 80; two 4-in; Wm
Gray & Co, West Hartlepool, 1937;
b/up Preston 1950.
Glorious: Courageous cls aircraft
carrier; 22,500; 786¼ x 100; 30; 1216;
48 aircraft, sixteen 4.7-in; Harland &
Wolff, Belfast, completed 1916 as light
battlecruiser, converted into aircraft
carrier HM Dockyards, Rosyth and
Devonport, 1924-30; sunk in action
with German battlecruisers
Scharnhorst and *Gneisenau* near
Narvik, June 8, 1940.
Glory: Colossus cls aircraft carrier;
13,190; 694½ x 112½; 25; 1350; 39-44
aircraft; Harland & Wolff, Belfast,
1945; b/up Inverkeithing 1961.
Gloucester: Southampton cls cruiser;
9400; 591½ x 62⅓; 32; 830; twelve
6-in, eight 4-in, six 21-in tt; HM
Dockyard, Devonport, 1939; bombed
and sunk by German aircraft off Crete,
May 22, 1941.
Glowworm: G cls destroyer; 1345; 323
x 33; 35½; 145; four 4.7-in, ten 21-in tt;
J. I. Thornycroft & Co, Southampton,
1936; sunk by German cruiser *Admiral
Hipper* off Norway, Apr 8, 1940.
Gloxinia: Flower cls corvette; 925; 205
x 33; 16; 85; one 4-in; Harland & Wolff,
Belfast, 1940; b/up Purfleet 1947.
Gnat: Insect cls river gunboat; 625;
237½ x 36; 14; 65; two 6-in, one 3-in;
Lobnitz & Co, Renfrew, 1916;
damaged by torpedo from *U-79* off
Bardia, Oct 21, 1941, and beached
Alexandria; b/up 1945.
Goathland: Hunt cls destroyer —

Albrighton type; 1050; 280 x 31½; 27; 168; four 4-in, two 21-in tt; Fairfield SB & E Co, Govan, 1942; damaged by mine off Normandy, July 24, 1944; b/up Troon 1945.

Godetia: Flower cls corvette; 925; 205 x 33; 16; 85; one 4-in; Smith's Dock Co, Middlesbrough, 1940; lost in collision off Northern Ireland, Sept 6, 1940.

Godetia: Flower cls corvette; 925; 205 x 33; 16; 85; one 4-in; J. Crown & Sons, Sunderland, 1942; ex-*Dart,* 1941; b/up Grays 1947.

Golden Fleece: Algerine cls minesweeper; 950; 235 x 35½; 16½; 104; one 4-in; Redfern Construction Co, Toronto, 1944; ex-*Humberstone* (RCN) 1943; b/up Llanelly 1960.

Gold Ranger: Ranger cls oiler; 3313 grt; 355¼ x 47; 14; 47; --; Caledon SB & E Co, Dundee, 1941; 1974, Tunas (Pte) Ltd, Singapore.

Goodall: Captain cls frigate; 1140; 289½ x 35; 21; 200; three 3-in; Navy Yard, Boston, 1943; ex-USN Evarts cls destroyer-escort *Reybold, DE-275,* transferred Lease/Lend to RN 1943; torpedoed by U-boat bound for Russia, Apr 29, 1945.

Goodson: Captain cls frigate; 1140; 289½ x 35; 21; 200; three 3-in; Navy Yard, Boston, 1943; ex-USN Evarts cls destroyer-escort *George, DE-276,* transferred Lease/Lend to RN 1943; irreparably damaged by U-boat off Cherbourg, June 25, 1944, rtnd USN 1945; b/up Whitchurch 1948.

Gore: Captain cls frigate; 1140; 289½ x 35; 21; 200; three 3-in; Navy Yard, Boston, 1943; ex-USN Evarts cls destroyer-escort *Herzog, DE-277,* transferred Lease/Lend to RN 1943, rtnd USN 1946, b/up.

Gorgon: Catherine cls minesweeper; 890; 221 x 32; 18; 109; one 3-in; Savannah Machine & Foundry Co, Savannah, 1943; ex-USN Auk cls minesweeper *BAM-18* transferred Lease/Lend to RN 1943, rtnd USN 1946; sold 1946 to Greece, nothing more known.

Gorleston: Lulworth cls escort; 1546; 250 x 42; 16; 200; one 5-in, two 3-in; Gen Eng & DD Co, Oakland, 1930; ex-US Coast Guard cutter *Itasca,*

transferred Lease/Lend to RN 1941, rtnd USCG 1946, rnd *Itasca;* sold Baltimore shipbreakers 1950.

Gorregan: Isles cls trawler; 560; 164 x 27½; 12; 40; one 12-pdr; Ardrossan Dockyard Ltd, Ardrossan, 1944; b/up Charlestown 1957.

Gossamer: Halcyon cls minesweeper; 835; 245 x 33½; 17; 80; two 4-in; Wm Hamilton & Co, Port Glasgow, 1938; sunk by German aircraft in Kola Inlet, June 24, 1942.

Gould: Captain cls frigate; 1140; 289½ x 35; 21; 200; three 3-in; Navy Yard, Boston, 1943; ex-USN Evarts cls destroyer-escort *Lovering, DE-272,* transferred Lease/Lend to RN 1943; torpedoed and sunk by *U-358,* north-east of Azores, Mar 1, 1944.

Gozo: Algerine cls minesweeper; 950; 235 x 35½; 16½; 104; one 4-in; Redfern Construction Co, Toronto, 1943; ex-USN, transferred Lease/Lend to RN 1943, rtnd USN 1946; transferred 1947 to Royal Hellenic Navy, rnd *Polemistis;*

Graemsay: Isles cls trawler; 560; 164 x 27½; 12; 40; one 12-pdr; Ardrossan Dockyard Ltd, Ardrossan, 1942;

Grafton: G cls destroyer; 1335; 323 x 33; 35½; 145; four 4.7-in, eight 21-in tt; J. I. Thornycroft & Co, Southampton, 1936; damaged by *U-62* off Dunkirk, May 29, 1940, and sunk by RN.

Grain: Isles cls trawler; 560; 164 x 27½; 12; 40; one 12-pdr; Cochrane & Sons, Selby, 1943; transferred 1946 to Italian Navy, rnd *RD-309;* used as target, mid-1960s.

Grampus: Porpoise cls minelaying submarine; 1520/2117; 293 x 25½; 15¾/8¾; 55; 50 mines, six 21-in tt, one 4-in; HM Dockyard, Chatham, 1937; sunk by Italian surface craft off Syracuse, June 24, 1940.

Graph: submarine; 770/870; 218¼ x 19⅔; 16½/8; 44; five 21-in tt, one 3.5-in; Blohm & Voss, Hamburg, 1941; ex-German *U-570,* surrendered Aug 27, 1941, after being disabled off Iceland by RAF Hudson aircraft; entered RN service, Sept, 1941; wrecked, when in tow, on west coast of Islay, Mar 20, 1944.

Grassholm: Isles cls trawler; 560; 164 x 27½; 12; 40; one 12-pdr; J. Lewis &

Sons, Aberdeen, 1943; 1946, A/S Skarreholmen, Norway, no name change; 1956, G. Arcoulis, Greece, rnd *Evangelistria;* 1961, Atlantic Fishing Enterprises 'Evangelistria', Greece, no name change;

Grasshopper: Locust cls gunboat; 585; 197 x 33; 17; 74; two 4-in, one 3.7-in howitzer; J. I. Thornycroft & Co, Southampton, 1939; driven ashore by Japanese aircraft Sianpeng Island, Sumatra, Feb 14, 1942.

Grayling: Fish cls trawler; 670; 162 x 25¼; 11; 35; one 4-in; Cochrane & Sons, Selby, 1942; 1946, Consolidated Fisheries, Grimsby, rnd *Barry Castle;* lost, Nov 1, 1955.

Gray Ranger: Ranger cls oiler; 3313 grt; 355¼ x 47; 14; 47; --; Caledon SB & E Co, Dundee, 1941; torpedoed by *U-435* on passage from North Russia, Sept 22, 1942.

Grecian: Catherine cls minesweeper; 890; 221 x 32; 18; 109; one 3-in; Savannah Machine & Foundry Co, Savannah, 1943; ex-USN Auk cls minesweeper *BAM-19* transferred Lease/Lend to RN 1943, rtnd USN 1946; transferred 1947 to Turkish Navy, rnd *Edincik;*

Greenock: Bangor cls minesweeper; 656; 174 x 28½; 16; 60; one 3-in; Blyth SB & DD Co, Blyth, 1942; transferred 1942 to Royal Indian Navy, rnd *Baluchistan;* b/up.

Green Ranger: Ranger cls oiler; 3313 grt; 355¼ x 47; 14; 47; --; Caledon SB & E Co, Dundee, 1941; wrecked near Hartland Point, Nov 17, 1962, after tow parted.

Greenwich: destroyer depot ship; 8100; 402 x 52; 11; 244; four 4-in, one 3-in; Wm Dobson & Co, Newcastle, 1916; purchased RN on stocks 1915; 1946, Cia de Cabotagem de Pernambuco, Brazil, converted to passenger-cargo liner, rnd *Hembury;* 1955, Navegacao Mercantil SA, Brazil, rnd *Navem Hembury;*

Grenade: G cls destroyer; 1335; 323 x 33; 35½; 145; four 4.7-in, eight 21-in tt; A. Stephen & Sons, Linthouse, 1936; sunk by German aircraft off Dunkirk, May 29, 1940.

Grenadier: Military cls trawler; 750; 193 x 30; 11; 40; one 4-in; Cook

Welton & Gemmell, Beverley, 1943; 1946, Great Grimsby & East Coast Steam Fishing Co, Grimsby, rnd *Isernia;* b/up Hendrik Ido Ambacht 1966.

Grenville: G cls destroyer; 1485; 330 x 34½; 36; 175; five 4.7-in, eight 21-in tt; Yarrow & Co, Scotstoun, 1936; mined in North Sea, Jan 19, 1940.

Grenville: U cls destroyer; 1730; 362⅔ x 35¾; 36; 230; four 4.7-in, eight 21-in tt; Swan Hunter & Wigham Richardson, Wallsend, 1943;

Greyhound: G cls destroyer; 1335; 323 x 33; 35½; 145; four 4.7-in, eight 21-in tt; Vickers-Armstrongs, Barrow, 1936; sunk by German aircraft off Crete, May 22, 1941.

Griffin: G cls destroyer; 1335; 323 x 33; 35½; 145; four 4.7-in, eight 21-in tt; Vickers-Armstrongs, Barrow, 1936; transferred 1943 to Royal Canadian Navy, rnd *Ottawa;* sold Hamilton, Ont, shipbreakers, 1945.

Grilse: Fish cls trawler; 670; 162 x 25¼; 11; 35; one 4-in; Cochrane & Sons, Selby, 1943; 1946, Consolidated Fisheries, Grimsby, rnd *Cardiff Castle;* 1952, Clifton Steam Trawlers, Fleetwood, rnd *Julia Brierley;* b/up Belgium 1961.

Grimsby: Grimsby cls sloop; 990; 266 x 36; 16½; 100; two 4.7-in, one 3-in; HM Dockyard, Devonport, 1933; sunk by aircraft off Tobruk, May 25, 1941.

Grindall: Captain cls frigate; 1140; 289½ x 35; 21; 200; three 3-in; Navy Yard, Boston, 1943; ex-USN Evarts cls destroyer-escort *Sanders, DE-273,* transferred Lease/Lend to RN 1943, rtnd USN 1945; b/up Philadelphia 1946.

Griper: Assurance cls tug; 1045; 157 x 35; 13; 31; one 3-in; Cochrane & Sons, Selby, 1942; 1946, Singapore Harbour Board, no name change; 1962, P. N. Pelajaran Bahtera Adhiguna, Indonesia, rnd *Surabajah,* rnd *Selat Surabaja;*

Grove: Hunt cls destroyer — Blankney type; 1050; 280 x 31½; 27; 168; six 4-in; Swan Hunter & Wigham Richardson, Wallsend, 1941; torpedoed and sunk by *U-77* in central Mediterranean, June 12, 1942.

Growler: Bustler cls tug; 1800; 205 x

38½; 15; 42; one 3-in; H. Robb, Leith, 1943; 1947, on charter, rnd *Caroline Moller;* 1952, on charter, rnd *Castle Peak;* 1954, rnd *Growler;* 1958, on charter, rnd *Welshman;* 1963, rnd *Cyclone;*
Gruinard: Isles cls trawler; 560; 164 x 27½; 12; 40; one 12-pdr; J. Crown & Sons, Sunderland, 1943; transferred 1943 to Portuguese Navy, rnd *P-7,* rtnd RN 1944; 1946, NV Oostendsche Reederij, Belgium, rnd *President F. D. Roosevelt;* 1950, Kohlenberg & Putz Seefischerei AG, Germany, rnd *Odin;* 1956, G. Arcoulis, Greece, rnd *Evangelistria 11;* 1961, Atlantic Fishing Enterprises 'Evangelistria', Greece, no name change;
Guardian: net layer; 2860; 338 x 53; 18; 181; two 4-in; HM Dockyard, Chatham, 1933; b/up Troon 1963.
Guardsman: Military cls trawler; 750; 193 x 30; 11; 40; one 4-in; Cook, Welton & Gemmell, Beverley, 1944; 1946, Great Grimsby & East Coast Steam Fishing Co, Grimsby, rnd *Thuringia;* b/up Dunston 1966.
Guava: trawler; 134 grt, 100¾ x 21; --; --; one 6-pdr; Richards Ironworks, Lowestoft, 1935; ex-*British Columbia* (Grimsby Motor Trawlers, Grimsby) bought RN, 1939; 1946, Colne Fishing Co, Lowestoft, rnd *British Columbia;* sank in collision in North Sea, Sept 29, 1957.
Guillemot: Guillemot cls sloop; 580; 233¼ x 26½; 20; 60; one 4-in; Wm Denny & Bros, Dumbarton, 1939; b/up Grays 1950.
Gulland: Isles cls trawler; 560; 164 x 27½; 12; 40; one 12-pdr; Cook Welton & Gemmell, Beverley, 1943; sold Belgian owners 1946, (nothing more known).
Gurkha: Tribal cls destroyer; 1870; 377 x 36½; 36½; 190; eight 4.7-in, four 21-in tt; Fairfield SB & E Co, Govan, 1938; sunk by German aircraft off Norwegian coast, south of Trondheim, Apr 9, 1940.
Gurkha: L cls destroyer; 1920; 362¼ x 37; 36½; 190; eight 4-in, eight 21-in tt; Cammell Laird, Birkenhead, 1941; ex-*Larne,* 1940; torpedoed and sunk by *U-133* off Libyan coast, Jan 17, 1942.

Guysborough: Bangor cls minesweeper; 672; 180 x 28½; 16; 60; one 3-in; North Vancouver Ship Repairs, North Vancouver, 1941; transferred to Royal Canadian Navy; torpedoed and sunk by *U-878* off Ushant, Mar 17, 1945.
Gweal: Isles cls trawler; 560; 164 x 27½; 12; 40; one 12-pdr; Cook, Welton & Gemmell, Beverley, 1942; ex-*Broreray* 1942; 1947, Johannes Ostensjo & Co, A/S, Norway, rnd *Velox;* 1960, People's Republic of China, no name change.

H-28: H cls submarine; 410/500; 171¾ x 15¼; 13/10½; 22; four 21-in tt; Vickers-Armstrongs, Barrow, 1918; b/up Troon 1944.
H-31: H cls submarine; 410/500; 171¾ x 15¼; 13/10½; 22; four 21-in tt; Vickers-Armstrongs, Barrow, 1919; lost in Bay of Biscay, December, 1941.
H-32: H cls submarine; 410/500; 171¾ x 15¼; 13/10½; 22; four 21-in tt; Vickers-Armstrongs, Barrow, 1919; b/up Troon 1944.
H-33: H cls submarine; 410/500; 171¾ x 15¼; 13/10½; 22; four 21-in tt; Cammell Laird, Birkenhead, 1919; b/up Troon 1944.
H-34: H cls submarine; 410/500; 171¾ x 15¼; 13/10½; 22; four 21-in tt; Cammell Laird, Birkenhead, 1919; b/up Troon 1945.
H-43: H cls submarine; 410/500; 171¾ x 15¼; 13/10½; 22; four 21-in tt; Armstrong Whitworth & Co, Newcastle, 1919; b/up Troon 1944.
H-44: H cls submarine; 410/500; 171¾ x 15¼; 13/10½; 22; four 21-in tt; Armstrong Whitworth & Co, Newcastle, 1920; b/up Troon 1945.
H-49: H cls submarine; 410/500; 171¾ x 15¼; 13/10½; 22; four 21-in tt; W. Beardmore, Dalmuir, 1919; sunk by German surface force near Terschelling, Oct 18, 1940.
H-50: H cls submarine; 410/500; 171¾ x 15¼; 13/10½; 22; four 21-in tt; W. Beardmore, Dalmuir, 1920; b/up Troon 1945.
Hadleigh Castle: Castle cls corvette;

1010; 252 x 36¾; 16½; 120; one 4-in;
Smith's Dock Co, Middlesbrough,
1943; b/up Gateshead 1959.
Halcyon: Halcyon cls minesweeper;
815; 245 x 33½; 17; 80; two 4-in; J.
Brown & Co, Clydebank, 1934; b/up
Milford Haven 1950.
Haldon: Hunt cls destroyer —
Albrighton type; 1050; 280 x 31½; 27;
168; four 4-in, two 21-in tt; Fairfield SB
& E Co, Govan, 1942; transferred 1942
to French Navy, rnd La Combattante;
lost in North Sea, Feb 23, 1945.
Halladale: River cls frigate; 1370;
301½ x 36½; 19; 140; two 4-in; A. & J.
Inglis, Glasgow, 1944; 1948,
Townsend Bros, London, converted
to passenger-car ferry, no name
change; 1962, W. Rostedt, Finland,
rnd Norden; 1962, W. M. Heinonen,
Finland, rnd Turist Expressen; 1963,
Ferryboats Margarita C.A. 'Ferrymar',
Venezuela, rnd Ferrymar III;
Halsted: Captain cls frigate; 1400;
306 x 36¾; 23½; 220; three 3-in;
Bethlehem-Hingham Shipyard, 1943;
ex-USN Buckley cls destroyer-escort
Reynolds, DE-91, transferred
Lease/Lend to RN 1943; irreparably
damaged by German E-boats, June
11, 1944, rtnd USN 1946; sold
Dordrecht shipbreakers 1947.
Hambledon: Hunt cls destroyer —
Atherstone type; 1000; 280 x 29; 27½;
146; four 4-in; Swan Hunter & Wigham
Richardson, Wallsend, 1940; b/up
Dunston 1959.
Hamilton: Town cls destroyer; 1060;
314⅓ x 30½; 122; one 4-in, three 21-in
tt; Bethlehem SB, Fore River, 1919;
ex-USN Kalk, ex-USN Rodgers,
transferred 1940 to RN, transferred
1941 to Royal Canadian Navy; b/up
Baltimore 1945.
Hamlet: Shakespearian cls trawler;
545; 164 x 27¾; 12; 35; one 12-pdr;
Cook Welton & Gemmell, Beverley,
1940; 1947, Partrederiet Reidun,
Norway, rnd Eifonn; 1950, Soc Nav
Caennaise, France, converted to
cargo ship, rnd Fort Lamalgue; 1954,
Paolo Caruso & Co, Italy, rnd Union,
rnd Itaca 1956;
Hannaray: Isles cls trawler; 560; 164
x 27½; 12; 40; one 12-pdr; Cook
Welton & Gemmell, Beverley, 1944;

1947, Friedrich Beutelrock, West
Germany, converted to cargo ship,
rnd Wodan; 1965, Johannes Nagel,
West Germany, no name change;
1969, Reederei Wodan, West
Germany, no name change;
Hardy: H cls destroyer; 1455; 330 x
34; 36; 175; five 4.7-in, eight 21-in tt;
Cammell Laird, Birkenhead, 1936;
beached and abandoned at Narvik,
Apr 10, 1940.
Hardy: V cls destroyer; 1730; 362¾ x
35¾; 36; 220; four 4.7-in, eight 21-in tt;
John Brown & Co, Clydebank, 1943;
sunk by U-278 off Bear Island, Jan 30,
1944.
Hare: Algerine cls minesweeper; 950;
235 x 35½; 16½; 104; one 4-in;
Harland & Wolff, Belfast, 1944;
transferred 1959 to Nigerian Navy,
rnd Nigeria; b/up Faslane 1962.
Hargood: Captain cls frigate; 1400;
306 x 36¾; 23½; 220; three 3-in;
Bethlehem-Hingham Shipyard, 1944;
ex-USN Buckley cls destroyer-escort
DE-573, transferred Lease/Lend to
RN 1944, rtnd USN 1946; b/up 1947.
Harrier: Halcyon cls minesweeper;
815; 245 x 33½; 17; 80; two 4-in; J. I.
Thornycroft & Co, Southampton,
1934; b/up Gateshead 1950.
Harris: Isles cls trawler; 560; 164 x
27½; 12; 40; one 12-pdr; Cook Welton
& Gemmell, Beverley, 1944;
ex-Gilsay, 1947, A/S
Sandskaars Rederi, Norway,
converted to cargo ship, rnd Lyngas;
1950, Soc Nav Caennaise, France,
rnd Fort Malbousquet; 1952, Gill Amin
& Co, India, rnd Sheila Margaret;
believed b/up Bombay 1965.
Harrow: Hunt cls minesweeper; 800;
231 x 28½; 16; 74; one 4-in, one 3-in;
J. T. Eltringham & Co, South Shields,
1918; b/up Genoa 1950.
Hart: Modified Black Swan cls sloop;
1430; 299½ x 38; 20; 192; six 4-in; A.
Stephen & Sons, Linthouse, 1943;
transferred 1958 to West German
Navy, rnd Scheer; b/up 1969.
Hartland: Lulworth cls escort; 1546;
250 x 42; 16; 200; one 5-in, two 3-in;
Bethlehem SB, Quincy, 1928; ex-US
Coast Guard cutter Pontchartrain,
transferred Lease/Lend to RN 1941;
sunk forcing entry into harbour at Oran,

Nov 8, 1942, raised and sunk in deep water, October 1949.
Hartland Point: landing craft repair ship; 8580; 441½ x 57; 11; 440; sixteen 20-mm; Burrard DD Co, Vancouver, 1945; 1974, Marine Oil Industry Repairs Ltd, UK, conversion to oil rig repair ship;
Hartlepool: Bangor cls minesweeper; 656; 174 x 28½; 16; 60; one 3-in; Blyth SB & DD Co, Blyth, 1942; transferred 1942 to Indian Navy, rnd *Kathiawar;* transferred 1948 to Pakistan Navy, rnd *Chittagong;* b/up 1956.
Harvester: Havant cls destroyer; 1340; 323 x 33; 36; 145; three 4.7-in, eight 21-in tt; Vickers-Armstrongs, Barrow, 1940; ex-Brazilian *Jurua,* taken over while building by RN 1939, rnd *Handy,* rnd *Harvester* 1940; torpedoed and sunk by *U-432* in Western Atlantic, Mar 11, 1943.
Harwich: Bangor cls minesweeper; 656; 174 x 28½; 16; 60; one 3-in; Wm Hamilton & Co, Port Glasgow, 1942; transferred 1942 to Indian Navy, rnd *Khyber;* reported b/up 1949.
Hascosay: Isles cls trawler; 560; 164 x 27½; 12; 40; one 12-pdr; Cook Welton & Gemmell, Beverley, 1944; 1947, E. Karavias & G. Manolessos, Greece, converted to cargo ship, rnd *Ypapandi;* lost on voyage from Alexandropoulis to Piraeus, mid-Jan 1952.
Hastings: Hastings cls sloop; 1045; 266 x 34; 16; 100; two 4-in; HM Dockyard, Devonport, 1930; b/up Troon 1946.
Hasty: H cls destroyer; 1340; 323 x 33; 36; 145; four 4.7-in, eight 21-in tt; Wm Denny & Bros, Dumbarton, 1936; damaged by German E-boat in Mediterranean, June 15, 1942, sunk by RN.
Hatherleigh: Hunt cls destroyer — Albrighton type; 1050; 280 x 31½; 27; 168; four 4-in, two 21-in tt; Vickers-Armstrongs, Tyne, 1942; transferred 1942 to Royal Hellenic Navy, rnd *Kanaris,* rtnd RN 1959; b/up Greece 1960.
Havant: Havant cls destroyer; 1340; 323 x 33; 36; 145; three 4.7-in, eight 21-in tt; J. S. White & Co, Cowes, 1940; ex-Brazilian *Javary,* taken over

1939 while building by RN; sunk by German aircraft off Dunkirk, June 1, 1940.
Havelock: Havant cls destroyer; 1340; 323 x 33; 36; 145; three 4.7-in, eight 21-in tt; J. S. White & Co, Cowes, 1940; ex-Brazilian *Jutahy,* taken over 1939 while building by RN; b/up Inverkeithing 1946.
Havock: H cls destroyer; 1340; 323 x 33; 36; 145; four 4.7-in, eight 21-in tt; Wm Denny & Bros, Dumbarton, 1936; wrecked, aground near Kelibia, Apr 6, 1942, destroyed by Italian submarine.
Hawkins: Hawkins cls cruiser; 9800; 605 x 65; 29½; 749; seven 7.5-in, four 4-in, four 21-in tt; HM Dockyard, Chatham, 1919; b/up Dalmuir 1947.
Hawthorn: Berberis cls trawler; 593; 140 x 24½; 11; 18; one 12-pdr; Cochrane & Sons, Selby, 1930; ex-*Cape Guardafui* (Hudson Steam Fishing Co, Hull) bought RN 1935; 1946, P/F Saelingahella, Denmark, rnd *Havborgin;*
Haydon: Hunt cls destroyer — Albrighton type; 1050; 280 x 31½; 27; 168; four 4-in, two 21-in tt; Vickers-Armstrongs, Tyne, 1942; b/up Dunston 1958.
Hayling: Isles cls trawler; 560; 164 x 27½; 12; 40; one 12-pdr; Cook Welton & Gemmell, Beverley, 1942; transferred 1943 to Portuguese Navy, rnd *P-3,* rnd *Terceira,* 1946; for disposal and breaking-up 1957.
Hazard: Halcyon cls minesweeper; 835; 245 x 33½; 17; 80; two 4-in; Wm Gray & Co, West Hartlepool, 1937; b/up Grays 1949.
Hazel: Tree cls trawler; 530; 164 x 27½; 11½; 35; one 12-pdr; H. Robb, Leith, 1940; sold 1946, buyers not known.
Heartsease: Flower cls corvette; 925; 205 x 33; 16; 85; one 4-in; Harland & Wolff, Belfast, 1945; ex-*Pansy;* transferred 1942 to US Navy, rnd *Courage,* rtnd 1945; 1946, sold, converted to merchant ship, rnd *Roskva;* 1956, rnd *Douglas;* 1958, rnd *Seabird;* lost Dec 1958. (See *Pansy*)
Heather: Flower cls corvette; 925; 205 x 33; 16; 85; one 4-in; Harland & Wolff, Belfast, 1940; b/up Grays 1947.
Hebe: Halcyon cls minesweeper; 835;

245 x 33½; 17; 80; two 4-in; HM Dockyard, Devonport, 1937; mined in Adriatic, Nov 22, 1943.

Hecla: destroyer depot ship; 11,000; 623 x 66; 17; 1000; eight 4.5-in; J. Brown & Co, Clydebank, 1940; torpedoed and sunk by U-515 off Morocco, Nov 12, 1942.

Hedingham Castle: Castle cls corvette; 1010; 252 x 36¾; 16; 120; one 4-in; J. Crown & Sons, Sunderland, 1945; ex-Gorey Castle, 1945; b/up Granton 1958.

Helford: River cls frigate; 1370; 301½ x 36½; 19; 140; two 4-in; Hall Russell & Co, Aberdeen, 1943; b/up Troon 1956.

Heliotrope: Flower cls corvette; 925; 205 x 33; 16; 85; one 4-in; J. Crown & Sons, Sunderland, 1940; transferred 1942 to US Navy, rnd Surprise, rtnd RN 1945, rnd Heliotrope; 1946, Wheelock Marden, Hong Kong, converted to cargo ship, rnd Heliolock; 1947, Chinese owners, rnd Ziang Teh; rearmed by China, rnd Lin I (nothing more known).

Hellisay: Isles cls trawler; 560; 164 x 27½; 12; 40; one 12-pdr; Cochrane & Sons, Selby, 1944; 1947, A. G. Chalaris & Co, Greece, converted to cargo ship, rnd Elpis; 1954, P. Dacoutros, A. Dacoutros, G. Dacoutros, Malta, rnd Elpis II; (no trace after 1958).

Helmsdale: River cls frigate; 1370; 301½ x 36½; 19; 140; two 4-in; A. & J. Inglis, Glasgow, 1943; b/up Faslane 1957.

Help: Kin cls coastal salvage vessel; 950; 179½ x 35¾; 9; 34; two 20-mm; Smith's Dock Co, Middlesbrough, 1943; 1959, G. Wimpey & Co, London, no name change; 1960, NV Bureau Wijsmuller, Holland, no name change; b/up Wormerveer 1968.

Hengist: Assurance cls tug; 1045; 157 x 35; 13; 31; one 3-in; Cochrane & Sons, Selby, 1942; 1965, Tsavliris (Salvage & Towage), Greece, rnd Nisos Crete; b/up Greece 1972.

Hepatica: Flower cls corvette; 925; 205 x 33; 16; 85; one 4-in; Davie SB & Repairing Co, Levis, 1940; transferred 1941 to Royal Canadian Navy, no name change, rtnd RN 1945;

b/up Llanelly 1947.

Herald: '24' cls sloop; 1320; 276½ x 34¾; 17; 132; one 4-in; Blyth SB & DD Co, Blyth, 1919; ex-Merry Hampton, converted to survey ship and rnd 1923; scuttled at Seletar, Feb 1942, salved by Japan, rnd Heiyo; mined in Java Sea, Nov 14, 1944.

Hereward: H cls destroyer; 1340; 323 x 33; 36; 145; four 4.7-in, eight 21-in tt; Vickers-Armstrongs, Tyne, 1936; sunk by Italian aircraft off Crete, May 29, 1941.

Hermes: aircraft carrier; 10,850; 598 x 70; 25; 664; twelve aircraft, six 5.5-in, three 4-in; Armstrong Whitworth & Co, Newcastle/HM Dockyard, Devonport, 1923; sunk by Japanese aircraft south of Ceylon, Apr 9, 1942.

Hermetray: Isles cls trawler; 560; 164 x 27½; 12; 40; one 12-pdr; Cochrane & Sons, Selby, 1944; 1947, NV Visscherij Maats 'Prinses Beatrix' Holland, rnd Coimbra; 1952, Lloyd-Seeschiffahrts AG, Switzerland, converted to cargo ship, rnd Furka; 1957, E. H. Smith, Panama, rnd Nenter; 1965, Navieros de Yucatan SA, Mexico, rnd T'Ho;

Hermione: Dido cls cruiser; 5450; 512 x 50½; 33; 620; ten 5.25-in, six 21-in tt; A. Stephen & Sons, Linthouse, 1941; torpedoed and sunk by U-205 south of Crete, June 16, 1942.

Hero: H cls destroyer; 1340; 323 x 33; 36; 145; four 4.7-in, eight 21-in tt; Vickers-Armstrongs, Tyne, 1936; transferred 1943 to Royal Canadian Navy, rnd Chaudiere; sold Halifax Shipyards 1945; sold Sydney NS shipbreakers 1950.

Herring: Fish cls trawler; 670; 162 x 25¼; 11; 35; one 4-in; Cochrane & Sons, Selby, 1943; lost in collision in North Sea, Apr 22, 1943.

Herschell: Isles cls trawler; 560; 164 x 27½; 12; 40; one 12-pdr; G. T. Davie & Sons, Lauzon, 1943; 1946 (owner not known) rnd Eirikur Hin Reidi; 1947, P/F Logn, Denmark, rnd Radni; 1956, L. T. Thadani, Nigeria, no name change; b/up Nigeria 1961.

Hesperia: Bustler cls tug; 1800; 205 x 38½; 15; 42; one 3-in; H. Robb, Leith, 1943; wrecked on coast of Libya, Feb 9, 1945.

Hesperus: Havant cls destroyer; 1340;

323 x 33; 36; 145; three 4.7-in, eight 21-in tt; J. I. Thornycroft & Co, Southampton, 1940; ex-Brazilian *Juruena,* taken over 1939 while building by RN, rnd *Hearty,* rnd *Hesperus* 1940; b/up Grangemouth 1947.

Heythrop: Hunt cls destroyer — Blankney type; 1050; 280 x 31½; 27; 168; six 4-in; Swan Hunter & Wigham Richardson, Wallsend, 1941; sunk by *U-652* north of Sollum, Mar 20, 1942.

Hibiscus: Flower cls corvette; 925; 205 x 33; 16; 85; one 4-in; Harland & Wolff, Belfast, 1940; transferred 1942 to US Navy, rnd *Spry,* rtnd RN 1945 rnd *Hibiscus;* 1947, Cia Panamena Monagre SA, Panama, converted to cargo ship rnd *Madonna;* b/up Hong Kong 1955.

Hickorol: Elmol cls oiler; 2410; 220 x 34⅔; 9½; 19; --; A. McMillan & Sons, Dumbarton, 1918; 1948, Hemsley Bell & Co, Southampton, rnd *Hemsley II;* 1950, N. T. Pappadatos, Greece, rnd *Grammos;* 1956, D'Alesio & Castaldi, Italy, rnd *Ardenza;* 1967, O. Novella, Italy, rnd *Pannesi;*

Hickory: Tree cls trawler; 530; 164 x 27½; 11½; 35; one 12-pdr; H. Robb, Leith, 1940; mined in English Channel, Nov 22, 1940.

Highlander: Havant cls destroyer; 1340; 323 x 33; 36; 145; three 4.7-in, eight 21-in tt; J. I. Thornycroft & Co, Southampton, 1940; ex-Brazilian *Jaguaribe,* taken over 1939 while building by RN, rnd; b/up Rosyth 1947.

Highway: landing ship, dock; 7930; 457¾ x 72; 15; 260; one 4-in; Newport News SB & DD Co, Newport News, 1943; ex-USN *Claymore, LSD-10,* transferred Lease/Lend to RN 1943, rnd, rtnd USN 1946; 1953, Suwanee SS Co, Florida, converted to rail ferry, rnd *Antonio Maceo;* 1957, TMT Trailer Ferry Inc, US, converted to vehicle ferry, rnd *TMT Florida Queen;* b/up 1959.

Hildasay: Isles cls trawler; 560; 164 x 27½; 12; 40; one 12-pdr; Cook Welton & Gemmell, Beverley, 1941; wrecked near Kilindini, June 21, 1945.

Hind: Modified Black Swan cls sloop; 1430; 299½ x 38; 20; 192; six 4-in; Wm

Denny & Bros, Dumbarton, 1944; b/up Dunston 1958.

Hogue: Battle cls destroyer; 2315; 379 x 40¼; 36; 247; four 4.5-in, eight 21-in tt; Cammell Laird, Birkenhead, 1945; b/up Singapore 1962.

Holcombe: Hunt cls destroyer — Albrighton type; 1050; 280 x 31½; 27; 168; four 4-in, two 21-in tt; A. Stephen & Sons, Linthouse, 1942; torpedoed and sunk by *U-593* off Bougie, Dec 12, 1943.

Holderness: Hunt cls destroyer — Atherstone type; 1000; 280 x 29; 27½; 146; four 4-in; Swan Hunter & Wigham Richardson, Wallsend, 1940; b/up Preston 1956.

Holly: Berberis cls trawler; 590; 140¼ x 24½; 11; 18; one 12-pdr; Cook Welton & Gemmell, Beverley, 1930; ex-*Kingston Coral* (Kingston Steam Trawling Co, Hull) bought RN 1935; 1947, J. F. Kjolbro, Denmark, rnd *Dragaberg;* 1955, Lars Gundersen & Per Olsen, Norway, no name change; struck rocks and sank off Faeringehavn, Greenland, July 28, 1961.

Hollyhock: Flower cls corvette; 925; 205 x 33; 16; 85; one 4-in; J. Crown & Sons, Sunderland, 1940; sunk by Japanese aircraft south of Ceylon, Apr 9, 1942.

Holmes: Captain cls frigate; 1400; 306 x 36⅝; 23½; 220; three 3-in; Bethlehem-Hingham Shipyard, 1944; ex-USN Buckley cls destroyer-escort *DE-572,* transferred Lease/Lend to RN 1944, rtnd USN 1945; sold Detroit shipbreakers 1947.

Holm Sound: aircraft component repair ship; 7340 grt; 447¾ x 56¼; 11; --; twelve 20-mm; W. Gray & Co, West Hartlepool, 1945; 1948, Aviation & Shipping Co, London, converted to cargo ship, rnd *Avisbay;* 1950, Elder Dempster Lines, Liverpool, rnd *Prah;* 1959, Atlantska Plovidba, Yugoslavia, rnd *Naprijed;* b/up Split 1969.

Home Guard: Military cls trawler; 750; 193 x 30; 11; 40; one 4-in; Cook Welton & Gemmell, Beverley, 1944; 1946, Loyal Steam Fishing Co, Grimsby, rnd *Loyal;* b/up Belgium 1966.

Honesty: Modified Flower cls

corvette; 980; 208¼ x 33; 16; 109; one 4-in; Kingston SB Co, Kingston, 1943; was to be US Navy *Caprice* not transferred; 1951, Balleneros Ltd SA, Uruguay, for conversion to whale catcher, not converted, laid up Hamburg; b/up Hamburg 1961.

Honeysuckle: Flower cls corvette; 925; 205 x 33; 16; 85; one 4-in; Ferguson Bros, Port Glasgow, 1940; b/up Grays 1950.

Hood: battlecruiser; 42,100; 860¾ x 105¼; 31; 1341; eight 15-in, twelve 5.5-in, eight 4-in; J. Brown & Co, Clydebank, 1920; sunk by German battleship *Bismarck* in North Atlantic, May 24, 1941.

Horatio: Shakespearian cls trawler; 545; 164 x 27¾; 12; 35; one 12-pdr; Cook Welton & Gemmell, Beverley, 1940; sunk in Western Mediterranean, Jan 7, 1943.

Hornbeam: Berberis cls trawler; 346 grt; 140 x 24; 11; 18; one 12-pdr; Cochrane & Sons, Selby, 1929; ex-*Lord Trent* (Pickering & Haldane's Steam Trawling Co, Hull) bought RN 1939; 1946, A/S Rankin, Denmark, rnd *Rankin;* b/up Denmark 1959.

Hornpipe: Dance cls trawler; 530; 160½ x 27½; 11½; 35; one 4-in; Cook Welton & Gemmell, Beverley, 1940; transferred 1946 to Italian Navy, rnd *RD-316;* used as target, mid-1960s.

Horsa: Assurance cls tug; 1045; 157 x 35; 13; 31; one 3-in; Cochrane & Sons, Selby, 1942; wrecked Iceland, Mar 17, 1943.

Hoste: Captain cls frigate; 1140; 289½ x 35; 21; 200; three 3-in; Navy Yard, Boston 1943 ex-USN Evarts cls destroyer-escort *DE-521,* transferred Lease/Lend to RN, rnd *Mitchell,* rnd *Hoste* 1943, rtnd USN 1945; b/up Philadelphia 1946.

Hostile: H cls destroyer; 1340; 323 x 33; 36; 145; four 4.7-in, eight 21-in tt; Scotts SB & E Co, Greenock, 1936; mined in central Mediterranean Aug 23, 1940.

Hotham: Captain cls frigate; 1400; 306 x 36⅝; 23½; 220; three 3-in; Bethlehem-Hingham Shipyard, 1944; ex-USN Buckley cls destroyer-escort *DE-574,* transferred Lease/Lend to RN 1944, rtnd USN 1956; b/up Holland 1956.

Hotspur: H cls destroyer; 1340; 323 x 33; 36; 145; four 4.7-in, eight 21-in tt; Scotts SB & E Co, Greenock, 1936; transferred 1948 to Dominican Republic, rnd *Trujillo,* rnd *Duarte* 1962; withdrawn from service 1972.

Hound: Algerine cls minesweeper; 950; 235 x 35½; 16½; 104; one 4-in; Lobnitz & Co, Renfrew, 1942; b/up Troon 1963.

Howe: King George V cls battleship; 35,000; 745 x 103; 28; 1900; ten 14-in, sixteen 5.25-in; Fairfield SB & E Co, Govan, 1942; ex-*Beatty,* 1940; b/up Inverkeithing 1958.

Hoxa: Isles cls trawler; 560; 164 x 27½; 12; 40; one 12-pdr; Cook Welton & Gemmell, Beverley, 1941; 1946, Ming Sung Industrial Co, China, rnd *Sung Hwei;*

Hoy: Isles cls trawler; 560; 164 x 27½; 12; 40; one 12-pdr; Cook Welton & Gemmell, Beverley, 1941; 1946, USSR, converted to cargo ship, rnd *Dunay;* (nothing known after 1959).

Hunda: Isles cls trawler; 560; 164 x 27½; 12; 40; one 12-pdr; Ferguson Bros, Port Glasgow, 1942; sold Norwegian owner 1946, nothing more known.

Hunter: H cls destroyer; 1340; 323 x 33; 36; 145; four 4.7-in, eight 21-in tt; Swan Hunter & Wigham Richardson, Wallsend, 1936; sunk in collision at Narvik, Apr 10, 1940.

Hunter: Attacker cls escort carrier; 10,200; 496 x 69½; 16; 650; 15-20 aircraft; Ingalls SB Corp, Pascagoula, 1943; ex-cargo liner *Mormacpenn,* ex-USN *Block Island, BAVG-8,* transferred Lease/Lend to RN 1943, rnd *Trailer,* rnd *Hunter,* rtnd USN 1945; 1948, Holland America Line, Holland, converted to cargo liner, rnd *Almdyk;* b/up Valencia 1965.

Huntley: Hunt cls minesweeper; 800; 231 x 28½; 16; 74; one 4-in, one 3-in; J. T. Eltringham & Co, South Shields, 1919; ex-*Helmsdale* 1918; sunk by aircraft in eastern Mediterranean, Jan 31, 1941.

Hurricane: Havant cls destroyer; 1340; 323 x 33; 36; 145; three 4.7-in, eight 21-in tt; Vickers-Armstrongs, Barrow, 1940; ex-Brazilian *Japarua,* taken over

1939 while building by RN; torpedoed and sunk by U-boat, north-east of Azores, Dec 24, 1943.

Hursley: Hunt cls destroyer — Blankney type; 1050; 280 x 31½; 27; 168; six 4-in; Swan Hunter & Wigham Richardson, Wallsend, 1941; transferred 1943 to Royal Hellenic Navy, rnd *Kriti,* rtnd RN 1959; b/up Greece 1960.

Hurst Castle: Castle cls corvette; 1010; 252 x 36¾; 16½; 120; one 4-in; Caledon SB & E Co, Dundee, 1944; torpedoed and sunk by *U-482* off Tory Island, Sept 1, 1944.

Hurworth: Hunt cls destroyer — Blankney type; 1050; 280 x 31½; 27; 168; six 4-in; Vickers-Armstrongs, Tyne, 1941; mined east of Kalymnos, Oct 22, 1943.

Hussar: Halcyon cls minesweeper; 815; 245 x 33; 17; 80; one 4-in; J. I. Thornycroft & Co, Southampton, 1935; bombed in error off Normandy, Aug 27, 1944.

Hyacinth: Flower cls corvette; 925; 205 x 33; 16; 85; one 4-in; Harland & Wolff, Belfast, 1940; transferred 1943 to Royal Hellenic Navy rnd *Apostolis;* rtnd RN, b/up Italy 1961.

Hyderabad: Flower cls corvette; 925; 205 x 33; 16; 85; one 4-in; A. Hall & Co, Aberdeen, 1941; ex-*Nettle* 1941; b/up Portaferry 1948.

Hydra: Algerine cls minesweeper; 950; 235 x 35½; 16½; 104; one 4-in; Lobnitz & Co, Renfrew, 1942; irreparably damaged by mine in English Channel, Nov 10, 1944; b/up Grays 1947.

Hydrangea: Flower cls corvette; 925; 205 x 33; 16; 85; one 4-in; Ferguson Bros, Port Glasgow, 1941; 1948, Wheelock Marden, Hong Kong, converted to cargo ship, rnd *Hydralock;* aground in Formosa Strait, Feb 25, 1957, and sank.

Hyperion: H cls destroyer; 1340; 323 x 33; 36; 145; four 4.7-in, eight 21-in tts; Swan Hunter & Wigham Richardson, Wallsend, 1936; torpedoed by Italian submarine *Serpente* off Pantellaria, Dec 22, 1940, sunk by RN.

Hythe: Bangor cls minesweeper; 656; 174 x 28½; 16; 60; one 3-in; Ailsa SB Co, Troon, 1941; ex-*Banff,* 1941; torpedoed and sunk by *U-371* in

Mediterranean, Oct 11, 1943.

Ibis: Black Swan cls sloop; 1350; 299½ x 38; 19¼; 180; six 4-in; Furness SB Co, Haverton Hill, 1941; sunk by German aircraft off Algeria, Nov 10, 1942.

Icarus: I cls destroyer; 1370; 323 x 33; 35½; 145; four 4.7-in, ten 21-in tt; J. Brown & Co, Clydebank, 1937; b/up Troon 1946.

Ilex: I cls destroyer; 1370; 323 x 33; 35½; 145; four 4.7-in, ten 21-in tt; J. Brown & Co, Clydebank 1937; b/up Italy 1948.

Ilfracombe: Bangor cls minesweeper; 656; 174 x 28½; 16; 60; one 3-in; Wm Hamilton & Co, Port Glasgow, 1941; b/up Dunston 1948.

Illustrious: Illustrious cls aircraft carrier; 23,000; 753 x 95; 31; 1600; 54 aircraft, sixteen 4.5-in; Vickers-Armstrongs, Barrow, 1940; b/up Faslane 1956.

Imersay: Isles cls trawler; 560; 164 x 27½; 12; 40; one 12-pdr; Cochrane & Sons, Selby, 1944; 1959, Piangos Bros, Greece, converted to cargo ship, rnd *Michael;* 1969, A. Riza Yakup, Aksoy, Turkey, rnd *Mehmet Aksoy;* 1973, Iltas Kollektif Sirketi, Turkey, no name change;

Imogen: I cls destroyer; 1370; 323 x 33; 35½; 145; four 4.7-in, ten 21-in tt; Hawthorn Leslie, Hebburn, 1937; sunk after collision in Pentland Firth, July 16, 1940.

Imperial: I cls destroyer; 1370; 323 x 33; 35½; 145; four 4.7-in, ten 21-in tt; Hawthorn Leslie, Hebburn, 1937; damaged by German aircraft near Crete, May 28, 1941, sunk next day by RN.

Implacable: Implacable cls aircraft carrier; 26,000; 766 x 95¾; 32; 2000; 60 aircraft, sixteen 4.5-in; Fairfield SB & E Co, Govan, 1944; b/up Inverkeithing 1955.

Impulsive: I cls destroyer; 1370; 323 x 33; 35½; 145; four 4.7-in, ten 21-in tt; J. S. White & Co, Cowes, 1938; b/up Sunderland 1946.

Inchcolm: Isles cls trawler; 560; 164 x 27½; 12; 40; one 12-pdr; Cook Welton

& Gemmell, Beverley, 1941; transferred 1946 to War Dept, converted to cargo ship; 1953, Giacomo Federici di Giovanni, Italy, rnd *Celeste Aida;* 1966, A. Schiano di Cola, Italy, rnd *Anna Gemma;*
Inchkeith: Isles cls trawler; 560; 164 x 27½; 12; 40; one 12-pdr; J. Lewis & Sons, Aberdeen, 1941; transferred 1942 to Royal New Zealand Navy; sold Auckland shipbreakers 1958.

Inchmarnock: Isles cls trawler; 560; 164 x 27½; 12; 40; one 12-pdr; J. Lewis & Sons, Aberdeen, 1941; transferred 1944 to Royal Norwegian Navy, rnd *Karmoy,* rtnd RN 1946; 1947, Skibs A/S Tilthorn, Norway, converted to cargo ship, rnd *Tilthorn;* 1952, Sov Navale de Maghreb, Morocco, rnd *Nador;* 1955, Cie Armoricaine de Transports Marit, France, rnd *Servannaise;* 1963, C. Garofano, Italy, rnd *Marteresa;* 1970, J. Olwa, Italy, no name change;

Inconstant: destroyer; 1360; 323 x 33; 35½; 145; four 4.7-in, four 21-in tt; Vickers-Armstrongs, Barrow, 1942; ex-Turkish *Muavenet,* taken over 1939 while building by RN; delivered to Turkish Navy, rnd *Muavenet,* 1945; discarded 1960.

Indefatigable: Implacable cls aircraft carrier; 26,000; 766 x 95¾; 32; 2000; 60 aircraft, sixteen 4.5-in; J. Brown & Co, Clydebank, 1944; b/up Dalmuir 1956.

Indomitable: Illustrious cls aircraft carrier; 23,000; 754 x 95¾; 31; 1600; 54 aircraft, sixteen 4.5-in; Vickers-Armstrongs, Barrow, 1941; b/up Faslane 1955.

Inglefield: I cls destroyer; 1455; 330 x 34; 36; 175; five 4.7-in, ten 21-in tt; Cammell Laird, Birkenhead, 1937; sunk by German aircraft off Anzio, Feb. 25, 1944.

Inglis: Captain cls frigate; 1140; 289½ x 35; 21; 200; three 3-in; Navy Yard Boston, 1943; ex-USN Evarts cls destroyer-escort *DE-525,* transferred Lease/Lend to RN 1943, rtnd USN 1946; b/up 1947.

Ingonish: Bangor cls minesweeper; 672; 180 x 28½; 16; 60; one 3-in; North Vancouver Ship Repairs, North Vancouver, 1941; transferred RCN

1942, rtnd 1945; b/up Dunston 1948.
Inkpen: Hills cls trawler; 750; 181¼ x 28; 11; 35; one 12-pdr; Cook Welton & Gemmell, Beverley, 1942; sold 1946.

Inman: Captain cls frigate; 1140; 289½ x 35; 21; 200; three 3-in; Navy Yard, Boston, 1944; ex-USN Evarts cls destroyer-escort *DE-526,* transferred Lease/Lend to RN 1944, rtnd USN 1946; sold New York shipbreakers 1946.

Integrity: BAT cls tug; 783; 143 x 33; 14; 34; one 3-in; Levingston SB, Orange, 1942; ex-USN, transferred Lease/Lend to RN 1942, rtnd USN 1946; sold 1948.

Intrepid: I cls destroyer; 1370; 323 x 33; 35½; 145; four 4.7-in, ten 21-in tt; J. S. White & Co, Cowes, 1937; sunk by German aircraft in Leros Harbour, Sept 27, 1943.

Inver: River cls frigate; 1370; 301½ x 36½; 19; 140; two 4-in; Canadian Vickers, Montreal, 1943; ex-USN *PG-107,* transferred Lease/Lend to RN 1943, rtnd USN 1946; sold 1946.

Ironbound: Isles cls trawler; 560; 164 x 27½; 12; 40; one 12-pdr; Kingston SB, Kingston, Ont, 1942; transferred RCN 1942; rtnd 1945; 1946, A/S M/S Turoy, Norway, converted to cargo ship rnd *Turoy;* 1949, Rederi A/B Universal Line, Sweden, rnd *Christina;* 1954, Rederi A/B Kirsta, Finland, rnd *Korso;* lost by mine, November 1957.

Iron Duke: gunnery training ship; 21,250; 623 x 89½; 18; 580; six 13.5-in, twelve 6-in; HM Dockyard, Portsmouth, 1914; former Iron Duke cls battleship converted to gunnery training ship 1931, became depot ship 1939; b/up Faslane 1946.

Isis: I cls destroyer; 1370; 323 x 33; 35½; 145; four 4.7-in, ten 21-in tt; Yarrow & Co. Scotstoun, 1937; sunk (possibly mined) off Normandy, July 20, 1944.

Islay: Isles cls trawler; 560; 164 x 27½; 12; 40; one 12-pdr; Smith's Dock Co, Middlesbrough, 1941; 1946 (owners not known) rnd *Isly;* 1949, (owners not known) rnd *St Anne;* lost Mar 14, 1950.

Isleford: armament store carrier; 350 dwt; 149¾ x 25½; 8; --; --; Ardrossan DD & SB Co, Ardrossan, 1913; lost near Wick, Jan, 1942.

Itchen: River cls frigate; 1370; 301½ x 36½; 19; 140; two 4-in; Fleming & Ferguson, Paisley, 1942; torpedoed and sunk by *U-260* in North Atlantic, Sept 22, 1943.
Ithuriel: destroyer; 1360; 323 x 33; 35½; 145; four 4.7-in, four 21-in tt; Vickers-Armstrongs, Barrow, 1942; ex-Turkish *Gayret,* taken over 1939 while building by RN; irreparably damaged by aircraft at Bone, Nov 28, 1942; b/up Bo'ness 1946.
Ivanhoe: I cls destroyer; 1370; 323 x 33; 35½; 145; four 4.7-in, ten 21-in tt; Yarrow & Co, Scotstoun, 1937; mined north-west of Texel, Aug 31, 1940, sunk by RN.

Jackal: J cls destroyer; 1760; 356½ x 35¾; 36; 183; six 4.7-in, ten 21-in tt; J. Brown & Co, Clydebank, 1939; damaged by German aircraft off Malta, May 11, 1942, and sunk next day by RN.
Jade: Gem cls trawler; 615; 151¾ x 25½; 12; 18; one 4-in; Cook Welton & Gemmell, Beverley, 1933; ex-*Lady Lillian* (Jutland Amalgamated Trawlers, Hull) bought RN 1939; sunk at Malta, Apr 10, 1942, wreck raised and scuttled 1943.
Jaguar: J cls destroyer; 1760; 356½ x 35¾; 36; 183; six 4.7-in, ten 21-in tt; Wm Denny & Bros, Dumbarton, 1939; sunk by U-boat off Libya, Mar 26, 1942.
Jamaica: Fiji cls cruiser; 8525; 555½ x 62; 33; 980; twelve 6-in, eight 4-in, six 21-in tt; Vickers-Armstrongs, Barrow, 1942; b/up Dalmuir 1960.
James Ludford: Mersey cls trawler: 551; 148 x 22¾; 11; 20; two 3-in; Cochrane & Sons, Selby, 1919; mined off the Tyne, Dec 14, 1939.
Janus: J. cls destroyer; 1760; 356½ x 35¾; 36; 183; six 4.7-in, ten 21-in tt; Swan Hunter & Wigham Richardson, Wallsend, 1939; sunk by German aircraft off Anzio, Jan 23, 1944.
Jaseur: Algerine cls minesweeper; 950; 235 x 35½; 16½; 104; one 4-in; Redfern Construction Co, Toronto, 1944; b/up Blyth 1956.
Jasmine: Flower cls corvette; 925; 205 x 33; 16; 85; one 4-in; Ferguson Bros,

Port Glasgow, 1941; sold 1948 to French owners, nothing more known.
Jason: Halcyon cls minesweeper; 835; 245 x 33½; 17; 80; two 4-in; Ailsa SB Co, Troon, 1938; 1946, Wheelock Marden, Hong Kong, for conversion to merchant ship, rnd *Jaslock,* not completed; b/up Grays 1950.
Jasper: Gem cls trawler; 581; 145¾ x 25; 12; 18; one 4-in; Cook Welton & Gemmell, Beverley, 1932; ex-*Balthasar* (Hull Northern Fishing Co, Hull) bought RN 1935; sunk by E-boat in English Channel, Dec 1, 1942.
Jasper: Catherine cls minesweeper; 890; 221 x 32; 18; 109; one 3-in; Associated Shipbuilders, Seattle, 1944; ex-USN Auk cls minesweeper *BAM-29,* transferred Lease/Lend to RN 1944, rtnd USN 1946; 1947, Foustanos Bros, Greece, rnd *Pandelis;* b/up Split 1968.
Jaunty: Assurance cls tug; 1045; 157 x 35; 13; 31; one 3-in; Cochrane & Sons, Selby, 1941; sold 1966, buyers not known.
Javelin: J cls destroyer; 1760; 356½ x 35¾; 36; 183; six 4.7-in, ten 21-in tt; J. Brown & Co, Clydebank, 1939; ex-*Kashmir* 1937; b/up Troon 1949.
Jed: River cls frigate; 1370; 301½ x 36½; 19; 140; two 4-in; C. Hill & Sons, Bristol, 1942; b/up Milford Haven 1957.
Jennet: boom working vessel; 358 grt; 140¼ x 24; --; 15; --; Cook Welton & Gemmell, Beverley, 1926; ex-trawler *Bunsen* (F. & T. Ross, Hull) bought RN 1939; 1946, J. C. Llewellyn (Trawlers), Milford Haven, converted to trawler rnd *Westheron* 1949; 1950, Associated Fisheries Trawling Co, Hull, rnd *Lord Bann,* b/up 1951-52.
Jersey: J cls destroyer; 1760; 356½ x 35¾; 36; 183; six 4.7-in, ten 21-in tt; J. S. White & Co, Cowes, 1939; mined in Malta Harbour, May 2, 1941.
Jervis: J cls destroyer; 1760; 356½ x 35¾; 36; 218; six 4.7-in, ten 21-in tt; Hawthorn Leslie, Hebburn, 1939; b/up Troon 1949.
Jewel: Algerine cls minesweeper; 950; 235 x 35½; 16½; 104; one 4-in; Harland & Wolff, Belfast, 1944; b/up Inverkeithing 1967.
John Evelyn: armament carrier; 435

grt; 142 x 25; --; --; --; Colby Bros, Lowestoft, 1920; ex-*Fort Lavernock* (Fort Shipping Co, Cardiff) 1924; 1946, W. N. Lindsay Ltd, Leith, no name change; 1957 Beaufort Shipping Co, Guernsey, rnd *Maryston;* b/up Portsmouth 1960.

Jonquil: Flower cls corvette; 925; 205 x 33; 16; 85; one 4-in; Fleming & Ferguson, Paisley, 1940; 1948, Greek government, rnd *Lemnos;* 1951, Balleneros Ltd SA, Uruguay, converted to whale catcher, rnd *Olympic Rider;* lost in collision in South Atlantic. Dec 1, 1955.

Juliet: Shakespearian cls trawler; 545; 164 x 27¾; 12; 35; one 12-pdr; Cook Welton & Gemmell, Beverley, 1941; 1947, Regent Shipping Co, London, converted to cargo ship, rnd *Peterjon;* 1951; Limerick SS Co, Limerick, rnd *Plassy;* lost aground Aran Island, May 8, 1960.

Juniper: Tree cls trawler; 530; 164 x 27½; 11½; 35; one 12-pdr; Ferguson Bros, Port Glasgow, 1940; sunk by German surface force in Norwegian waters, June 8, 1940.

Juno: J cls destroyer; 1760; 356½ x 35¾; 36; 183; six 4.7-in, ten 21-in tt; Fairfield SB & E Co, Govan, 1939; bombed and sunk by German aircraft near Crete, May 21, 1941.

Jupiter: J cls destroyer; 1760; 356½ x 35¾; 36; 183; six 4.7-in, ten 21-in tt; Yarrow & Co, Scotstoun, 1939; sunk by Japanese surface force in Java Sea, Feb 27, 1942.

Jura: Isles cls trawler; 560; 164 x 27½; 12; 40; one 12-pdr; Ardrossan Dockyard Ltd, Ardrossan, 1942; sunk by *U-371* in western Mediterranean, Jan 7, 1943.

Justice: Justice cls tug; 1360; 165 x 34; 12; 32; one 3-in; Camden SB, New Jersey, 1943; ex-USN, transferred Lease/Lend to RN 1943, rtnd USN 1946; 1947, L. Simoncini, Buenos Aires, rnd *St Christopher* (no trace after 1950).

Kale: River cls frigate; 1370; 301½ x 36½; 19; 140; two 4-in; A. & J. Inglis, Glasgow, 1942; b/up Newport 1956.

Kandahar: K cls destroyer; 1760; 356½ x 35¾; 36; 183; six 4.7-in, ten 21-in tt; Wm Denny & Bros, Dumbarton, 1939; mined off Tripoli, Dec 19, 1941, sunk next day by RN.

Kashmir: K cls destroyer; 1760; 356½ x 35¾; 36; 183; six 4.7-in, ten 21-in tt; J. I. Thornycroft & Co, Southampton, 1939; ex-*Javelin,* 1939; bombed and sunk by German aircraft near Crete, May 23, 1941.

Keats: Captain cls frigate; 1140; 289½ x 35; 21; 200; three 3-in; Navy Yard, Boston, 1943; ex-USN Evarts cls destroyer-escort *Tisdale, DE-278,* transferred Lease/Lend to RN 1943, rtnd USN 1946; b/up.

Keith: B cls destroyer; 1400; 323 x 32¼; 35; 157; four 4.7-in, eight 21-in tt; Vickers-Armstrongs, Barrow, 1931; sunk by German aircraft off Dunkirk, June 1, 1940.

Kellett: Hunt cls minesweeper; 800; 231 x 28½; 16; 74; one 4-in, one 3-in; Wm Simons & Co, Renfrew, 1919; ex-*Uppingham,* 1919; former survey ship; b/up Sunderland 1945.

Kelly: K cls destroyer; 1760; 356½ x 35¾; 36; 218; six 4.7-in, ten 21-in tt; Hawthorn Leslie, Hebburn, 1939; bombed and sunk by German aircraft near Crete, May 23, 1941.

Kelvin: K cls destroyer; 1760; 356½ x 35¾; 36; 183; six 4.7-in, ten 21-in tt; Fairfield SB & E Co, Govan, 1939; used in underwater explosion tests, and b/up Troon 1949.

Kempenfelt: W cls destroyer; 1730; 362¾ x 35¾; 36; 220; four 4.7-in, eight 21-in tt; J. Brown & Co, Clydebank, 1943; ex-*Valentine,* 1944; transferred 1956 to Yugoslavia rnd *Kotor;* b/up Split 1970.

Kempthorne: Captain cls frigate; 1140; 289½ x 35; 21; 200; three 3-in; Navy Yard, Boston, 1943; ex-USN Evarts cls destroyer-escort *Trumpeter, DE-279,* transferred Lease/Lend to RN 1943, rtnd USN 1945; b/up.

Kenilworth Castle: Castle cls corvette; 1010; 252 x 36¾; 16½; 120; one 4-in; Smith's Dock Co, Middlesbrough, 1943; b/up Llanelly 1959.

Kennet: Axe cls trawler; 407; 139 x 23½; 10½; 18; one 3-in; Smith's Dock Co, Middlesbrough, 1916; ex-Russian

T-17, acquired by RN 1918, rnd *Iceaxe*, rnd *Kennet* 1920; b/up 1946.

Kent: Kent cls cruiser; 10,570; 630 x 68⅓; 31½; 679; eight 8-in, eight 4-in, eight 21-in tt; HM Dockyard, Chatham, 1928; b/up Troon 1948.

Kenya: Fiji cls cruiser; 8525; 555½ x 62; 33; 980; twelve 6-in, eight 4-in, six 21-in tt; A. Stephen & Sons, Linthouse, 1940; b/up Faslane 1962.

Keppel: Shakespeare cls destroyer; 1480; 329 x 31¾; 31; 183; two 4.7-in six 21-in tt; J. I. Thornycroft & Co, Southampton/HM Dockyard, Portsmouth, 1925; b/up Barrow 1945.

Kerrera: Isles cls trawler; 560; 164 x 27½; 12; 40; one 12-pdr; Fleming & Ferguson, Paisley, 1941; transferred 1944 to Royal Norwegian Navy, rnd *Oksoy*, rtnd RN 1946; 1946, Norsk Bjergningskompagni A/S, Norway, rnd *Jason*; stranded and sank off Svolvaer, Mar 1, 1950.

Khartoum: K cls destroyer; 1760; 356½ x 35¾; 36; 183; six 4.7-in, ten 21-in tt; Swan Hunter & Wigham Richardson, Wallsend, 1939; beached off Perim harbour after explosion during action with Italian submarine *Torricelli*, June 23, 1940.

Khedive: Smiter cls escort carrier; 11,420; 496 x 69½; 16; 650; 20 aircraft, two 5-in; Seattle-Tacoma SB Corp, Tacoma, 1943; ex-USN *Cordova*, *BCVE-39*, transferred Lease/Lend to RN 1943, rtnd USN 1946; 1947, Stoom Maats 'Nederland', Holland, converted to cargo ship, rnd *Rempang*; 1968, Atlas Enterprises Inc, Panama, rnd *Daphne*;

Kilbirnie: Kil cls escort; 795; 184½ x 33; 18; 100; one 3-in; Pullman Standard Car Mfg Co, Chicago, 1943; ex-USN *PCE-827*, transferred Lease/Lend to RN 1943, rtnd USN 1946; 1947, Det Stavangerske Damps, Norway, converted to passenger-cargo ship rnd *Haugesund*; 1973, A. Lauro, Italy, rnd *Lauro Express*;

Kilbride: Kil cls escort; 795; 184½ x 33; 18; 100; one 3-in; Pullman Standard Car Mfg Co, Chicago, 1943; ex-USN *PCE-828*, transferred Lease/Lend to RN 1943, rtnd USN 1946; 1946 A/S Kristiansands Damps,

Norway, converted to passenger-cargo ship, rnd *Jylland*; 1967, E. Zammit, Malta, no name change;

Kilchattan: Kil cls escort; 795; 184½ x 33; 18; 100; one 3-in; Pullman Standard Car Mfg Co, Chicago, 1943; ex-USN *PCE-829*, transferred Lease/Lend to RN 1943, rtnd USN 1946; 1947, Det Stavangerske D/S, Norway, converted to passenger-cargo ship, rnd *Stavanger*, rnd *Kong Sverre*, 1973;

Kilchrenan: Kil cls escort; 795; 184½ x 33; 18; 100; one 3-in; Pullman Standard Car Mfg Co, Chicago, 1943; ex-USN *PCE-830*, transferred Lease/Lend to RN 1943, rtnd USN 1946; 1947, Hardanger Sunnhordlandske Damps, Norway, converted to passenger-cargo ship, rnd *Sunnhordland*;

Kildary: Kil cls escort; 795; 184½ x 33; 18; 100; one 3-in; Pullman Standard Car Mfg Co, Chicago, 1943; ex-USN *PCE-831*, transferred Lease/Lend to RN 1943, rtnd USN 1946; 1952, Empresa de Pesca de Aviero, Portugal, converted to trawler, rnd *Rio Vouga*;

Kildwick: Kil cls escort; 795; 184½ x 33; 18; 100; one 3-in; Pullman Standard Car Mfg Co, Chicago, 1943; ex-USN *PCE-832*, transferred Lease/Lend to RN 1943, rtnd USN 1946; 1947, Fylkesbaatane I Sogn og Fjordane, Norway, converted to passenger-cargo ship, rnd *Sunnfjord*;

Kilham: Kil cls escort; 795; 184½ x 33; 18; 100; one 3-in; Pullman Standard Car Mfg Co, Chicago, 1943; ex-USN *PCE-833*, transferred Lease/Lend to RN 1943, rtnd USN 1946; 1947, A/S Investment, Norway, converted to passenger-cargo ship, rnd *Sognefjord*;

Kilkenzie: Kil cls escort; 795; 184½ x 33; 18; 100; one 3-in; Pullman Standard Car Mfg Co, Chicago, 1944; ex-USN *PCE-834*, transferred Lease/Lend to RN 1943, rtnd USN 1946; 1947, Giertsen & Co, Norway, converted to cargo ship, rnd *Nadodd*; 1952, Southern Lines, Philippines, rnd *Governor Wright*; 1967, Sweet Lines, Philippines, rnd *Sweet Sail*;

Kilkhampton: Kil cls escort; 795; 184½ x 33; 18; 100; one 3-in; Pullman Standard Car Mfg Co, Chicago, 1944; ex-USN *PCE-835,* transferred Lease/Lend to RN 1944, rtnd USN 1946; 1948, Foustanis Bros, Greece, converted to cargo ship, rnd *Georgios F;* b/up Greece 1970.

Killegray: Isles cls trawler; 560; 164 x 27½; 12; 40; one 12-pdr; Cook Welton & Gemmell, Beverley, 1941; transferred 1942 to Royal New Zealand Navy; sold Auckland shipbreakers 1958.

Kilmalcolm: Kil cls escort; 795; 184½ x 33; 18; 100; one 3-in; Pullman Standard Car Mfg Co, Chicago, 1944; ex-USN *PCE-836,* transferred Lease/Lend to RN 1944, rtnd USN 1946; 1952, Empresa de Pesca de Aviero, Portugal, converted to trawler, rnd *Rio Agueda;*

Kilmarnock: Kil cls escort; 795; 184½ x 33; 18; 100; one 3-in; Pullman Standard Car Mfg Co, Chicago, 1946; ex-USN *PCE-837,* transferred Lease/Lend to RN 1944, rtnd USN 1946; 1947, Greek government no name change; 1949, P. G. Skourlitis, Greece, converted to cargo ship, rnd *Arion;* wrecked off Morocco, Jan 5, 1951.

Kilmartin: Kil cls escort; 795; 184½ x 33; 18; 100; one 3-in; Pullman Standard Car Mfg Co, Chicago, 1944; ex-USN *PCE-838,* transferred Lease/Lend to RN 1943, rtnd USN 1946; 1947, Th. Constantopoulis, Greece, converted to cargo ship, no name change; 1957, Marigoula Mitsios & Co, Greece, rnd *Marigoula;* b/up Greece 1970.

Kilmelford: Kil cls escort; 795; 184½ x 33; 18; 100; one 3-in; Pullman Standard Car Mfg Co, Chicago, 1944; ex-USN *PCE-839,* transferred Lease/Lend to RN 1944, rtnd USN 1946; 1946, Greek government, no name change; 1949(?) Zacharis Bros & Co, Greece, converted to cargo ship (1954) rnd *Aghios Spyridon;* 1971, Saint Matthew Shpg Co, Cyprus, rnd *Saint Matthew;*

Kilmington: Kil cls escort; 795; 184½ x 33; 18; 100; one 3-in; Pullman Standard Car Mfg Co, Chicago, 1944; ex-USN *PCE-840,* transferred

Lease/Lend to RN 1944, rtnd USN 1946; 1949, N. Gavalas, Greece, no name change; 1951, Madame A. G. Klaspis, Greece, converted to ferry, rnd *Athinai;* 1955, Larnaca Navigation Co, Cyprus, rnd *Trias;* 1960, Christos S. Pagoulatos & Others, Greece, rnd *Agios Gerassimos;*

Kilmore: Kil cls escort; 795; 184½ x 33; 18; 100; one 3-in; Pullman Standard Car Mfg Co, Chicago, 1944; ex-USN *PCE-841,* transferred Lease/Lend to RN 1944, rtnd USN 1946; 1947, Foustanos Bros, Greece, converted to cargo ship, rnd *Despina;* 1969, G. Kouzouniadis, Greece, rnd *Evangelistria;*

Kilmun: cable ship; 890; 182 x 30; 12; 30; two 20-mm; Smith's Dock Co, Middlesbrough, 1920; former Kil cls patrol gunboat completed as cable ship; 1947, A/S Rask, Norway, converted to cargo ship rnd *Rask;* lost, aground near Berwick High Light, Jan 31, 1950.

Kimberley: K cls destroyer; 1760; 356½ x 35¾; 36; 183; six 4.7-in, ten 21-in tt; J. I. Thornycroft & Co, Southampton, 1939; b/up Troon 1949.

Kimmerol: Elmol cls oiler; 2410; 220 x 34⅔; 9½; 19; --; Craig Taylor & Co, Stockton-on-Tees, 1916; 1949, Ocean Freighters (Ceylon) Ltd, Ceylon, rnd *Lanka Bahu;* 1951, Wallem & Co, Hong Kong, rnd *Tenena* (no trace 1954-55).

Kinbrace: Kin cls coastal salvage vessel; 950; 179½ x 35¾; 9; 34; two 20-mm; Alex Hall & Co, Aberdeen, 1945;

Kingarth: Kin cls coastal salvage vessel; 950; 179½ x 35¾; 9; 34; two 20-mm; Alex Hall & Co, Aberdeen, 1944; ex-*Sledway,* 1944;

Kingcup: Flower cls corvette; 925; 205 x 33; 16; 85; one 4-in; Harland & Wolff, Belfast, 1941; 1946 Soc Anon John Cockerill, Belgium, converted to fruit carrier, rnd *Rubis;* 1954, Seismograph Services (Bahamas), converted to survey ship, rnd *Seislim;* b/up 1959-60.

Kingfisher: Kingfisher cls sloop; 510; 243⅙ x 26½; 20; 60; one 4-in; Fairfield SB & E Co, Govan, 1935; b/up Middlesbrough 1947.

King George V: King George V cls

battleship; 35,000; 745 x 103; 28; 1900; ten 14-in, sixteen 5.25-in; Vickers-Armstrongs, Tyne, 1940; b/up Dalmuir 1958.

King Salvor: King Salvor cls salvage vessel; 1400; 216 x 37¾; 12; 72; four 20-mm; Wm Simons & Co, Renfrew, 1942; converted to submarine rescue ship rnd *Kingfisher,* 1954; transferred 1960 to Argentine Navy, rnd *Tehuelche,* rnd *Guardiamarina Zicari* 1963;

Kingsmill: Captain cls frigate; 1140; 289½ x 35; 21; 200; three 3-in; Navy Yard, Boston, 1943; ex-USN Evarts cls destroyer- escort *DE-280,* transferred Lease/Lend to RN 1943, rtnd USN 1945; b/up.

Kingston: K cls destroyer; 1760; 356½ x 35¾; 36; 183; six 4.7-in, ten 21-in tt; J. S. White & Co, Cowes, 1939; damaged when in drydock at Malta by German aircraft, Apr 11, 1942, and sunk as blockship.

Kinloss: Kin cls coastal salvage vessel; 950; 179½ x 35¾; 9; 34; two 20-mm; Alex Hall & Co, Aberdeen, 1945;

Kinterbury: coastal ammunition ship; 1488; 199¾ x 34½; 11; --; --; Philip & Son, Dartmouth 1943;

Kintyre: Isles cls trawler; 560; 164 x 27½; 12; 40; one 12-pdr; Ardrossan Dockyard Ltd, Ardrossan, 1942; 1946, Cia Ricuperi Altomare 'Ricalmare', Italy, converted to salvage ship, rnd *Fiocina;* 1957 Dr. Camillo Bartoli, Italy, rnd *Adele Bartoli;* 1967, A. Scotto di Santolo, Italy, rnd *Silvana Otto;* foundered Mar 1971.

Kipling: K cls destroyer; 1760; 356½ x 35¾; 36; 183; six 4.7-in, ten 21-in tt; Yarrow & Co, Scotstoun, 1939; sunk by German aircraft in eastern Mediterranean, May 11, 1942.

Kite: Modified Black Swan cls sloop; 1430; 299½ x 38; 20; 192; six 4-in; Cammeil Laird, Birkenhead, 1943; torpedoed and sunk by *U-344* bound for Russia, Aug 21, 1944.

Kittern: Isles cls trawler; 560; 164 x 27½; 12; 40; one 12-pdr; Cook Welton & Gemmell, Beverley, 1943; 1946, Ahlgren & Cappellens Rederi A/S, Norway, converted to cargo ship, rnd *Bonita;* 1949, NorskSkibs

Hypothekbank A/S, Norway, rnd *Stat;* 1950, British owners, rnd *Helen Tola;* 1951, owners not known, rnd *Stat;* 1951, Ezra Deep Sea Fishing Co, Israel, rnd *D'Vora;* (year not known) C & H Products, London, no name change; 1955, Mercury Fisheries, Canada, no name change; 1957, Canadian Government, no name change; 1958, R. Duval, Canada, no name change; lost, beached near Fox River, Gaspe, Dec 27, 1968.

Kittiwake: Kingfisher cls sloop; 530; 243⅙ x 26½; 20; 60; one 4-in; J. I. Thornycroft & Co, Southampton, 1937; 1947, Chinese owners, believed converted to merchant ship, nothing more known.

Knaresborough Castle: Castle cls corvette; 1010; 252 x 36¾; 16½; 120; one 4-in; Blyth SB & DD Co, Blyth, 1943; b/up Port Glasgow 1956.

L-23: L cls submarine; 760/1080; 238½ x 23½; 17½/10½; 35; four 21-in tt, one 4-in; Vickers-Armstrongs, Barrow/HM Dockyard, Chatham, 1924; lost off Nova Scotia in tow to shipbreakers, 1946.

L-26: L cls submarine; 760/1080; 238½ x 23½; 17½/10½; 35; four 21-in tt, one 4-in; Vickers-Armstrongs, Barrow/HM Dockyard, Devonport 1926; b/up Canada 1946.

L-27: L cls submarine; 760/1080; 238½ x 23½; 17½/10½; 35; four 21-in tt, one 4-in; Vickers-Armstrongs, Barrow/HM Dockyard, Sheerness, 1925; b/up Canada 1947.

Labuan: Colony cls frigate; 1430; 304 x 37½; 18; 120; three 3-in; Walsh-Kaiser Co, Providence, 1943; ex-USN *PF-80,* transferred Lease/Lend to RN 1943, rnd *Harvey,* rnd *Gold Coast,* rnd *Labuan* 1943, rtnd USN 1946; sold Dorchester, Mas, shipbreakers 1947.

Laburnum: Flower cls sloop; 1165; 262½ x 33; 16; 104; two 4-in; C. Connell & Co, Scotstoun, 1915; lost at Singapore, Feb, 1942.

Ladybird: Insect cls river gunboat; 625; 237½ x 36; 14; 65; two 6-in, one 3-in; Lobnitz & Co, Renfrew, 1916;

sunk by Italian aircraft off Tobruk, May 12, 1941.

Laertes: Shakespearian cls trawler; 545; 164 x 27¾; 12; 35; one 12-pdr; Cook Welton & Gemmell, Beverley, 1941; sunk by *U-201* off Freetown, July 25, 1942.

Laertes: Algerine cls minesweeper; 950; 235 x 35½; 16½; 104; one 4-in; Redfern Construction Co, Toronto, 1944; b/up Barrow 1959.

Laforey: L cls destroyer; 1935; 362¼ x 37; 36½; 224; six 4.7-in, one 4-in, four 21-in tt; Yarrow & Co, Scotstoun, 1941; torpedoed and sunk by *U-223* off north coast of Sicily, Mar 30, 1944.

Lagan: River cls frigate; 1370; 301½ x 36½; 19; 140; two 4-in; Smith's Dock Co, Middlesbrough, 1942; stern blown off by torpedo, Sept 20, 1943, b/up Troon 1946.

La Malouine: Flower cls corvette; 925; 205 x 33; 16; 85; one 4-in; Smith's Dock Co, Middlesbrough, 1940; transferred 1940 from French Navy; b/up Gelleswick Bay 1947.

Lamerton: Hunt cls destroyer — Blankney type; 1050; 280 x 31½; 27; 168; six 4-in; Swan Hunter & Wigham Richardson, Wallsend, 1941; transferred 1953 to Indian Navy, rnd *Gomati;*

Lamont: infantry landing ship; 9512; 487¾ x 66¼; --; --; one 4-in; Greenock Dockyard Co, Greenock, 1939; ex-cargo liner *Clan Lamont* (Clan Line, London) purchased RN and converted, rnd *Ardpatrick* 1945; 1946, Clan Line, London, converted to cargo liner, rnd *Clan Lamont;* b/up Hong Kong 1961.

Lancaster: Town cls destroyer; 1090; 314⅓ x 30½; 30; 122; one 4-in, six 21-in tt; Bath Iron Works, Bath, 1918; ex-USN *Philip,* transferred 1940 to RN; b/up Blyth 1947.

Lancaster Castle: Castle cls corvette; 1010; 252 x 36¾; 16½; 120; one 4-in; Fleming & Ferguson, Paisley, 1944; b/up Gateshead 1960.

Lance: L cls destroyer; 1920; 362¼ x 37; 36½; 190; eight 4-in, eight 21-in tt; Yarrow & Co, Scotstoun, 1941; bombed in drydock at Malta and reduced to a wreck, Apr-Oct, 1942, towed to UK, b/up Grays 1944.

Lancer: Military cls trawler; 750; 193 x 30; 11; 40; one 4-in; Cook Welton & Gemmell, Beverley, 1943; 1946, East Riding Trawlers, Hull, rnd *Stella Orion;* lost, aground near Maaloy, Nov 7, 1955.

Landguard: Lulworth cls escort; 1546; 250 x 42; 16; 200; one 5-in, two 3-in; Gen Eng & DD Co, Oakland, 1930; ex-US Coast Guard cutter *Shoshone,* transferred Lease/Lend to RN 1941, rtnd USCG 1946; b/up Colombo 1949.

Lapwing: Modified Black Swan cls sloop; 1430; 299½ x 38; 20; 192; six 4-in; Scotts SB & E Co, Greenock, 1943; torpedoed and sunk by U-boat in Kola Inlet, Mar 20, 1945.

Larch: Berberis cls trawler; 360 grt; 140¼ x 24; 11; 18; one 12-pdr; Cook Welton & Gemmell, Beverley, 1928; ex-*St Alexandria* (T. Hamling & Co, Hull) bought RN 1939; 1946, J. C. Llewellyn (Trawlers), Milford Haven, rnd *Westhill;* b/up Sunderland 1952.

Larchol: Elmol cls oiler; 2410; 220 x 34⅔; 9½; 19; --; Lobnitz & Co, Renfrew, 1917; 1958, R. S. Hayes, Pembroke Dock, no name change; b/up Boom 1959.

Lariat: BAT cls tug; 783; 143 x 33; 14; 34; one 3-in; Levingston SB, Orange, 1942; ex-USN, transferred Lease/Lend to RN 1942, rtnd USN 1946; 1946, China Merchants SN Co, Shanghai, rnd *Ming 108* (no trace 1953).

Lark: Modified Black Swan cls sloop; 1430; 299½ x 38; 20; 192; six 4-in; Scotts SB & E Co, Greenock, 1943; torpedoed by U-boat, Feb 17, 1945, and beached at Murmansk; salved by Soviet Union, refitted, rnd *Neptun;* now b/up.

Larkspur: Flower cls corvette; 925; 205 x 33; 16; 85; one 4-in; Fleming & Ferguson, Paisley, 1941; transferred 1942 to US Navy, rnd *Fury,* rtnd RN 1945; 1946, Wheelock Marden, Hong Kong, converted to cargo ship, rnd *Larkslock;* b/up Hong Kong 1953.

Larne: Algerine cls minesweeper; 950; 235 x 35½; 16½; 104; one 4-in; Lobnitz & Co, Renfrew, 1943; transferred 1946 to Italian Navy, rnd *Ammiraglio Magnaghi,* rnd *Eritrea,* 1948, rnd *Alabarda,* 1951; b/up Genoa 1968.

Lasso: cable ship; 903; 205 x 35; 13;

--; one 12-pdr; J. I. Thornycroft & Co, Southampton, 1939; b/up Burght 1959.

Latona: Manxman cls minelayer; 4000; 418 x 39; 40; 246; 160 mines, six 4.7-in; J. I. Thornycroft & Co, Southampton,1941; sunk by German aircraft off Bardia, Oct 25, 1941.

Lauderdale: Hunt cls destroyer — Blankney type; 1050; 280 x 31½; 27; 168; six 4-in; J. I. Thornycroft & Co, Southampton, 1941; transferred 1946 to Royal Hellenic Navy, rnd *Aigaion,* rtnd RN 1959; b/up Greece 1960.

Launceston Castle: Castle cls corvette; 1010; 252 x 36¾; 16½; 120; one 4-in; Blyth SB & DD Co, Blyth, 1944; b/up St Davids on Forth 1959.

Laurel: Berberis cls trawler; 590; 140¼ x 24½; 11; 18; one 12-pdr; Cook Welton & Gemmell, Beverley, 1930; ex-*Kingston Cyanite* (Kingston Steam Trawling Co, Hull) bought RN 1935; 1947, Granton Trawling Co, Granton, rnd *Strathyre;* 1951, Clifton Steam Trawlers, Fleetwood, rnd *Patricia Hague;* b/up Troon 1955.

Lavender: Flower cls corvette; 925; 205 x 33; 16; 85; one 4-in; A. Hall & Co, Aberdeen, 1941; 1948, NV Ned Maats voor de Walvischvaart, Holland, converted to whale catcher, rnd *Eugene W. Vinke;* b/up South Africa 1964.

Lawford: Captain cls frigate; 1140; 289½ x 35; 21; 200; three 3-in; Navy Yard, Boston, 1943; ex-USN Evarts cls destroyer-escort *DE-516,* transferred Lease/Lend to RN 1943; sunk by German aircraft off Normandy, June 8, 1944.

Lawson: Captain cls frigate; 1140; 289½ x 35; 21; 200; three 3-in; Navy Yard, Boston, 1943; ex-USN Evarts cls destroyer-escort *DE-518,* transferred Lease/Lend to RN 1943, rtnd USN 1946; b/up.

Leamington: Town cls destroyer; 1090; 314⅓ x 30½; 30; 122; one 4-in, six 21-in tt; New York SB Co, New York, 1919; ex-USN *Twiggs,* transferred 1940 to RN; transferred 1944 to Soviet Union, rnd *Zhguchi,* rtnd RN 1950; b/up Newport 1951.

Leander: Leander cls cruiser; 7270; 554½ x 55¼; 32½; 680; eight 6-in,

eight 4-in, eight 21-in tt; HM Dockyard, Devonport, 1933; b/up Blyth 1950.

Leda: Halcyon cls minesweeper; 835; 245 x 33½; 17; 80; two 4-in; HM Dockyard, Devonport, 1937; torpedoed and sunk by *U-435* in Russian convoy, Sept 20, 1942.

Ledbury: Hunt cls destroyer — Blankney type; 1050; 280 x 31½; 27; 168; six 4-in; J. I. Thornycroft & Co, Southampton, 1941; b/up Rosyth 1958.

Leeds: Town cls destroyer; 1020; 315½ x 30⅔; 30; 122; two 4-in, one 3-in; Wm Cramp & Sons, Philadelphia, 1918; ex-USN *Conner,* transferred 1940 to RN; b/up Grays 1947.

Leeds Castle: Castle cls corvette; 1010; 252 x 36¾; 16½; 120; one 4-in; Wm Pickersgill & Sons, Sunderland, 1944; b/up Grays 1958.

Legion: L cls destroyer; 1920; 362¼ x 37; 36½; 190; eight 4-in, eight 21-in tt; Hawthorn Leslie, Hebburn, 1940; irreparably damaged by German aircraft at Malta, Mar 26, 1942; b/up prior to 1945.

Leith: Grimsby cls sloop; 990; 266 x 36; 16½; 100; two 4.7-in, one 3-in; HM Dockyard, Devonport, 1934; 1947, Cia de Nav Torecha SA, Panama, converted to passenger ship, rnd *Byron;* 1948, Tuxen & Hageman, Denmark, rnd *Friendship;* 1949, Danish Navy, converted to survey ship, rnd *Galathea;* b/up Odense 1954.

Lennox: Algerine cls minesweeper; 950; 235 x 35½; 16½; 104; one 4-in; Lobnitz & Co, Renfrew, 1944; b/up Gateshead 1961.

Lewes: Town cls destroyer; 1020; 315½ x 30⅔; 30; 122; one 3-in; Navy Yard, Norfolk, 1918; ex-USN *Craven* 1939; ex-USN *Conway,* transferred 1940 to RN; scuttled off Australia, May 1946.

Liberty: Algerine cls minesweeper; 950; 235 x 35½; 16½; 104; one 4-in; Harland & Wolff, Belfast, 1945; transferred 1949 to Belgian Navy, rnd *Adrien de Gerlache;* b/up Bruges 1970.

Liddesdale: Hunt cls destroyer — Blankney type; 1000; 280 x 29; 27½; 146; four 4-in; Vickers-Armstrongs, Tyne, 1940; b/up Tyne 1948.

Lifeline: Kin cls coastal salvage vessel; 950; 179½ x 35¾; 9; 34; two 20-mm; Smith's Dock Co, Middlesbrough, 1943; 1959, Risdon, Beazley, Southampton, no name change;

Liffey: Axe cls trawler; 373; 139 x 23½; 10½; 18; one 3-in; Smith's Dock Co, Middlesbrough, 1916; ex-Russian *T-14,* acquired by RN 1918, rnd *Stoneaxe,* rnd *Liffey* 1920; b/up Northam 1953.

Lightfoot: Algerine cls minesweeper; 950; 235 x 35½; 16½; 104; one 4-in; Redfern Construction Co, Toronto, 1943; ex-USN, transferred Lease/Lend to RN 1943, rtnd USN 1946; transferred 1947 to Royal Hellenic Navy, rnd *Navmachos;*

Lightning: L cls destroyer; 1920; 362¼ x 37; 36½; 190; six 4.7-in, one 4-in, four 21-in tt; Hawthorn Leslie, Hebburn, 1941; sunk by Italian MTB off North Africa, Mar 12, 1943.

Lilac: Berberis cls trawler; 593; 150½ x 25½; 11; 18; one 12-pdr; Cochrane & Sons, Selby, 1930; ex-*Beachflower* (Yorkshire Steam Fishing Co, Hull) bought RN 1935; 1946, Great Northern Fishing Co, Fleetwood, rnd *Robert Hewett;* b/up UK 1961.

Limbourne: Hunt cls destroyer — Albrighton type; 1050; 280 x 31½; 27; 168; four 4-in, two 21-in tt; A. Stephen & Sons, Linthouse, 1942; torpedoed by German surface force in Channel, sunk by RN, Oct 23, 1943.

Limol: Elmol cls oiler; 2,410; 220 x 34⅔; 9½; 19; --; Lobnitz & Co, Renfrew, 1917; b/up Briton Ferry 1959.

Linaria: Modified Flower cls corvette; 980; 208 x 33; 16; 109; one 4-in; Midland Shipyards, Midland, 1943; was to be US Navy *Clash* not transferred; sold Italian owners 1948.

Lincoln: Town cls destroyer; 1090; 314⅓ x 30½; 30; 122; one 4-in, six 21-in tt; Wm Cramp & Sons, Philadelphia, 1918; ex-USN *Yarnall,* transferred 1940 to RN; transferred 1944 to Soviet Union, rnd *Druzni,* rtnd RN 1952; b/up Rosyth 1952.

Lincoln Salvor: salvage vessel; 800; 183¼ x 37; 12; 35; one 3-in; Bellingham Marine Railway &

Boatbuilding Co, Bellingham, 1943; ex-USN, transferred Lease/Lend to RN 1943, rtnd USN 1946; 1947, Greek Government, rnd *Agerochos;* 1955, Greek owners (nothing more known).

Lindisfarne: Isles cls trawler; 560; 164 x 27½; 12; 40; one 12-pdr; Cook Welton & Gemmell, Beverley, 1943; b/up Dover 1958.

Lingay: Isles cls trawler; 560; 164 x 27½; 12; 40; one 12-pdr; Cochrane & Sons, Selby, 1944; 1947, British Wheeler Process, Liverpool, converted to oil sludge vessel, rnd *Tulipdale;* b/up Belgium 1965.

Linnet: Linnet cls coastal minelayer; 498; 163¾ x 27⅙; 10½; 24; one 20-mm; Ardrossan Dockyard Ltd, Ardrossan, 1938; b/up Dunston 1964.

Lioness: Algerine cls minesweeper; 950; 235 x 35½; 16½; 104; one 4-in; Redfern Construction Co, Toronto, 1944; ex-*Petrolia* (RCN) 1943; b/up Rosyth 1956.

Liscomb: Isles cls trawler; 560; 164 x 27½; 12; 40; one 12-pdr; Kingston SB Co, Kingston, Ont, 1942; transferred to RCN 1942; rtnd 1945; 1946, Aalesunds Rederi A/S Norway, converted to cargo ship, rnd *Aalesund;* 1967, L. Nyvoll, Norway, rnd *Lars Nyvoll;*

Lively: L cls destroyer; 1920; 362¼ x 37; 36½; 190; eight 4-in, eight 21-in tt; Cammell Laird, Birkenhead, 1941; sunk by German aircraft in eastern Mediterranean, May 11, 1942.

Liverpool: Southampton cls cruiser; 9400; 591½ x 62⅓; 32; 830; twelve 6-in, eight 4-in, six 21-in tt; Fairfield SB & E Co, Govan, 1938; b/up Bo'ness 1958.

Llandudno: Bangor cls minesweeper; 656; 174 x 28½; 16; 60; one 3-in; Wm Hamilton & Co, Port Glasgow, 1942; 1947, Rorvik Syndicate, London, for conversion to merchant ship, rnd *Rorvik,* conversion not completed, b/up Southampton 1950.

Lobelia: Flower cls corvette; 925; 205 x 33; 16; 85; one 4-in; A. Hall & Co, Aberdeen, 1941; transferred 1941, French Navy, no name change, rtnd RN 1947; 1947, Bryde & Dahls Hvalfangerselskap A/S, Norway, converted to whale catcher, rnd *Thorgeir;* b/up Norway 1970.

Loch Achanalt: Loch cls frigate; 1435; 307 x 38½; 19½; 140; one 4-in; H. Robb, Leith, 1944; ex-*Naver,* 1943; transferred 1948 Royal New Zealand Navy, rnd *Pukaki;* b/up Hong Kong 1965.

Loch Achray: Loch cls frigate; 1435; 307 x 38½; 19½; 140; one 4-in; Smith's Dock Co, Middlesbrough, 1945; transferred 1948 Royal New Zealand Navy, rnd *Kaniere;* b/up Hong Kong 1967.

Loch Alvie: Loch cls frigate; 1435; 307 x 38½; 19½; 140; one 4-in; Barclay Curle & Co, Glasgow, 1944; b/up Far East (Singapore?) 1965.

Loch Ard: Loch cls frigate; 1435; 307 x 38½; 19½; 140; one 4-in; Harland & Wolff, Belfast, 1945; transferred 1945, South African Navy, rnd *Transvaal;*

Loch Arkaig: Loch cls frigate; 1435; 307 x 38½; 19½; 140; one 4-in; Caledon SB & E Co, Dundee, 1945; b/up Gateshead 1960.

Loch Boisdale: Loch cls frigate; 1435; 307 x 38½; 19½; 140; one 4-in; Blyth SB & DD Co, Blyth, 1944; transferred 1944, South African Navy, rnd *Good Hope;*

Loch Craggie: Loch cls frigate; 1435; 307 x 38½; 19½; 140; one 4-in; Harland & Wolff, Belfast, 1944; b/up Lisbon 1963.

Loch Cree: Loch cls frigate; 1435; 307 x 38½; 19½; 140; one 4-in; Swan Hunter & Wigham Richardson, Wallsend, 1945; transferred 1945, South African Navy, rnd *Natal,* converted to survey ship 1957;

Loch Dunvegan: Loch cls frigate; 1435; 307 x 38½; 19½; 140; one 4-in; C. Hill & Sons, Bristol, 1944; b/up Briton Ferry 1960.

Loch Eck: Loch cls frigate; 1435; 307 x 38½; 19½; 140; one 4-in; Smith's Dock Co, Middlesbrough, 1944; transferred 1948, Royal New Zealand Navy, rnd *Hawea;* b/up Hong Kong 1965.

Loch Fada: Loch cls frigate; 1435; 307 x 38½; 19½; 140; one 4-in; J. Brown & Co, Clydebank, 1944; b/up Faslane 1970.

Loch Fyne: Loch cls frigate; 1435; 307 x 38½; 19½; 140; one 4-in; Burntisland SB Co, Burntisland, 1944; b/up Newport 1970.

Loch Glendhu: Loch cls frigate; 1435; 307 x 38½; 19½; 140; one 4-in; Burntisland SB Co, Burntisland, 1945; b/up Dunston 1957.

Loch Gorm: Loch cls frigate; 1435; 307 x 38½; 19½; 140; one 4-in; Harland & Wolff, Belfast, 1944; 1961, Kavounides Shipping Co, Greece, converted to passenger ship, rnd *Orion;* b/up Yugoslavia 1966.

Loch Insh: Loch cls frigate; 1435; 307 x 38½; 19½; 140; one 4-in; H. Robb, Leith, 1944; transferred 1964, Malaysian Navy, rnd *Hang Tuah;*

Loch Katrine: Loch cls frigate; 1435; 307 x 38½; 19½; 140; one 4-in; H. Robb, Leith, 1944; transferred 1949, Royal New Zealand Navy, rnd *Rotoiti;* b/up Hong Kong 1967.

Loch Killin: Loch cls frigate; 1435; 307 x 38½; 19½; 140; one 4-in; Burntisland SB Co, Burntisland, 1944; b/up Newport 1960.

Loch Killisport: Loch cls frigate; 1435; 307 x 38½; 19½; 140; one 4-in; Harland & Wolff, Belfast, 1945; b/up Blyth 1970.

Loch Lomond: Loch cls frigate; 1435; 307 x 38½; 19½; 140; one 4-in; Caledon SB & E Co, Dundee, 1944; b/up Faslane 1968.

Loch More: Loch cls frigate; 1435; 307 x 38½; 19½; 140; one 4-in; Caledon SB & E Co, Dundee, 1945; b/up Inverkeithing 1963.

Loch Morlich: Loch cls frigate; 1435; 307 x 38½; 19½; 140; one 4-in; Swan Hunter & Wigham Richardson, Wallsend 1944; transferred 1949, Royal New Zealand Navy, rnd *Tutira;* b/up Hong Kong 1962.

Loch Quoich: Loch cls frigate; 1435; 307 x 38½; 19½; 140; one 4-in; Blyth SB & DD Co, Blyth, 1945; b/up Dunston 1957.

Loch Ruthven: Loch cls frigate; 1435; 307 x 38½; 19½; 140; one 4-in; C. Hill & Sons, Bristol, 1944; b/up Plymouth 1966.

Loch Scavaig: Loch cls frigate; 1435; 307 x 38½; 19½; 140; one 4-in; C. Hill & Sons, Bristol, 1945; b/up Genoa 1959.

Loch Shin: Loch cls frigate; 1435; 307 x 38½; 19½; 140; one 4-in; Swan Hunter & Wigham Richardson, Wallsend, 1944; transferred 1948,

Royal New Zealand Navy, rnd *Taupo;*
b/up Hong Kong 1962.

Loch Tarbert: Loch cls frigate; 1435;
307 x 38½; 19½; 140; one 4-in; Ailsa
SB Co, Troon, 1945; b/up Genoa 1959.

Loch Tralaig: Loch cls frigate; 1435;
307 x 38½; 19½; 140; one 4-in;
Caledon SB & E Co, Dundee, 1945;
b/up Bo'ness 1963.

Lochy: River cls frigate; 1370; 301½ x
36½; 19; 140; two 4-in; Hall Russell
Aberdeen, 1944; b/up Troon 1956.

Locust: Locust cls gunboat; 585; 197 x
33; 17; 74; two 4-in, one 3.7-in
howitzer; Yarrow & Co, Scotstoun,
1939; RNVR drillship 1951; b/up
Newport 1968.

London: London cls cruiser; 9850; 633
x 66; 32¼; 850; eight 8-in, eight 4-in,
eight 21-in tt; HM Dockyard,
Portsmouth, 1929; b/up Barrow 1950.

Londonderry: Grimsby cls sloop; 990;
266 x 36; 16½; 100; two 4.7-in, one
3-in; HM Dockyard, Devonport, 1935;
b/up Llanelly 1948.

Longa: Isles cls trawler; 560; 164 x
27½; 12; 40; one 12-pdr; Cochrane &
Sons, Selby, 1944; 1947, Scottish
Home Dept as fisheries patrol ship, no
name change; b/up Inverkeithing
1973.

Lookout: L cls destroyer; 1920; 362¼ x
37; 36½; 190; six 4.7-in, one 4-in, four
21-in tt; Scotts SB & E Co, Greenock,
1941; b/up Newport 1948.

Loosestrife: Flower cls corvette; 925;
205 x 33; 16; 85; one 4-in; Hall Russell,
Aberdeen, 1941; 1947, P/F Kimbil,
Norway, converted to trawler, rnd
Kallsevni; b/up Masnedo 1962.

Loring: Captain cls frigate; 1140;
289½ x 35; 21; 200; three 3-in; Navy
Yard, Boston, 1943; ex-USN Evarts cls
destroyer-escort *DE-520,* transferred
Lease/Lend to RN 1943, rtnd USN
1947; b/up Greece 1947.

Lossie: River cls frigate; 1370; 301½ x
36½; 19; 140; two 4-in; Canadian
Vickers, Montreal, 1943; ex-USN
PG-108, transferred Lease/Lend to RN
1943, rtnd USN 1946; 1947, Cadio Cia
de Nav SA, Panama, converted to
cargo ship, rnd *Teti;* 1955, Typaldos
Bros SA, Greece, rnd *Adriatiki;*
stranded and sunk in Aegean Sea, Jan
16, 1968.

Lotus: Flower cls corvette; 925; 205 x
33; 16; 85; one 4-in; C. Hill & Sons,
Bristol, 1942; transferred 1942 French
Navy, rnd *Commandant D'Estienne
D'Orves,* rtnd RN 1947; b/up Troon
1951.

Lotus: Flower cls corvette; 925; 205 x
33; 16; 85; one 4-in; H. Robb, Leith,
1942; ex-*Phlox,* 1942; 1948, South
Georgia Co (C. Salvesen) Leith,
converted to whale catcher, rnd
Southern Lotus; lost, aground
Jutland, Dec 18, 1966, after breaking
tow on way to shipbreakers at Ghent.

Louis: Captain cls frigate; 1140; 289½
x 35; 21; 200; three 3-in; Navy Yard,
Boston, 1943; ex-USN Evarts cls
destroyer-escort *DE-517,* transferred
Lease/Lend to RN 1943, rtnd USN
1946; b/up.

Lowestoft: Grimsby cls sloop; 990;
266 x 36; 16½; 100; two 4.7-in, one
3-in; HM Dockyard, Devonport, 1934;
1947, Cie Maritima Geojunior SA,
Panama, for conversion to merchant
ship, rnd *Miraflores;* conversion not
completed, b/up Boom 1955.

Loyal: L cls destroyer; 1920; 362¼ x
37; 36½; 190; six 4.7-in, one 4-in, four
21-in tt; Scotts SB & E Co, Greenock,
1942; irreparably damaged by mine in
north Adriatic, Oct 12, 1944, b/up
Milford Haven 1948.

Loyalty: Algerine cls minesweeper;
950; 235 x 35½; 16½; 104; one 4-in;
Harland & Wolff, Belfast, 1943;
ex-*Rattler,* 1943; torpedoed and sunk
by *U-480* in English Channel, Aug 22,
1944.

LST-3001: landing ship, tank; 4980;
345 x 54; 13; 115; ten 20-mm;
Vickers-Armstrongs, Tyne, 1945;
transferred 1946, War Dept, rnd
Frederick Clover; 1966, Liana Naviera
SA, Panama, rnd *Pacific Pioneer;* b/up
Hong Kong 1968.

LST-3006: landing ship, tank; 4980;
345 x 54; 13; 115; ten 20-mm; Harland
& Wolff, Belfast, 1944; rnd *Tromso,*
1947; transferred 1956, Ministry of
Transport, rnd *Empire Gannet;* b/up
Singapore 1968.

LST-3007: landing ship, tank; 4980;
345 x 54; 13; 115; ten 20-mm; Harland
& Wolff, Belfast, 1944; transferred
1947, Royal Hellenic Navy, md *Axios,*

rtnd RN 1962; b/up Genoa 1962.

LST-3008: landing ship, tank; 4980; 345 x 54; 13; 115; ten 20-mm; Harland & Wolff, Belfast, 1944; transferred 1946 Royal Australian Navy, no name change; 1950, R. R. Coots, Sydney (nothing further known).

LST-3009: landing ship, tank; 4980; 345 x 54; 13; 115; ten 20-mm; Harland & Wolff, Belfast, 1945; transferred 1946, War Dept, rnd *Reginald Kerr;* b/up Singapore 1966.

LST-3010: landing ship, tank; 4980; 345 x 54; 13; 115; ten 20-mm; Harland & Wolff, Belfast, 1944; rnd *Attacker,* 1947; transferred 1954, Ministry of Transport, rnd *Empire Cymric;* b/up Faslane 1963.

LST-3011: landing ship, tank; 4980; 345 x 54; 13; 115; ten 20-mm; Harland & Wolff, Belfast, 1945; rnd *Avenger* 1947; transferred 1949, Indian Navy, rnd *Magar,* 1951;

LST-3012: landing ship, tank; 4980; 345 x 54; 13; 115; ten 20-mm; Harland & Wolff, Belfast, 1945; rnd *Ben Nevis* 1947; b/up Faslane 1965.

LST-3014: landing ship, tank; 4980; 345 x 54; 13; 115; ten 20-mm; Barclay Curle & Co, Glasgow, 1945; transferred 1946, Royal Australian Navy, no name change; 1950, R. R. Coots, Sydney (nothing further known).

LST-3016: landing ship, tank; 4980; 345 x 54; 13; 115; ten 20-mm; Hawthorn Leslie, Hebburn, 1945; rnd *Dieppe,* 1947; on sale list 1968.

LST-3017: landing ship, tank; 4980; 345 x 54; 13; 115; ten 20-mm; Hawthorn Leslie, Hebburn, 1945; transferred 1948 to Royal Australian Navy, rnd *Tarakan;* 1954, E. A. Marr, Sydney, (nothing further known).

LST-3019: landing ship, tank; 4980; 345 x 54; 13; 115; ten 20-mm; Swan Hunter & Wigham Richardson, Wallsend, 1944; rnd *Vaagso* 1947; b/up Faslane 1959.

LST-3020: landing ship, tank; 4980; 345 x 54; 13; 115; ten 20-mm; Swan Hunter & Wigham Richardson, Wallsend, 1945; transferred 1947 to Royal Hellenic Navy, rnd *Alfios,* rtnd RN 1962; b/up Spezia 1963.

LST-3021: landing ship, tank; 4980;

345 x 54; 13; 115; ten 20-mm; Lithgows Ltd, Port Glasgow, 1945; transferred 1946 to War Dept. rnd *Charles McLeod;* b/up Spezia 1968.

LST-3022: landing ship, tank; 4980; 345 x 54; 13; 115; ten 20-mm; Lithgows Ltd, Port Glasgow, 1945; transferred 1946 to Royal Australian Navy; no name change; 1950, Queensland Cement & Lime Co, Australia, converted to dumb suction cutter dredger, rnd *Coral;*

LST-3024: landing ship, tank; 4980; 345 x 54; 13; 115; ten 20-mm; Smith's Dock Co, Middlesbrough, 1945; transferred 1946 to War Dept, rnd *Maxwell Brander;* 1968, F. M. V. Holding SA, Panama, rnd *Fedredge Isabel;* b/up Hong Kong 1969.

LST-3025: landing ship, tank; 4980; 345 x 54; 13; 115; ten 20-mm; Smith's Dock Co, Middlesbrough, 1945; rnd *Bruizer,* 1947; sold 1954 at Singapore (breaking up?).

LST-3026: landing ship, tank; 4980; 345 x 54; 13; 115; ten 20-mm; Blyth SB & DD Co, Blyth, 1944; rnd *Charger,* 1947; transferred 1956 to Ministry of Transport rnd *Empire Nordic;* b/up Bilbao 1968.

LST-3028: landing ship, tank; 4980; 345 x 54; 13; 115; ten 20-mm; Alex Stephen & Sons, Linthouse, 1945; transferred 1946 to War Dept, rnd *Snowden Smith;* 1964, Compagnia Sardia di Navigazione SpA, Italy, rnd *Elbano Primo;* 1968, Cia di Nav Mista, Italy, no name change; 1971, Cia Sanda di Nav Marittima SpA, Italy, no name change; b/up Italy 1971.

LST-3031: landing ship, tank; 4980; 345 x 54; 13; 115; ten 20-mm; Hall Russell & Co, Aberdeen, 1945; b/up Spain 1972-73.

LST-3033: landing ship, tank; 4980; 345 x 54; 13; 115; ten 20-mm; Wm Pickersgill & Sons, Sunderland, 1945; transferred 1956 to Ministry of Transport, rnd *Empire Shearwater;* b/up Ghent 1962.

LST-3035: landing ship, tank; 4980; 345 x 54; 13; 115; ten 20-mm; Wm Denny & Bros, Dumbarton, 1945; transferred 1946 to Royal Australian Navy, rnd *Lae,* 1948; sold 1955 and stranded on North Queensland coast on passage in tow to Japan for breaking-up.

LST-3036: landing ship, tank; 4980; 345 x 54; 13; 115; ten 20-mm; Ailsa SB Co, Troon, 1945; rnd *Puncher,* 1947; b/up Ghent 1961.

LST-3037: landing ship, tank; 4980; 345 x 54; 13; 115; ten 20-mm; Fairfield SB & E Co, Govan, 1945; transferred 1946 to War Dept, rnd *Evan Gibb;* b/up Spezia 1963.

LST-3038: landing ship, tank; 4980; 345 x 54; 13; 115; ten 20-mm; Fairfield SB & E Co, Govan, 1945; rnd *Fighter,* 1947; transferred 1956 to Ministry of Transport, rnd *Empire Grebe;* b/up Singapore 1968.

LST-3041: landing ship, tank; 4980; 345 x 54; 13; 115; ten 20-mm; Harland & Wolff, Govan, 1945; transferred 1954 to Ministry of Transport, rnd *Empire Doric;* b/up Port Glasgow 1960.

LST-3043: landing ship, tank; 4980; 345 x 54; 13; 115; ten 20-mm; Scotts SB & E Co, Greenock, 1945; rnd *Messina* 1947; for b/up 1967.

LST-3501: landing ship, tank; 4980; 345 x 54; 13; 115; four 40-mm; Canadian Vickers, Montreal, 1944; transferred 1946 to Royal Australian Navy, rnd *Labuan,* 1949; b/up Hikari 1956.

LST-3502: landing ship, tank; 4980; 345 x 54; 13; 115; four 40-mm; Canadian Vickers, Montreal, 1944; transferred 1947 to Royal Hellenic Navy, rnd *Strymon,* rtnd RN 1962; b/up Spezia 1962.

LST-3503: landing ship, tank; 4980; 345 x 54; 13; 115; four 40-mm; Canadian Vickers, Montreal, 1944; transferred 1947 to Royal Hellenic Navy, rnd *Acheloos;* b/up Spezia 1971.

LST-3504: landing ship, tank; 4980; 345 x 54; 13; 115; four 40-mm; Canadian Vickers, Montreal, 1945; rnd *Pursuer,* 1947; transferred 1956 to Ministry of Transport, rnd *Empire Tern;* b/up Singapore 1968.

LST-3506: landing ship, tank; 4980; 345 x 54; 13; 115; four 40-mm; Canadian Vickers, Montreal, 1945; transferred 1947 to Royal Hellenic Navy, rnd *Pinios;* b/up Piraeus 1972.

LST-3507: landing ship, tank; 4980; 345 x 54; 13; 115; four 40-mm; Davie

SB & Repair Co, Lauzon, 1945; transferred 1954 to Ministry of Transport, rnd *Empire Gaelic;* b/up Belgium 1960.

LST-3508: landing ship, tank; 4980; 345 x 54; 13; 115; four 40-mm; Davie SB & Repair Co, Lauzon, 1945; rnd *Searcher,* 1947; b/up Milford Haven 1949.

LST-3512: landing ship, tank; 4980; 345 x 54; 13; 115; four 40-mm; Davie SB & Repair Co, Lauzon, 1945; transferred 1956 to Ministry of Transport, rnd *Empire Celtic;* b/up Spezia 1962.

LST-3514: landing ship, tank; 4980; 345 x 54; 13; 115; four 40-mm; Yarrow, Esquimalt, 1945; rnd *Smiter* 1947; in tow Algiers for Tyne for breaking up, broke adrift and aground Lages, Portugal, total loss, Apr 25, 1949.

LST-3515: landing ship, tank; 4980; 345 x 54; 13; 115; four 40-mm; Yarrows Esquimalt, 1945; rnd *Stalker,* 1947;

LST-3516: landing ship, tank; 4980; 345 x 54; 13; 115; four 40-mm; Yarrows, Esquimalt, 1945; rnd *Striker,* 1947; b/up Valencia 1971.

Lucia: submarine depot ship; 5805; 367½ x 45¼; 12½; 262; --; Furness Withy, West Hartlepool, 1908; ex-Hamburg Amerika Line passenger ship *Spreewald,* captured 1914 by RN, converted by Clyde SB Co, 1916; 1948, Cia Maritima Geojunior SA, Panama, rnd *Sinai;* b/up Spezia 1951.

Lucigen: oiler; 4979 grt; 388 x 50½; --; --; --; Armstrong Whitworth, Newcastle, 1909; ex-tanker (Lucigen SS Co, Liverpool) bought RN 1939; used as fuel hulk at Lagos; towed out to sea and sunk, 1945.

Ludlow: Town cls destroyer; 1020; 315½ x 30⅔; 30; 122; two 4-in; one 3-in; Wm Cramp & Sons, Philadelphia, 1917; ex-USN *Stockton,* transferred 1940 to RN; expended as target, June 1945.

Lulworth: Lulworth cls escort; 1546; 250 x 42; 16; 200; one 5-in, two 3-in; Bethlehem SB, Quincy, 1928; ex-US Coast Guard cutter *Chelan,* transferred Lease/Lend to RN 1941, rtnd USCG 1946; sold New York buyers (shipbreakers?) 1947.

Lundy: Isles cls trawler; 560; 164 x 27½; 12; 40; one 12-pdr; Cook Welton & Gemmell, Beverley, 1942;

Lupin: Flower cls sloop; 1175; 267¾ x 33½; 16½; 98; two 4-in; Wm Simons & Co, Renfrew, 1916; b/up Portchester 1947.

Lydd: Hunt cls minesweeper; 800; 231 x 28½; 16; 74; one 4-in, one 3-in; Fairfield SB & E Co, Govan, 1919; ex-*Lydney*, 1918; b/up Belgium 1947.

Lyme Regis: Bangor cls minesweeper; 672; 180 x 28½; 16; 60; one 3-in; Lobnitz & Co, Renfrew, 1942; transferred 1942 to Indian Navy, rnd *Rajputana*; b/up 1961.

Lyme Regis: Bangor cls minesweeper; 656; 174 x 28½; 16; 60; one 3-in; Alex Stephen & Sons, Linthouse, 1942; ex-*Sunderland* 1942; b/up Sunderland 1948.

Lysander: Algerine cls minesweeper; 950; 235 x 35½; 16½; 104; one 4-in; Port Arthur SB Co, Port Arthur, 1944; ex-*Hespeler* (RCN) 1943; b/up Blyth 1957.

Macbeth: Shakespearian cls trawler; 545; 164 x 27¾; 12; 35; one 12-pdr; Goole SB & Repairing Co, Goole, 1941; 1947, Skibs A/S Macbeth, Norway, no name change; lost Oct 10, 1950.

Mackay: Scott cls destroyer; 1530; 332½ x 31¾; 31; 183; four 4.7-in, one 3-in; Cammell Laird, Birkenhead, 1919; b/up Charlestown 1949.

Maenad: Algerine cls minesweeper; 950; 235 x 35½; 16½; 104; one 4-in; Redfern Construction Co, Toronto, 1944; b/up Grays 1957.

Magdalen: Isles cls trawler; 560; 164 x 27½; 12; 40; one 12-pdr; Midland Shipyards, Midland, Ont, 1942; 1946, L. Myreboe A/S, Norway, converted to cargo ship, rnd *Maroy*; 1951, Gabriele Zunini, Italy, rnd *Cinzia*; 1958, M. Minnici in Picardi, Italy, rnd *Sabina*; aground near Marsala, Dec 10, 1960.

Magic: Catherine cls minesweeper; 890; 221 x 32; 18; 109; one 3-in; Savannah Machine & Foundry Co, Savannah, 1943; ex-USN Auk cls minesweeper *BAM-20* transferred

Lease/Lend to RN 1943; sunk off Normandy, July 6, 1944.

Magicienne: Algerine cls minesweeper; 950; 235 x 35½; 16½; 104; one 4-in; Redfern Construction Co, Toronto, 1944; b/up Newport 1956.

Magnet: Bayonet cls boom defence vessel; 530; 135 x 30½; 11½; 32; one 3-in; Smith's Dock Co, Middlesbrough, 1939; ex-*Barnsley*, 1938; sold Italian buyers 1959.

Magnolia: Berberis cls trawler; 557; 150¼ x 24½; 11; 18; one 12-pdr; Cochrane & Sons, Selby, 1930; ex-*Lord Brentford* (Pickering & Haldane's Steam Trawling Co, Hull) bought RN 1935; 1948, East Fisheries, South Africa, rnd *Oranjezicht*; b/up 1966-67.

Magpie: Modified Black Swan cls sloop; 1430; 299½ x 38; 20; 192; six 4-in; J. I. Thornycroft & Co, Southampton, 1943; b/up Blyth 1959.

Mahratta: M cls destroyer; 1920; 362½ x 37; 36½; 190; six 4.7-in, one 4-in, four 21-in tt; Scotts SB & E Co, Greenock, 1942; ex-*Marksman*, 1942; sunk by *U-956* in Barentz Sea, Feb 25, 1944.

Maidstone: submarine depot ship; 8900; 531 x 75; 17; 502; eight 4.5-in; J. Brown & Co, Clydebank, 1938;

Maine: hospital ship; 10,100; 401 x 58⅓; 13; --; --; Fairfield SB & E Co, Glasgow, 1902; ex-passenger liner *Panama* (Pacific SN Co, Liverpool) bought RN 1920; b/up Bo'ness 1948.

Malaya: Queen Elizabeth cls battleship; 31,100; 639¾ x 104; 24; 1184; eight 15-in, twelve 6-in, eight 4-in; Armstrong Whitworth & Co, Newcastle, 1916; b/up Faslane 1948.

Malcolm: Scott cls destroyer; 1530; 332½ x 31¾; 31; 183; two 4.7-in, three 21-in tt; Cammell Laird, Birkenhead, 1919; b/up Barrow 1945.

Mallard: Kingfisher cls sloop; 510; 243⅙ x 26½; 20; 60; one 4-in; Alex Stephen & Sons, Linthouse, 1936; b/up Gateshead 1947.

Mallow: Flower cls corvette; 925; 205 x 33; 16; 85; one 4-in; Harland & Wolff, Belfast, 1940; transferred 1943 to Yugoslav Navy, rnd *Nada*, rnd *Partizanska*, rtnd RN 1949; transferred

1949 to Egypt, rnd *El Sudan;*
Mameluke: Algerine cls minesweeper;
950; 235 x 35½; 16½; 104; one 4-in;
Redfern Construction Co, Toronto,
1944; b/up Middlesbrough 1950.
Manchester: Southampton cls
cruiser; 9400; 591½ x 62⅓; 32; 830;
twelve 6-in, eight 4-in, six 21-in tt;
Hawthorn Leslie, Hebburn, 1938;
torpedoed and sunk by Italian motor
boats off Tunisia, Aug 13, 1942.
Mandate: Algerine cls minesweeper;
950; 235 x 35½; 16½; 104; one 4-in;
Redfern Construction Co, Toronto,
1944; b/up Charlestown 1957.
Mandrake: Modified Flower cls
corvette; 980; 208¼ x 33; 16; 109; one
4-in; Morton Eng & DD Co, Quebec,
1943; transferred 1943 to US Navy, rnd
Haste; 1949, Soc Anon Navigazione
Toscana, Italy, converted to cargo
ship, rnd *Porto Azzuro;* b/up Italy
1971.
Mangrove: Tree cls trawler; 530; 164 x
27½; 11½; 35; one 12-pdr; Ferguson
Bros, Port Glasgow, 1940; transferred
1943 to Portuguese Navy, rnd *P-2,*
bought 1946, rnd *Faial;* for disposal
and breaking-up 1967.
Manitoulin: Isles cls trawler; 560; 164
x 27½; 12; 40; one 12-pdr; Midland
Shipyards, Midland, Ont, 1942; 1946,
Red A/B M/S Ran, Norway, converted
to cargo ship, rnd *Ran;* 1951, Blue Peter
Steamships, Canada, rnd *Ran B,* rnd
Blue Peter II, rnd *Blue Bay,* 1964; 1965,
R. J. Sumarah. Canada, rnd *William S;*
1973, A. Vicenti, Panama, rnd *Queen
Patricia;*
Manners: Captain cls frigate; 1140;
289½ x 35; 21; 200; three 3-in; Navy
Yard, Boston, 1943; ex-USN Evarts cls
destroyer-escort *DE-523,* transferred
Lease/Lend to RN 1943; irreparably
damaged by U-boat off west coast UK,
Jan 26, 1945, rtnd USN 1945; b/up
Piraeus 1947.
Mansfield: Town cls destroyer; 1090;
314⅓ x 30½; 30; 122; one 4-in, three
21-in tt; Bath Iron Works, Bath, 1919;
ex-USN *Evans,* transferred 1940 to RN;
b/up Baltimore 1945.
Mantis: Insect cls river gunboat; 625;
237½ x 36; 14; 65; two 6-in, one 3-in;
Sunderland SB Co, Sunderland, 1916;
1940, sold, China (nothing more

known).
Manxman: Manxman cls minelayer;
4000; 418 x 39; 40; 246; 160 mines, six
4.7-in; Alex Stephen & Sons,
Linthouse, 1941; b/up Newport 1972.
Maori: Tribal cls destroyer; 1870; 377
x 36½; 36½; 190; eight 4.7-in, four 21-in
tt; Fairfield SB & E Co, Govan, 1939;
sunk by German aircraft at Dockyard
Creek, Malta, Feb 12, 1942; raised and
set down off Sliema in deeper water,
1942; raised and sunk in even deeper
water off Malta, 1945.
Maple: Berberis cls trawler; 550; 140¼
x 24; 11; 18; one 12-pdr; Cook Welton
& Gemmell, Beverley, 1929; ex-*St
Gerontius* (T. Hamling & Co, Hull),
bought RN 1939; 1947, De Ven NV,
Holland, rnd *Sumatra;* b/up Holland
1956.
Marauder: Brigand cls tug; 840; 174 x
32; 15½; 43; one 3-in; Fleming &
Ferguson, Paisley, 1939; 1958, Collins
Submarine Pipelines, London, rnd
Emerson K; b/up South Africa 1966.
Marguerite: Flower cls corvette; 925;
205 x 33; 16; 85; one 4-in; Hall Russell,
Aberdeen, 1940; transferred 1947 to
Air Ministry. converted to weather
ship, rnd *Weather Observer;* b/up
Ghent 1961.
Marigold: Flower cls corvette; 925;
205 x 33; 16; 85; one 4-in; Hall Russell,
Aberdeen, 1941; sunk by Italian
aircraft off Algiers, Dec 9, 1942.
Mariner: Algerine cls minesweeper;
950; 235 x 35½; 16½; 104; one 4-in;
Port Arthur SB Co, Port Arthur, 1945;
ex-*Kincardine,* 1944; transferred 1958
to Burma, rnd *Yan Myo Aung;*
Marmion: Algerine cls minesweeper;
950; 235 x 35½; 16½; 104; one 4-in;
Port Arthur SB Co, Port Arthur, 1944;
ex-*Orangeville* (RCN) 1943; b/up Tyne
1959.
Marne: M cls destroyer; 1920; 362½ x
37; 36½; 190; six 4.7-in, one 4-in, four
21-in tt; Vickers-Armstrongs, Tyne,
1941; transferred 1959 to Turkey, rnd
Maresal Fevzi Cakmak; for disposal
1971.
Marshal Ney: depot ship; 6700; 355⅔
x 90¼; 6.7; 280; --; Palmers SB & Iron
Co, Hebburn, 1915; ex-Marshal Ney cls
monitor, converted to depot ship
1922; b/up Milford Haven 1957.

Battleships were the pride of the Royal Navy. Here the *King George V,* completed in 1940, (**above**) contrasts with the *Revenge* of 1916.

The aircraft carrier ousted the battleship as the capital ship of every fleet during the Second World War. Its development is shown in these four photographs.
Above The *Argus,* completed in 1918 from a merchant ship's hull. **Below** The *Eagle* was laid down as a battleship in 1913 and completed as an aircraft carrier in 1923.

The *Indomitable* (above) was completed in 1941, while the *Fencer* was an ex-US escort carrier transferred to the Royal Navy under Lease/Lend.

Inter-war cruisers are represented by the *Cairo* (**above**), dating from 1919, and the *Cumberland* (**below**), built in 1928.

Above The *Skate* was completed in 1917. **Below** The *Fame* of 1935.

Above The escort destroyer *Easton,* completed in 1942. **Below** The *Wager* of 1944.

The *Wear* was one of the many anti-submarine frigates.

Above The pre-war construction of escort vessels included the *Fowey*. **Below** The Flower class corvettes were the most famous North Atlantic convoy escorts. Here is the *Thyme*.

Above This photograph of the *Upstart* was taken after the war, when her 3-inch gun had been removed. **Below** The *Solent.*

Some fleet minesweepers doubled as convoy escorts. However, the *Ossory* (**above**) was completed too late to see active service. Minesweeping was also carried out by trawlers, including the *Steepholm,* seen here as a wreck dispersal vessel.

The *Sefton* was one of the big infantry landing ships supplied under the Lease/Lend agreement.

Above The Bar class of boom defence vessels included the *Barrage*. **Below** Oilers, represented here by the *Abbeydale,* formed a vital part of the fleet train.

This is the fleet repair ship *Resource*, completed in 1929.

Above The *Salvestor* was a big salvage ship. **Below** The tug *Bustler* was specially designed for ocean work.

Marshal Soult: gunnery training ship; 6400; 355⅔ x 90¼; 6.7; 280; two 15-in, eight 4-in; Palmers SB & Iron Co, Hebburn, 1915; ex-Marshal Ney cls monitor; b/up Troon 1946.

Martin: M cls destroyer; 1920; 362½ x 37; 36½; 190; six 4.7-in, one 4-in, four 21-in tt; Vickers-Armstrongs, Tyne, 1941; torpedoed and sunk by U-431 off Algeria, Nov 10. 1942.

Martinet: Bayonet cls boom defence vessel; 530; 135 x 30½; 11½; 32; one 3-in; Smith's Dock Co, Middlesbrough, 1939; ex-Barnstone 1938; sold Portsmouth shipbreakers 1958.

Marvel: Algerine cls minesweeper; 950; 235 x 35½; 16½; 104; one 4-in; Redfern Construction Co, Toronto, 1944; b/up Charlestown 1958.

Mary Rose: Algerine cls minesweeper; 950; 235 x 35½; 16½; 104; one 4-in; Redfern Construction Co, Toronto, 1943; ex-Toronto (RCN) 1943; b/up Gateshead 1957.

Mashona: Tribal cls destroyer; 1870; 377 x 36½; 36½; 190; eight 4.7-in, four 21-in tt; Vickers-Armstrongs, Tyne, 1939; damaged by German aircraft off west coast of Ireland, sunk by RN, May 28, 1941.

Masterful: BAT cls tug; 783; 143 x 33; 14; 34; one 3-in; Levingston SB, Orange 1942; ex-USN, transferred Lease/Lend to RN 1942, rtnd USN 1946; 1948, Moran Towing Corp, US, rnd Eugenia M Moran; 1960, Pacific Inland Nav Co, US, rnd Comanche;

Mastiff: Basset cls trawler; 520; 163½ x 27½; 13; 33; one 4-in; H. Robb, Leith, 1938; mined in Thames Estuary, Nov 20, 1939.

Matabele: Tribal cls destroyer; 1870; 377 x 36½; 36½; 190; eight 4.7-in, four 21-in tt; Scotts SB & E Co, Greenock, 1939; torpedoed and sunk by U-454 in Barentz Sea, Jan 17, 1942.

Matchless: M cls destroyer; 1920; 362½ x 37; 36½; 190; six 4.7-in, one 4-in, four 21-in tt; Alex Stephen & Sons, Linthouse, 1942; transferred 1958 to Turkey, rnd Kilic Ali Pasa; for disposal 1971.

Mauritius: Fiji cls cruiser; 8525; 555½ x 62; 33; 980; twelve 6-in, eight 4-in, six 21-in tt; Swan Hunter & Wigham Richardson, Wallsend, 1940; b/up Inverkeithing 1965.

Mayflower: Flower cls corvette; 925; 205 x 33; 16; 85; one 4-in; Canadian Vickers, Montreal, 1940; transferred 1941 to Royal Canadian Navy, rtnd RN 1945; b/up Inverkeithing 1949.

Mazurka: Dance cls trawler; 530; 160½ x 27½; 11½; 35; one 4-in; Ferguson Bros, Port Glasgow, 1941; sold Belgian owners 1946.

Meadowsweet: Flower cls corvette; 925; 205 x 33; 16; 85; one 4-in; C. Hill & Sons, Bristol, 1942; 1951, Ned Mij voor de Walvishaart NV, Holland, converted to whale catcher, rnd Gerrit W Vinke; b/up South Africa 1965.

Mediator: Bustler cls tug; 1800; 205 x 38½; 15; 42; one 3-in; H. Robb, Leith, 1944; 1965, Tsavliris (Salvage & Towage), Greece, rnd Nisos Zakynthos;

Medusa: coastal minelayer; 535; 177 x 31; 12; 52; 52 mines; Harland & Wolff, Belfast, 1915; ex-coastal monitor M-29, 1925; converted depot ship, rnd Talbot, 1941; rnd Medway II, 1943; rnd Medusa, 1944; b/up Dover 1947.

Medway: submarine depot ship; 14,600; 580 x 85; 16; 400; six 4-in; Vickers-Armstrongs, Barrow, 1929; torpedoed and sunk by U-372 off Port Said, June 30, 1942.

Melbreak: Hunt cls destroyer — Albrighton type; 1050; 280 x 31½; 27; 168; four 4-in, two 21-in tt; Swan Hunter & Wigham Richardson, Wallsend, 1942; b/up Grays 1956.

Melita: Algerine cls minesweeper; 950; 235 x 35½; 16½; 104; one 4-in; Redfern Construction Co, Toronto, 1943; rnd Satellite (RNVR drillship) 1947, rnd Melita, 1951; b/up Llanelly 1959.

Melpomene: coastal minelayer; 535; 177 x 31; 12; 52; 52 mines; Harland & Wolff, Belfast, 1915; ex-coastal monitor M-31, 1925; rnd Menelaus, 1941; b/up Llanelly 1948.

Mendip: Hunt cls destroyer — Atherstone type; 1000; 280 x 29; 27½; 146; four 4-in; Swan Hunter & Wigham Richardson, Wallsend, 1940; transferred 1948 to China, rnd Lin Fu, rtnd RN 1949, rnd Mendip; transferred 1949 to Egypt, rnd Mohamed Ali El Kebir, rnd Ibraham El Awal, 1951;

captured off Haifa by Israel, Oct 31, 1956, rnd *Haifa;* withdrawn from service 1972.

Meon: River cls frigate; 1370; 301½ x 36½; 19; 140; two 4-in; A. & J. Inglis, Glasgow, 1943; b/up Blyth 1966.

Mermaid: Modified Black Swan cls sloop; 1430; 299½ x 38; 20; 192; six 4-in; Wm Denny & Bros, Dumbarton, 1944; transferred 1959 to West German Navy, rnd *Scharnhorst;* b/up 1972.

Meteor: M cls destroyer; 1920; 362½ x 37; 36½; 190; six 4.7-in, one 4-in, four 21-in tt; Alex Stephen & Sons, Linthouse 1942; transferred 1958 to Turkey, rnd *Piyale Pasa;* de-commissioned 1972.

Mewstone: Isles cls trawler; 560; 164 x 27½; 12; 40; one 12-pdr; Cook Welton & Gemmell, Beverley, 1943; sold 1946, buyers not known.

Meynell: Hunt cls destroyer — Atherstone type; 1000; 280 x 29; 27½; 146; four 4-in; Swan Hunter & Wigham Richardson, Wallsend, 1940; transferred 1955 to Ecuador, rnd *Presidente Velasco Ibarra;*

Michael: Algerine cls minesweeper; 950; 235 x 35½; 16½; 104; one 4-in; Redfern Construction Co, Toronto, 1944; b/up Bo'ness 1956.

Middlesbrough: Bangor cls minesweeper; 656; 174 x 28½; 16; 60; one 3-in; Wm Hamilton & Co, Port Glasgow, 1942; transferred 1942 to Indian Navy, rnd *Kumaon;* b/up 1949(?).

Middleton: Hunt cls destroyer — Blankney type; 1050; 280 x 31½; 27; 168; six 4-in; Vickers-Armstrongs, Tyne, 1941; b/up Blyth 1957.

Mignonette: Flower cls corvette; 925; 205 x 33½; 16; 85; one 4-in; Hall Russell, Aberdeen, 1941; transferred 1946 to Greek Navy (nothing more known).

Milfoil: Modified Flower cls corvette; 980; 208¼ x 33; 16; 109; one 4-in; Morton Eng & DD Co, Quebec, 1942; transferred 1942 to US Navy, rnd *Intensity;* 1950, Balleneros Ltd SA, Uruguay, converted to whale catcher, rnd *Olympic Promoter;* 1956, Kyokuyo Hogei KK, Japan, rnd *Otori Maru No 5;* b/up Japan 1966.

Milford: Falmouth cls sloop; 1060; 266 x 34; 16; 100; two 4-in; HM Dockyard, Devonport, 1932; b/up Hayle 1949.

Milne: M cls destroyer; 1935; 362½ x 37; 36½; 224; six 4.7-in, one 4-in, four 21-in tt; Scotts SB & E Co, Greenock/John Brown & Co, Clydebank, 1942; transferred 1959 to Turkey, rnd *Alp Arslan;* for disposal 1971.

Mimosa: Flower cls corvette; 925; 205 x 33; 16; 85; one 4-in; C. Hill & Sons, Bristol, 1941; transferred 1941 to French Navy, no name change; torpedoed and sunk by *U-124* in North Atlantic, June 9, 1942.

Minalto: Isles cls trawler; 560; 164 x 27½; 12; 40; one 12-pdr; Cook Welton & Gemmell, Beverley, 1943; 1947, S. Sorvigs Reederi A/S, Norway, converted to cargo ship, rnd *Lillen;* 1956, Partenreed m.s. 'Agricola', West Germany, rnd *Agricola;* 1958, O. Arens, West Germany, rnd *Holstentor;* 1961, H. Melz, West Germany, rnd *Trave;* 1964, Mediteranska Plovdba, Yugoslavia, rnd *Perna;*

Mincarlo: Isles cls trawler; 560; 164 x 27½; 12; 40; one 12-pdr; Ardrossan Dockyard Ltd, Ardrossan, 1944; transferred 1944 to Royal Norwegian Navy, rnd *Tromoy,* rtnd RN 1946; 1948, Skibs A/S Rapid, Norway, converted to cargo ship, rnd *Kristianborg;* 1950, A/S Nordlandslinjen, Norway, rnd *Sverre Hund;* 1961, A/S Grindhaugs Fiskeriselskap, Norway, rnd *Camelia;* 1965, O. Koch, Norway, rnd *Oborg;*

Mindful: BAT cls tug; 783; 143 x 33; 14; 34; one 3-in; Levingston SB, Orange, 1943; ex-USN, transferred Lease/Lend to RN 1943, rtnd USN 1946, rnd *ATR-48;* 1947, Tug Harriet Moran Inc, US, rnd *Gay Moran;* 1949, Tug Sea Lion Inc, US, rnd *Sea Lion;* 1955, Gulf Canal Lines Inc, US, rnd *Harry J. Mosser;* 1957, Mobile Towing & Wrecking Co, US, rnd *Margaret Walsh;* 1966, Foss Launch & Tug Co, US, rnd *Margaret Foss;* 1974, Cementos California SA, Mexico, rnd *CC-7;*

Miner I: coastal minelayer; 350; 122½ x 26½; 10; 24; 10 mines; Philip & Son, Dartmouth, 1939; rnd *Minstrel,* 1962;

sold UK buyers 1966.

Miner II: coastal minelayer; 350; 122½ x 26½; 10; 24; 10 mines; Philip & Son, Dartmouth, 1940; rnd *Gossamer,* 1949; sunk off Dorset coast 1970 after use as target.

Miner III: coastal minelayer; 350; 122½ x 26½; 10; 24; 10 mines; Philip & Son, Dartmouth, 1940;

Miner IV: coastal minelayer; 350; 122½ x 26½; 10; 24; 10 mines; Philip & Son, Dartmouth, 1940; b/up 1964.

Miner V: coastal minelayer; 350; 122½ x 26½; 10; 24; 10 mines; Philip & Son, Dartmouth, 1941; converted to cable lighter, rnd *Britannic, 1960;*

Miner VI: coastal minelayer; 350; 122½ x 26½; 10; 24; 10 mines; Philip & Son, Dartmouth, 1942; 1966, E. Zammit, Malta, converted to ferry, rnd *Minor Eagle;*

Miner VII: coastal minelayer; 350; 122½ x 26½; 10; 24; 10 mines; Philip & Son, Dartmouth, 1944; converted to trials ship, rnd *ETV 7,* then rnd *Steady,* 1959.

Miner VIII: coastal minelayer; 350; 122½ x 26½; 10; 24; 10 mines; Philip & Son, Dartmouth, 1943; rnd *Mindful* 1963; sold UK buyers 1965.

Minerva: coastal minelayer; 535; 177 x 31; 12; 52; 52 mines; Harland & Wolff, Belfast, 1915; ex-coastal monitor *M-33,* 1925; hulked, rnd *C-23,* 1940;

Minstrel: Algerine cls minesweeper; 950; 235 x 35½; 16½; 104; one 4-in; Redfern Construction Co, Toronto, 1945; transferred 1947 to Royal Siamese Navy, rnd *Phosamton;*

Minuet: Dance cls trawler; 530; 160½ x 27½; 11½; 35; one 4-in; Ferguson Bros, Port Glasgow, 1941; transferred 1946 to Italian Navy, rnd *RD-307;* used as target mid-1960s.

Miscou: Isles cls trawler; 560; 164 x 27½; 12; 40; one 12-pdr; Collingwood Shipyards, Collingwood, Ont, 1942; ex-*Campenia,* 1942; ex-*Bowell,* 1942; 1946, Hvides Rederi A/S, Norway, converted to cargo ship, rnd *Cleveland;* 1950, A/S Nordlandslinjen, Norway, rnd *Sigurd Hund;* 1964, A/S Vestfar, Norway, rnd *Vestfar;* 1971, A. Hansen, Norway, rnd *Hans Hansen;*

Mixol: oiler; 4326; 270 x 38½; 11½; --; --; Caledon SB & E Co, Dundee, 1916;

1948, Counties Ship Management, London, rnd *Whitebrook;* 1953, Nolido Compania de Navegacion SA, Panama, rnd *Irene M;* b/up Belgium 1953.

Modbury: Hunt cls destroyer — Albrighton type; 1050; 280 x 31½; 27; 168; four 4-in, two 21-in tt; Swan Hunter & Wigham Richardson, Wallsend, 1942; transferred 1942 to Royal Hellenic Navy, rnd *Miaoulis,* rtnd RN 1960; b/up Greece 1960.

Mohawk: Tribal cls destroyer; 1870; 377 x 36½; 36½; 190; eight 4.7-in, four 21-in tt; J. I. Thornycroft & Co, Southampton, 1938; torpedoed by Italian destroyer *Tarigo* in central Mediterranean, Apr 16, 1941, and sunk by RN.

Monkshood: Flower cls corvette; 925; 205 x 33; 16; 85; one 4-in; Fleming & Ferguson, Paisley, 1941; 1948, Union Whaling Co, South Africa, converted to whale catcher, rnd *W. R. Strang;* 1957, Taiyo Kyokyo KK, Japan, rnd *Toshi Maru No 1,* rnd *Toshi Maru,* 1960; b/up Japan 1965-66.

Monnow: River cls frigate; 1370; 301½ x 36½; 19; 140; two 4-in; C. Hill & Sons, Bristol, 1944; transferred 1945 to Denmark, rnd *Holger Danske;* sold Odense shipbreakers 1960.

Montbretia: Flower cls corvette; 925; 205 x 33; 16; 85; one 4-in; Fleming & Ferguson, Paisley, 1941; transferred 1941 to Royal Norwegian Navy, no name change; sunk by U-boat in North Atlantic, Nov 18, 1942.

Montclare: depot ship; 16,314 grt; 570 x 70; 16; 480; four 4-in; J. Brown & Co, Clydebank, 1922; ex-passenger liner (Canadian Pacific SS Co, Montreal), bought RN 1942 and converted; b/up Inverkeithing 1958.

Montenol: Belgol cls oiler; 5620; 335 x 41½; 14; 39; --; Wm Gray & Co, West Hartlepool, 1917; torpedoed off Africa, May 21, 1942, and sunk by RN.

Montgomery: Town cls destroyer; 1090; 314⅓ x 30½; 30; 122; one 4-in, three 21-in tt; Bath Iron Works, Bath, 1918; ex-USN *Wickes,* transferred 1940 to RN; b/up Tyne 1945.

Montrose: Scott cls destroyer; 1530; 332½ x 31¾; 31; 183; two 4.7-in, three 21-in tt; Hawthorn Leslie, Hebburn,

1918; b/up Blyth 1946.

Montserrat: Colony cls frigate; 1430; 304 x 37½; 18; 120; three 3-in; Walsh Kaiser Co, Providence, 1944; ex-USN *PF-82,* transferred Lease/Lend to RN rnd *Hornby,* rnd *Montserrat* 1944, rtnd USN 1946; sold Quincy shipbreakers 1947.

Moon: Algerine cls minesweeper; 950; 235 x 35½; 16½; 104; one 4-in; Redfern Construction Co, Toronto, 1943; ex-*Mimico* (RCN), 1943; b/up Gateshead 1957.

Moonstone: Gem cls trawler; 615; 154½ x 25½; 12; 18; one 4-in; Cook Welton & Gemmell, Beverley, 1934; ex-*Lady Madeleine* (Jutland Amalgamated Trawlers, Hull) bought RN 1939; 1946, Iago Steam Trawler Co, London, rnd *Red Lancer;* b/up Glasson Dock 1964.

Moor: Moor cls mooring vessel; 720; 148 x 29; 9; --; one 12-pdr; Bow McLachlan & Co, Paisley, 1919; mined at Malta, Apr 8, 1942.

Moorburn: Admiralty type mooring vessel; 1000; 163½ x 37; 9; --; one 12-pdr; Goole SB & Repairing Co, Goole, 1942; sold Glasgow buyers 1962.

Moorcock: Admiralty type mooring vessel; 1000; 163½ x 37; 9; --; one 12-pdr; Goole SB & Repairing Co, Goole, 1942; b/up Troon 1963.

Moordale: Moor cls mooring vessel; 720; 148 x 29; 9; --; one 12-pdr; Bow McLachlan & Co, Paisley, 1919; 1961, Matthews Wrightson Burbidge, London, (for re-sale?).

Mooress: Admiralty type mooring vessel; 1000; 163½ x 37; 9; --; one 12-pdr; Goole SB & Repairing Co, Goole, 1943; 1962, Davies & Newman, London, (for re-sale?).

Moorfield: Admiralty type mooring vessel; 1000; 163½ x 37; 9; --; one 12-pdr; Wm Simons & Co, Renfrew, 1941; sold Portsmouth shipbreakers, 1963.

Moorfire: Admiralty type mooring vessel; 1000; 163½ x 37; 9; --; one 12-pdr; HM Dockyard, Devonport, 1941; b/up St Davids on Forth 1963.

Moorfly: Admiralty type mooring vessel; 1000; 163½ x 37; 9; --; one 12-pdr; Goole SB & Repairing Co,

Goole, 1942; 1963, A. Georgacacos & Co, Greece, rnd *Sophia G;* sprang leak, foundered near Skopelos Island, Nov 12, 1967.

Moorfowl: Moor cls mooring vessel; 720; 148 x 29; 9; --; one 12-pdr; Bow McLachlan & Co, Paisley, 1919; 1962, Matthews Wrightson Burbidge, London (for re-sale?).

Moorgrass: Admiralty type mooring vessel; 1000; 163½ x 37; 9; --; one 12-pdr; Goole SB & Repairing Co, Goole, 1942; b/up Troon 1963.

Moorgrieve: Admiralty type mooring vessel; 1000; 163½ x 37; 9; --; one 12-pdr; Goole SB & Repairing Co, Goole, 1945; 1963, NV Bureau Wijsmuller, Holland, converted to salvage ship, rnd *Octopus;* b/up West Germany 1971.

Moorhen: Admiralty type mooring vessel; 1000; 163½ x 37; 9; --; one 12-pdr; Goole SB & Repairing Co, Goole, 1943;

Moorhill: Moor cls mooring vessel; 720; 148 x 29; 9; --; one 12-pdr; Bow McLachlan & Co, Paisley, 1920; sold Madrid buyers 1963.

Moorlake: Moor cls mooring vessel; 720; 148 x 29; 9; --; one 12-pdr; Bow McLachlan & Co, Paisley, 1920; 1946, unknown Ceylon company for wreck removal work off island, (nothing more known).

Moorland: mooring vessel; 720; 145 x 31; 10; --; two 20-mm; Wm Simons & Co, Renfrew, 1939;

Moormyrtle: Admiralty type mooring vessel; 1000; 163½ x 37; 9; --; one 12-pdr; Goole SB & Repairing Co, Goole, 1945; b/up Passage West 1963.

Moorpout: Admiralty type mooring vessel; 1000; 163½ x 37; 9; --; one 12-pdr; HM Dockyard, Chatham, 1944; b/up Belgium 1968.

Moorsman: Admiralty type mooring vessel; 1000; 163½ x 37; 9; --; one 12-pdr; HM Dockyard, Chatham, 1944;

Moorsom: Captain cls frigate; 1140; 289½ x 35; 21; 200; three 3-in; Navy Yard, Boston, 1943; ex-USN Evarts cls destroyer-escort *DE-522,* transferred Lease/Lend to RN 1943, rtnd USN 1945; b/up.

Moorstone: Moor cls mooring vessel; 720; 148 x 29; 9; --; one 12-pdr; Bow

McLachlan & Co, Paisley, 1920; 1950, Mediterranean Shipbreaking & Salvage Co, Malta, no name change; 1951, M. Azmi Alpmen ve Ortaklar-Kollektif Sirketi, Turkey, rnd *Kurtaran;* 1962, M. Taviloglu, Turkey, rnd *Cikaran;*

Morpeth Castle: Castle cls corvette; 1010; 252 x 36¾; 16½; 120; one 4-in; Wm Pickersgill & Sons, Sunderland, 1944; b/up Llanelly 1960.

Morris Dance: Dance cls trawler; 530; 160½ x 27½; 11½; 35; one 4-in; Goole SB & Repairing Co, Goole, 1940; sold Belgian owners 1946.

Mosquito: Locust cls river gunboat; 585; 197 x 33; 17; 74; two 4-in, one 3.7-in howitzer; J. I. Thornycroft & Co, Southampton, 1939; sunk by German aircraft off Dunkirk, June 1, 1940.

Moth: Insect cls river gunboat; 625; 237½ x 36; 14; 65; two 6-in, one 3-in; Sunderland SB Co, Sunderland, 1916; scuttled at Hong Kong, Dec 12, 1941; salved by Japanese and refitted, rnd *Suma;* mined Mar 19, 1945.

Mounsey: Captain cls frigate; 1140; 289½ x 35; 21; 200; three 3-in; Navy Yard, Boston, 1943; ex-USN Evarts cls destroyer-escort *DE-524,* transferred Lease/Lend to RN 1943, rtnd USN 1946; sold Philadelphia shipbreakers 1946.

Mourne: River cls frigate; 1370; 301½ x 36½; 19; 140; two 4-in; Smith's Dock Co, Middlesbrough, 1943; torpedoed and sunk by *U-767* off the Lizard, June 15, 1944.

Mousa: Isles cls trawler; 560; 164 x 27½; 12; 40; one 12-pdr; Goole SB & Repairing Co, Goole, 1942; transferred 1946 to Italian Navy, rnd *RD-311;* used as target, mid-1960s.

Moy: Mersey cls trawler; 551; 148 x 22¾; 11; 20; two 3-in; Cochrane & Sons, Selby, 1917; ex-*Alexander Hills,* 1920; 1945, Oddson & Co, Hull, rnd *Coral Island,* rnd *Arnarnes,* 1949; 1949, Ocean Steam Trawling Co, Anlaby, rnd *Forbes;* 1950, Boyd Line, Hull, rnd *Arctic Trapper;* b/up Sunderland 1952.

Moyola: River cls frigate; 1370; 301½ x 36½; 19; 140; two 4-in; Smith's Dock Co, Middlesbrough, 1943; transferred 1944 to French Navy, rnd *Tonkinois,*

rnd *La Confiance,* 1953; condemned 1961, rnd *Q-308;* b/up Brest.

Mull: Isles cls trawler; 560; 164 x 27½; 12; 40; one 12-pdr; Cook Welton & Gemmell, Beverley, 1941; transferred 1947 to Army Dept, converted to cargo ship no name change;

Mullet: Fish cls trawler; 670; 162 x 25¼; 11; 35; one 4-in; Cochrane & Sons, Selby, 1942; 1946, Consolidated Fisheries, Grimsby, rnd *Neath Castle;* b/up Dunston 1960.

Mullion Cove: repair ship; 9700; 447¾ x 56; 11; --; twelve 20-mm; Bartram & Sons, Sunderland, 1945; 1948, Clunies Shipping Co, Greenock, converted to cargo ship, rnd *Margaret Clunies;* 1951, Turnbull Scott & Co, London, rnd *Waynegate;* 1961, Pacifico Cia Naviera SA, Greece, rnd *Katingo;* 1964, Philippine President Lines, Philippines, rnd *President Magsaysay,* rnd *Magsaysay* 1968; caught fire off southern Korea coast, July 19, 1968, towed to Pusan, condemned and b/up.

Mull of Galloway: escort repair ship; 8580; 441½ x 57; 11; 440; eleven 40-mm; North Vancouver Ship Repairs, Vancouver, 1945; launched as *Kinnaird Head;* b/up Hamburg 1965.

Musk: Modified Flower cls corvette; 980; 208¼ x 33; 16; 109; one 4-in; Morton Eng & DD Co, Quebec, 1942; transferred 1943 to US Navy, rnd *Might;* 1950, Balleneros Ltd SA, Uruguay, converted to whale catcher, rnd *Olympic Explorer;* 1956, Kyokuyo Hogei KK, Japan, rnd *Otori Maru No 3,* rnd *Kyo Maru No 12,* 1957;

Musketeer: M cls destroyer; 1920; 362½ x 37; 36½; 190; six 4.7-in, one 4-in, four 21-in tt; Fairfield SB & E Co, Govan, 1942; b/up Sunderland 1955.

Mutine: Algerine cls minesweeper; 950; 235 x 35½; 16½; 104; one 4-in; Harland & Wolff, Belfast, 1943; b/up Barrow 1967.

Myngs: Z cls destroyer; 1730; 362¾ x 35; 36; 220; four 4.5-in, eight 21-in tt; Vickers-Armstrongs, Tyne, 1944; transferred 1955 to Egypt, rnd *El Qaher;* sunk by Israeli aircraft at Berenice, May 16, 1970.

Myosotis: Flower cls corvette; 925;

205 x 33; 16; 85; one 4-in; J. Lewis &
Sons, Aberdeen, 1941; 1946, P/f
Kimbil, Norway, converted to trawler,
rnd *Grunningur;* 1949, A/S Thor Dahl,
Norway, converted to whale catcher,
rnd *Thororn;* b/up Norway 1969.

Myrmidon: M cls destroyer; 1920;
362½ x 37; 36½; 190; six 4.7-in, one
4-in, four 21-in tt; Fairfield SB & E Co,
Govan, 1942; transferred 1942 to
Poland, rnd *Orkan;* torpedoed and
sunk by *U-610,* south of Iceland, Oct 8,
1943.

Myrmidon: Algerine cls minesweeper;
950; 235 x 35½; 16½; 104; one 4-in;
Redfern Construction Co, Toronto,
1945; b/up Briton Ferry 1958.

Myrtle: Berberis cls crawler; 357 grt;
140⅓ x 24; 11; 18; one 12-pdr; Cook
Welton & Gemmell, Beverley, 1928;
ex-*St Irene* (T. Hamling & Co, Hull),
bought RN 1939; mined in Thames
Estuary, June 14, 1940.

Mystic: Algerine cls minesweeper;
950; 235 x 35½; 16½; 104; one 4-in;
Redfern Construction Co, Toronto,
1945; b/up Llanelly 1958.

Nabob: Smiter cls escort carrier;
11,420; 496 x 69½; 16; 650; 20 aircraft,
two 5-in; Seattle-Tacoma SB Corp.
Tacoma, 1943; ex-USN *Edisto,*
BCVE-41, transferred Lease/Lend to
RN 1943; transferred to RCN;
damaged by torpedo from *U-354* off
North Cape, Aug 22, 1944; towed to
Hendrik Ido Ambacht, Holland, 1947,
for breaking-up; hull bought 1951,
converted into merchant ship for
Roland Linie Schiff-Gesellschaft,
Bremen, no name change; 1967,
Chi-Shihi Nav Corp, Taiwan, rnd
Glory;

Nadder: River cls frigate; 1370; 301½
x 36½; 19; 140; two 4-in; Smith's Dock
Co, Middlesbrough, 1944; transferred
1944 to Indian Navy, rnd *Shamsher;*
transferred 1948 to Pakistan Navy, no
name change; b/up 1959.

Naiad: Dido cls cruiser; 5450; 512 x
50½; 33; 620; ten 5.25-in, six 21-in tt;
Hawthorn Leslie, Hebburn, 1940;
torpedoed and sunk by *U-565* in
Mediterranean, Mar 11, 1942.

Nairana: escort carrier; 14,046; 528½
x 68¼; 17; 558; 20-24 aircraft, two 4-in;
John Brown & Co, Clydebank, 1943;
building for Port Line, London,
purchased by Admiralty 1939;
transferred 1946 to Royal Netherlands
Navy, rnd *Karel Doorman,* rtnd RN
1948; 1948, Port Line, London,
converted to cargo ship, rnd *Port
Victor;* b/up Faslane 1971.

Napier: N cls destroyer; 1760; 348 x
35¾; 36; 218; six 4.7-in, one 4-in, five
21-in tt; Fairfield SB & E Co, Govan,
1941; transferred to RAN; rtnd 1945;
b/up Briton Ferry 1956.

Narborough: Captain cls frigate; 1400;
306 x 36⅝; 23½; 220; three 3-in;
Bethlehem-Hingham Shipyard, 1944;
ex-USN Buckley cls destroyer-escort
DE-569, transferred Lease/Lend to RN
1944, rtnd USN 1946; b/up.

Narcissus: Flower cls corvette; 925;
205 x 33; 16; 85; one 4-in; J. Lewis &
Sons, Aberdeen, 1941; 1946, Soc Anon
Maritime & Commerciale, Switzerland,
converted to cargo ship, rnd *Este;*
1960, Diogo & Cia, Brazil, rnd *Planeta;*
aground near Ilheus, Brazil, June 27,
1969, total loss.

Narwhal: Porpoise cls minelaying
submarine; 1520/2117; 293 x 25½;
15¾/8¾; 55; 50 mines, six 21-in tt, one
4-in; Vickers-Armstrongs, Barrow,
1936; lost (mined?) off Norway, July
1940.

Nasprite: petrol carrier; 1600; 214 x
33¼; 11; 23; --; Blythswood SB & E Co,
Scotstoun, 1941; b/up Willebroek
1964.

Nasturtium: Flower cls corvette; 925;
205 x 33; 16; 85; one 4-in; Smith's
Dock Co, Middlesbrough, 1940; ex-*La
Paimpolaise,* 1940; 1948, Greek
government, rnd *Cania;* transferred to
Royal Hellenic Navy, converted to
lighthouse tender, rnd *St Lykoudis;*

Neave: Isles cls trawler; 560; 164 x
27½; 12; 40; one 12-pdr; Cook Welton
& Gemmell, Beverley, 1942; 1951,
British Wheeler Process, Liverpool,
converted to oil sludge vessel, rnd
Tulipbank; 1963, Elderslie Tank &
Boiler Cleaning Co, Glasgow, no name
change;

Nelson: Nelson cls battleship; 33,950;
710 x 106; 23; 1640; nine 16-in, twelve

6-in, six 4.7-in, two 24.5-in tt;
Armstrong Whitworth & Co,
Newcastle, 1927; b/up Inverkeithing
1949.

Nene: River cls frigate; 1370; 301½ x
36½; 19; 140; two 4-in; Smith's Dock
Co, Middlesbrough, 1943; b/up Briton
Ferry 1955.

Nepal: N cls destroyer; 1760; 348 x
35¾; 36; 183; six 4.7-in, one 4-in, five
21-in tt; J. I. Thornycroft & Co,
Southampton, 1942; ex-*Norseman,*
1942; b/up Briton Ferry 1956.

Nepeta: Modified Flower cls corvette;
980; 208¼ x 33; 16; 109; one 4-in;
Morton Eng & DD Co, Quebec, 1943;
transferred 1943 to US Navy, rnd *Pert;*
1950, Balleneros Ltd SA, Uruguay,
converted to whale catcher, rnd
Olympic Leader; 1956, Kyokuyo Hogei
KK, Japan, rnd *Otori Maru No 1,* rnd
Kyo Maru No 15, 1957;

Neptune: Leander cls cruiser; 7175;
554½ x 55¼; 32½; 680; eight 6-in,
eight 4-in, eight 21-in tt; HM Dockyard,
Portsmouth, 1934; sunk off Libyan
coast by mine, Dec 19, 1941.

Nerissa: N cls destroyer; 1760; 348 x
35¾; 36; 183; six 4.7-in, one 4-in, five
21-in tt; John Brown & Co, Clydebank,
1940; transferred 1940 to Poland rnd
Piorun, rtnd RN 1946, rnd *Noble;* b/up
Dunston 1955.

Ness: River cls frigate; 1370; 301½ x
36½; 19; 140; two 4-in; H. Robb, Leith,
1942; b/up Newport 1956.

Nestor: N cls destroyer; 1760; 348 x
35¾; 36; 183; six 4.7-in, one 4-in, five
21-in tt; Fairfield SB & E Co, Govan,
1941; transferred to RAN; sunk by
German aircraft in central
Mediterranean, June 15, 1942.

Newark: Town cls destroyer; 1060;
315½ x 30½; 30; 122; one 4-in, three
21-in tt; Union Iron Works, San
Francisco, 1918; ex-USN *Ringgold,*
transferred 1940 to RN; b/up Bo'ness
1947.

Newcastle: Southampton cls cruiser;
9100; 591½ x 61⅔; 32; 830; twelve
6-in, eight 4-in, six 21-in tt;
Vickers-Armstrongs, Tyne, 1937;
ex-*Minotaur,* 1936; b/up Faslane 1959.

Newfoundland: Uganda cls cruiser;
8875; 555½ x 62; 31½; 950; nine 6-in,
eight 4-in, six 21-in tt; Swan Hunter &

Wigham Richardson, Wallsend, 1942;
transferred 1959 to Peru, rnd
Almirante Grau, rnd *Capitan Quinones*
1973;

Newhaven: Bangor cls minesweeper;
656; 174 x 28½; 16; 60; one 3-in; Wm
Hamilton & Co, Port Glasgow, 1942;
transferred 1942 to Indian Navy, rnd
Carnatic; b/up 1949(?).

Newmarket: Town cls destroyer;
1060; 315½ x 30½; 30; 122; one 4-in,
three 21-in tt; Union Iron Works, San
Francisco, 1918; ex-USN *Robinson,*
transferred 1940 to RN; b/up Llanelly
1946.

Newport: Town cls destroyer; 1060;
315½ x 30½; 30; 122; three 4-in, six
21-in tt; Bethlehem SB, Fore River,
1918; ex-USN *Sigourney,* transferred
1940 to RN; b/up Granton 1947.

Niagara: Town cls destroyer; 1060;
314⅓ x 30½; 30; 122; three 4-in, six
21-in tt; Bethlehem SB, Fore River,
1919; ex-USN *Thatcher,* transferred
1940 to Royal Canadian Navy; sold
Hamilton, Ont, shipbreakers 1948.

Nigella: Flower cls corvette; 925; 205
x 33; 16; 85; one 4-in; Philip & Son,
Dartmouth, 1941; 1947, Wheelock
Marden, Hong Kong, converted to
cargo ship, rnd *Nigelock;* lost Min
River, March 1955.

Niger: Halcyon cls minesweeper; 815;
245 x 33½; 17; 80; two 4-in; J. S. White
& Co, Cowes, 1936; mined off Iceland,
July 5, 1942.

Nigeria: Fiji cls cruiser; 8525; 555½ x
62; 33; 980; twelve 6-in, eight 4-in, six
21-in tt; Vickers-Armstrongs, Tyne,
1940; transferred 1957 to India, rnd
Mysore;

Nimble: Nimble cls tug; 890; 175 x
35¾; 16; 43; one 3-in; Fleming &
Ferguson, Paisley, 1942;

Nith: River cls frigate; 1370; 301½ x
36½; 19; 140; two 4-in; H. Robb, Leith,
1943; transferred 1950 to Egypt, rnd
Domiat; sunk by cruiser
Newfoundland off Suez, Nov 1, 1956.

Nizam: N cls destroyer; 1760; 348 x
35¾; 36; 183; six 4.7-in, one 4-in,
five 21-in tt; John Brown & Co,
Clydebank, 1941; transferred to RAN;
rtnd 1945; b/up Grays 1955.

Noble: N cls destroyer; 1760; 348 x
35¾; 36; 183; six 4.7-in, one 4-in, five

21-in tt; Wm Denny & Bros,
Dumbarton, 1941; transferred 1942 to
Royal Netherlands Navy, rnd *Van
Galen;* b/up Hendrik Ido Ambacht
1957.
Nonpareil: N cls destroyer; 1760; 348
x 35¾; 36; 183; six 4.7-in, one 4-in, five
21-in tt; Wm Denny & Bros,
Dumbarton, 1941; transferred 1942 to
Royal Netherlands Navy, rnd *Tjerk
Hiddes;* transferred 1951 to
Indonesian Navy, rnd *Gadja Mada;*
b/up Surabaya Harbour 1961.
Norfolk: Norfolk cls cruiser; 9925; 630
x 66; 32¼; 820; eight 8-in, eight 4-in,
eight 21-in tt; Fairfield SB & E Co,
Govan, 1930; b/up Newport 1950.
Norman: N cls destroyer; 1760; 348 x
35¾; 36; 183; six 4.7-in, one 4-in, five
21-in tt; J. I. Thornycroft & Co,
Southampton, 1941; transferred to
RAN; rtnd 1945; b/up Newport 1958.
Northway: landing ship, dock; 7930;
457¾ x 72; 15; 260; one 4-in; Newport
News SB & DD Co, Newport News,
1943; ex-USN *Cutlass, (LSD-11),*
transferred Lease/Lend to RN 1943,
rtnd USN 1946; 1953, Suwanee SS Co,
Florida, partly converted to rail ferry,
rnd *Jose-Marti;* 1956, West Indies Fruit
SS Co, Florida, converted to
passenger-car ferry, rnd *City of
Havana;* 1962, West German Navy,
converted to accommodation ship,
rnd *WS-1;* 1966, Atlantic SN Co,
London, rnd *Celtic Ferry;* sold
Hamburg shipbreakers 1974.
Nubian: Tribal cls destroyer; 1870; 377
x 36½; 36½; 190; eight 4.7-in, four
21-in tt; J. I. Thornycroft & Co,
Southampton, 1938; b/up Briton Ferry
1949.
Nyasaland: Colony cls frigate; 1430;
304 x 37½; 18; 120; three 3-in;
Walsh-Kaiser Co, Providence, 1944;
ex-USN *PF-83,* transferred
Lease/Lend to RN, rnd *Hoste* rnd
Nyasaland 1944, rtnd USN 1946; sold
Chester, Pa, shipbreakers 1947.

Oak: Berberis cls trawler; 357 grt;
140⅓ x 24; 11; 18; one 12-pdr; Cook
Welton & Gemmell, Beverley, 1928;
ex-*St Romanus* (T. Hamling & Co,

Hull), acquired by RN 1939; 1946,
Unity Fishing Co, Hull, rnd *St Stephen;*
1949, Cairo Fishing Co, Hull, rnd *Lady
June;* 1952, G. F. Sleight & Sons,
Grimsby, rnd *Recepto;* b/up Belgium
1956.
Oakham Castle: Castle cls corvette;
1010; 252 x 36¾; 16½; 120; one 4-in;
A. & J. Inglis, Glasgow, 1944;
transferred 1958 to Air Ministry,
converted to weather ship, rnd
Weather Reporter;
Oakley: Hunt cls destroyer —
Blankney type; 1050; 280 x 31½; 27;
168; six 4-in; Vickers-Armstrongs,
Tyne, 1941; transferred 1941 to
Poland, rnd *Kujawiak;* mined off
Malta, June 16, 1942.
Oakley: Hunt cls destroyer —
Blankney type; 1050; 280 x 31½; 27;
168; six 4-in; Yarrow & Co, Scotstoun,
1942; ex-*Tickham,* 1942; transferred
1957 to West German Navy, rnd
Gneisenau; b/up 1972.
Obdurate: O cls destroyer; 1540; 345 x
35; 36; 176; four 4-in, 60 mines; Wm
Denny & Bros, Dumbarton, 1942; b/up
Inverkeithing 1964.
Obedient: O cls destroyer; 1540; 345 x
35; 36; 176; four 4-in, 60 mines; Wm
Denny & Bros, Dumbarton, 1943; b/up
Blyth 1962.
Oberon: O cls submarine; 1311/1892;
275 x 28; 15/9; 54; eight 21-in tt, one
4-in; HM Dockyard, Chatham, 1927;
ex-*O-1,* 1924; b/up Dunston 1945.
Ocean: Colossus cls aircraft carrier;
13,190; 694½ x 112½; 25; 1350; 39-44
aircraft; Alex Stephen & Sons,
Linthouse, 1945; b/up Faslane 1962.
Ocean Salvor: King Salvor cls salvage
vessel; 1440; 216 x 37¾; 12; 72; four
20-mm; Wm Simons & Co, Renfrew,
1943; 1960, Ship & Cargo (Salvage),
London, no name change; b/up
Karachi 1967.
Oceanway: landing ship, dock; 7930;
457¾ x 72; 15; 260; one 4-in; Newport
News SB & DD Co, Newport News,
1944; ex-USN *Dagger, (LSD-12);*
transferred Lease/Lend to RN 1944,
rtnd USN 1946; transferred 1946 to
Greece, rnd *Okeanos,* rtnd USN 1952;
transferred 1952 to France, rnd
Foudre; withdrawn 1970.
Octavia: Algerine cls minesweeper;

950; 235 x 35½; 16½; 104; one 4-in;
Redfern Construction Co, Toronto,
1943; b/up Gateshead 1950.

Odin: O cls submarine; 1475/2030;
283½ x 28; 17½/9; 54; eight 21-in tt,
one 4-in; HM Dockyard, Chatham,
1928; sunk by Italian destroyer in Gulf
of Taranto, June 13, 1940.

Odzani: River cls frigate; 1370; 301½ x
36½; 19; 140; two 4-in; Smith's Dock
Co, Middlesbrough, 1943; b/up
Newport 1957.

Offa: O cls destroyer; 1540; 345 x 35;
36; 176; four 4.7-in, one 4-in, four 21-in
tt; Fairfield SB & E Co, Govan, 1941;
transferred 1949 to Pakistan, rnd
Tariq; b/up Sunderland 1959.

Olcades: oiler; 15,030; 430 x 57; 11;
--; --; Workman Clark, Belfast, 1918;
ex-*British Beacon,* 1937; b/up Blyth
1953.

Oleander: oiler; 15,000; 430 x 57; 11;
--; --; HM Dockyard, Pembroke, 1922;
damaged and beached Harstad Bay,
May 26, 1940, sunk later.

Oligarch: oiler; 15,000; 430 x 57; 11;
--; --; Workman Clark, Belfast, 1918;
ex-*British Lantern,* 1937; loaded with
obsolete ammunition and scuttled in
Red Sea, June 1946.

Olive: Tree cls trawler; 530; 164 x 27½;
11½; 35; one 12-pdr; Hall Russell,
Aberdeen, 1940; 1949, S. A. Olsson,
Sweden, converted to cargo ship, rnd
Samba; lost, aground near Lerwick,
Dec 28, 1956.

Olna: oiler; 15,000; 430 x 57; 11; --; --;
HM Dockyard, Devonport, 1921; sunk
by aircraft, Suda Bay, May 18, 1941.

Olna: oiler; 25,096; 562 x 70; 17; 77;
one 4-in; Swan Hunter & Wigham
Richardson, Wallsend, 1945; b/up
Castellon 1967.

Olwen: oiler; 13,690; 419½ x 54½; 10;
--; --; Palmers SB & Iron Co, Jarrow,
1917; ex-*British Light,* bought by
Admiralty 1922; 1949, Gulf SS,
Karachi, rnd *Mushtari;* b/up Pakistan
1959.

Olympus: O cls submarine;
1475/2030; 283½ x 28; 17½/9; 54;
eight 21-in tt, one 4-in; Wm
Beardmore, Dalmuir, 1929; sunk by
mine off Malta, May 8, 1942.

Olynthus: oiler; 15,000; 430; x 57; 11;
--; --; Swan Hunter & Wigham

Richardson, Wallsend, 1918;
ex-*British Star,* bought by Admiralty
1922; 1947, Rapp Hatch & Co, London,
no name change; 1947, Ditta Luigi
Rittaluga Vapori, Italy, rnd
Pensilvania; b/up Italy 1960.

Onslaught: O cls destroyer; 1540; 345
x 35; 36; 176; four 4.7-in, one 4-in, four
21-in tt; Fairfield SB & E Co, Govan,
1942; ex-*Pathfinder,* 1941: transferred
1950 to Pakistan, rnd *Tughril;*

Onslow: O cls destroyer; 1550; 345 x
35; 36; 217; four 4.7-in, one 4-in, four
21-in tt; John Brown & Co, Clydebank,
1941; ex-*Pakenham,* 1941; transferred
1949 to Pakistan, rnd *Tippu Sultan;*

Onyx: Algerine cls minesweeper; 950;
235 x 35½; 16½; 104; one 4-in;
Harland & Wolff, Belfast, 1943; b/up
Inverkeithing 1967.

Ophelia: Shakespearian cls trawler;
545; 164 x 27¾; 12; 35; one 12-pdr;
Goole SB & Repairing Co, Goole,
1940; 1946, Partrederiet Engerbretsen
& Hauan, Norway, rnd *Tottan,*
converted to sealer, 1951; 1960, A/S
Rieber & Co, Norway, rnd *Kvitfjell;*
1968, Carino Co, Canada, no name
change; 1972, interfish Ltd, Canada,
no name change;

Opossum: Modified Black Swan cls
sloop; 1430; 299½ x 38; 20; 192; six
4-in; Wm Denny & Bros, Dumbarton,
1945; b/up Plymouth 1960.

Opportune: O cls destroyer; 1540; 345
x 35; 36; 176; four 4-in, 60 mines; J. I.
Thornycroft & Co, Southampton, 1942;
b/up Milford Haven 1955.

Orangeleaf: Leaf cls oiler; 12,370; 425
x 54½; 14; 26; --; Sir J. L. Thompson &
Sons, Sunderland, 1917; ex-*Bornol,*
1917; b/up Briton Ferry 1948.

Orcadia: Algerine cls minesweeper;
950; 235 x 35½; 16½; 104; one 4-in;
Port Arthur SB Co, Port Arthur, 1944;
b/up Briton Ferry 1958.

Orchis: Flower cls corvette; 925; 205 x
33; 16; 85; one 4-in; Harland & Wolff,
Belfast, 1940; irreparably damaged by
mine or torpedo off Normandy, Aug
21, 1944, beached as total loss.

Orestes: Algerine cls minesweeper;
950; 235 x 35½; 16½; 104; one 4-in;
Lobnitz & Co, Renfrew, 1943; b/up
Troon 1963.

Orfasy: Isles cls trawler; 560; 164 x

27½; 12; 40; one 12-pdr; A. Hall,
Aberdeen, 1942; sunk by U-boat off
West Africa, Oct 22, 1943.
Oriana: BAT cls tug; 783; 143 x 33; 14;
34; one 3-in; Gulfport Boilerworks &
Eng Co, Port Arthur, 1942; ex-USN
BAT-1, transferred Lease/Lend to RN
1942, rtnd USN 1946; 1946, (owners
not known) rnd *Ocean Pride;* 1947,
(owners not known) rnd *Pan America;*
1956, N. V. Bureau Wijsmuller,
Holland, rnd *Zeeland;* 1964, Tunisia
Navy, rnd *Ras Adar;*
Oribi: O cls destroyer; 1540; 345 x 35;
36; 176; four 4.7-in, one 4-in, four 21-in
tt; Fairfield SB & E Co, Govan, 1941;
transferred 1946 to Turkey, rnd
Gayret; decommissioned.
Orion: Leander cls cruiser; 7215;
554½ x 55½; 32½; 680; eight 6-in,
eight 4-in, eight 21-in tt; HM Dockyard,
Devonport, 1934; b/up Troon 1949.
Oronsay: Isles cls trawler; 560; 164 x
27½; 12; 40; one 12-pdr; Cochrane &
Sons, Selby, 1944; sold 1946, buyers
not known.
Orpheus: O cls submarine;
1475/2030; 283½ x 28; 17½/9; 54;
eight 21-in tt, one 4-in; Wm
Beardmore, Dalmuir, 1929; sunk by
Italian destroyer off Tobruk, June 27,
1940.
Orsay: Isles cls trawler; 560; 164 x
27½; 12; 40; three 20-mm; Cochrane &
Sons, Selby, 1945; sold Dutch owners
1958.
Orwell: O cls destroyer; 1540; 345 x
35; 36; 176; four 4-in, 60 mines; J. I.
Thornycroft & Co, Southampton, 1942;
b/up Newport 1965.
Osiris: O cls submarine; 1475/2030;
283½ x 28; 17½/9; 54; eight 21-in tt,
one 4-in; Vickers-Armstrongs, Barrow,
1928; b/up Durban 1946.
Oswald: O cls submarine; 1475/2030;
283½ x 28; 17½/9; 54; eight 21-in tt,
one 4-in; Vickers-Armstrongs, Barrow,
1929; rammed and sunk by Italian
destroyer *Ugolino Vivaldi* in Ionian
Sea, Aug 1, 1940.
Othello: Shakespearian cls trawler;
545; 164 x 27¾; 12; 35; one 12-pdr;
Hall Russell, Aberdeen, 1942;
transferred 1946 to Italian Navy, rnd
RD-310; used as target, mid-1960s.
Otus: O cls submarine; 1475/2030;

283½ x 28; 17½/9; 54; eight 21-in tt,
one 4-in; Vickers-Armstrongs, Barrow,
1929; sold and scuttled off Durban,
1946.
Otway: O cls submarine; 1350/1870;
278½ x 27¾; 15½/9; 54; eight 21-in tt,
one 4-in; Vickers-Armstrongs, Barrow,
1927; ex-*AO-2,* transferred from Royal
Australian Navy to RN 1931; b/up
Inverkeithing 1945.
Ouse: Mersey cls trawler; 551; 148 x
22¾; 11; 20; two 3-in; Cochrane &
Sons, Selby, 1917; ex-*Andrew King,*
1920; mined off North Africa, Feb 20,
1941.
Oxford Castle: Castle cls corvette;
1010; 252 x 36¾; 16½; 120; one 4-in;
Harland & Wolff, Belfast, 1944; b/up
Briton Ferry 1960.
Oxley: O cls submarine; 1350/1870;
278½ x 27¾; 15½/9; 54; eight 21-in tt,
one 4-in; Vickers-Armstrongs, Barrow,
1927; ex-*AO-1,* transferred from Royal
Australian Navy to RN 1931; sunk in
collision with HMS *Triton* off Norway,
Sept 10, 1939.
Oxlip: Flower cls corvette; 925; 205 x
33; 16; 85; one 4-in; A. & J. Inglis,
Glasgow, 1941; transferred 1946 to
Eire, rnd *Maev;* b/up Passage West
1972.
Oxna: Isles cls trawler; 560; 164 x
27½; 12; 40; one 12-pdr; A. & J. Inglis,
Glasgow, 1943; transferred 1946 to
War Dept, converted to cargo ship;
b/up 1958-59.

P-32: U cls submarine; 545/735; 196¾
x 16; 11/9; 31; four 21-in tt, one 3-in;
Vickers-Armstrongs, Barrow, 1941;
mined off Tripoli, Aug 18, 1941.
P-33: U cls submarine; 545/735; 196¾
x 16; 11/9; 31; four 21-in tt, one 3-in;
Vickers-Armstrongs, Barrow, 1941;
sunk by Italian surface craft off
Pantelleria, Aug 23, 1941.
P-36: U cls submarine; 545/735; 196¾
x 16; 11/9; 31; four 21-in tt, one 3-in;
Vickers-Armstrongs, Barrow, 1941;
sunk by Italian aircraft at Malta, Mar
31, 1942; raised and beached August
1958, towed out to deep water off
Malta and scuttled.
P-38: U cls submarine; 545/735; 196¾

x 16; 11/9; 31; four 21-in tt, one 3-in,
Vickers-Armstrongs, Barrow, 1941;
sunk by Italian surface craft off
Tunisia, Feb 25, 1942.

P-39: U cls submarine; 545/735; 196¾
x 16; 11/9; 31; four 21-in tt, one 3-in;
Vickers-Armstrongs, Barrow, 1942;
sunk in air attack at Malta, Mar 26,
1942; raised and beached 1943; b/up
1954.

P-47: U cls submarine; 545/735; 196¾
x 16; 11/9; 31; four 21-in tt, one 3-in;
Vickers-Armstrongs, Barrow, 1942;
transferred 1942 to Royal
Netherlands Navy, rnd *Dolfijn,* rtnd RN
1947; b/up 1947.

P-48: U cls submarine; 545/735; 196¾
x 16; 11/9; 31; four 21-in tt, one 3-in;
Vickers-Armstrongs, Barrow, 1942;
sunk by Italian surface craft off Tunis,
Dec 25, 1942.

P-52: U cls submarine; 545/735; 196¾
x 16; 11/9; 31; four 21-in tt, one 3-in;
Vickers-Armstrongs, Barrow, 1943;
transferred 1942 to Poland, rnd *Dzik,*
rtnd RN 1946; transferred 1946 to
Denmark, rnd *U-1,* rnd *Springeren,*
1947, rtnd RN 1957; b/up Faslane
1958.

P-222: S cls submarine; 715/1000; 217
x 23½; 14½/10; 44; seven 21-in tt, one
3-in; Vickers-Armstrongs, Barrow,
1942; ex-*P-72;* sunk by Italian surface
craft off Naples, Dec 12, 1942.

P-311: T cls submarine; 1090/1575;
273½ x 26½; 15¼/9; 59; eleven 21-in
tt, one 4-in; Vickers-Armstrongs,
Barrow, 1942; ex-*P-91,*
ex-*Tutankhamen,* 1942; missing
Mediterranean, Jan, 1943.

P-511: submarine; 530/684; 186¼ x
18; 13½/10½; 33; four 21-in tt, one
3-in; Fore River SB Co, Quincy, 1919;
ex-USN R cls *R-3,* transferred
Lease/Lend to RN, 1941, rtnd USN
1944; sunk Kames Bay, Nov, 1947,
salved, b/up Troon 1948.

P-512: submarine; 530/684; 186¼ x
18; 13½/10½; 33; four 21-in tt, one
3-in; Union Iron Works, San Francisco,
1918; ex-USN R cls *R-17,* transferred
Lease/Lend to RN 1942, rtnd USN
1944; sold Philadelphia shipbreakers
1945.

P-514: submarine; 530/684; 186¼ x
18; 13½/10½; 33; four 21-in tt, one

3-in; Union Iron Works, San Francisco,
1919; ex-USN R cls *R-19,* transferred
Lease/Lend to RN 1942; lost in
collision with minesweeper *Georgian*
in North Atlantic, June 21, 1942.

P-551: submarine; 854/1062; 219¼ x
20¾; 14½/11; 42; four 21-in tt, one
4-in; Bethlehem SB, Quincy, 1923;
ex-USN S cls *S-25,* transferred
Lease/Lend to RN 1941; transferred
1941 to Poland, rnd *Jastrzab;* sunk in
error by RN surface force off north
Norway, May 2, 1942.

P-552: submarine; 854/1062; 219¼ x
20¾; 14½/11; 42; four 21-in tt, one
4-in; Fore River SB Co, Quincy, 1919;
ex-USN S cls *S-1,* transferred
Lease/Lend to RN 1942, rtnd USN
1944; b/up Durban 1946.

P-553: submarine; 854/1062; 219¼ x
20¾; 14½/11; 42; four 21-in tt, one
4-in; Bethlehem SB, Quincy, 1921;
ex-USN S cls *S-21,* transferred
Lease/Lend to RN 1942, rtnd USN
1944; sunk as target, Mar, 1945.

P-554: submarine; 854/1062; 219¼ x
20¾; 14½/11; 42; four 21-in tt, one
4-in; Bethlehem SB, Quincy, 1921;
ex-USN S cls *S-22,* transferred
Lease/Lend to RN, 1942, rtnd USN
1944; sold Philadelphia shipbreakers
1945.

P-555: submarine; 854/1062; 219¼ x
20¾; 14½/11; 42; four 21-in tt, one
4-in; Bethlehem SB, Quincy, 1923;
ex-USN S cls *S-24,* transferred
Lease/Lend to RN 1942, rtnd USN
1945; sunk as target off Portland, 1947.

P-556: submarine; 854/1062; 219¼ x
20¾; 14½/11; 42; four 21-in tt, one
4-in; Bethlehem SB, Quincy, 1923;
ex-USN S cls *S-29,* transferred
Lease/Lend to RN 1942, rtnd USN
1946; stranded Portsmouth harbour
on way to shipbreakers, 1947, salved
and b/up Portsmouth 1965.

P-611: submarine; 624/856; 201½ x
22½; 13¾/9; 40; five 21-in tt, one 3-in;
Vickers-Armstrongs, Barrow, 1942;
ex-*Oruc Reis,* building for Turkey,
taken over by RN; transferred 1942 to
Turkey, rnd *Oruc Reis;* discarded
1957.

P-612: submarine; 624/856; 201½ x
22½; 13¾/9; 40; five 21-in tt, one 3-in;
Vickers-Armstrongs, Barrow, 1942;

ex-*Murat Reis,* building for Turkey, taken over by RN; transferred 1942 to Turkey, rnd *Murat Reis;* discarded 1957.

P-614: submarine; 624/856; 201½ x 22½; 13¾/9; 40; five 21-in tt, one 3-in; Vickers-Armstrongs, Barrow, 1942; ex-*Burak Reis,* building for Turkey, taken over by RN; transferred 1945 to Turkey, rnd *Burak Reis;* discarded 1957.

P-615: submarine; 624/856; 201½ x 22½; 13¾/9; 40; five 21-in tt, one 3-in; Vickers-Armstrongs, Barrow, 1941; ex-*Uluc Ali Reis,* building for Turkey, taken over by RN; sunk by U-boat off Freetown Apr 18, 1943.

P-711: submarine; 880/1260; 231¾ x 22½; 17/8½; 53; eight 21-in tt, two 3.9-in; Cant Nav F. Tosi, Taranto, 1934; ex-Italian *Galilei,* captured in Red Sea by HMS *Moonstone,* June 19, 1940; rnd *X-2;* b/up Port Said 1946.

P-712: submarine; 620/853; 197½ x 21; 14/8½; 45; six 21-in tt, one 3.9-in; Cant Riuniti del Adriatico, Monfalcone, 1936; ex-Italian *Perla,* captured July 1942 in eastern Mediterranean; transferred 1943 to Royal Hellenic Navy, rnd *Matrozos;* b/up 1954.

P-714: submarine; 630/860; 197½ x 20; 14/7.7; 50; four 21-in tt, one 3.9-in; Cant Nav F. Tosi, Taranto, 1942; ex-Italian *Bronzo,* captured intact off Augusta, July 1943; transferred 1944 to French Navy, rnd *Narval;* b/up France 1949.

Padstow: Bangor cls minesweeper; 656; 174 x 28½; 16; 60; one 3-in; Wm Hamilton & Co, Port Glasgow, 1943; transferred 1943 to Indian Navy, rnd *Rohilkhand;* believed b/up India 1961.

Pakenham: P cls destroyer; 1540; 345 x 35; 36; 228; five 4-in, four 21-in tt; Hawthorn Leslie, Hebburn, 1941; ex-*Onslow,* 1941; sunk by Italian MTBs off Sicily, Apr 16, 1943.

Paladin: P cls destroyer; 1540; 345 x 35; 36; 176; four 4-in, eight 21-in tt; John Brown & Co, Clydebank, 1942; b/up Dunston 1962.

Palomares: fighter direction ship; 1900grt; 306½ x 45; 16; --; six 4-in; Wm Doxford & Sons, Sunderland, 1938; ex-refrigerated cargo ship

(MacAndrews & Co, London) bought RN 1941 and converted; 1946, MacAndrews & Co, London, converted to refrigerated cargo ship, no name change; 1959, Red Oluv Svendsen, Denmark, rnd *Mary Sven;* 1961, S.A. Olsson Handels AB, Sweden, rnd *Sarabande;* ashore near Sur after fire, Oct 5, 1961, lost.

Pandora: P cls submarine; 1475/2040; 290 x 28; 17½/9; 50; eight 21-in tt, one 4-in; Vickers-Armstrongs, Barrow, 1930; sunk in air attack at Malta, Mar 31, 1942, raised and beached September, 1943; b/up as lay, 1955.

Pangbourne: Hunt cls minesweeper; 800; 231 x 28½; 16; 74; one 4-in, one 3-in; Lobnitz & Co, Renfrew, 1918; ex-*Padstow,* 1918; b/up Belgium 1947.

Pansy: Flower cls corvette; 925; 205 x 33; 16; 85; one 4-in; Harland & Wolff, Belfast, 1940; rnd *Heartsease,* 1940; transferred 1942 to USN, rnd *Courage,* rtnd RN 1945, rnd *Heartsease;* 1951, Giertsen & Co, A/S, Norway, converted, rnd *Roskva;* 1956, Statius Jansens Rederi A/S, Norway, rnd *Douglas;* 1958, Carrara v Cia, Panama, rnd *Seabird;* lost Celebes between December 1958 and January 1959.

Panther: P cls destroyer; 1540; 345 x 35; 36; 176; five 4-in, four 21-in tt; Fairfield SB & E Co, Govan, 1942; sunk by German aircraft near Scarpanto Oct 9, 1943.

Papua: Colony cls frigate; 1430; 304 x 37½; 18; 120; three 3-in; Walsh-Kaiser Co, Providence, 1944; ex-USN *PF-84,* transferred Lease/Lend to RN 1944, rnd *Howlett,* rnd *Papua,* rtnd USN 1946; 1950, Khedivial Mail Line, Egypt, for conversion to passenger ship, not completed; b/up Bitter Lakes 1956.

Parret: River cls frigate; 1370; 301½ x 36½; 19; 140; two 4-in; Canadian Vickers, Montreal, 1943; ex-USN *PG-109,* transferred Lease/Lend to RN 1943, rtnd USN 1946; sold 1948, b/up.

Parrsborough: Bangor cls minesweeper; 672; 180 x 28½; 16; 60; one 3-in; Dufferin SB Co, Toronto, 1941; b/up Pembroke Dock 1948.

Parthian: P cls submarine; 1475/2040; 290 x 28; 17½/9; 50; eight 21-in tt, one 4-in; HM Dockyard, Chatham, 1930; lost off Sicily, August 1943.

Partridge: P cls destroyer; 1540; 345 x 35; 36; 176; five 4-in, four 21-in tt; Fairfield SB & E Co, Govan, 1942; torpedoed and sunk by *U-565* in western Mediterranean, Dec 18, 1942.

Pasley: Captain cls frigate; 1140; 289½ x 35; 21; 200; three 3-in; Navy Yard, Boston, 1943; ex-USN Evarts cls destroyer-escort *DE-519,* transferred Lease/Lend to RN 1943 rnd *Lindsay,* rnd *Pasley* 1943, rtnd USN 1945; b/up.

Pathfinder: P cls destroyer; 1540; 345 x 35; 36; 176; four 4-in, eight 21-in tt; Hawthorn Leslie, Hebburn, 1942; ex-*Onslaught* 1941; irreparably damaged by Japanese aircraft at Ramree Island, Feb 11, 1945; used in explosion tests UK, 1948; b/up UK 1949.

Patroclus: BAT cls tug; 783; 143 x 33; 14; 34; one 3-in; Levingston SB, Orange, 1943; ex-USN, transferred Lease/Lend to RN 1943, rtnd USN 1946, rnd *ATR-91;* 1947, Tug Marion Moran Inc, US, rnd *Kevin Moran;* 1960, Pacific Inland Nav Co, US, rnd *Mohawk;*

Patroller: Smiter cls escort carrier; 11,420; 496 x 69½; 16; 650; 20 aircraft, two 5-in; Seattle-Tacoma SB Corp, Tacoma, 1944; ex-USN *Keeweenaw, BCVE-44,* transferred Lease/Lend to RN 1944, rtnd USN 1946; 1948, NV Vereenigde Nederlandsche Scheeps Maats, Holland, converted to cargo liner, rnd *Almkerk;* 1968, Thai Hwa Nav Corp, SA, Panama, rnd *Pacific Alliance;* b/up Kaohsiung 1974.

PC-74: PC cls sloop; 610; 247 x 26¾; 20; 56; one 4-in, two 3-in; J. S. White & Co, Cowes, 1918; design modified when building to submarine decoy ship, or Q-boat; b/up Pembroke Dock, 1947.

Peacock: Modified Black Swan cls sloop; 1430; 299½ x 38; 20; 192; six 4-in; J. I. Thornycroft & Co, Southampton, 1944; b/up Rosyth 1958.

Pearl: Gem cls trawler; 649; 154½ x 25½; 12; 18; one 4-in; Cook Welton & Gemmell, Beverley, 1934; ex-*Dervish* (Hellyer Bros, Hull) bought RN 1935; 1946, J. Marr & Sons, Hull, rnd *Westella;* 1949, Pegasus Trawling Co, Hull, no name change; 1951, Dinas

Steam Trawling Co, Fleetwood, no name change, b/up Ghent 1959.

Pearleaf: Leaf cls oiler; 12,370; 425 x 54½; 14; 26; --; Wm Gray & Co, West Hartlepool, 1917; ex-*Gypol,* 1917; b/up Blyth 1947.

Pegasus: catapult trials and maintenance ship; 6900; 366 x 50; 11; 139; four 12-pdr; Blyth SB & DD Co, Blyth, 1915; purchased during construction, 1914; ex-seaplane carrier *Ark Royal,* rnd 1934; 1947, Soc Anon 'Ellanita', Panama, rnd *Anita I,* for conversion into merchant ship, conversion not completed; 1949, NV Holland, Holland, no name change; 1949, Mons Engelea, of Boom, no name change; 1949, Armement Cornelis, Ghent, no name change; conversion not continued, b/up Grays 1950.

37½; 19¼; 188; eight 4-in; J. I. Thornycroft & Co, Southampton, 1939; b/up Preston 1958.

Pelorus: Algerine cls minesweeper; 950; 235 x 35½; 16½; 104; one 4-in; Lobnitz & Co, Renfrew, 1943; transferred 1947 to South African Navy, rnd *Pietermaritzburg;*

Penelope: Arethusa cls cruiser; 5270; 506 x 51; 32¼; 450; six 6-in, eight 4-in, six 21-in tt; Harland & Wolff, Belfast, 1936; torpedoed and sunk by *U-410* off Anzio, Feb 18, 1944.

Penn: P cls destroyer; 1540; 345 x 35; 36; 176; four 4-in, eight 21-in tt; Vickers-Armstrongs, Tyne, 1941; b/up Troon 1950.

Pennywort: Flower cls corvette; 925; 205 x 33; 16; 85; one 4-in; A. & J. Inglis, Glasgow, 1942; b/up Troon 1949.

Pentstemon: Flower cls corvette; 925; 205 x 33; 16; 85; one 4-in; Philip & Son, Dartmouth, 1941; 1947, Greek government, rnd *Galaxidi;* 1951, G. & A. K. Vlassis, Greece, converted to cargo ship, rnd *Rosa Vlassis;* 1960, Hellenic Atlantic Fishing Co, Greece, converted to trawler, rnd *Athina;* lost, aground Plettenberg Bay, July 31, 1967.

Penylan: Hunt cls destroyer — Albrighton type; 1050; 280 x 31½; 27; 168; four 4-in, two 21-in tt; Vickers-Armstrongs, Barrow, 1942; sunk by E-boat in English Channel,

Dec 3, 1942.

Penzance: Hastings cls sloop; 1045; 266 x 34; 16; 100; two 4-in; HM Dockyard, Devonport, 1930; torpedoed and sunk by U-boat in North Atlantic, Aug 24, 1940.

Peony: Flower cls corvette; 925; 205 x 33; 16; 85; one 4-in; Harland & Wolff, Belfast, 1940; transferred 1943 to Greek Navy, rnd *Sakhtouris,* rtnd RN 1952; b/up Dunston 1952.

Perim: Colony cls frigate; 1430; 304 x 37½; 18; 120; three 3-in; Walsh-Kaiser Co, Providence, 1944; ex-USN *PF-89,* transferred Lease/Lend to RN, rnd *Phillimore,* rnd *Sierra Leone,* rnd *Perim* 1944, rtnd USN 1946; sold Chester Pa shipbreakers 1947.

Periwinkle: Flower cls corvette; 925; 205 x 33; 16; 85; one 4-in; Harland & Wolff, Belfast, 1940; transferred 1942 to US Navy, rnd *Restless,* rtnd RN 1945, rnd *Periwinkle;* 1947, Wheelock Marden, Hong Kong, converted to cargo ship, rnd *Perilock;* b/up Hong Kong 1953.

Perseus: P cls submarine; 1475/2040; 290 x 28; 17½/9; 50; eight 21-in tt, one 4-in; Vickers-Armstrongs, Barrow, 1930; torpedoed and sunk by Italian submarine *Enrico Toti* off Zante, Dec 1, 1941.

Perseus: aircraft maintenance ship; 12,265; 694½ x 80⅓; 25; 700; --; Vickers-Armstrongs, Tyne, 1945; ex-*Edgar,* 1944; b/up Port Glasgow, 1958.

Persian: Algerine cls minesweeper; 950; 235 x 35½; 16½; 104; one 4-in; Redfern Construction Co, Toronto, 1943; ex-USN, transferred Lease/Lend to RN 1943, rtnd USN 1946; sold 1948.

Petard: P cls destroyer; 1540; 345 x 35; 36; 176; four 4-in, eight 21-in tt; Vickers-Armstrongs, Tyne, 1942; ex-*Persistent,* 1941; b/up Bo'ness 1967.

Peterel: Peterel cls river gunboat; 310; 184⅔ x 29; 16; 55; two 3-in; Yarrow & Co, Scotstoun, 1927; sunk in action with Japanese coast defence ship *Idzumo* at Shanghai, Dec 8, 1941.

Peterhead: Bangor cls minesweeper; 672; 180 x 28½; 16; 60; one 3-in; Blyth SB & DD Co, Blyth, 1941; irreparably damaged by mine off Normandy, June 8, 1944, b/up Pembroke Dock 1948.

Petrella: petrol carrier; 1024; 164 x 28; 9½; 16; --; Dunlop, Bremner & Co, Port Glasgow, 1918; 1946, Lucinda Cia Panamena de Nav SA, Panama, rnd *Captain Mikes;* about 1961, Hydrotiki Etaireia SA, Greece, rnd *Evros;* 1970, Demetrios Raviolos & Petros Dalcas, Greece, rnd *Megalohari;*

Petrobus: petrol carrier; 1024; 164 x 28; 9½; 16; --; Dunlop, Bremner & Co, Port Glasgow, 1918; b/up Grays 1959.

Petronel: water carrier; 1024; 164 x 28; 9½; 16; --; Dunlop, Bremner & Co, Port Glasgow, 1918; 1945, Bulk Oil SS Co, London, rnd *Pass of Glencoe,* 1947; 1949, Athel Line, London, rnd *Athelglen;* 1954, Pure Cane Molasses Co, British Guiana, rnd *Molaglen;* b/up British Guiana 1958.

Petunia: Flower cls corvette; 925; 205 x 33; 16; 85; one 4-in; H. Robb, Leith, 1940; transferred 1945 to China, rnd *Fu Po;* sunk in collision, Mar 19, 1947.

Pevensey Castle: Castle cls corvette; 1010; 252 x 36¾; 16½; 120; one 4-in; Harland & Wolff, Belfast, 1944; transferred 1960 to Air Ministry, converted to weather ship, rnd *Weather Monitor;*

Pheasant: Modified Black Swan cls sloop; 1430; 299½ x 38; 20; 192; six 4-in; Yarrow & Co, Scotstoun, 1943; b/up Troon 1963.

Philoctetes: destroyer depot ship; 11,431 grt; 528½ x 63; 14; --; four 4-in; Scotts SB & E Co, Greenock, 1922; ex-cargo liner (Ocean SS Co, Liverpool), bought RN 1940, converted; b/up Newport 1948.

Philol: Elmol cls oiler; 2410; 220 x 34⅔; 9½; 19; --; Tyne Iron Shipbuilding Co, Willington Quay, 1916; used as hulk, 1956; b/up Belgium 1967.

Phoebe: Dido cls cruiser; 5450; 512 x 50½; 33; 620; eight 5.25-in, six 21-in tt; Fairfield SB & E Co, Govan, 1940; b/up Blyth 1956.

Phoenix: P cls submarine; 1475/2040; 290 x 28; 17½/9; 50; eight 21-in tt, one 4-in; Cammell Laird, Birkenhead, 1930; sunk by Italian torpedo boat off Augusta, July 17, 1940.

Pickle: Algerine cls minesweeper; 950; 235 x 35½; 16½; 104; one 4-in;

Harland & Wolff, Belfast, 1943; transferred 1959 to Ceylon, rnd *Parakrama;* b/up Singapore 1964.

Picotee: Flower cls corvette; 925; 205 x 33; 16; 85; one 4-in; Harland & Wolff, Belfast, 1940; torpedoed and sunk by *U-568* off Iceland, Aug 12, 1941.

Pimpernel: Flower cls corvette; 925; 205 x 33; 16; 85; one 4-in; Harland & Wolff, Belfast, 1941; b/up Portaferry 1948.

Pincher: Algerine cls minesweeper; 950; 235 x 35½; 16½; 104; one 4-in; Harland & Wolff, Belfast, 1943; b/up Dunston 1962.

Pine: Tree cls trawler; 530; 164 x 27½; 11½; 35; one 12-pdr; Hall Russell, Aberdeen, 1940; sunk by E-boat off Selsey Bill, Jan 31, 1944.

Pink: Flower cls corvette; 925; 205 x 33; 16; 85; one 4-in; H. Robb, Leith, 1942; irreparably damaged by mine off Normandy, June 27, 1944, b/up Llanelly 1947.

Pintail: Guillemot cls sloop; 580; 243½ x 26½; 20; 60; one 4-in; Wm Denny & Bros, Dumbarton, 1940; mined in Humber, June 10, 1941.

Pioneer: aircraft maintenance ship; 12,000; 694½ x 80⅓; 25; 700; --; Vickers-Armstrongs, Barrow, 1945; ex-*Mars,* 1944; b/up Inverkeithing 1954.

Pique: Catherine cls minesweeper; 890; 221 x 32; 18; 109; one 3-in; Assoc Shipbuilding Seattle, 1943; ex-USN Auk cls minesweeper *BAM-II,* transferred Lease/Lend to RN 1943, rtnd USN 1946; transferred 1947 to Turkey, rnd *Eregli;*

Pirouette: Dance cls trawler; 530; 160½ x 27½; 11½; 35; one 4-in; Goole SB & Repairing Co, Goole, 1940; 1947, Ricuperi Altomare 'Ricalmare', Italy, converted to salvage ship, rnd *Tridente;* 1957, Dr C. Bartoli, Italy, rnd *Federico Bartoli;* 1958, Soc di Navigazione 'S. Pietro', Italy, rnd *Tabarchin;*

Pitcairn: Colony cls frigate; 1430; 304 x 37½; 18; 120; three 3-in; Walsh-Kaiser Co, Providence, 1944; ex-USN *PF-85,* transferred Lease/Lend to RN, rnd *Pilford,* rnd *Pitcairn* 1944, rtnd USN 1946; sold Quincy shipbreakers 1947.

Pladda: Isles cls trawler; 560; 164 x 27½; 12; 40; one 12-pdr; Cook Welton & Gemmell, Beverley, 1941; 1946, Gythfeldt & Co, Singapore, no name change; 1949, Siamese owners, nothing more known.

Planet: Bayonet cls boom defence vessel; 530; 135 x 30½; 11½; 32; one 3-in; Lobnitz & Co, Renfrew, 1939; ex-*Barnwell,* 1938; sold Portsmouth shipbreakers 1958.

Plantagenet: Bayonet cls boom defence vessel; 530; 135 x 30½; 11½; 32; one 3-in; Lobnitz & Co, Renfrew, 1939; ex-*Barwood,* 1938; 1959, Metal Industries (Salvage), Faslane, for commercial use, no name change; 1962, Soc d'Etude du Transports et de la Valorisation des Gas Naturels du Sahara, France, converted to hydrographic research ship, rnd *Amalthee;* 1966, Developpement Operationnel des Richesses Sous-Marines, France, no name change; 1969, French Navy, converted to survey ship, rnd *La Decouverte;*

Plover: coastal minelayer; 805; 195¼ x 37½; 14¾; 69; one 12-pdr; Wm Denny & Bros, Dumbarton, 1937; b/up Inverkeithing 1969.

Plucky: Algerine cls minesweeper; 950; 235 x 35½; 16½; 104; one 4-in; Harland & Wolff, Belfast, 1943; b/up Dunston 1962.

Plumleaf: Leaf cls oiler; 12,370; 425 x 54½; 14; 26; --; Swan Hunter & Wigham Richardson, Wallsend, 1917; ex-*Trinol,* 1917; bombed and sunk, Apr 4, 1942 at Malta; raised August, 1947 and b/up.

Pluto: Algerine cls minesweeper; 950; 235 x 35½; 16½; 104; one 4-in; Port Arthur SB Co, Port Arthur, 1945; b/up Dalmuir 1972.

Plym: River cls frigate; 1370; 301½ x 36½; 19; 140; two 4-in; Smith's Dock Co, Middlesbrough, 1943; destroyed in atomic tests Oct 3, 1952.

Polka: Dance cls trawler; 530; 160½ x 27½; 11½; 35; one 4-in; Hall Russell, Aberdeen, 1941; sold Belgian owners 1946.

Pollack: Fish cls trawler; 670; 162 x 25¼; 11; 35; one 4-in; Cochrane & Sons, Selby, 1943; 1946, Consolidated Fisheries, Grimsby, rnd *Swansea*

Castle; b/up Sunderland 1960.

Polruan: Bangor cls minesweeper; 656; 174 x 28½; 16; 60; one 3-in; Ailsa SB Co, Troon, 1940; b/up Sunderland 1950.

Polyanthus: Flower cls corvette; 925; 205 x 33; 16; 85; one 4-in; H. Robb, Leith, 1941; torpedoed by U-boat, south of Iceland, Sept 20, 1943.

Poole: Bangor cls minesweeper; 656; 174 x 28½; 16; 60; one 3-in; Alex Stephen & Sons, Linthouse, 1941; b/up Pembroke Dock, 1948.

Poppy: Flower cls corvette; 925; 205 x 33; 16; 85; one 4-in; Alex Hall & Co, Aberdeen, 1942; 1946, Soc Anon Maritime et Commercial, Switzerland, converted to merchant ship, rnd *Rami;* hulked 1955.

Porcher: Isles cls trawler; 560; 164 x 27½; 12; 40; one 12-pdr; Midland Shipyards, Midland, 1942; ex-*Procher,* 1942; 1951, British Wheeler Process, Liverpool, converted to oil sludge vessel, rnd *Tulipglen;* b/up Belgium 1965.

Porcupine: P cls destroyer; 1540; 345 x 35; 36; 176; five 4-in, four 21-in tt; Vickers-Armstrongs, Tyne 1942; irreparably damaged by torpedo from U-boat in Mediterranean, Dec 9, 1942; towed to UK 1943, and used as base ship; b/up Plymouth 1947.

Porpoise: Porpoise cls minelaying submarine; 1500/2060; 288 x 29¾; 15¾/8¾; 55; 50 mines, six 21-in tt, one 4-in; Vickers-Armstrongs, Barrow, 1933; sunk by Japanese aircraft in Straits of Malacca, Jan 19, 1945.

Portchester Castle: Castle cls corvette; 1010; 252 x 36¾; 16½; 120; one 4-in; Swan Hunter & Wigham Richardson, Wallsend, 1943; b/up Troon, 1958.

Portsdown: Hills cls trawler; 750; 181¼ x 28; 11; 35; one 12-pdr; Cook Welton & Gemmell, Beverley, 1942; 1946, Hull Merchants Amalgamated Trawlers, Hull, rnd *Sollum;* 1949, Grimsby Motor Trawlers, Grimsby, rnd *Hargood;* 1955, Iago Steam Trawler Co, London, rnd *Red Sabre;* b/up Passage West 1964.

Postillion: Algerine cls minesweeper; 950; 235 x 35½; 16½; 104; one 4-in; Redfern Construction Co, Toronto,

1943; ex-USN, transferred Lease/Lend to RN 1943, rtnd USN 1946; transferred 1947 to Greek Navy, rnd *Machitis;*

Potentilla: Flower cls corvette; 925; 205 x 33; 16; 85; one 4-in; Wm Simons & Co, Renfrew, 1942; transferred 1942 to Norwegian Navy, no name change, rtnd RN 1944; b/up Tyne 1946.

Pozarica: A-A ship; 1893 grt; 306½ x 45; --; --; six 4-in; Wm Doxford & Sons, Sunderland, 1938; ex-cargo ship (MacAndrews & Co, London) bought RN 1940; sunk in air attack off Bougie, Feb 13, 1943; raised and b/up Italy 1951.

Precept: Prefect cls boom defence vessel; 1215; 194½ x 34½; 14; 44; one 3-in; Barbour Boat Works, New Bern, 1944; ex-USN Bitterbush cls net layer, transferred Lease/Lend to RN 1944, rtnd USN 1946; sold 1947.

Precise: Prefect cls boom defence vessel; 1215; 194½ x 34½; 14; 44; one 3-in; Barbour Boat Works, New Bern, 1944; ex-USN Bitterbush cls net layer, transferred Lease/Lend to RN 1944, rtnd USN 1945; 1947, A. R. Reid, Jamaica, no name change; foundered 40 miles south-east of Puerto Cabezas, Oct 13, 1958.

Prefect: Prefect cls boom defence vessel; 1215; 194½ x 34½; 14; 44; one 3-in; American Car & Foundry Corp, Wilmington, 1944; ex-USN Bitterbush cls net layer, transferred Lease/Lend to RN 1944, rtnd USN 1945; 1947, W. Stubbs Bradley, Panama, rnd *Arctic Prowler;* 1951, Sea Traders Ltd, Canada, no name change; 1962 W. Sumarah Jr, Canada, rnd *North Star VI;*

Premier: Smiter cls escort carrier; 11,420; 496 x 69½; 16; 650; 20 aircraft, two 5-in; Seattle-Tacoma SB Corp, Tacoma, 1944; ex-USN *Estero, BCVE-42,* 1943, transferred Lease/Lend to RN 1944, rtnd USN 1946; 1948, Blue Star Line, London, converted to cargo liner, rnd *Rhodesia Star;* 1967, International Export Lines, Hong Kong, rnd *Hongkong Knight;* b/up Kaohsiung 1974.

Prestol: Belgol cls oiler; 5620; 335 x 41½; 14; 39; --; Napier & Miller, Glasgow, 1917; b/up St David's on

Forth, 1958.
Pretext: Prefect cls boom defence vessel; 1215; 194½ x 34½; 14; 44; one 3-in; American Car & Foundry Corp, Wilmington, 1944; ex-USN Bitterbush cls net layer, transferred Lease/Lend to RN 1944, rtnd USN 1946; 1948, Falkland Island Dependencies Committee, Falkland Islands, converted to research ship, rnd *John Biscoe;* 1956, New Zealand Navy, rnd *Endeavour;* 1962, A.M.C. Shaw, Canada, rnd *Arctic Endeavour;* 1969, Mayhaven Shipping, Canada, no name change;
Pretoria Castle: escort carrier-training aircraft carrier; 17,390 grt; 594½ x 76½; 17; --; fifteen aircraft, four 4-in; Harland & Wolff, Belfast, 1939; fitted out as armed merchant cruiser, converted 1942 to aircraft carrier; 1946, Union-Castle Line, London, converted to passenger ship, rnd *Warwick Castle;* b/up Barcelona 1962.
Preventer: Prefect cls boom defence vessel; 1215; 194½ x 34½; 14; 44; one 3-in; American Car & Foundry Corp, Wilmington, 1944; ex-USN Bitterbush cls net layer, transferred Lease/Lend to RN 1944, rtnd USN 1946; 1947, Wills Export Line SA, US, no name change; 1952 (owners not known) rnd *Electron;* burned and sunk north-east of Port Limon, Aug 28, 1970.
Primrose: Flower cls corvette; 925; 205 x 33; 16; 85; one 4-in; Wm Simons & Co, Renfrew, 1940; 1949, Hvalfangerselsk Polaris A/S, Hvalfangerselskapet Globus, Norway, converted to whale catcher, rnd *Norfinn;* b/up Belgium 1966.
Primula: Flower cls corvette; 925; 205 x 33; 16; 85; one 4-in; Wm Simons & Co, Renfrew, 1940; 1947, Wheelock Marden, Hong Kong, converted to cargo ship, rnd *Marylock;* b/up Hong Kong 1953.
Prince of Wales: King George V cls battleship; 35,000; 745 x 103; 28; 1900; ten 14-in, sixteen 5.25-in; Cammell Laird, Birkenhead, 1941; sunk by Japanese aircraft off east coast of Malaya, Dec 10, 1941.
Prince Salvor: King Salvor cls salvage vessel; 1440; 216 x 37¾; 12; 72; four

20-mm; Goole SB & Repairing Co, Goole, 1943; 1965, Vamvounakis Bros, Greece, no name change; awaiting commencement of demolition.
Privet: Modified Flower cls corvette; 980; 208¼ x 33; 16; 109; one 4-in; Morton Eng & DD Co, Montreal, 1943; transferred 1943 to USN, rnd *Prudent;* transferred 1949 to Italian Navy, converted to survey ship, rnd *Elbano,* rnd *Staffetta,* 1951; withdrawn 1972.
Probe: Professor cls trawler; 550; 148 x 27¾; 11; 30; one 12-pdr; Alfeite Arsenal, Lisbon, 1942; ex-*Portaferry,* 1942; 1946, Soc de Pesca 'Polo Norte', Portugal, rnd *Polo Norte;*
Proctor: Professor cls trawler; 550; 148 x 27¾; 11; 30; one 12-pdr; Alfeite Arsenal, Lisbon, 1943; ex-*Portadown,* 1943; 1946, Soc Pescarias Arrabida, Portugal, rnd *Arrabida;*
Prodigal: Professor cls trawler; 550; 148 x 27¾; 11; 30; one 12-pdr; Cia Uniao Fabril, Lisbon, 1941; ex-*Porthleven,* 1943; sold Bergen owners 1946.
Product: Professor cls trawler; 550; 148 x 27¾; 11; 30; one 12-pdr; Cia Uniao Fabril, Lisbon, 1941; ex-*Port Jackson,* 1943; converted 1943 to repair ship; transferred 1946 to Greek Navy, rnd *Hermes;*
Professor: Professor cls trawler; 550; 148 x 27¾; 11; 30; one 12-pdr; Cia Uniao Fabril, Lisbon, 1943, ex-*Portmadoc,* 1943; 1946, Cia Portuguesa de Pesca, Portugal, rnd *Algenib;*
Promise: Professor cls trawler; 550; 148 x 27¾; 11; 30; one 12-pdr; Cia Uniao Fabril, Lisbon, 1943; ex-*Port Natal,* 1943; 1946, Cia Portuguesa de Pesca, Portugal, rnd *Aldebaran;*
Prompt: Algerine cls minesweeper; 950; 235 x 35½; 16½; 104; one 4-in; Redfern Construction Co, Toronto, 1944; ex-*Huntsville* (RCN), 1943; irreparably damaged by mine off Ostend, May 9, 1945, b/up Rainham 1947.
Prong: Professor cls trawler; 525; 139 x 27¾; 11; 30; one 12-pdr; Antonio Monica, Aveiro, 1942; ex-*Port Stanley,* 1943; 1946, Richard Lundberg & Co, Norway, rnd *Sjosterk;* b/up Norway 1953.

Proof: Professor cls trawler; 525; 139 x 27¾; 11; 30; one 12-pdr; Antonio Monica, Aveiro, 1942; ex-*Port Royal,* 1943; sold Glasgow owners 1946.

Property: Professor cls trawler; 525; 139 x 27¾; 11; 30; one 12-pdr; Antonio Monica, Aveiro, 1942; ex-*Portrush,* 1943; 1947, Jacob P. Sandoy & Others, Norway, no name change; 1955, Erling Wagsholm, Norway, rnd *Vaagnes;* converted for use as breakwater in Norway 1961.

Prophet: Professor cls trawler; 525; 139 x 27¾; 11; 30; one 12-pdr; Manuel Maria Bolais Monica, Aveiro 1942; ex-*Portobello,* 1943; sold Icelandic owners 1946.

Prospect: Isles cls trawler; 560; 164 x 27½; 12; 40; one 12-pdr; Midland Shipyards, Midland 1942; 1946, transferred to War Dept, converted to cargo ship; 1962, P. Stefanis & Co, Greece, rnd *Angelis S;* 1960, A. Gatzanis & Co, Greece, rnd *Tris Ierarchal II;* 1973, P. Stefanis & Co, Greece, rnd *Angelis S;*

Prosperous: Assurance cls tug; 1045; 157 x 35; 13; 31; one 3-in; Cochrane & Sons, Selby, 1942; 1965, Aegean Steam Nav Typaldos Bros, Greece, rnd *Eyforia;* 1967 rnd *Eforia;* 1968, Seka SA, Greece, rnd *Captain Spyromilios;*

Protector: net layer; 2900; 338 x 50; 20; 190; one 4-in; Yarrow & Co, Scotstoun, 1936; b/up Inverkeithing 1970.

Protest: Professor cls trawler; 525; 139 x 27¾; 11; 30; one 12-pdr; Manuel Maria Bolais Monica, Aveiro, 1942; ex-*Portpatrick,* 1943; sold Icelandic owners 1946.

Proteus: P cls submarine; 1475/2040; 290 x 28; 17½/9; 50; eight 21-in tt, one 4-in; Vickers-Armstrongs, Barrow, 1930; b/up Troon 1946.

Providence: Algerine cls minesweeper; 950; 235 x 35½; 16½; 104; one 4-in; Redfern Construction Co, Toronto, 1944; ex-*Forest Hill* (RCN) 1943; b/up Sunderland 1958.

Prowess: Professor cls trawler; 525; 139 x 27¾; 11; 30; one 12-pdr; Manuel Maria Bolais Monica, Aveiro, 1941; ex-*Provost,* ex-*Portreath,* 1943; 1948, Norwegian owners; wrecked Aug 4, 1948.

Prudent: Assurance cls tug; 1045; 157 x 35; 13; 31; one 3-in; Cochrane & Sons, Selby, 1940; rnd *Cautious,* 1947; 1965, M. R. Cliff Tugboat Co, Canada, rnd *Rivtow Lion;* 1972, Rivtow Marine Ltd, Canada, no name change;

Puckeridge: Hunt cls destroyer — Blankney type; 1050; 280 x 31½; 27; 168; six 4-in; J. S. White & Co, Cowes, 1941; torpedoed by *U-617* in western Mediterranean, Sept 6, 1943.

Puffin: Kingfisher cls sloop; 510; 243⅙ x 26½; 20; 60; one 4-in; Alex Stephen & Sons, Linthouse, 1936; b/up Grays 1947.

Puncher: Smiter cls escort carrier; 11,420; 496 x 69½; 16; 650; 20 aircraft, two 5-in; Seattle-Tacoma SB Corp, Tacoma, 1944; ex-USN *Willapa, BCVE-53,* transferred Lease/Lend to RN 1944, rtnd USN 1946; 1948, Lancashire Shipping Co, Hong Kong, converted to cargo liner, rnd *Muncaster Castle;* rnd *Bardic,* 1954; 1957, Ben Line Steamers, Edinburgh, no name change, rnd *Bennevis,* 1959; b/up Kaohsiung 1973.

Punjabi: Tribal cls destroyer; 1870; 377 x 36½; 36½; 190; eight 4.7-in, four 21-in tt; Scotts SB & E Co, Greenock, 1939; lost after collision with HMS *King George V* in North Atlantic, May 1, 1942.

Punnet: boom working vessel; 321 grt; 140¼ x 24; 10½; 15; --; Cochrane & Sons, Selby, 1925; ex-trawler *Cape Matapan* (Hudson Steam Fishing Co, Hull) bought RN 1939; transferred 1941 to Turkey, rnd *Erdek,* rtnd RN 1946; 1946, Nordic Fishing Co, Aberdeen, converted to trawler, rnd *Cape Matapan;* 1951, B. Gelcer & Co, South Africa, no name change; sunk in collision off Cape Town, Apr 20, 1960.

Pursuer: Attacker cls escort carrier; 10,200; 496 x 69½; 16; 650; 15-20 aircraft; Ingalls SB Corp, Pascagoula, 1942; ex-cargo liner *Mormacland,* ex-USN *St George, BAVG-17,* transferred Lease/Lend to RN 1942, rtnd USN 1946; b/up 1946.

Pylades: Catherine cls minesweeper; 890; 221 x 32; 18; 109; one 3-in; Savannah Machine & Foundry Co, Savannah, 1943; ex-USN Auk cls minesweeper *BAM-21,* transferred Lease/Lend to RN 1943; sunk off Normandy, July 8, 1944.

Pytchley: Hunt cls destroyer — Atherstone type; 1000; 280 x 29; 27½; 146; four 4-in; Scotts SB & E Co, Greenock, 1940; b/up Llanelly 1956.

Quadrant: Q cls destroyer; 1705; 358¼ x 35¾; 36; 176; four 4.7-in, eight 21-in tt; Hawthorn Leslie, Hebburn, 1942; transferred 1945 to Royal Australian Navy; b/up Japan 1963.

Quadrille: Dance cls trawler; 530; 160½ x 27½; 11½; 35; one 4-in; Hall Russell, Aberdeen, 1941; 1946, Skibs A/S Storhaug, Norway, converted to cargo ship, rnd *Elsa;* 1950, Keller Shipping, Switzerland, rnd *Murten;* 1956, U. Gennari Fu Torquato & C, Italy, rnd *Remex;* 1967, De Marzo Bros, Ethiopia, rnd *Ghedem;*

Quail: Q cls destroyer; 1705; 358¼ x 35¾; 36; 176; four 4.7-in, eight 21-in tt; Hawthorn Leslie, Hebburn, 1942; damaged by mine, south of Calabria, Nov 15, 1943; foundered in tow, central Mediterranean, June 18, 1944.

Qualicum: Bangor cls minesweeper; 672; 180 x 28½; 16; 60; one 3-in; Dufferin SB Co, Toronto, 1941; b/up Charlestown 1949.

Quality: Q cls destroyer; 1705; 358¼ x 35¾; 36; 176; four 4.7-in, eight 21-in tt; Swan Hunter & Wigham Richardson, Wallsend, 1942; transferred 1945 to Royal Australian Navy; b/up Japan 1958.

Quannet: boom working vessel; 350 grt; 140¼ x 24; 10½; 15; --; Cochrane & Sons, Selby, 1926; ex-trawler *Dairycoates* (City Steam Fishing Co, Hull), bought RN 1939; 1946, Northburn (Fishing) Aberdeen, converted to trawler, rnd *Dairycoates;* 1948, NV Visscherij Maats 'De Daad', Holland, rnd *Klaas Wyker;* b/up 1958.

Quantock: Hunt cls destroyer — Atherstone type; 1000; 280 x 29; 27½; 146; four 4-in; Scotts SB & E Co, Greenock, 1941; transferred 1955 to Ecuador, rnd *Presidente Alfaro;*

Queen: Smiter cls escort carrier; 11,420; 496 x 69½; 16; 650; 20 aircraft two 5-in; Seattle-Tacoma SB Corp, Tacoma, 1943; ex-USN *St Andrews, BCVE-49;* transferred Lease/Lend to RN 1943, rtnd USN 1946; 1947, NV Stoom Maats 'Nederland', Holland, converted to cargo liner, rnd *Roebiah;* 1966, Philippine President Line, Philippines, rnd *President Marcos;* rnd *Lucky One,* 1972, same owners; b/up Kaohsiung 1972.

Queenborough: Q cls destroyer; 1705; 358¼ x 35¾; 36; 176; four 4.7-in, eight 21-in tt; Swan Hunter & Wigham Richardson, Wallsend, 1942; transferred 1945 to Royal Australian Navy; awaiting placement on disposal list, 1972.

Queen Elizabeth: Queen Elizabeth cls battleship; 32,700; 643¾ x 104; 24; 1184; eight 15-in, twenty 4.5-in; HM Dockyard, Portsmouth, 1915; b/up Dalmuir 1948.

Queenworth: mine destructor vessel; 2047 grt; 275 x 39¾; --; --; --; S. P. Austin & Son, Sunderland, 1925; ex-cargo ship (Watergate Steam Shipping Co, Newcastle) bought RN 1940; sunk by German aircraft in North Sea, May 9, 1941.

Quentin: Q cls destroyer; 1705; 358¼ x 35¾; 36; 176; four 4.7-in, eight 21-in tt; J. S. White & Co, Cowes, 1942; sunk by Italian aircraft off Galita Island, Dec 2, 1942.

Quiberon: Q cls destroyer; 1705; 358¼ x 35¾; 36; 176; four 4.7-in, eight 21-in tt; J. S. White & Co, Cowes, 1942; transferred 1943 to Royal Australian Navy; b/up Japan 1972.

Quickmatch: Q cls destroyer; 1705; 358¼ x 35¾; 36; 176; four 4.7-in, eight 21-in tt; J. S. White & Co, Cowes, 1942; transferred 1943 to Royal Australian Navy; b/up Osaka 1972.

Quilliam: Q cls destroyer; 1705; 358¼ x 35¾; 36; 225; four 4.7-in, eight 21-in tt; Hawthorn Leslie, Hebburn, 1942; transferred 1945 to Netherlands Navy, rnd *Banckert;* b/up Burght 1957.

Quorn: Hunt cls destroyer — Atherstone type; 1000; 280 x 29; 27½; 146; four 4-in; J. S. White & Co, Cowes, 1940; sunk by German explosive boat off Normandy, Aug 3, 1944.

Racehorse: R cls destroyer; 1705; 358¼ x 35¾; 36; 176; four 4.7-in, eight 21-in tt; John Brown & Co, Clydebank, 1942; b/up Troon 1950.

Raider: R cls destroyer; 1705; 358¼ x 35¾; 36; 176; four 4.7-in, eight 21-in tt; Cammell Laird, Birkenhead, 1942; transferred 1949 to India, rnd *Rana;*

Rainbow: R cls submarine; 1475/2015; 210 x 28; 17½/9; 50; eight 21-in tt, one 4-in; HM Dockyard, Chatham, 1932; sunk off Calabria, October, 1940.

Rajah: Smiter cls escort carrier; 11,420; 496 x 69½; 16; 650; 20 aircraft, two 5-in; Seattle-Tacoma SB Corp, Tacoma, 1944; ex-US *Prince,* ex-*McLure, BCVE-45;* transferred Lease/Lend to RN 1944, rtnd USN 1946; 1948, NV Kon Rotterdamsche Lloyd, Holland, converted to cargo ship, rnd *Drente;* 1966, Cia Nav Odiseo SA, Panama, rnd *Lambros;* 1969, Atlas Enterprises Inc, Panama, rnd *Ulisse;* 1971, Comaran Africa Line, Ivory Coast, no name change;

Ramillies: Royal Sovereign cls battleship; 29,150; 620 x 102½; 21; 1146; eight 15-in, twelve 6-in, eight 4-in; Wm Beardmore, Dalmuir/Cammell Laird, Birkenhead, 1917; b/up Cairnryan 1948.

Rampant: wreck disposal ship; 619 grt; 180 x 27; --; --; --; G. Seebeck AG, Bremerhaven, 1898; ex-*Phaedra,* (Dampfshiffahrts Ges Neptun, Bremen) seized 1939, rnd *Empire Sentinel;* converted to wreck disposal ship 1943, rnd *Rampant;* transferred 1946 to Ministry of Transport; 1947, Wizard Shipping Co, London, rnd *Yiaghos;* 1948, De Malglaive Shipping, Honduras, rnd *Raymond Olivier;* 1952, Costa Rican Navigation Ltd, Guatemala, rnd *Maria Paolina,* 1955; b/up Italy 1960.

Ramsey: Town cls destroyer; 1190; 314½ x 30½; 30; 122; three 4-in, six 21-in tt; Bethlehem SB Squantum, 1919; ex-USN *Meade,* transferred to RN 1940; b/up Bo'ness 1947.

Ranee: Smiter cls escort carrier; 11,420; 496 x 69½; 16; 650; 20 aircraft, two 5-in; Seattle-Tacoma SB Corp, Tacoma, 1944; ex-USN *Niantic, BCVE-46;* transferred Lease/Lend to RN 1944, rtnd USN 1946; 1948; NV Kon Rotterdamsche Lloyd, Holland, converted to cargo ship, rnd *Friesland;* 1967, United Overseas Marine Corp, Japan, rnd *Pacific Breeze;*

Ranpura: destroyer depot ship; 16,120; 570 x 71¼; 17; 600; twenty 20-mm; Hawthorn Leslie, Hebburn, 1925; ex-passenger liner (P & O SN Co, London); bought RN 1943 and converted; b/up Spezia 1961.

Ranunculus: Flower cls corvette; 925; 205 x 33; 16; 85; one 4-in; Wm Simons & Co, Renfrew, 1942; transferred 1942 to French Navy, rnd *Renoncule,* rtnd RN 1946; 1947, South Georgia Co (C. Salvesen) Leith, converted to whale catcher, rnd *Southern Lily;* b/up Bruges, 1967.

Rapid: R cls destroyer; 1705; 358¼ x 35¾; 36; 176; four 4.7-in, eight 21-in tt; Cammell Laird, Birkenhead, 1943; converted to target ship 1974.

Rapidol: Belgol cls oiler; 5620; 335 x 41½; 14; 39; --; Wm Gray & Co, West Hartlepool, 1917; 1946, Mollers Ltd, London, rnd *Louise Moller,* rnd *Mount Cameron,* 1950; b/up Hong Kong 1955.

Rattlesnake: Algerine cls minesweeper; 950; 235 x 35½; 16½; 104; one 4-in; Lobnitz & Co, Renfrew, 1943; b/up Grangemouth 1959.

Ravager: Smiter cls escort carrier; 11,420; 496 x 69½; 16; 650; 20 aircraft; Seattle-Tacoma SB Corp, Tacoma, 1942; ex-USN *Charger, BAVG-24;* transferred Lease/Lend to RN 1942, rtnd USN 1946; 1948, Seas Shipping Co, US, converted to cargo ship, rnd *Robin Trent;* 1957, Moore-McCormack Lines, US, no name change; 1969, States Marine Corp, US, no name change; 1971, Verity Marine Corp, US, rnd *Trent;* b/up Kaohsiung 1973.

Reading: Town cls destroyer; 1190; 314½ x 30½; 30; 122; three 4-in, six 21-in tt; Bethlehem SB, Squantum, 1919; ex-USN *Bailey,* transferred 1940 to RN; b/up Inverkeithing 1945.

Ready: Algerine cls minesweeper; 950; 235 x 35½; 16½; 104; one 4-in; Harland & Wolff, Belfast, 1943; transferred 1951 to Belgium, rnd *Jan E. Van Haverbeke;* b/up Bruges 1961.

Reaper: Smiter cls escort carrier; 11,420; 496 x 69½; 16; 650; 20 aircraft, two 5-in; Seattle-Tacoma SB Corp, Tacoma, 1944; ex-USN *Winjah, BCVE-54;* transferred Lease/Lend to RN 1944, rtnd USN 1946; 1948, Blue Star Line, London, converted to cargo liner, rnd *South Africa Star;* b/up Miihara 1967.

Recruit: Algerine cls minesweeper; 950; 235 x 35½; 16½; 104; one 4-in; Harland & Wolff, Belfast, 1944; b/up Barrow 1965.

Redmill: Captain cls frigate; 1400; 306 x 36⅚; 23½; 220; three 3-in; Bethlehem-Hingham Shipyard, 1943; ex-USN Buckley cls destroyer-escort *DE-89,* transferred Lease/Lend to RN 1943; irreparably damaged by U-boat off west coast of Ireland, Apr 27, 1945; rtnd USN 1947; b/up 1947.

Redoubt: R cls destroyer; 1705; 358¼ x 35¾; 36; 176; four 4.7-in, eight 21-in tt; John Brown & Co, Clydebank, 1942; transferred 1949 to India, rnd *Ranjit;*

Redpole: Modified Black Swan cls sloop; 1430; 229½ x 38; 20; 192; six 4-in; Yarrow & Co, Scotstoun, 1943; b/up St Davids on Forth, 1960.

Redshank: Bird cls controlled minelayer; 670; 162 x 25¼; 11; 35; one 4-in; Cochrane & Sons, Selby, 1942; ex-Fish cls trawler *Turbot,* 1942; b/up Sunderland 1957.

Redstart: Linnet cls coastal minelayer; 498; 163¾ x 27⅙; 10½; 24; 12 mines, one 12-pdr; H. Robb, Leith, 1938; scuttled at Hong Kong, Dec 19, 1941.

Redwood: Berberis cls trawler; 540; 140¼ x 24; 11; 18; one 12-pdr; Cook Welton & Gemmell, Beverley, 1928; ex-*St Rose* (T. Hamling & Co, Hull) bought RN 1939; 1946, De Vem NV, Netherlands, rnd *Mary;* b/up Holland 1956.

Regent: R cls submarine; 1475/2015; 290 x 28; 17½/9; 50; eight 21-in tt, one 4-in; Vickers-Armstrongs, Barrow, 1930; missing in Mediterranean April 1943.

Regulus: R cls submarine; 1475/2015; 290 x 28; 17½/9; 50; eight 21-in tt, one 4-in; Vickers-Armstrongs, Barrow, 1930; lost Adriatic, December 1940.

Regulus: Algerine cls minesweeper; 950; 235 x 35½; 16½; 104; one 4-in; Toronto Shipyard, Toronto, 1943; ex-*Longbranch* (RCN) 1943; mined off Corfu, Jan 12, 1945.

Relentless: R cls destroyer; 1705; 358¼ x 35¾; 36; 176; four 4.7-in, eight 21-in tt; John Brown & Co, Clydebank, 1942; b/up Inverkeithing 1971.

Reliant: store ship; 17,000; 471½ x 58; 14; --; --; Furness SB Co, Haverton Hill, 1922; ex-cargo ship *London Importer* (Furness Withy, London) bought RN 1933; 1948, Malta Cross SS Co, Malta, converted to cargo ship, rnd *Anthony G;* 1949, East & West SS Co, Pakistan, rnd *Firdausa;* b/up Pakistan 1963.

Rennet: boom working vessel; 335 grt; 140¼ x 24; 10½; 15; --; Cochrane & Sons, Selby, 1928; ex-trawler *Deepdale Wyke* (West Dock Steam Fishing Co, Hull) bought RN 1939; 1946, Iago Steam Trawler Co, London, converted to trawler, rnd *Red Archer;* b/up Barrow 1958.

Renown: Repulse cls battlecruiser; 32,000; 794 x 102⅔; 29; 1260; six 15-in, twenty 4.5-in, eight 21-in tt; Fairfield SB & E Co, Govan, 1916; b/up Faslane 1948.

Repulse: Repulse cls battlecruiser; 32,000; 794 x 102⅔; 29; 1260; six 15-in, fifteen 4-in, eight 21-in tt; John Brown & Co, Clydebank, 1916; sunk by Japanese aircraft off east coast of Malaya, Dec 10, 1941.

Resolution: Royal Sovereign cls battleship; 29,150; 620 x 102½; 21; 1146; eight 15-in, twelve 6-in, eight 4-in; Palmers SB & Iron Co, Hebburn, 1916; b/up Faslane 1948.

Resolve: Rollicker cls tug; 1400; 182 x 34; 14; 24; one 12-pdr; Ayrshire Dockyard Co, Irvine, 1918; sold 1950.

Resource: fleet repair ship; 12,300; 530 x 83; 15; 450; four 4-in; Vickers-Armstrongs, Barrow, 1929; b/up Inverkeithing 1954.

Respond: Rollicker cls tug; 1400; 182 x 34; 14; 24; one 12-pdr; Ayrshire Dockyard Co, Irvine, 1919; b/up Italy 1956.

Restive: Assurance cls tug; 1045; 157 x 35; 13; 31; one 3-in; Cochrane & Sons, Selby, 1940; 1965, Branco

Salvage, Cyprus, rnd *Ventura;* 1966,
Goldsworthy Mining Pty, Australia, rnd
Nullagine; 1971, Brunei Shipping &
Shipbuilding Panama SA, Panama,
rnd *Man Soon;*
Retalick: Captain cls frigate; 1400; 306
x 36⅚; 23½; 220; three 3-in;
Bethlehem-Hingham Shipyard, 1943;
ex-USN Buckley cls destroyer-escort
DE-90, transferred Lease/Lend to RN
1943, rtnd USN 1945, b/up.

Retort: Rollicker cls tug; 1400; 182 x
34; 14; 24; one 12-pdr; Day Summers &
Co, Southampton, 1919; sold 1958.

Revenge: Royal Sovereign cls
battleship; 29,150; 624½ x 102½; 21;
1146; eight 15-in, twelve 6-in, eight
4-in, two 21-in tt; Vickers-Armstrongs,
Barrow, 1916; ex-*Renown,* 1913; b/up
Inverkeithing 1948.

Reward: Bustler cls tug; 1800; 205 x
38½; 15; 42; one 3-in; H. Robb, Leith,
1945;

Rhododendron: Flower cls corvette;
925; 205 x 33; 16; 85; one 4-in; Harland
& Wolff, Belfast, 1940; 1950 Nederl
Maats voor de Walvischvaart, Holland,
converted to whale catcher, rnd *Maj
Vinke;* b/up South Africa 1968.

Rhyl: Bangor cls minesweeper; 672;
180 x 28½; 16; 60; one 3-in; Lobnitz &
Co, Renfrew, 1940; b/up Gateshead
1948.

Ribble: River cls frigate; 1370; 301½ x
36½; 19; 140; two 4-in; Wm Simons &
Co, Renfrew, 1943; transferred 1943 to
Netherlands Navy, rnd *Johan Maurits
van Nassau;* sold Diemen
shipbreakers 1959.

Ribble: River cls frigate; 1370; 301½ x
36½; 19; 140; two 4-in; Blyth SB & DD
Co, Blyth, 1944; ex-*Duddon,* 1943;
b/up Blyth 1957.

Richmond: Town cls destroyer; 1090;
314⅓ x 30½; 30; 122; three 4-in, six
21-in tt; Navy Yard, Mare Island, 1918;
ex-USN *Fairfax,* transferred 1940 to
RN; transferred 1944 to Russia, rnd
Zhivuchi, rtnd RN 1949; b/up Bo'ness
1949.

Rifleman: Algerine cls minesweeper;
950; 235 x 35½; 16½; 104; one 4-in;
Harland & Wolff, Belfast, 1944; b/up
Barrow 1972.

Rinaldo: Algerine cls minesweeper;
950; 235 x 35½; 16½; 104; one 4-in;

Harland & Wolff, Belfast, 1943; b/up
Gateshead 1961.

Ringdove: Linnet cls coastal
minelayer; 498; 163¾ x 27⅙; 10½; 24;
12 mines; H. Robb, Leith, 1938; 1951,
Pakistan government, converted to
pilot vessel;

Riou: Captain cls frigate; 1400; 306 x
36⅚; 23½; 220; three 3-in;
Bethlehem-Hingham Shipyard, 1943;
ex-USN Buckley cls destroyer-escort
DE-92, transferred Lease/Lend to RN
1943, rtnd USN 1946, b/up.

Ripley: Town cls destroyer; 1190;
314½ x 30½; 30; 122; one 4-in, three
21-in tt; Bethlehem SB Squantum,
1919; ex-USN *Shubrick,* transferred
1940 to RN; b/up Sunderland 1945.

Robert Dundas: store ship; 1900;
222½ x 35; 10½; 17; --; Grangemouth
Dockyard Co, Grangemouth 1938;
b/up Grays 1972.

Robert Middleton: store ship; 1900;
220 x 35; 10½; 17; --; Grangemouth
Dockyard Co, Grangemouth 1938;

Roberts: Abercrombie cls monitor;
7970; 373⅓ x 89¾; 12; 350; two 15-in;
John Brown & Co, Clydebank, 1941;
b/up Inverkeithing 1965.

Robin: river gunboat; 226; 151 x 26⅔;
12¾; 35; one 3.7-in howitzer; Yarrow &
Co, Scotstoun, 1935; scuttled at Hong
Kong, December 1941.

Rochester: Shoreham cls sloop; 1105;
266 x 34; 16; 100; two 4-in; HM
Dockyard, Chatham, 1932; b/up
Dunston 1951.

Rocket: R cls destroyer; 1705; 358¼ x
35¾; 36; 220; four 4.7-in, eight 21-in tt;
Scotts SB & E Co, Greenock, 1943;
b/up Dalmuir 1967.

Rockingham: Town cls destroyer;
1190; 314½ x 30½; 30; 122; one
4-in, three 21-in tt; Bethlehem SB,
Squantum, 1919; ex-USN *Swasey,*
transferred 1940 to RN; mined off
Aberdeen, Sept 27, 1944.

Rockrose: Flower cls corvette; 925;
205 x 33; 16; 85; one 4-in; C. Hill &
Sons, Bristol, 1941; transferred 1947
to South Africa Navy, converted to
survey ship, rnd *Protea;* 1962, sold to
commercial interests and scrapped.

Rocksand: Empire cls infantry landing
ship; 11,650; 418 x 60; 14; 898; one
4-in; Consolidated Steel Corp,

Wilmington, 1944; launched as *Cape Argus* (US Maritime Commission, Washington) transferred Lease/Lend to Ministry of War Transport, London, 1944, rnd *Empire Anvil,* transferred 1944 RN, rnd; rtnd MoWT rnd *Empire Anvil* 1946, rtnd USMC rnd *Cape Argus,* 1946; 1948, was to be sold to China and rnd *Hai Ya;* 1950, USMC, rnd *Empire Anvil;* 1960, China Merchants SN Co, Taiwan, converted to cargo ship, rnd *Hai Ya;* 1973, Yangming Marine Transport Corp, Taiwan, rnd *Fu Ming;*

Rockwood: Hunt cls destroyer — Albrighton type; 1050; 280 x 31½; 27; 168; four 4-in, two 21-in tt; Vickers-Armstrongs, Barrow, 1942; irreparably damaged by German aircraft in Aegean, Nov 11, 1943; b/up Gateshead 1946.

Rodney: Nelson cls battleship; 33,900; 710 x 106; 23; 1640; nine 16-in, twelve 6-in, eight 4.7-in, two 24.5-in tt; Cammell Laird, Birkenhead, 1927; b/up Inverkeithing 1948.

Roebuck: R cls destroyer; 1705; 358¼ x 35¾; 36; 176; four 4.7-in, eight 21-in tt; Scotts SB & E Co, Greenock, 1943; b/up Inverkeithing 1968.

Rollicker: Rollicker cls tug; 1400; 182 x 34; 14; 24; one 12-pdr; Ferguson Bros, Port Glasgow, 1919; b/up Dunston 1952.

Romeo: Shakespearian cls trawler; 545; 164 x 27¾; 12; 35; one 12-pdr; A. & J. Inglis, Glasgow, 1941; sold 1946 Belgian owners; 1952 Guard Salvage & Wrecking Co, Canada, rnd *Guard Mavoline;* 1955, J. A. Anderson, Canada, no name change; 1960, Levis Shipping Canada, no name change; 1966, Rail & Water Terminal of Montreal, Canada no name change;

Romney: Bangor cls minesweeper; 672; 180 x 28½; 16; 60; one 3-in; Lobnitz & Co, Renfrew, 1940; b/up Granton 1950.

Romola: Algerine cls minesweeper; 950; 235 x 35½; 16½; 104; one 4-in; Port Arthur SB Co, Port Arthur 1945; b/up Plymouth 1957.

Ronaldsay: Isles cls trawler; 560; 164 x 27½; 12; 40; one 12-pdr; Cochrane & Sons, Selby, 1941; 1946, Tin Tai Nav Co, China, rnd *Dah Lai;*

Ronay: Isles cls trawler; 560; 164 x 27½; 12; 40; three 20-mm; Cochrane & Sons, Selby, 1945; b/up Troon 1967.

Rorqual: Porpoise cls minelaying submarine; 1520/2117; 293 x 25½; 15¾/8¾; 55; 50 mines, six 21-in tt, one 4-in; Vickers-Armstrongs, Barrow, 1937; b/up Newport 1946.

Rosalind: Shakespearian cls trawler; 545; 164 x 27¾; 12; 35; one 12-pdr; A. & J. Inglis, Glasgow, 1941; transferred 1946 to Royal East African Navy; 1963, African Marine & General Engineering Co, Mombasa (nothing more known).

Rosario: Algerine cls minesweeper; 950; 235 x 35½; 16½; 104; one 4-in; Harland & Wolff, Belfast, 1943; transferred 1953 to Belgium, rnd *De Moor;* b/up Bruges 1970.

Rose: Flower cls corvette; 925; 205 x 33; 16; 85; one 4-in; Wm Simons & Co, Renfrew, 1941; transferred 1941 to Norwegian Navy, no name change; lost in collision in North Atlantic, Oct 26, 1944.

Rosebay: Modified Flower cls corvette; 980; 208¼ x 33; 16; 109; one 4-in; Kingston SB Co, Kingston, 1943; ex-USN *Splendor,* transferred Lease/Lend to RN 1943, rtnd USN 1946; 1947, Banana Shipping Co, US, converted to cargo ship, rnd *Benmark;* 1950, Transportes Maritimes y Refrigerados SA, Mexico, rnd *Frida;* b/up Sweden 1954.

Rosemary: Flower cls sloop; 1175; 267¾ x 33½; 16½; 98; two 4-in; Richardson Duck & Co, Stockton-on-Tees, 1916; b/up Milford Haven 1948.

Rosevean: Isles cls trawler; 560; 164 x 27½; 12; 40; one 12-pdr; Cook Welton & Gemmell, Beverley, 1943; sold 1946.

Ross: Hunt cls minesweeper; 800; 231 x 28½; 16; 74; one 4-in, one 3-in; Lobnitz & Co, Renfrew, 1919; ex-*Ramsey,* 1918; 1947 sold Liege shipbreakers.

Rother: River cls frigate; 1370; 301½ x 36½; 19; 140; two 4-in; Smith's Dock Co, Middlesbrough, 1942; b/up Troon 1955.

Rotherham: R cls destroyer; 1750; 358¼ x 35¾; 36; 230; four 4.7-in, eight 21-in tt; John Brown & Co, Clydebank, 1942; transferred 1949 to India, rnd

Rajput;
Rothesay: Bangor cls minesweeper;
656; 174 x 28½; 16; 60; one 3-in; Wm
Hamilton & Co, Port Glasgow, 1941;
b/up Milford Haven 1950.
Rousay: Isles cls trawler; 560; 164 x
27½; 12; 40; one 12-pdr; Goole SB &
Repairing Co, Goole, 1942; 1947,
Rederi A/S Fortuna, Sweden,
converted to cargo ship, rnd *Tova;*
1954, A/S Nordlandslinjen, Norway,
rnd *Einar Hund;* 1970, O. Berg,
Norway, rnd *Tangvik;*
Rover: R cls submarine; 1475/2015;
290 x 28; 17½/9; 50; eight 21-in tt, one
4-in; Vickers-Armstrongs, Barrow,
1931; b/up Durban 1946.
Rowan: Tree cls trawler; 530; 164 x
27½; 11½; 35; one 12-pdr; Smith's
Dock Co, Middlesbrough, 1940; 1947,
Froyland & Hatlestad, Norway,
converted to cargo ship, rnd *Maiken;*
1956, A/S Tanja, Norway, rnd *Talis;*
1963, Transocean Shipping Co, Hong
Kong, no name change; 1964,
Indonesian government, rnd *Musi;*
Rowena: Algerine cls minesweeper;
950; 235 x 35½; 16½; 104; one 4-in;
Lobnitz & Co, Renfrew, 1944; b/up
Gateshead 1958.
Rowley: Captain cls frigate; 1400; 306
x 36⅝; 23½; 220; three 3-in;
Bethlehem-Hingham Shipyard, 1943;
ex-USN Buckley cls destroyer-escort
DE-95, transferred Lease/Lend to RN
1943, rtnd USN 1945, b/up.
Roxburgh: Town cls destroyer; 1060;
314⅓ x 30½; 30; 122; one 4-in, six
21-in tt; Bethlehem SB, Fore River,
1919; ex-USN *Foote,* transferred 1940
to RN; transferred 1944 to Russia, rnd
Doblestni, rtnd RN 1949; b/up
Dunston 1949.
Royalist: Improved Dido cls cruiser;
5770; 512 x 50½; 33; 620; eight 5.25-in,
six 21-in tt; Scotts SB & E Co,
Greenock, 1943; transferred 1956 to
Royal New Zealand Navy, rtnd RN
1967; b/up Japan 1968.
Royal Marine: Military cls trawler;
750; 193 x 30; 11; 40; one 4-in; Cook
Welton & Gemmell, Beverley, 1944;
1946, Standard Steam Fishing Co,
Grimsby, rnd *Sisapon;* b/up Belgium
1967.
Royal Oak: Royal Sovereign cls

battleship; 29,150; 620 x 102½; 21;
1146; eight 15-in, twelve 6-in, eight
4-in; HM Dockyard, Devonport, 1916;
torpedoed and sunk by *U-47* in Scapa
Flow, Oct 14, 1939.
Royal Sovereign: Royal Sovereign cls
battleship; 29,150; 620 x 102½; 21;
1146; eight 15-in, twelve 6-in, eight
4-in; HM Dockyard, Portsmouth, 1916;
transferred 1944 to Russia, rnd
Archangelsk, rtnd RN 1949; b/up
Inverkeithing 1949.
Roysterer: Rollicker cls tug; 1400; 182
x 34; 14; 24; one 12-pdr; J. I.
Thornycroft & Co, Southampton, 1919;
b/up Italy 1954.
Ruby: Gem cls trawler; 568; 152 x
25½; 12; 18; one 4-in; Cochrane &
Sons, Selby, 1933; ex-*Cape Bathurst*
(Hudson Steam Fishing Co, Hull)
bought RN 1935; 1947, J. Marr & Son,
Fleetwood, rnd *Carella;* 1952, Dinas
Steam Trawling Co, Fleetwood, no
name change; b/up Troon 1959.
Ruler: Smiter cls escort carrier;
11,420; 496 x 88; 16; 650; 20 aircraft,
two 5-in; Seattle-Tacoma SB Corp,
Tacoma, 1944; ex-USN *St Joseph,*
BCVE-50, transferred Lease/Lend to
RN 1944, rtnd USN 1946; b/up US
1947.
Rumba: Dance cls trawler; 530; 160½
x 27½; 11½; 35; one 4-in; A. & J. Inglis,
Glasgow, 1940; 1946, A/S Estella,
Norway, converted to cargo ship, no
name change; 1951, Costa Ricande
Productos Maritima, Costa Rica, no
name change; 1953, Republic of
Korea, rnd *Buk Hae Ho;* 1956, Korea
Shipping Corp, Korea, rnd *Buk Hae;*
1959, Hyop-Sung Shipping Corp,
Korea, no name change;
Rupert: Captain cls frigate; 1400; 306
x 36⅝; 23½; 220; three 3-in;
Bethlehem-Hingham Shipyard, 1943;
ex-USN Buckley cls destroyer-escort
DE-96, transferred Lease/Lend to RN
1943, rtnd USN 1946, b/up.
Rushen Castle: Castle cls corvette;
1010; 252 x 36¾; 16½; 120; one 4-in;
Swan Hunter & Wigham Richardson,
Wallsend, 1944; transferred 1960 to Air
Ministry, converted to weather ship,
rnd *Weather Surveyor;*
Ruskholm: Isles cls trawler; 560; 164 x
27½; 12; 40; one 12-pdr; Goole SB &

Repairing Co, Goole, 1942; transferred 1947 to Portuguese Navy, rnd *Baldaque da Silva;* b/up 1961.

Ruthenia: oiler; 7394; 446 x 52; --; --; --; Barclay Curle & Co, Glasgow, 1903; ex-passenger liner *Lake Champlain* (Canadian Pacific Railway Co, Montreal) rnd *Ruthenia,* 1913; bought by Admiralty 1914; converted 1915 to water carrier, 1916 to oiler; scuttled 1942 at Singapore as oil fuel jetty; refloated by Japanese, refitted, rnd *Choran Maru* and used as troopship; recovered by RN 1945; b/up Dalmuir 1949.

Rutherford: Captain cls frigate; 1400; 306 x 36⅝; 23½; 220; three 3-in; Bethlehem-Hingham Shipyard, 1943; ex-USN Buckley cls destroyer-escort *DE-93,* transferred Lease/Lend to RN 1943, rtnd USN 1945, b/up.

Rye: Bangor cls minesweeper; 656; 174 x 28½; 16; 60; one 3-in; Ailsa SB Co, Troon, 1940; b/up Purfleet 1948.

Rysa: Isles cls trawler; 560; 164 x 27½; 12; 40; one 12-pdr; Cochrane & Sons, Selby, 1941; mined off Maddalena, Dec 8, 1943.

Sabre: S cls destroyer; 905; 276 x 26¾; 31; 98; one 4-in; Alex Stephen & Sons, Linthouse, 1918; b/up Grangemouth 1946.

Safari: S cls submarine; 715/1000; 217 x 23½; 14½/10; 44; six 21-in tt, one 3-in; Cammell Laird, Birkenhead, 1942; ex-*P-61;* foundered off St Abbs Head in tow for b/up at Newport, Jan 7, 1946.

Saga: S cls submarine; 715/1000; 217 x 23½; 14½/10; 44; six 21-in tt, one 4-in; Cammell Laird, Birkenhead, 1945; transferred 1948 to Portugal, rnd *Nautilo;* for disposal and breaking up, 1969.

Sahib: S cls submarine; 715/1000; 217 x 23½; 14½/10; 44; six 21-in tt, one 3-in; Cammell Laird, Birkenhead, 1942, ex-*P-62;* sunk by Italian corvette *Gabbiano* off Sicily, Apr 24, 1943.

Sainfoin: Empire cls infantry landing ship; 11,650; 418 x 60; 14; 898; one 4-in; Consolidated Steel Corp, Wilmington, 1944; launched as *Cape*

Washington (US Maritime Commission, Washington), transferred Lease/Lend to Ministry of War Transport, London, 1944, rnd *Empire Crossbow,* transferred 1944 to RN, rnd; rtnd MoWT rnd *Empire Crossbow,* 1946, rtnd USMC rnd *Cape Washington,* 1947; sold 1964, Portsmouth Va shipbreakers.

St Abbs: Saint cls tug; 820; 143 x 29; 12; 21; one 12-pdr; Ferguson Bros, Port Glasgow, 1918; sunk by aircraft off Dunkirk, June 1, 1940.

St Agnes: Isles cls trawler; 560; 164 x 27½; 12; 40; one 12-pdr; J. Lewis & Sons, Aberdeen, 1943; 1947, Soc Anon Armement Ostendais, Belgium, rnd *Captain Arsene Blonde;* 1950, Kohlenberg & Putz Seefischerei, AG, West Germany, rnd *Thor;* capsized and sank, March 1952.

St Albans: Town cls destroyer; 1060; 314⅓ x 30½; 30; 122; three 4-in, three 21-in tt; Newport News SB & DD Co, Newport News, 1919; ex-USN *Thomas,* transferred 1940 to RN; transferred 1944 to Russia, rnd *Dostoini,* rtnd RN 1949; b/up Charlestown 1949.

St Austell Bay: Bay cls frigate; 1580; 307½ x 38½; 19½; 157; four 4-in; Harland & Wolff, Belfast, 1945; ex-*Loch Lydoch,* 1944; b/up Rosyth 1959.

St Blazey: Saint cls tug; 820; 143 x 29; 12; 21; one 12-pdr; Cran & Somerville, Leith, 1919; sunk as target off Bermuda, July 1946.

St Breock: Saint cls tug; 820; 143 x 29; 12; 21; one 12-pdr; Hong Kong & Whampoa Dock Co, Hong Kong, 1918; sunk by Japanese aircraft off Sumatra Feb 14, 1942.

St Brides Bay: Bay cls frigate; 1580; 307½ x 38½; 19½; 157; four 4-in; Harland & Wolff, Belfast, 1945; ex-*Loch Achilty,* 1944; b/up Faslane 1962.

St Clair: Town cls destroyer; 1060; 314⅓ x 30½; 30; 122; three 4-in, six 21-in tt; Union Iron Works, San Francisco, 1919; ex-USN *Williams,* transferred 1940 to Royal Canadian Navy, converted to submarine tender; sold Canadian shipbreakers 1947.

St Clears: Saint cls tug; 820; 143 x 29; 12; 21; one 12-pdr; Livingstone &

Cooper, Hessle, 1919; 1948, Risdon Beazley, Southampton (nothing more known).

St Croix: Town cls destroyer; 1190; 314½ x 30½; 30; 122; three 4-in, six 21-in tt; Bethlehem SB, Quincy, 1919; ex-USN *McCook,* transferred 1940 to Royal Canadian Navy; torpedoed and sunk by *U-305* in North Atlantic, Sept 20, 1943.

St Cyrus: Saint cls tug; 820; 143 x 29; 12; 21; one 12-pdr; Crichton & Co, Chester 1919; mined off the Humber, Jan 22, 1941.

St Day: Saint cls tug; 820; 143 x 29; 12; 21; one 12-pdr; Taikoo Dockyard Co, Hong Kong, 1919; 1948, Soc Anon Rimorchiatori Riuniti Panfido & Co, Italy, rnd *Ursus;* 1962, Imprese Cesare Davanzaliso, Italy, rnd *San Ciriaco;*

St Dogmael: Saint cls tug; 820; 143 x 29; 12; 21; one 12-pdr; Taikoo Dockyard Co, Hong Kong, 1918; sold 1950.

St Fagan: Saint cls tug; 820; 143 x 29; 12; 21; one 12-pdr; Lytham SB & E Co, Lytham, 1919; sunk by German aircraft off Dunkirk, June 1, 1940.

St Francis: Town cls destroyer; 1190; 314½ x 30½; 30; 122; three 4-in, six 21-in tt; Bethlehem SB, Quincy, 1919; ex-USN *Bancroft,* transferred 1940 to RCN; sunk after collision off Sagonnet Point on way to shipbreakers at Philadelphia, July 14, 1945.

St Helena: Colony cls frigate; 1430; 304 x 37½; 18; 120; three 3-in; Walsh-Kaiser Co Providence, 1943; ex-US *PF-86,* transferred Lease/Lend to RN, rnd *Pasley,* rnd *St Helena,* 1943, rtnd USN 1946; sold Chester, Pa, shipbreakers 1947.

St Issey: Saint cls tug; 820; 143 x 29; 12; 21; one 12-pdr; Napier & Miller, Glasgow, 1918; lost off Benghazi, Dec 28, 1942.

St Just: Saint cls tug; 820; 143 x 29; 12; 21; one 12-pdr; Napier & Miller, Glasgow, 1918; sunk by Japanese aircraft near Singapore, Feb 14, 1942.

St Kilda: Isles cls trawler; 560; 164 x 27½; 12; 40; one 12-pdr; Alex Hall & Co, Aberdeen, 1942; 1948, NV Verre Visscherij Maats, Holland, rnd *Claes Compaen;* 1952, Schlienz-Hagemann Hochsee & Gefrierfisch, West

Germany, rnd *Prof Hensen;* 1957, W. Marsen & D. Marsen, West Germany, converted to cargo ship, rnd *Donar;*

St Margarets: Bull cls cable ship; 2600; 252 x 36½; 12; 46; one 4-in; Swan Hunter & Wigham Richardson, Wallsend, 1944;

St Martin: Saint cls tug; 820; 143 x 29; 12; 21; one 12-pdr; Livingstone & Cooper, Hessle, 1919; sold 1947.

St Mary's: Town cls destroyer; 1060; 314⅓ x 30½; 30; 122; one 4-in, six 21-in tt; Newport News SB & DD Co, Newport News, 1919; ex-USN *Bagley,* ex-*Doran,* 1939, transferred 1940 to RN; b/up Rosyth 1945.

St Mellons: Saint cls tug; 820; 143 x 29; 12; 21; one 12-pdr; Harland & Wolff, Govan, 1918; sold Portsmouth shipbreakers, 1948.

St Monance: Saint cls tug; 820; 143 x 29; 12; 21; one 12-pdr; Hong Kong & Whampoa Dock Co, Hong Kong, 1919; sold 1948.

St Omar: Saint cls tug; 820; 143 x 29; 12; 21; one 12-pdr; Ferguson Bros, Port Glasgow, 1919; sold 1948.

Saladin: S cls destroyer; 905; 276 x 26¾; 31; 98; one 4-in; Alex Stephen & Sons, Linthouse, 1919; b/up Llanelly 1947.

Salamander: Halcyon cls minesweeper; 815; 245 x 33½; 17; 80; two 4-in; J. S. White & Co, Cowes, 1936; irreparably damaged by Allied aircraft off Havre, Aug 27, 1944; b/up Blyth 1947.

Salisbury: Town cls destroyer; 1090; 314⅓ x 30½; 30; 122; one 4-in, three 21-in tt; Navy Yard, Mare Island, 1919; ex-USN *Claxton,* transferred 1940 to RN; b/up Baltimore 1945.

Salmon: S cls submarine; 670/960; 208¾ x 24; 13¾/10; 40; six 21-in tt, one 3-in; Cammell Laird, Birkenhead, 1935; mined off south-west Norway, July 9, 1940.

Saltarelo: Dance cls trawler; 530; 160½ x 27½; 11½; 35; one 4-in; H. Robb, Leith, 1940; transferred 1947 to Portuguese Navy, converted to minesweeper, then survey ship, rnd *Salvador Correia;* de-commissioned 1967.

Saltash: Hunt cls minesweeper; 800; 231 x 28½; 16; 74; one 4-in, one 3-in;

Murdoch & Murray, Port Glasgow, 1918; sold Liege shipbreakers 1947.

Saltburn: Hunt cls minesweeper; 800; 231 x 28½; 16; 74; one 4-in, one 3-in; Murdoch & Murray, Port Glasgow, 1919; foundered in gale at Spithead, October 1945, raised; wrecked Hartland Point, December 1946 on way to shipbreakers at Briton Ferry, demolished as she lay.

Salvage Duke: King Salvor cls salvage vessel; 1440; 216 x 37¾; 12; 72; four 20-mm; Wm Simons & Co, Renfrew, 1944; 1948, chartered to Turkish Salvage Administration, rnd *Imroz;* gutted by fire Jan 13-14, 1959, following explosion on board tanker *Mirador,* which she was engaged in salvaging.

Salveda: salvage vessel; 1250; 194 x 34¾; 12; 62; four 20-mm; Cammell Laird, Birkenhead, 1943; 1972, Pounds Shipowners & Shipbreakers, Old Portsmouth; 1972, G. Vamvounakis, Greece;

Salventure: King Salvor cls salvage ship; 1440; 216 x 37¾; 12; 72; four 20-mm; Wm Simons & Co, Renfrew, 1942; transferred 1950 to Greek Navy, rnd *Sotir.*

Salvestor: King Salvor cls salvage vessel; 1440; 216 x 37¾; 12; 72; four 20-mm; Wm Simons & Co, Renfrew, 1942; b/up Briton Ferry 1970.

Salvia: Flower cls corvette; 925; 205 x 33; 16; 85; one 4-in; Wm Simons & Co, Renfrew, 1940; torpedoed and sunk by U-568 west of Alexandria, Dec 24, 1941.

Salvictor: King Salvor cls salvage vessel; 1440; 216 x 37¾; 12; 72; four 20-mm; Wm Simons & Co, Renfrew, 1944; b/up Briton Ferry 1970.

Salviking: King Salvor cls salvage vessel; 1440; 216 x 37¾; 12; 72; four 20-mm; Wm Simons & Co, Renfrew, 1943; sunk by U-boat in Indian Ocean, Feb 14, 1944.

Samphire: Flower cls corvette; 925; 205 x 33; 16; 85; one 4-in; Smith's Dock Co, Middlesbrough, 1941; torpedoed and sunk by submarine off Bougie, Jan 30, 1943.

Samsonia: Bustler cls tug; 1800; 205 x 38½; 15; 42; one 3-in; H. Robb, Leith, 1942; 1947, on charter, rnd

Foundation Josephine, rtnd RN 1952, rnd *Samsonia;* 1974, Brodospas, Yugoslavia, rnd *Jaki;*

Sanda: Isles cls trawler; 560; 164 x 27½; 12; 40; one 12-pdr; Goole SB & Repairing Co, Goole, 1941; transferred 1942 to Royal New Zealand Navy; sold Auckland shipbreakers 1958.

Sandhurst: depot ship; 11,500; 485 x 58; 10½; 357; four 4-in; Harland & Wolff, Belfast, 1906; ex-cargo liner *Manipur* (T. & J. Brocklebank, Liverpool) bought RN 1915, converted and rnd; b/up Dalmuir 1946.

Sandpiper: river gunboat; 185; 160 x 30⅔; 11¼; 35; one 3.7-in howitzer; J. I. Thornycroft & Co, Southampton, 1933; presented to Nationalist China, February 1942, rnd *Ying Hao,* (nothing more known).

Sandray: Isles cls trawler; 560; 164 x 27½; 12; 40; three 20-mm; Cook Welton & Gemmell, Beverley, 1944; 1961, Honduras-flag interests, no name change; b/up Bruges, 1962.

Sandwich: Bridgewater cls sloop; 1045; 266 x 34; 16; 100; two 4-in; Hawthorn Leslie, Hebburn, 1928; sold 1946.

Sanguine: S cls submarine; 715/1000; 217 x 23½; 14½/10; 44; seven 21-in tt, one 4-in; Cammell Laird, Birkenhead, 1945; transferred 1958 to Israel, rnd *Rahav;* believed b/up Haifa 1969.

Sansovino: Empire cls infantry landing ship; 11,650; 418 x 60; 14; 898; one 4-in; Consolidated Steel Corp, Wilmington, 1943; launched as *Cape Compass* (US Maritime Commission, Washington), transferred Lease/Lend to Ministry of War Transport London, 1943, rnd *Empire Cutlass,* transferred 1944 to RN and rnd; rtnd MoWT rnd *Empire Cutlass,* 1946, rtnd USMC 1946; 1948, was to be sold to China and rnd *Hai Aw;* 1950, USMC, Washington, rnd *Empire Cutlass;* 1960, China Merchants SN Co, Taiwan, converted to cargo ship, rnd *Hai Ou;* b/up Kaohsiung 1970.

Sapper: Military cls trawler; 750; 193 x 30; 11; 40; one 4-in; Cook Welton & Gemmell, Beverley, 1943, 1946, Hudson Bros Trawlers, Hull, rnd *Cape Gloucester;* 1957, Henriksen & Co, Hull, rnd *Admetus;* b/up Belgium

1966.

Sapphire: Gem cls trawler; 608; 160¼ x 26½; 12; 18; one 4-in; Smith's Dock Co, Middlesbrough, 1935; ex-*Mildenhall* (H. Croft Baker & Sons, Grimsby) bought RN 1935; 1946, Seddon Fishing Co, Hull, rnd *Dunsby;* 1953, Hammerfest Havfiske A/L, Norway, rnd *Findus I,* rnd *Skaidi* 1954;

Sarabande: Dance cls trawler; 530; 160½ x 27½; 11½; 35; one 4-in; A. & J. Inglis, Glasgow, 1940; 1946, Rederi A/S Vollen, Norway, converted to cargo ship, rnd *Vollen;* 1953, Gabriele Zunini, Italy, rnd *Betty;* 1956, Soc di Monteponi SpA, Italy, rnd *Monteponi;* b/up Italy 1968.

Saracen: S cls submarine; 715/1000; 217 x 23½; 14½/10; 44; six 21-in tt, one 3-in; Cammell Laird, Birkenhead, 1942; ex-*P-247,* ex-*P-63;* sunk by Italian surface craft off Bastia, Aug 18, 1943.

Sarawak: Colony cls frigate; 1430; 304 x 37½; 18; 120; three 3-in; Walsh-Kaiser Co, Providence, 1944; ex-USN *PF-87,* transferred Lease/Lend to RN rnd *Patton,* rnd *Sarawak,* 1944, rtnd USN 1946; sold Chester, Pa, shipbreakers 1947.

Sardonyx: S cls destroyer; 905; 276 x 26¾; 31; 98; one 4-in; Alex Stephen & Sons, Linthouse, 1919; b/up Preston 1945.

Satyr: S cls submarine; 715/1000; 217 x 23½; 14½/10; 44; six 21-in tt, one 3-in; Scotts SB & E Co, Greenock, 1943; ex-*P-64;* transferred 1952 to French Navy, rnd *Saphir,* rtnd RN 1961; b/up Charlestown 1962.

Saucy: Assurance cls tug; 1045; 157 x 35; 13; 31; one 3-in; Cochrane & Sons, Selby, 1942; 1965, Tsavliris (Salvage & Towage), Greece, rnd *Nisos Chios;* b/up Greece 1973.

Saumarez: S cls destroyer; 1730; 362¾ x 35¾; 36; 220; four 4.7-in, eight 21-in tt; Hawthorn Leslie, Hebburn, 1943; badly damaged by mine in Corfu Channel, October 1946; b/up Charlestown 1950.

Savage: S cls destroyer; 1710; 362¾ x 35¾; 36; 180; four 4.5-in, eight 21-in tt; Hawthorn Leslie, Hebburn, 1943; b/up Newport 1962.

Saxifrage: Flower cls corvette; 925; 205 x 33; 16; 85; one 4-in; C. Hill & Sons, Bristol, 1942; 1947, Den Norske Stat, Norway, converted to weather ship, rnd *Polarfront I;*

Scalpay: Isles cls trawler; 560; 164 x 27½; 12; 40; one 12-pdr; Cook Welton & Gemmell, Beverley, 1942; 1947, W. Rippon, London, converted to salvage ship, no name change; 1951, 'Sorima'; Soc Ricuperi Marittimi, Italy, no name change; 1958, Pasquale di Donna, Italy, no name change; about 1964, C. Garofano, Italy, no name change; beached near Capo Mannu, August 1967 after grounding, total loss.

Scarab: Insect cls river gunboat; 625; 237½ x 36; 14; 65; two 6-in, one 3-in; Wood, Skinner & Co, Newcastle, 1916; b/up Singapore 1948.

Scaravay: Isles cls trawler; 560; 164 x 27½; 12; 40; three 20-mm; Cook Welton & Gemmell, Beverley, 1944; sold Belgian owners 1946.

Scarba: Isles cls trawler; 560; 164 x 27½; 12; 40; one 12-pdr; Cook Welton & Gemmell, Beverley, 1941; transferred 1942 to Royal New Zealand Navy; sold Auckland shipbreakers 1958.

Scarborough: Hastings cls sloop; 1045; 266 x 34; 16; 100; two 4-in; Swan Hunter & Wigham Richardson, Wallsend, 1930; b/up Thornaby-on-Tees 1949.

Sceptre: S cls submarine; 715/1000; 217 x 23½; 14½/10; 44; six 21-in tt, one 3-in; Scotts SB & E Co, Greenock, 1943; ex-*P-65;* b/up Gateshead 1949.

Scimitar: S cls destroyer; 905; 276 x 26¾; 31; 98; one 4-in; John Brown & Co, Clydebank, 1918; b/up Briton Ferry 1947.

Scorcher: S cls submarine; 715/1000; 217 x 23½; 14½/10; 44; seven 21-in tt, one 4-in; Cammell Laird, Birkenhead, 1945; b/up Charlestown 1962.

Scorpion: river gunboat; 700; 208¾ x 34¾; 17; 93; two 4-in, one 3.7-in howitzer; J. S. White & Co, Cowes, 1938; sunk by Japanese destroyer in Banka Strait Feb 13, 1942.

Scorpion: S cls destroyer; 1710; 362¾ x 35¾; 36; 180; four 4.7-in, eight 21-in tt; Cammell Laird, Birkenhead, 1943; transferred 1945 to Netherlands Navy, rnd *Kortenaer;* b/up Ghent 1963.

Scotol: Elmol cls oiler; 2410; 220; x 34⅔; 9½; 19; --; Tyne Iron Shipbuilding Co, Willington Quay, 1916; 1948, Hemsley Bell & Co, Southampton, rnd *Hemsley I;* lost, aground at Porthconan, May 12, 1969 on way to Belgium for breaking-up.

Scotsman: S cls submarine; 715/1000; 217 x 23½; 14½/10; 44; seven 21-in tt, one 4-in; Scotts SB & E Co, Greenock, 1944; b/up Troon 1964.

Scott: Halcyon cls minesweeper; 875; 245 x 33½; 17; 80; two 4-in; Caledon SB & E Co, Dundee, 1939; completed as survey ship but converted 1939 to minesweeper; b/up Troon 1965.

Scottish American: oiler; 6981 grt; 425 x 57; --; --; --; Sir J. Laing & Co, Sunderland, 1920; ex-tanker (Tankers Ltd, London) bought RN 1939; 1947, Tankers Ltd, London, no name change; 1949, Cia Atlantica y Pacifica SA, Panama, rnd *Fairwater;* b/up Italy 1954.

Scourge: S cls destroyer; 1710; 362¾ x 35¾; 36; 180; four 4.7-in, eight 21-in tt; Cammell Laird, Birkenhead, 1943; transferred 1945 to Netherlands Navy, rnd *Evertsen;* b/up Holland 1963.

Scout: S cls destroyer; 905; 276 x 26¾; 31; 98; one 4-in; John Brown & Co, Clydebank, 1918; b/up Briton Ferry 1946.

Scylla: Dido cls cruiser; 5450; 512 x 50½; 33; 620; eight 4.5-in, six 21-in tt; Scotts SB & E Co, Greenock, 1942; b/up Barrow 1950.

Scythian: S cls submarine; 715/1000; 217 x 23½; 14½/10; 44; seven 21-in tt, one 3-in; Scotts SB & E Co, Greenock, 1944; b/up Charlestown 1960.

Seabear: Algerine cls minesweeper; 950; 235 x 35½; 16½; 104; one 4-in; Redfern Construction Co, Toronto, 1944; ex-*St Thomas* (RCN) 1943; b/up Preston 1958.

Sea Devil: S cls submarine; 715/1000; 217 x 23½; 14½/10; 44; seven 21-in tt, one 4-in; Scotts SB & E Co, Greenock, 1945; b/up Newhaven 1965.

Seadog: S cls submarine; 715/1000; 217 x 23½; 14½/10; 44; seven 21-in tt, one 3-in; Cammell Laird, Birkenhead, 1942; ex-*P-66;* b/up Troon 1948.

Seagull: Halcyon cls minesweeper; 835; 245 x 33½; 17; 80; two 4-in; HM Dockyard, Devonport, 1938; b/up Plymouth 1956.

Seaham: Bangor cls minesweeper; 672; 180 x 28½; 16; 60; one 3-in; Lobnitz & Co, Renfrew, 1941; 1947, Rangoon Port Commissioners, Burma, converted to pilot cutter and tender, rnd *Chinthe;* sunk by mine, November 1948.

Seahorse: S cls submarine; 640/935; 202½ x 24; 13¾/10; 40; six 21-in tt, one 3-in; HM Dockyard, Chatham, 1933; sunk by German surface force in North Sea, Jan 7, 1940.

Seal: Porpoise cls minelaying submarine; 1520/2117; 293 x 25½; 15¾/8¾; 55; 50 mines, six 21-in tt, one 4-in; HM Dockyard, Chatham, 1939; captured after being disabled by German aircraft in Kattegat, May 5, 1940; became German *UB;* blown up by own crew at Kiel, May 3, 1945.

Sealion: S cls submarine; 670/960; 208¾ x 24; 13¾/10; 40; six 21-in tt, one 3-in; Cammell Laird, Birkenhead, 1934; sunk as target off Isle of Arran, March, 1945.

Seamew: Tern cls river gunboat; 262; 167½ x 27; 14; 55; two 3-in; Yarrow & Co, Scotstoun, 1928; sold 1947 at Singapore.

Sea Nymph: S cls submarine; 715/1000; 217 x 23½; 14½/10; 44; seven 21-in tt, one 3-in; Cammell Laird, Birkenhead, 1942; ex-*P-73;* b/up Troon 1948.

Searcher: Smiter cls escort carrier; 11,420; 496 x 69½; 16; 650; 20 aircraft; Seattle-Tacoma SB corp, Tacoma, 1942; ex-USN, *BAVG-22,* transferred Lease/Lend to RN 1942, rtnd USN 1946; 1952, Cia Mar Ador SA, Panama, converted to cargo ship, rnd *Captain Theo;* 1964, Atlantic Far East Lines, Japan, rnd *Oriental Banker;*

Sea Rover: S cls submarine; 715/1000; 217 x 23½; 14½/10; 44; seven 21-in tt, one 3-in; Scotts SB & E Co, Greenock, 1943; ex-*P-68;* b/up Faslane 1949.

Sea Salvor: King Salvor cls salvage vessel; 1440; 216 x 37¾; 12; 72; four 20-mm; Goole SB & Repairing Co, Goole, 1943; b/up Grays 1973.

Sea Scout: S cls submarine; 715/1000; 217 x 23½; 14½/10; 44;

seven 21-in tt, one 4-in; Cammell
Laird, Birkenhead, 1944; b/up Briton
Ferry 1965.

Seawolf: S cls submarine; 670/960;
208¾ x 24; 13¾/10; 40; six 21-in tt,
one 3-in; Scotts SB & E Co, Greenock,
1936; sold Montreal shipbreakers
1948.

Sefton: Empire cls infantry landing
ship; 11,650; 418 x 60; 14; 898; one
4-in; Consolidated Steel Corp,
Wilmington, 1944; launched as *Cape
Comorin* (US Maritime Commission,
Washington) transferred Lease/Lend
to Ministry of War Transport, London,
1944, rnd *Empire Gauntlet,* transferred
1944 to RN and rnd; rtnd MoWT, rnd
Empire Gauntlet 1945, rtnd USMC rnd
Cape Comorin 1945; b/up Portsmouth
Va, 1964.

Selene: S cls submarine; 715/1000;
217 x 23½; 14½/10; 44; seven 21-in tt,
one 4-in; Cammell Laird, Birkenhead,
1944; b/up Gateshead 1961.

Selkirk: Hunt cls minesweeper; 800;
231 x 28½; 16; 74; one 4-in, one 3-in;
Murdoch & Murray, Port Glasgow,
1919; sold Liege shipbreakers 1947.

Sennen: Lulworth cls escort; 1546;
250 x 42; 16; 200; one 5-in, two 3-in;
Bethlehem SB Corp, Quincy, 1928;
ex-US Coast Guard cutter *Champlain,*
transferred Lease/Lend to RN 1941,
rtnd USCG 1946, rnd *Champlain;* sold
New York shipbreakers 1948.

Seraph: S cls submarine; 715/1000;
217 x 23½; 14½/10; 44; seven 21-in tt,
one 3-in; Vickers-Armstrongs, Barrow,
1942; ex-*P-69;* b/up Briton Ferry 1965.

Serapis: S cls destroyer; 1710; 362¾ x
35¾; 36; 180; four 4.7-in, eight 21-in tt;
Scotts SB & E Co, Greenock, 1943;
transferred 1945 to Netherlands Navy,
rnd *Piet Hein;* b/up Bruges 1962.

Serene: Algerine cls minesweeper;
950; 235 x 35½; 16½; 104; one 4-in;
Redfern Construction Co, Toronto,
1944; ex-*Leaside* (RCN) 1943; b/up
Llanelly 1959.

Serbol: Belgol cls oiler; 5620; 335 x
41½; 14; 39; --; Caledon SB & E Co,
Dundee, 1917; b/up Blyth 1958.

Sesame: Assurance cls tug; 1045; 157
x 35; 13; 31; one 3-in; Cochrane &
Sons, Selby, 1944; sunk by E-boat off
Normandy, June 11, 1944.

Severn: River cls submarine;
1850/2710; 345 x 28¼; 22½/10; 60; six
21-in tt, one 4-in; Vickers-Armstrongs,
Barrow, 1935; b/up Trincomalee
Dockyard 1945.

Seychelles: Colony cls frigate; 1430;
304 x 37½; 18; 120; three 3-in;
Walsh-Kaiser Co, Providence, 1944;
ex-USN *PF-88,* transferred
Lease/Lend to RN 1944 rnd *Pearl,* rnd
Seychelles, rtnd USN 1946; sold
Chester, Pa, shipbreakers 1947.

Seymour: Captain cls frigate; 1400;
306 x 36⅝; 23½; 220; three 3-in;
Bethlehem-Hingham Shipyard, 1943;
ex-USN Buckley cls destroyer-escort
DE-98, transferred Lease/Lend to RN
1943, rtnd USN 1946, b/up.

Shah: Smiter cls escort carrier;
11,420; 496 x 69½; 16; 650; 20 aircraft,
two 5-in; Seattle-Tacoma SB Corp,
Tacoma, 1943; ex-USN *Jamaica,*
BCVE-43, transferred Lease/Lend to
RN 1943, rtnd USN 1946; 1949, Dodero
Line, Argentine, converted to
passenger liner, rnd *Salta;* b/up
Buenos Aires 1966.

Shakespeare: S cls submarine;
715/1000; 217 x 23½; 14½/10; 44;
seven 21-in tt, one 3-in;
Vickers-Armstrongs, Barrow, 1942;
ex-*P-71;* irreparably damaged by
Japanese aircraft in Nankauri Strait,
Jan 3, 1945; b/up Briton Ferry 1946.

Shalimar: S cls submarine; 715/1000;
217 x 23½; 14½/10; 44; seven 21-in tt,
one 3-in; HM Dockyard, Chatham
1943; b/up Troon 1950.

Shapinsay: Isles cls trawler; 560; 164
x 27½; 12; 40; one 12-pdr; Cochrane &
Sons, Selby, 1941; 1946, Scerif Abo
Imanchio, Italy, converted to cargo
ship, rnd *El Hascimy;* 1955, Hussein
Fayez, Saudi Arabia, rnd *Al Fayez;*
1958, G. & N. Angelakis & A. Petras,
Greece, rnd *Aghia Marina;* lost off
Cape Doro, July 5, 1967.

Shark: S cls submarine; 670/960;
208¼ x 24; 13¾/10; 40; six 21-in tt,
one 3-in; HM Dockyard, Chatham,
1934; damaged by German aircraft off
Skudesnes and sunk by surface craft,
July 6, 1940.

Shark: S cls destroyer; 1710; 362¾ x
35¾; 36; 180; four 4.7-in, eight 21-in tt;
Scotts SB & E Co, Greenock, 1944;

transferred 1944 to Norwegian Navy, rnd *Svenner;* sunk by German TBs off Normandy June 6, 1944.

Sharpshooter: Halcyon cls minesweeper; 835; 245 x 33½; 17; 80; two 4-in; HM Dockyard, Devonport, 1937; converted to survey ship rnd *Shackleton,* 1953; b/up Troon 1965.

Shearwater: Guillemot cls sloop; 580; 243¼ x 26½; 20; 60; one 4-in; J. S. White & Co, Cowes, 1939; b/up Thornaby-on-Tees 1947.

Sheffield: Southampton cls cruiser; 9100; 591½ x 61⅔; 32; 830; twelve 6-in, eight 4-in, six 21-in tt; Vickers-Armstrongs, Tyne, 1937; b/up Rosyth 1967.

Sheldrake: Kingfisher cls sloop; 530; 243⅙ x 26½; 20; 60; one 4-in; J. I. Thornycroft & Co, Southampton, 1937; 1946, San Peh S.N. Co, Shanghai (nothing more known).

Sheppey: Isles cls trawler; 560; 164 x 27½; 12; 40; one 12-pdr; Cook Welton & Gemmell, Beverley, 1942; ex-*Raasay,* 1942; b/up Plymouth 1959.

Sherwood: Town cls destroyer; 1190; 314½ x 30½; 30; 122; three 4-in, six 21-in tt; Bethlehem SB, Quincy, 1919; ex-USN *Rodgers,* ex-*Kalk,* transferred 1940 to RN; sunk in Humber as target, 1943.

Shiant: Isles cls trawler; 560; 164 x 27½; 12; 40; one 12-pdr; Goole SB & Repairing Co, Goole, 1941; transferred 1944 to Norwegian Navy, rnd *Jeloy;* 1946, L. W. Tornoe A/S, Norway, rnd *Artemis;* lost, aground near Obbia, July 31, 1960.

Shiel: River cls frigate; 1370; 301½ x 36½; 19; 140; two 4-in; Canadian Vickers, Montreal, 1943; ex-USN *PG-110,* transferred Lease/Lend to RN 1943, rtnd USN 1946; sold 1946.

Shikari: S cls destroyer; 905; 276 x 26¾; 31; 98; one 4-in; Wm Doxford & Sons, Sunderland/HM Dockyard, Chatham, 1924; b/up Newport, 1945.

Shillay: Isles cls trawler; 560; 164 x 27½; 12; 40; three 20-mm; Cook Welton & Gemmell, Beverley, 1945; 1958, C. Bartoli, Italy, converted to cargo ship, rnd *Federico Bartoli,* 1966, converted to wine tanker rnd *Mont Blanc,* same owners; 1968, G. Messina, Italy, no name change;

Shippigan: Bangor cls minesweeper; 672; 180 x 28½; 16; 60; one 3-in; Dufferin SB Co, Toronto, 1941; b/up Charlestown 1949.

Shoreham: Shoreham cls sloop; 1105; 266 x 34; 16; 100; two 4-in; HM Dockyard, Chatham, 1931; 1947, Cia de Vapores Jorge SA, Panama, for conversion to merchant ship, rnd *Jorge F El Joven,* work not completed; b/up Boom 1950.

Shrewsbury Castle: Castle cls corvette; 1010; 252 x 36¾; 16½; 120; one 4-in; Swan Hunter & Wigham Richardson, Wallsend, 1944; transferred 1944 to Norwegian Navy, rnd *Tunsberg Castle;* mined in Kola Inlet, Dec 12, 1944.

Shropshire: London cls cruiser; 9830; 633 x 66; 32¼; 850; eight 8-in, eight 4-in, eight 21-in tt; Wm Beardmore, Dalmuir, 1929; transferred 1943 to Royal Australian Navy; b/up Troon 1955.

Sibyl: S cls submarine; 715/1000; 217 x 23½; 14½/10; 44; seven 21-in tt, one 3-in; Cammell Laird, Birkenhead, 1942; ex-*P-67;* b/up Troon 1948.

Sickle: S cls submarine; 715/1000; 217 x 23½; 14½/10; 44; seven 21-in tt, one 3-in; Cammell Laird, Birkenhead, 1942; ex-*P-74;* reported lost in Aegean, June 1944.

Sidmouth: Bangor cls minesweeper; 672; 180 x 28½; 16; 60; one 3-in; H. Robb, Leith, 1941; b/up Charlestown 1950.

Sidon: S cls submarine; 715/1000; 217 x 23½; 14½/10; 44; seven 21-in tt, one 4-in; Cammell Laird, Birkenhead, 1945; sank after a torpedo explosion at Portland in 1955, raised and sunk as seabed target off Portland, June 1957.

Signet: Bayonet cls boom defence vessel; 530; 135 x 30½; 11½; 32; one 3-in; Blyth SB & DD Co, Blyth, 1939; sold Portsmouth shipbreakers 1958.

Sikh: Tribal cls destroyer; 1870; 377 x 36½; 36½; 190; eight 4.7-in, four 21-in tt; Alex Stephen & Sons, Linthouse, 1938; sank after being badly damaged by Tobruk shore batteries, Sept 14, 1942.

Silverton: Hunt cls destroyer — Blankney type; 1050; 280 x 31½; 27; 168; six 4-in; J. S. White & Co, Cowes,

1941; transferred 1941 to Poland, rnd *Krakowiak,* rtnd RN 1945 and rnd *Silverton;* b/up Grays 1959.

Silvio: Empire cls infantry landing ship; 11,650; 418 x 60; 14; 898; one 4-in; Consolidated Steel Corp, Wilmington, 1943; launched as *Cape Gregory* (US Maritime Commission, Washington) transferred Lease/Lend to Ministry of War Transport, London, rnd *Empire Halberd,* transferred 1944 to RN and rnd; rtnd MoWT 1945 rnd *Empire Halberd,* rtnd USMC 1948 rnd *Cape Gregory;* sold Baltimore shipbreakers 1965.

Simoon: S cls submarine; 715/1000; 217 x 23½; 14½/10; 44; seven 21-in tt, one 3-in; Cammell Laird, Birkenhead, 1943; ex-*P-75;* reported lost in Aegean, November 1943.

Sir Agravaine: Round Table cls trawler; 440; 137¾ x 23¾; 12; 35; one 12-pdr; J. Lewis & Sons, Aberdeen, 1942; 1946, Great Western Fishing Co, Fleetwood, no name change; 1954, Nils Utheim, Norway, rnd *Utheim;* 1971, Rolf Hansen Partrederi, Norway, rnd *Federal;* capsized and sank about 80 miles off Krakemeset, July 24, 1973.

Sirdar: S cls submarine; 715/1000; 217 x 23½; 14½/10; 44; seven 21-in tt, one 3-in; Scotts SB & E Co, Greenock, 1943; ex-*P-76;* used in experiments at Rosyth 1959; b/up Bo'ness 1965.

Sir Galahad: Round Table cls trawler; 440; 137¾ x 23¾; 12; 35; one 12-pdr; Hall Russell, Aberdeen, 1942; 1946, Walker Steam Trawl Fishing Co, Aberdeen, rnd *Star of Freedom;* 1956, O.W. Limbrick, Aberdeen, rnd *Robert Limbrick;* wrecked Ardmore Bay, Isle of Mull, Feb 5, 1957.

Sir Gareth: Round Table cls trawler; 440; 137¾ x 23¾; 12; 35; one 12-pdr; Hall Russell, Aberdeen, 1942; 1946, Walker Steam Trawl Fishing Co, Aberdeen, rnd *Star of the East;* 1958, Westward Trawlers, Milford Haven, rnd *Milford Star,* rnd *Rudlias,* 1964; b/up Passage West 1966.

Sir Geraint: Round Table cls trawler; 440; 137¾ x 23¾; 12; 35; one 12-pdr; J. Lewis & Sons, Aberdeen, 1942; 1946, Walker Steam Trawl Fishing Co, Aberdeen, rnd *Star of the South;* 1958, E. E. Carter, Milford Haven, rnd *Haven Star;* b/up Dublin 1964.

Sir Hugo: Empire cls infantry landing ship; 11,650; 418 x 60; 14; 898; one 4-in; Consolidated Steel Corp, Wilmington, 1944; launched as *Cape Pine* (US Maritime Commission, Washington), transferred Lease/Lend to Ministry of War Transport, London, 1944, rnd *Empire Lance,* transferred 1944 to RN and rnd, rtnd MoWT 1945 rnd *Empire Lance,* rtnd USMC 1948 rnd *Cape Pine;* sold Baltimore shipbreakers 1965.

Sirius: Dido cls cruiser; 5450; 512 x 50½; 33; 620; ten 5.25-in, six 21-in tt; HM Dockyard, Portsmouth, 1942; b/up Blyth 1956.

Sir Kay: Round Table cls trawler; 440; 137¾ x 23¾; 12; 35; one 12-pdr; Hall Russell, Aberdeen, 1943; 1946, Walker Steam Trawl Fishing Co, Aberdeen, rnd *Star of the North;* 1956, Joe Croan, Granton, rnd *Robert Croan;* b/up Grangemouth 1961.

Sir Lamorack: Round Table cls trawler; 440; 137¾ x 23¾; 12; 35; one 12-pdr; Hall Russell, Aberdeen, 1943; 1946, Don Fishing Co, Aberdeen, rnd *Braconbank;* 1954, C. Rango, Norway, rnd *Bracon;* 1968, B. A. Algroy Partrederi, Norway, no name change;

Sir Lancelot: Round Table cls trawler; 440; 137¾ x 23¾; 12; 35; one 12-pdr; J. Lewis & Sons, Aberdeen, 1942; transferred 1946 to Ministry of Agriculture, Fisheries & Food, London, as research trawler; 1962, Mrs K. M. A. Husseini, Hamburg, rnd *Hair-Ed-Din-Barbarosso;*

Sir Tristram; Round Table cls trawler; 440; 137¾ x 23¾; 12; 35; one 12-pdr; J. Lewis & Sons, Aberdeen, 1942; sold Aberdeen owners 1947.

Skate: R cls destroyer; 900; 276 x 26¾; 31; 98; one 4-in; John Brown & Co, Clydebank, 1917; b/up Newport, 1947.

Skipjack: Halcyon cls minesweeper; 815; 245 x 33½; 17; 80; one 4-in; John Brown & Co, Clydebank, 1934; sunk by German aircraft off Dunkirk, June 1, 1940.

Skipjack: Algerine cls minesweeper; 950; 235 x 35½; 16½; 104; one 4-in; Redfern Construction Co, Toronto, 1943; ex-*Solebay* (RCN) 1942; b/up

Blyth 1959.

Skokholm: Isles cls trawler; 560; 164 x 27½; 12; 40; one 12-pdr; Cook Welton & Gemmell, Beverley, 1943; 1946, Georg Stellberg, Norway, converted to cargo ship, rnd *Skogholm;* 1950, F. Preukschat, Germany, rnd *Hochmeister;* 1958, G. Iatrou, Greece, rnd *Grigorousa;* 1965, N. Diakos & Partners, Greece, rnd *Stelios;*

Skomer: Isles cls trawler; 560; 164 x 27½; 12; 40; one 12-pdr; J. Lewis & Sons, Aberdeen, 1943;

Skye: Isles cls trawler; 560; 164 x 27½; 12; 40; one 12-pdr; H. Robb, Leith, 1942; b/up Bo'ness 1958.

Slavol: Belgol cls oiler; 5620; 335 x 41½; 14; 39; --; Greenock & Grangemouth Dockyard, Co, Greenock, 1918; sunk by U-boat off Tobruk, Mar 26, 1942.

Sleuth: S cls submarine; 715/1000; 217 x 23½; 14½/10; 44; seven 21-in tt, one 4-in; Cammell Laird, Birkenhead, 1944; b/up Charlestown 1958.

Slinger: Smiter cls escort carrier; 11,420; 496 x 69½; 16; 650; 20 aircraft, two 5-in; Seattle-Tacoma SB Corp, Tacoma, 1943; ex-USN *Chatham, BCVE-32,* transferred Lease/Lend to RN 1943, rtnd USN 1946; 1948, Seas Shipping Co, US, converted to cargo ship, rnd *Robin Mowbray;* 1957, Moore-McCormack Lines, US, no name change; 1969, States Marine Corp, US, no name change; b/up Kaohsiung 1970.

Sluna: Isles cls trawler; 560; 164 x 27½; 12; 40; one 12-pdr; Cochrane & Sons, Selby, 1941; 1946, China owners, rnd *Shun Wa;* 1948, Hai Yung SS Co, China, converted to cargo ship, rnd *Hai Ma;* stranded Hainan Strait, Oct 13, 1950, refloated & b/up.

Smilax: Modified Flower cls corvette; 980; 208¼ x 33; 16; 109; one 4-in; Collingwood Shipyards, Collingwood, 1943; ex-USN *Tact* transferred Lease/Lend to RN 1943, rtnd USN 1946; transferred 1949 to Argentina, rnd *Republica;* b/up 1968.

Smiter: Smiter cls escort carrier; 11,420; 496 x 69½; 16; 650; 20 aircraft two 5-in; Seattle-Tacoma SB Corp, Tacoma, 1944; ex-USN *Vermillion, BCVE-52,* transferred Lease/Lend to RN 1944, rtnd USN 1946; 1948, Dodero Line, Argentine, converted to cargo liner, rnd *Artillero;* 1965, Philippine President Lines, Philippines, rnd *President Garcia;* aground Guernsey July 13, 1967, refloated but beyond repair, b/up Hamburg 1967.

Snapdragon: Flower cls corvette; 925; 205 x 33; 16; 85; one 4-in; Wm Simons & Co, Renfrew, 1940; sunk by German aircraft in eastern Mediterranean, Dec 19, 1942.

Snapper: S cls submarine; 670/960; 208¾ x 24; 13¾/10; 40; six 21-in tt, one 3-in; HM Dockyard, Chatham, 1935; lost (possibly mined) in Biscay area, February 1941.

Snowberry: Flower cls corvette; 925; 205 x 33; 16; 85; one 4-in; Davie SB & Repairing Co, Lauzon, 1940; transferred 1941 to Royal Canadian Navy, rtnd RN 1945; b/up Thornaby-on-Tees 1947.

Snowdrop: Flower cls corvette; 925; 205 x 33; 16; 85; one 4-in; Smith's Dock Co, Middlesbrough, 1941; 1947, Wheelock Marden, Hong Kong, no name change; b/up Clyde 1949.

Snowflake: Flower cls corvette; 925; 205 x 33; 16; 85; one 4-in; Smith's Dock Co, Middlesbrough, 1941; ex-*Zenobia,* 1941; transferred 1947 to Air Ministry, converted to weather ship, rnd *Weather Watcher;* b/up Dublin 1965.

Solent: S cls submarine; 715/1000; 217 x 23½; 14½/10; 44; seven 21-in tt, one 4-in; Cammell Laird, Birkenhead, 1944; b/up Troon 1961.

Solway Firth: repair ship; 7340 grt; 447 x 56¼; 11; --; twelve 20-mm; Short Bros, Sunderland, 1945; 1947, A. Gowart Olsen, Norway, converted to cargo ship, rnd *Kongsborg;* 1955, Rederibolaget Zachariassen & Co, Finland, rnd *Olofsborg;* 1959, Polish SS Co, Poland, rnd *Huta Florian;* b/up Spain 1971.

Somali: Tribal cls destroyer; 1870; 377 x 36½; 36½; 219; eight 4.7-in, four 21-in tt; Swan Hunter & Wigham Richardson, Wallsend, 1938; torpedoed by *U-703* in Arctic waters, Sept 20, 1943, foundered in tow four days later.

Somaliland: Colony cls frigate; 1430;

304 x 37½; 18; 120; three 3-in;
Walsh-Kaiser Co, Providence, 1944;
ex-USN *PF-90* transferred Lease/Lend
to RN, rnd *Popham,* rnd *Somaliland*
1944, rtnd USN 1946, sold 1947, b/up.

Sonnet: Bayonet cls boom defence
vessel; 530; 135 x 30½; 11½; 32; one
3-in; Blyth SB & DD Co, Blyth, 1939;
b/up Holland 1959.

Southampton: Southampton cls
cruiser; 9100; 591½ x 61⅔; 32; 830;
twelve 6-in, eight 4-in, six 21-in tt;
John Brown & Co, Clydebank, 1937;
ex-*Polyphemus* 1936; badly damaged
by German aircraft near Malta, Jan 11,
1941, sunk next day by RN.

Southampton Salvor: salvage ship;
800; 183¾ x 37; 12; 35; two 20-mm;
Bellingham Marine Railway &
Boatbuilding Co, Bellingham, 1943;
ex-USN transferred Lease/Lend to RN
1943, rtnd USN 1946; 1947, Greek
government, rnd *Alkimos;* b/up Greece
1953.

Southdown: Hunt cls destroyer —
Atherstone type; 1000; 280 x 29; 27½;
146; four 4-in; J. S. White & Co, Cowes,
1940; b/up Barrow 1956.

Southwold: Hunt cls destroyer —
Blankney type; 1050; 280 x 31½; 27;
168; six 4-in, two 21-in tt; J. S. White &
Co, Cowes, 1941; sunk by mine off
Malta, Mar 24 1942.

Spa: coastal water carrier; 1220; 172 x
30; 10; --; --; Philip & Son, Dartmouth
1941; b/up Passage West 1970.

Spabeck: coastal water carrier; 1220;
172 x 30; 10; --; --; Philip & Son,
Dartmouth, 1943; b/up Belgium 1966.

Spabrook: coastal water carrier; 1220;
172 x 30; 10; --; --; Philip & Son,
Dartmouth, 1944;

Spanker: Algerine cls minesweeper;
950; 235 x 35½; 16½; 104; one 4-in;
Harland & Wolff, Belfast, 1943;
transferred 1953 to Belgian Navy, rnd
De Brouwer; b/up Ghent 1968.

Spark: S cls submarine; 715/1000; 217
x 23½; 14½/10; 44; seven 21-in tt, one
3-in; Scotts SB & E Co, Greenock,
1944; b/up Faslane 1949.

Spartan: Improved Dido cls cruiser;
5770; 512 x 50½; 33; 620; eight 5.25-in,
six 21-in tt; Vickers-Armstrongs,
Barrow 1943; destroyed by German
aircraft at Anzio, Jan 29, 1944.

Speaker: Smiter cls escort carrier;
11,420; 496 x 69½; 16; 650; 20 aircraft,
two 5-in; Seattle-Tacoma SB Corp,
Tacoma, 1944; ex-USN *Delgada,*
BCVE-40, transferred Lease/Lend to
RN 1944, rtnd USN 1946; 1947, Dodero
Line, Argentine, converted to cargo
liner, rnd *Lancero;* 1965, Philippine
President Line, Philippines, rnd
President Osmena; rnd *Lucky Three*
1971, same owners; b/up Kaohsiung
1972.

Spearfish: S cls submarine; 670/960;
208¾ x 24; 13¾/10; 40; six 21-in tt,
one 3-in; Cammell Laird, Birkenhead,
1937; sunk by *U-34* off Norway, Aug 2,
1940.

Spearhead: S cls submarine;
715/1000; 217 x 23½; 14½/10; 44;
seven 21-in tt, one 4-in; Cammell
Laird, Birkenhead, 1945; transferred
1948 to Portugal, rnd *Neptuno;* for
disposal and breaking up 1967.

Speedwell: Halcyon cls minesweeper;
815; 245 x 33½; 17; 80; two 4-in; Wm
Hamilton & Co, Port Glasgow, 1935;
1947, Soc Anon John Cockerill,
Belgium, converted to fruit carrier, rnd
Topaze; b/up Hansweert 1954.

Speedy: Halcyon cls minesweeper;
875; 245 x 33½; 17; 80; two 4-in; Wm
Hamilton & Co, Port Glasgow, 1939;
1947, Cowasjee, Dinshaw & Bros,
Aden, converted to cargo ship, rnd
Speedon; b/up Aden 1957.

Spey: River cls frigate; 1370; 301½ x
36½; 19; 140; two 4-in; Smith's Dock
Co, Middlesbrough, 1942; transferred
1948 to Egypt, rnd *Rashid;*

Sphinx: Halcyon cls minesweeper;
875; 245 x 33½; 17; 80; two 4-in; Wm
Hamilton & Co, Port Glasgow, 1939;
sunk by German aircraft in Moray
Firth, Feb 3, 1940.

Spikenard: Flower cls corvette; 925;
205 x 33; 16; 85; one 4-in; Davie SB &
Repair Co, Lauzon, 1940; transferred
1941 to Royal Canadian Navy;
torpedoed and sunk by *U-136* in North
Atlantic, Feb 11, 1942.

Spiraea: Flower cls corvette; 925; 205
x 33; 16; 85; one 4-in; A. & J. Inglis,
Glasgow, 1941; 1948, Greek
government, rnd *Thessaloniki;* 1953,
D. Zavouris, Greece, converted to
cargo ship, no name change;

Spirit: S cls submarine; 715/1000; 217 x 23½; 14½/10; 44; seven 21-in tt, one 3-in; Cammell Laird, Birkenhead, 1943; b/up Grays 1950.

Spiteful: S cls submarine; 715/1000; 217 x 23½; 14½/10; 44; seven 21-in tt, one 3-in; Scotts SB & E. Co, Greenock, 1943; ex-*P-77;* transferred 1952 to France, rnd *Sirene,* rtnd RN 1958; b/up Faslane 1963.

Splendid: S cls submarine; 715/1000; 217 x 23½; 14½/10; 44; seven 21-in tt, one 3-in; HM Dockyard, Chatham, 1942; ex-*P-78;* damaged by German surface craft off Corsica, Apr 21, 1943 and scuttled.

Sportsman: S cls submarine; 715/1000; 217 x 23½; 14½/10; 44; seven 21-in tt, one 3-in; HM Dockyard, Chatham, 1942; ex-*P-79;* transferred 1951 to French Navy, rnd *Sibylle;* lost near Toulon, Sept 24, 1952.

Spragge: Captain cls frigate; 1400; 306 x 36⅝; 23½; 220; three 3-in; Bethlehem-Hingham Shipyard, 1944; ex-USN Buckley cls destroyer-escort *DE-563;* transferred Lease/Lend to RN 1944, rtnd USN 1946; sold 1947.

Springdale: mine destructor vessel; 1579 grt; 259¾ x 40¼; --; --; two 12-pdr; Short Bros, Sunderland, 1937; ex-cargo ship (Springwell Shipping Co, Hertford bought RN 1940; 1947, Springwell Shipping Co, Hertford, no name change; 1953, Eastboard Shipping Ltd, Canada, rnd *Eastdale;* 1954, Springwell Shipping Co, London, rnd *Springdale;* sank near Ornskoldsvik, June 18, 1959, after cargo shifted.

Springer: S cls submarine; 715/1000; 217 x 23½; 14½/10; 44; seven 21-in tt, one 4-in; Cammell Laird, Birkenhead, 1945; transferred 1958 to Israel, rnd *Tanin;* for disposal 1972.

Springtide: mine destructor vessel; 1579 grt; 259¾ x 40¼; --; --; two 12-pdr; Short Bros, Sunderland, 1937; ex-cargo ship (Springwell Shipping Co, Hertford) bought RN 1940; 1947, Springwell Shipping Co, Hertford, no name change; 1953, Eastboard Shipping Ltd, Canada, rnd *Eastide;* 1957. A. Bolten, Wm Miller's Nachf, West Germany, rnd *Sullberg;* 1960, Compania Maritima Angelikana,

Panama, rnd *Granny Marigo;* 1961, SANA So Abbruzzesi di Navigazione per Azioni, Italy, rnd *Giuseppe Riccardi;* b/up Italy 1972.

Spur: S cls submarine; 715/1000; 217 x 23½; 14½/10; 44; seven 21-in tt, one 4-in; Cammell Laird, Birkenhead, 1945; transferred 1948 to Portugal, rnd *Narval;* de-commissioned 1969.

Squirrel: Algerine cls minesweeper; 950; 235 x 35½; 16½; 104; one 4-in; Harland & Wolff, Belfast, 1944; mined off Phuket, Siam, and sunk by RN, July 24, 1945.

Staffa: Isles cls trawler; 560; 164 x 27½; 12; 40; one 12-pdr; H. Robb, Leith, 1942; transferred 1946 to Italian Navy, rnd *RD-304;* used as target, mid-1960s.

Stalker: Attacker cls escort carrier; 10,200; 496 x 69½; 16; 650; 15-20 aircraft; Western Pipe & Steel Co, San Francisco, 1942; ex-USN *Hamlin, BAVG-15,* transferred Lease/Lend to RN 1942, rtnd USN 1945; 1947, NV Stoom. Maats 'Nederland'; Holland, converted to cargo liner, rnd *Riouw;* 1967, Atlas Enterprises Inc, Panama, rnd *Lobito;* 1971, COMARAN Africa Line, Ivory Coast, no name change; b/up Bruges 1967.

Stanley: Town cls destroyer; 1190; 314½ x 30½; 30; 122; one 4-in, three 21-in tt; Bethlehem SB, Quincy, 1919; ex-USN *McCalla,* transferred 1940 to RN; torpedoed and sunk by *U-574* in North Atlantic, Dec 19, 1941.

Starfish: S cls submarine; 640/935; 202½ x 24; 13¾/10; 40; six 21-in tt, one 3-in; HM Dockyard, Chatham, 1933; sunk by German surface force in North Sea, Jan 9, 1940.

Starling: Modified Black Swan cls sloop; 1430; 299½ x 38; 20; 192; six 4-in; Fairfield SB & E Co, Govan, 1943; b/up Queenborough 1965.

Starwort: Flower cls corvette; 925; 205 x 33; 16; 85; one 4-in; A. & J. Inglis, Glasgow, 1941; 1948, South Georgia Co (C. Salvesen) Leith, converted to whale catcher, rnd *Southern Broom;* b/up Bruges 1967.

Statesman: S cls submarine; 715/1000; 217 x 23½; 14½/10; 44; seven 21-in tt, one 3-in; Cammell Laird, Birkenhead, 1944; transferred 1951 to French Navy rnd *Sultane,* rtnd RN

1959; reported b/up Portsmouth 1963.

Statice: Modified Flower cls corvette; 980; 208¼ x 33; 16; 109; one 4-in; Collingwood Shipyards, Collingwood, 1943; ex-USN *Vim,* transferred Lease/Lend to RN 1943, rtnd USN 1946; 1951, Balleneros Ltd SA, Uruguay, for conversion to whale catcher, work not carried out, laid up Hamburg; b/up Hamburg 1961.

Stayner: Captain cls frigate; 1400; 306 x 36⅝; 23½; 220; three 3-in; Bethlehem-Hingham Shipyard, 1943; ex-USN Buckley cls destroyer-escort *DE-564,* transferred Lease/Lend to RN 1943, rtnd USN 1945; b/up.

Steadfast: Catherine cls minesweeper; 890; 221 x 32; 18; 109; one 3-in; Gulf SB Corp, Houston, 1943; ex-USN Auk cls minesweeper, *BAM-31,* transferred Lease/Lend to RN 1943, rtnd USN 1946; 1947, Greek owners.

Steepholm: Isles cls trawler; 560; 164 x 27½; 12; 40; one 12-pdr; J. Lewis & Sons, Aberdeen, 1943; b/up Antwerp 1960.

Sterlet: S cls submarine; 670/960; 208¾ x 24; 13¾/10; 40; six 21-in tt, one 3-in; HM Dockyard, Chatham, 1937; sunk by German surface craft in Skagerrak, Apr 18, 1940.

Stevenstone: Hunt cls destroyer — Albrighton type; 1050; 280 x 31½; 27; 168; four 4-in, two 21-in tt; J. S. White & Co, Cowes, 1943; b/up Dunston 1959.

Stockham: Captain cls frigate; 1400; 306 x 36⅝; 23½; 220; three 3-in; Bethlehem-Hingham Shipyard, 1943; ex-USN Buckley cls destroyer-escort *DE-97,* transferred Lease/Lend to RN 1943, rtnd USN 1946; b/up US 1947.

Stoic: S cls submarine; 715/1000; 217 x 23½; 14½/10; 44; seven 21-in tt, one 3-in; Cammell Laird, Birkenhead, 1944; b/up Dalmuir 1950.

Stoke: Hunt cls minesweeper; 800; 231 x 28½; 16; 74; one 4-in, one 3-in; C. Rennoldson & Co, South Shields, 1918; sunk by aircraft at Tobruk, July 5, 1941.

Stonechat: Bird cls controlled minelayer; 560; 164 x 27½; 12; 40; one 4-in; Cook Welton & Gemmell, Beverley, 1944; ex-Isles cls trawler;

b/up Dalmuir 1967.

Stonecrop: Flower cls corvette; 925; 205 x 33; 16; 85; one 4-in; Smith's Dock Co, Middlesbrough, 1941; sold Hong Kong owners 1947.

Stonehenge: S cls submarine; 715/1000; 217 x 23½; 14½/10; 44; seven 21-in tt, one 3-in; Cammell Laird, Birkenhead, 1943; missing off Nicobar Islands, March, 1944.

Stork: Bittern cls sloop; 1190; 282 x 37; 18¾; 125; six 4-in; Wm Denny & Bros, Dumbarton, 1936; built as survey ship, refitted 1939; b/up Troon 1958.

Storm: S cls submarine; 715/1000; 217 x 23½; 14½/10; 44; seven 21-in tt, one 3-in; Cammell Laird, Birkenhead, 1944; b/up Troon 1949.

Stormcloud: Algerine cls minesweeper; 950; 235 x 35½; 16½; 104; one 4-in; Lobnitz & Co, Renfrew, 1944; b/up Gateshead 1959.

Stormking: Assurance cls tug; 1045; 157 x 35; 13; 31; one 3-in; Cochrane & Sons, Selby, 1943; 1959, Foremost Marine Transporters, Canada, rnd *Melanie Fair;* 1961, Imprese Marittime Portuali SpA, Italy, rnd *Toro;* b/up Italy 1969.

Stornoway: Bangor cls minesweeper 672; 180 x 28½; 16; 60; one 3-in; H. Robb, Leith, 1941; transferred 1946 to Egypt, rnd *Matrouh;* believed sunk 1968-69.

Stour: Mersey cls trawler; 551; 148 x 22¾; 11; 20; two 3-in; Cochrane & Sons, Selby, 1918; ex-*Daniel Fearall,* 1920; ex-*Stour,* 1922; ex-*Pembroke,* 1939; 1946, East Fisheries, South Africa, rnd *Storesse;* scuttled off South Africa, February 1967.

Stratagem: S cls submarine; 715/1000; 217 x 23½; 14½/10; 44; seven 21-in tt, one 3-in; Cammell Laird, Birkenhead, 1944; lost Far East December 1944.

Strathcoe: Strath cls trawler; 311; 12 x 22; 10½; 18; one 3-in; Hall Russell Aberdeen, 1917; ex-minelayer trawle *Vernon* 1938, ex-*Strathcoe* 1923; 1946 Granton Trawling Co, Granton, no name change; 1955, Bruce's Stores, Aberdeen, no name change; lost Feb 4, 1959.

Strenuous: Catherine cls minesweeper; 890; 221 x 32; 18; 109

one 3-in; Gulf SB Corp, Houston, 1943; ex-USN Auk cls minesweeper *Vital*, transferred Lease/Lend to RN 1943, rtnd USN 1946; 1948, Mr Summerscales, UK, for conversion to passenger ship to be rnd *Evening Star* — work stopped 1948; 1949, South Western Steam Navigation Co, Totnes, partly converted, rnd *Pride of the Nest;* b/up Hamburg 1956.

Striker: Attacker cls escort carrier; 10,200; 496 x 69½; 16; 650; 15-20 aircraft; Western Pipe & Steel Co, San Francisco, 1942; ex-USN *Prince William, BAVG-19,* transferred Lease/Lend to RN 1942, rtnd USN 1946; b/up Baltimore 1946.

Stroma: Isles cls trawler; 560; 164 x 27½; 12; 40; one 12-pdr; Hall Russell, Aberdeen, 1942; transferred 1946 to Italian Navy, rnd *RD-315;* used as target, mid-1960s.

Strongbow: S cls submarine; 715/1000; 217 x 23½; 14½/10; 44; seven 21-in tt, one 3-in; Scotts SB & E Co, Greenock, 1944; b/up Preston 1946.

Stronghold: S cls destroyer; 905; 276 x 26¾; 31; 98; two 4-in; Scotts SB & E Co, Greenock, 1919; sunk by Japanese surface force south of Java, Mar 2, 1942.

Stronsay: Isles cls trawler; 560; 164 x 27½; 12; 40; one 12-pdr; A. & J. Inglis, Glasgow, 1942; sunk (mined?) in western Mediterranean, Feb 5, 1943.

Strule: River cls frigate; 1370; 301½ x 36½; 19; 140; two 4-in; H. Robb, Leith, 1943; ex-*Glenarm*, 1944; transferred 1944 to French Navy, rnd *Croix de Lorraine;* condemned 1961, rnd *Q-306;* b/up Brest.

Stubborn: S cls submarine; 715/1000; 217 x 23½; 14½/10; 44; seven 21-in tt, one 3-in; Cammell Laird, Birkenhead, 1943; expended as target off Malta, April 1946.

Sturdy: S cls destroyer; 905; 276 x 26¾; 31; 98; two 4-in; Scotts SB & E Co, Greenock, 1919; wrecked on west coast of Scotland, Oct 30, 1940.

Sturdy: S cls submarine; 715/1000; 217 x 23½; 14½/10; 44; seven 21-in tt, one 3-in; Cammell Laird, Birkenhead, 1944; b/up Dunston 1958.

Sturgeon: S cls submarine; 640/935;

202½ x 24; 13¾/10; 40; six 21-in tt, one 3-in; HM Dockyard, Chatham, 1932; transferred 1943 to Netherlands Navy, rnd *Zeehond,* rtnd RN 1945; b/up Granton 1947.

Stygian: S cls submarine; 715/1000; 217 x 23½; 14½/10; 44; seven 21-in tt, one 3-in; Cammell Laird, Birkenhead, 1944; b/up Faslane 1949.

Subtle: S cls submarine; 715/1000; 217 x 23½; 14½/10; 44; seven 21-in tt, one 4-in; Cammell Laird, Birkenhead, 1944; b/up Charlestown 1959.

Success: S cls destroyer; 1710; 362¾ x 35¾; 36; 180; four 4.7-in, eight 21-in tt; J. S. White & Co, Cowes, 1943; transferred 1943 to Norwegian Navy, rnd *Stord;* b/up Burght 1959.

Succour: Kin cls coastal salvage vessel; 950; 179½ x 35¾; 9; 34; two 20-mm; Smith's Dock Co, Middlesbrough, 1943;

Suffolk: Kent cls cruiser; 10,800; 630 x 68⅓; 31½; 679; eight 8-in, six 4-in; HM Dockyard, Portsmouth, 1928; b/up Newport 1948.

Sundew: Flower cls corvette; 925; 205 x 33; 16; 85; one 4-in; J. Lewis & Sons, Aberdeen, 1941; transferred 1942 to French Navy, rnd *Roselys,* rtnd RN 1947; b/up Troon 1948.

Sunfish: S cls submarine; 670/960; 208¾ x 24; 13¾/10; 40; six 21-in tt, one 3-in; HM Dockyard, Chatham, 1936; transferred 1944 to Russia, rnd *B-1;* sunk in error by British aircraft while on passage to Russia, July 27, 1944.

Sunflower: Flower cls corvette; 925; 205 x 33; 16; 85; one 4-in; Smith's Dock Co, Middlesbrough 1941; b/up Hayle 1947.

Superb: Swiftsure cls cruiser; 8700; 555½ x 63; 31½; 1000; nine 6-in, ten 4-in, six 21-in tt, Swan Hunter & Wigham Richardson, Wallsend, 1945; b/up Dalmuir 1960.

Supreme: S cls submarine; 715/1000; 217 x 23½; 14½/10; 44; seven 21-in tt, one 4-in; Cammell Laird, Birkenhead, 1944; b/up Troon 1950.

Surf: S cls submarine; 715/1000; 217 x 23½; 14½/10; 44; seven 21-in tt, one 3-in; Cammell Laird, Birkenhead, 1943; b/up Faslane 1949.

Sursay: Isles cls trawler; 560; 164 x

27½; 12; 40; three 20-mm; Cook Welton & Gemmell, Beverley, 1945; b/up Troon 1967.

Sussex: London cls cruiser; 9830; 630 x 66; 32¼; 850; six 8-in, eight 4-in, eight 21-in tt; Hawthorn Leslie, Hebburn, 1929; b/up Dalmuir 1950.

Sutton: Hunt cls minesweeper; 800; 231 x 28½; 16; 73; one 4-in, one 3-in; A. McMillan & Son, Dumbarton, 1918; ex-*Salcombe*, 1918; sold Liege shipbreakers 1947.

Swale: River cls frigate; 1370; 301½ x 36½; 19; 140; two 4-in; Smith's Dock Co, Middlesbrough, 1942; b/up Faslane 1955.

Sweetbriar: Flower cls corvette; 925; 205 x 33; 16; 85; one 4-in; Smith's Dock Co, Middlesbrough, 1941; 1949, Hvalfanger A/S Rosshavet, Norway, converted to whale catcher, rnd *Star IX;* b/up Bruges 1966.

Swift; S cls destroyer; 1710; 362¾ x 35¾; 36; 180; four 4.7-in, eight 21-in tt; J. S. White & Co, Cowes, 1943; mined off Normandy, June 24, 1944.

Swiftsure: Swiftsure cls cruiser; 8700; 555½ x 63; 31½; 1000; nine 6-in, ten 4-in, six 21-in tt; Vickers-Armstrongs, Tyne, 1944; b/up Inverkeithing 1962.

Swin: Kin cls coastal salvage vessel; 950; 179½ x 35¾; 9; 34; two 20-mm; Alex Hall & Co, Aberdeen, 1944; ex-*Shipway*, 1944;

Switha: Isles cls trawler; 560; 164 x 27½; 12; 40; one 12-pdr; A. & J. Inglis, Glasgow, 1942;

Sword Dance: Dance cls trawler; 530; 160½ x 27½; 11½; 35; one 4-in; H. Robb, Leith, 1940; lost in collision in Moray Firth, July 5, 1942.

Swordfish: S cls submarine; 640/935; 202½ x 24; 13¾/10; 40; six 21-in tt, one 3-in; HM Dockyard. Chatham, 1932; missing Bay of Biscay, November 1940.

Sycamore: Berberis cls trawler; 573; 150½ x 25½; 11; 18; one 12-pdr; Cochrane & Sons, Selby, 1930; ex-*Lord Beaverbrook* (Pickering & Haldane's Steam Trawling Co, Hull) bought RN 1935; 1947, P/f Nevid, Denmark, rnd *Drattur;* 1957, P/f Degningur, Denmark, rnd *Jupiter;* b/up 1959/60.

Sylvia: Algerine cls minesweeper; 950; 235 x 35½; 16½; 104; one 4-in; Lobnitz & Co, Renfrew, 1944; b/up Tyne 1958.

Syringa: Berberis cls trawler; 574; 140 x 24½; 11; 18; one 12-pdr; Cochrane & Sons, Selby, 1930; ex-*Cape Kanin* (Hudson Steam Fishing Co, Hull), bought RN 1935; 1946, T. H. Scales & Sons, Edinburgh, rnd *Davarr Island;* 1948, Hudson Bros Trawlers, Hull, rnd *Cape Kanin;* b/up Boom 1954.

Syrtis: S cls submarine; 715/1000; 217 x 23½; 14½/10; 44; seven 21-in tt, one 3-in; Cammell Laird, Birkenhead, 1943; mined off Bodo, Mar 28, 1944.

Taciturn: T cls submarine; 1090/1575; 273½ x 26½; 15¼/9; 59; eleven 21-in tt, one 4-in; Vickers-Armstrongs, Barrow, 1944; b/up Briton Ferry 1971.

Tactician: T cls submarine; 1090/1575; 273½ x 26½; 15¼/9; 59; eleven 21-in tt, one 4-in; Vickers-Armstrongs, Barrow, 1942; ex-*P-94;* b/up Newport, 1964.

Tadoussac: Bangor cls minesweeper; 672; 180 x 28½; 16; 60; one 3-in; Dufferin SB Co, Toronto, 1941; 1946, C. N. Vernicos, Greece, converted to cargo ship, rnd *Alexandre;* hulked Greece 1952.

Taff: River cls frigate; 1370; 301½ x 36½; 19; 140; two 4-in; C. Hill & Sons, Bristol, 1944; b/up Newport 1957.

Tahay: Isles cls trawler; 560; 164 x 27½; 12; 40; three 20-mm; Cook Welton & Gemmell, Beverley, 1945; b/up Troon 1963.

Taku: T cls submarine; 1090/1575; 273½ x 26½; 15¼/9; 59; ten 21-in tt, one 4-in; Cammell Laird, Birkenhead, 1940; b/up Llanelly 1947.

Talent: T cls submarine; 1090/1575; 273½ x 26½; 15¼/9; 59; eleven 21-in tt, one 4-in; Vickers-Armstrongs, Barrow, 1944; transferred 1944 to Netherlands Navy, rnd *Zwaardvis;* sold Antwerp shipbreakers 1963.

Talent: T cls submarine; 1090/1575; 273½ x 26½; 15¼/9; 59; eleven 21-in tt, one 4-in; Vickers-Armstrongs, Barrow, 1945; ex-*Tasman*, 1945; b/up Troon 1970.

Talisman: T cls submarine; 1090/1575; 273½ x 26½; 15¼/9; 59; ten 21-in tt, one 4-in; Cammell Laird, Birkenhead, 1940; lost off Malta, September 1942.

Tally-Ho: T cls submarine; 1090/1575; 273½ x 26½; 15¼/9; 59; eleven 21-in tt, one 4-in; Vickers-Armstrongs, Barrow, 1943; ex-*P-97;* b/up Briton Ferry 1967.

Talybont: Hunt cls destroyer — Albrighton type; 1050; 280 x 31½; 27; 168; four 4-in, two 21-in tt; J. S. White & Co, Cowes, 1943; b/up Charlestown 1961.

Tamarisk: trawler; 352 grt; 140½ x 24; --;--;one4-in;CookWelton&Gemmell, Beverley, 1925; ex-*St Gatien* (T. Hamling & Co, Hull) bought RN 1939; sunk by German aircraft in Thames estuary, Aug 12, 1940.

Tamarisk: Flower cls corvette; 925; 205 x 33; 16; 85; one 4-in; Fleming & Ferguson, Paisley, 1941; ex-*Ettrick,* 1941; transferred 1943 to Greek Navy, rnd *Tompazis;* b/up Perama 1963.

Tanatside: Hunt cls destroyer — Albrighton type; 1050; 280 x 31½; 27; 168; four 4-in, two 21-in tt; Yarrow & Co, Scotstoun, 1942; transferred 1946 to Greek Navy, rnd *Adrias,* rtnd RN 1964; b/up Greece 1964.

Tanganyika: Algerine cls minesweeper; 950; 235 x 35½; 16½; 104; one 4-in; Lobnitz & Co, Renfrew, 1944; b/up Inverkeithing 1963.

Tango: Dance cls trawler; 530; 160½ x 27½; 11½; 35; one 4-in; Smith's Dock Co, Middlesbrough, 1941; sold 1946, Belgian owners.

Tantalus: T cls submarine; 1090/1575; 273½ x 26½; 15¼/9; 59; eleven 21-in tt, one 4-in; Vickers-Armstrongs, Barrow, 1943; b/up Milford Haven 1950.

Tantivy: T cls submarine; 1090/1575; 273½ x 26½; 15¼/9; 59; eleven 21-in tt, one 4-in; Vickers-Armstrongs, Barrow 1943; sunk as target in Cromarty Firth 1951.

Tapir: T cls submarine; 1090/1575; 273½ x 26½; 15¼/9; 59; eleven 21-in tt, one 4-in; Vickers-Armstrongs, Barrow, 1944; transferred 1948 to Netherlands Navy, rnd *Zeehond,* rtnd RN 1953; b/up Faslane 1967.

Tarantella: Dance cls trawler; 530; 160½ x 27½; 11½; 35; one 4-in; Smith's Dock Co, Middlesbrough 1941; rnd *Two Step,* 1943; transferred 1946 to Italian Navy, rnd *RD-308;* sold mid-1960s.

Tarantula: Insect cls river gunboat; 625; 237½ x 36; 14; 65; one 6-in, one 3-in; Wood, Skinner & Co, Newcastle, 1916; used as accommodation ship; sunk as target off Ceylon, May 1946.

Tarn: T cls submarine; 1090/1575; 273½ x 26½; 15¼/9; 59; eleven 21-in tt, one 4-in; Vickers-Armstrongs, Barrow, 1945; transferred 1946 to Netherlands, Navy, rnd *Tijgerhaai;* sold Amsterdam shipbreakers 1965.

Tarpon: T cls submarine; 1090/1575; 273½ x 26½; 15¼/9; 59; ten 21-in tt, one 4-in; Scotts SB & E Co, Greenock, 1940; sunk by German surface craft in North Sea, Apr 14, 1940.

Tartar: Tribal cls destroyer; 1870; 377 x 36½;36½;219;eight4.7-in,four21-intt; Swan Hunter & Wigham Richardson, Wallsend, 1939; b/up Newport, 1948.

Tattoo: Catherine cls minesweeper; 890; 221 x 32; 18; 109; one 3-in; Associated Shipbuilders, Seattle, 1943; ex-USN Auk cls minesweeper *BAM-32,* transferred Lease/Lend to RN 1943, rtnd USN 1946; transferred 1947 to Turkey, rnd *Carsamba;*

Taurus: T cls submarine; 1090/1575; 273½ x 26½; 15¼/9; 59; eleven 21-in tt, one 4-in; Vickers-Armstrongs, Barrow, 1942; ex-*P-93;* transferred 1948 to Netherlands Navy rnd *Dolfijn,* rtnd RN 1953; b/up Dunston 1960.

Tavy: River cls frigate; 1370; 301½ x 36½; 19; 140; two 4-in; C. Hill & Sons, Bristol, 1943; b/up Newport 1955.

Tay: River cls frigate; 1370; 301½ x 36½; 19; 140; two 4-in; Smith's Dock Co, Middlesbrough, 1942; b/up Rosyth 1956.

Teazer: T cls destroyer; 1710; 362¾ x 35¾; 36; 180; four 4.7-in, eight 21-in tt; Cammell Laird, Birkenhead, 1943; b/up Dalmuir 1965.

Tedworth: Hunt cls minesweeper; 750; 231 x 28; 16; 71; one 4-in; Wm Simons & Co, Renfrew, 1917; b/up Hayle 1946.

Tees: River cls frigate; 1370; 301½ x 36½; 19; 140; two 4-in; Hall Russell, Aberdeen, 1943; b/up Newport 1955.

Telemachus: T cls submarine: 1090/1575; 273½ x 26½; 15¼/9; 59; eleven 21-in tt, one 4-in; Vickers-Armstrongs, Barrow, 1943; b/up Charlestown 1961.

Teme: River cls frigate; 1370; 301½ x 36½; 19; 140; two 4-in; Smith's Dock Co, Middlesbrough, 1944; irreparably damaged by U-boat off Falmouth, Mar 29, 1945; b/up Llanelly 1946.

Tempest: T cls submarine; 1090/1575; 273½ x 26½; 15¼/9; 59; eleven 21-in tt, one 4-in; Cammell Laird, Birkenhead, 1941; sunk by Italian surface craft in Gulf of Taranto, Feb 13, 1942.

Templar: T cls submarine; 1090/1575; 273½ x 26½; 15¼/9; 59; eleven 21-in tt, one 4-in; Vickers-Armstrongs, Barrow, 1943; ex-*P-96;* sunk in Loch Striven as target for torpedoes, 1954; raised Dec 1958; b/up Troon 1959.

Tenacious: T cls destroyer; 1710; 362¾ x 35¾; 36; 180; four 4.7-in, eight 21-in tt; Cammell Laird, Birkenhead, 1943; b/up Troon 1965.

Tenacity: Assurance cls tug; 1045; 157 x 35; 13; 31; one 3-in; Cochrane & Sons, Selby, 1940; ex-*Diligent,* 1940; rnd *Adherent* 1947; 1962, Bergnings & Dykeri AB Neptun, Sweden, rnd *Hermes;* 1970, Rivtow Marine, Canada, rnd *Rivtow Viking;*

Tenby: Bangor cls minesweeper; 656; 174 x 28½; 16; 60; one 3-in; Wm Hamilton & Co, Port Glasgow, 1941; b/up Dunston 1948.

Tenedos: S cls destroyer; 905; 276 x 26¾; 31; 98; one 4-in; Hawthorn Leslie, Hebburn, 1919; sunk by Japanese aircraft at Colombo, Apr 5, 1942.

Termagant: T cls destroyer; 1710; 362¾ x 35¾; 36; 180; four 4.7-in, eight 21-in tt; Wm Denny & Bros, Dumbarton, 1943; b/up Dalmuir 1965.

Tern: Tern cls river gunboat; 262; 167½ x 27; 14; 55; two 3-in; Yarrow & Co, Scotstoun, 1928; scuttled Hong Kong Dec 19, 1941.

Terpsichore: T cls destroyer; 1710; 362¾ x 35¾; 36; 180; four 4.7-in, eight 21-in tt; Wm Denny & Bros, Dumbarton, 1944; b/up Troon 1966.

Terrapin: T cls submarine; 1090/1575; 273½ x 26½; 15¼/9; 59; eleven 21-in

tt, one 4-in; Vickers-Armstrongs, Barrow, 1944; irreparably damaged by Japanese surface force in South Pacific, May 19, 1945; b/up Troon 1946.

Terror: Erebus cls monitor; 7200; 405 x 88; 12; 315; two 15-in; Harland & Wolff, Belfast, 1916; sunk by aircraft off Derna, Feb 24, 1941.

Test: River cls frigate; 1370; 301½ x 36½; 19; 140; two 4-in; Hall Russell, Aberdeen, 1942; transferred 1946 to Indian Navy, rnd *Neza,* rtnd RN 1947; b/up Faslane 1955.

Tetcott: Hunt cls destroyer — Blankney type; 1050; 280 x 31½; 27; 168; six 4-in; J. S. White & Co, Cowes, 1941; b/up Milford Haven 1956.

Tetrarch: T cls submarine; 1090/1575; 273½ x 26½; 15¼/9; 59; ten 21-in tt, one 4-in; Vickers-Armstrongs, Barrow 1940; lost western Mediterranean November 1941.

Teviot: River cls frigate; 1370; 301½ x 36½; 19; 140; two 4-in; Hall Russell, Aberdeen, 1943; b/up Briton Ferry 1955.

Texada: Isles cls trawler; 560; 164 x 27½; 12; 40; one 12-pdr; Midland Shipyards, Midland, 1942; sold 1946.

Thames: River cls submarine; 1805/2680; 345 x 28¼; 21½/10; 60; six 21-in tt, one 4-in; Vickers-Armstrongs, Barrow, 1932; lost off Norway, July 1940.

Thane: Smiter cls escort carrier; 11,420; 496 x 69½; 16; 650; 20 aircraft, two 5-in; Seattle-Tacoma SB Corp, Tacoma, 1943; ex-USN *Sunset, BCVE-48,* transferred Lease/Lend to RN 1943; irreparably damaged by torpedo from *U-482* off Clyde Light Vessel, Jan 15, 1945; rtnd USN 1946; b/up Faslane 1946.

Thanet: S cls destroyer; 905; 276 x 26¾; 31; 98; one 4-in; Hawthorn Leslie, Hebburn, 1919/HM Dockyard, Sheerness, 1922; sunk by Japanese surface force off Endau, Jan 27, 1942.

Thermol: oiler; 4145; 270 x 38½; 11; 39; --; Greenock & Grangemouth Dockyard Co, Greenock, 1916; 1947, Harker (Coasters), London, rnd *Brocodale H;* 1948, Mirupanu SS Co, London, rnd *Julia C;* b/up Savona 1954.

Thirlmere: Lake cls trawler; 560; 147½ x 26½; 12½; 36; one 12-pdr; Smith's Dock Co, Middlesbrough; ex-whale catcher Kos XXVI (A. Jahre, Norway), bought RN 1939 and converted; 1946, A. Jahre & Co, Norway, converted to whale catcher, rnd Kos XXVI; b/up Grimstad 1964.

Thisbe: Algerine cls minesweeper; 950; 235 x 35½; 16½; 104; one 4-in; Redfern Construction Co, Toronto, 1943; b/up Charlestown 1957.

Thistle: T cls submarine; 1090/1575; 273½ x 26½; 15¼/9; 59; ten 21-in tt, one 4-in; Vickers-Armstrongs, Barrow, 1939; torpedoed and sunk by U-4 off Norway, Apr 10, 1940.

Thorn: T cls submarine; 1090/1575; 273½ x 26½; 15¼/9; 59; eleven 21-in tt, one 4-in; Cammell Laird, Birkenhead, 1941; sunk by Italian surface craft off Tobruk, Aug 6, 1942.

Thornbrough: Captain cls frigate; 1400; 306 x 36⅚; 23½; 220; three 3-in; Bethlehem-Hingham Shipyard, 1943; ex-USN Buckley cls destroyer-escort DE-565, transferred Lease/Lend to RN 1943, rtnd USN 1947; b/up Greece 1947.

Thorough: T cls submarine; 1090/1575; 273½ x 26½; 15¼/9; 59; eleven 21-in tt, one 4-in; Vickers-Armstrongs, Barrow, 1944; b/up Dunston 1961.

Thracian: S cls destroyer; 905; 276 x 26¾; 31; 98; two 4-in; Hawthorn Leslie, Hebburn/HM Dockyard, Sheerness 1922; damaged by Japanese aircraft and beached at Hong Kong Dec 24, 1941; salved by Japanese and commissioned as patrol vessel No 101; returned RN September 1945; b/up Hong Kong 1946.

Thrasher: T cls submarine; 1090/1575; 273½ x 26½; 15¼/9; 59; eleven 21-in tt, one 4-in; Cammell Laird, Birkenhead, 1941; b/up Briton Ferry 1947.

Throsk: coastal ammunition ship; 1488; 199¾ x 34½; 11½; --; --; Philip & Son Dartmouth, 1944;

Thruster: fighter direction ship; 5970; 400 x 49; 17; 500; eight 20-mm; Harland & Wolff, Belfast, 1943; transferred 1947 to Netherlands Navy,

rnd Pelikaan; b/up Bilbao 1973.

Thule: T cls submarine; 1090/1575; 273½ x 26½; 15¼/9; 59; eleven 21-in tt, one 4-in; HM Dockyard, Devonport, 1943; b/up Inverkeithing 1962.

Thunderbolt: T cls submarine; 1090/1575; 273½ x 26½; 15¼/9; 59; ten 21-in tt, one 4-in; Cammell Laird, Birkenhead, 1939; ex-Thetis, which foundered in Liverpool Bay, June 1, 1939, raised April 1940, refitted and rnd; sunk by Italian surface craft near Sicily, Mar 13, 1943.

Thyme: Flower cls corvette; 925; 205 x 33; 16; 85; one 4-in; Smith's Dock Co, Middlesbrough, 1941; transferred 1946 to Air Ministry, converted to weather ship, rnd Weather Reporter, rnd Weather Explorer, 1947; 1958, Mrs Evgenia J Chandris, Greece, rnd Epos;

Tigris: T cls submarine; 1090/1575; 273½ x 26½; 15¼/9; 59; ten 21-in tt, one 4-in; HM Dockyard, Chatham, 1940; lost off Naples, March 1943.

Tilbury: Bangor cls minesweeper; 672; 180 x 28½; 16; 60; one 3-in; Lobnitz & Co, Renfrew, 1942; transferred 1942 to Indian Navy, rnd Konkan; b/up mid-1960s.

Tintagel Castle: Castle cls corvette; 1010; 252 x 36¾; 16½; 120; one 4-in; Ailsa SB Co, Troon, 1944; b/up Troon 1958.

Tiptoe: T cls submarine; 1090/1575; 273½ x 26½; 15¼/9; 59; eleven 21-in tt, one 4-in; HM Dockyard, Barrow, 1944; sold Portsmouth shipbreakers 1972.

Tiree: Isles cls trawler; 560; 164 x 27½; 12; 40; one 12-pdr; Goole SB & Repairing Co, Goole, 1941; b/up Antwerp 1960.

Tireless: T cls submarine; 1090/1575; 273½ x 26½; 15¼/9; 59; eleven 21-in tt, one 4-in; HM Dockyard, Portsmouth, 1943; b/up Newport 1968.

Titania: submarine depot ship; 5250; 350 x 46¼; 14½; 249; --; Clyde SB & E Co, Port Glasgow, 1915; building for Italy, taken over by RN 1915, b/up Faslane 1949.

Tobago: Colony cls frigate; 1430; 304 x 37½; 18; 120; three 3-in; Walsh-Kaiser Co, Providence, 1944; ex-USN PF-81, transferred

Lease/Lend to RN 1944, rnd *Holmes,*
rnd *Hong Kong,* rnd *Tobago,* rtnd USN
1946; 1950, Khedivial Mail Line, Egypt,
for conversion to passenger ship —
not completed; b/up Bitter Lakes 1956.

Tocogay: Isles cls trawler; 560; 164 x
27½; 12; 40; three 20-mm; Cook
Welton & Gemmell, Beverley, 1945;
1958, (owner not known) rnd *Anna;*
1961, Stevanos M. Baxevais, Greece,
rnd *Elma;* 1968, D. Kallimasias & Co,
Greece, rnd *Kyriaki;*

Token: T cls submarine; 1090/1575;
273½ x 26½; 15¼/9; 59; eleven 21-in
tt, one 4-in; HM Dockyard,
Portsmouth, 1943; sold Portsmouth
shipbreakers 1970.

Topaze: Gem cls trawler; 608; 157 x
26¾; 12; 18; one 4-in; Smith's Dock
Co, Middlesbrough, 1935;
ex-*Melbourne* (H. Croft Baker & Sons,
Grimsby) bought RN 1935; lost in
collision off the Clyde, Apr 20, 1941.

Torbay: T cls submarine; 1090/1575;
273½ x 26½; 15¼/9; 56; ten 21-in tt,
one 4-in; HM Dockyard, Chatham,
1940; b/up Briton Ferry 1946.

Torridge: River cls frigate; 1370; 301½
x 36½; 19; 140; two 4-in; Blyth SB &
DD Co, Blyth, 1944; transferred 1944;
to French Navy, rnd *La Surprise;*
transferred 1964 to Morocco,
converted to Royal Yacht, rnd *Al
Maouna;*

Torrington: Captain cls frigate; 1400;
306 x 36⅝; 23½; 220; three 3-in;
Bethlehem-Hingham Shipyard, 1944;
ex-USN Buckley cls destroyer-escort
DE-568, transferred Lease/Lend to RN
1944, rtnd USN 1946, b/up.

Tortola: Colony cls frigate; 1430; 304 x
37½; 18; 120; three 3-in; Walsh-Kaiser
Co, Providence, 1944; ex-USN *PF-91,*
transferred Lease/Lend to RN, rnd
Peyton, rnd *Tortola,* 1944, rtnd USN
1946; sold 1947, b/up.

Totem: T cls submarine; 1090/1575;
273½ x 26½; 15¼/9;59; eleven 21-in tt,
one 4-in; HM Dockyard, Devonport,
1944; transferred 1967 to Israel, rnd
Dakar; lost in eastern Mediterranean,
Jan 25, 1968.

Totland: Lulworth cls escort; 1546;
250 x 42; 16; 200; one 5-in, three 3-in;
Gen Eng & DD Co, Oakland, 1932;
ex-US Coast Guard cutter *Cayuga,*

transferred Lease/Lend to RN 1941,
rtnd USCG 1946 rnd *Mocoma;*
damaged and decommissioned 1950,
used as barracks at Houston as *Coast
Guard Barge No 55;*

Tourmaline: Gem cls trawler; 641;
160¼ x 26¾; 12; 18; one 4-in; Smith's
Dock Co, Middlesbrough, 1935;
ex-*Berkshire* (Berkshire Fishing Co,
Grimsby) bought RN 1935; sunk by
German aircraft off North Foreland,
Feb 5, 1941.

Tourmaline: Catherine cls
minesweeper; 890; 221 x 32; 18; 109;
one 3-in; Gulf Shipbuilding Corp,
Houston, 1943; ex-USN Auk cls
minesweeper *Usage,* transferred
Lease/Lend to RN 1943, rtnd USN
1946; transferred 1947 to Turkey, rnd
Cardak;

Towy: River cls frigate; 1370; 301½ x
36½; 19; 140; two 4-in; Smith's Dock
Co, Middlesbrough, 1943; b/up Port
Glasgow 1956.

Tracker: Smiter cls escort carrier;
11,420; 496 x 69½; 16; 650; 20
aircraft; Seattle-Tacoma SB Corp,
Tacoma, 1942; ex-USN *BAVG-6,*
transferred Lease/Lend to RN 1942,
rtnd USN 1945; 1949, Dodero Line,
Argentine, converted to cargo liner,
rnd *Corrientes;* b/up Belgium 1964.

Tradewind: T cls submarine;
1090/1575; 273½ x 26½; 15¼/9; 59;
eleven 21-in tt, one 4-in; HM Dockyard,
Chatham, 1943; b/up Charlestown
1955.

Trafalgar: Battle cls destroyer; 2325;
379 x 40¼; 36; 308; four 4.5-in, eight
21-in tt; Swan Hunter & Wigham
Richardson, Wallsend, 1945; b/up
Dalmuir 1970.

Traveller: T cls submarine;
1090/1575; 273½ x 26½; 15¼/9; 59;
eleven 21-in tt, one 4-in; Scotts SB & E
Co, Greenock, 1941; missing in
Mediterranean, December 1942.

Trenchant: T cls submarine;
1090/1575; 273½ x 26½; 15¼/9; 59;
eleven 21-in tt, one 4-in; HM Dockyard,
Chatham, 1943; b/up Faslane 1963.

Trent: River cls frigate; 1370; 301½ x
36½; 19; 140; two 4-in; C. Hill & Sons,
Bristol, 1943; transferred 1946 to
Indian Navy, rnd *Kukri,* converted to
survey ship, rnd *Investigator* 1951;

Trespasser: T cls submarine; 1090/1575; 273½ x 26½; 15¼/9; 59; eleven 21-in tt, one 4-in; Vickers-Armstrongs, Barrow, 1942; ex-*P-92;* b/up Gateshead 1961.

Triad: T cls submarine; 1090/1575; 273½ x 26½; 15¼/9; 59; ten 21-in tt, one 4-in; Vickers-Armstrongs, Barrow, 1939; mined near Taranto, October 1940.

Tribune: T cls submarine; 1090/1575; 273½ x 26½; 15¼/9; 59; ten 21-in tt, one 4-in; Scotts SB & E Co, Greenock, 1939; b/up Milford Haven 1947.

Trident: T cls submarine; 1090/1575; 273½ x 26½; 15¼/9; 59; ten 21-in tt, one 4-in; Cammell Laird, Birkenhead, 1939; b/up Newport 1946.

Trillium: Flower cls corvette; 925; 205 x 33; 16; 85; one 4-in; Canadian Vickers, Montreal, 1940; transferred 1941 to Royal Canadian Navy, rtnd RN 1945; 1950, Balleneros Ltd SA, Uruguay, converted to whale catcher, rnd *Olympic Runner;* 1956, Kyokuyo Hogei KK, Japan, rnd *Otori Maru No 10,* rnd *Kyo Maru No 16,* 1959; b/up Japan 1971.

Trinidad: Fiji cls cruiser; 8525; 555½ x 62; 33; 980; twelve 6-in, eight 4-in, six 21-in tt; HM Dockyard, Devonport, 1940; damaged by German aircraft in Barentz Sea, sunk May 15, 1942, by RN.

Triton: T cls submarine; 1090/1575; 273½ x 26½; 15¼/9; 59; ten 21-in tt, one 4-in; Vickers-Armstrongs, Barrow, 1940; sunk by Italian surface craft in Strait of Otranto, Dec 18, 1940.

Triumph: T cls submarine; 1090/1575; 273½ x 26½; 15¼/9; 59; ten 21-in tt, one 4-in; Vickers-Armstrongs, Barrow, 1938; lost in Aegean, January 1942.

Trodday: Isles cls trawler; 560; 164 x 27½; 12; 40; three 20-mm; Cook Welton & Gemmell, Beverley, 1945; b/up Spezia 1960.

Trollope: Captain cls frigate; 1400; 306 x 36⅝; 23½; 220; three 3-in; Bethlehem-Hingham Shipyard, 1944; ex-USN Buckley cls destroyer-escort *DE-566,* transferred Lease/Lend to RN 1944; irreparably damaged by German E-boat off Normandy, July 6, 1944; b/up Troon 1951.

Trondra: Isles cls trawler; 560; 164 x 27½; 12; 40; one 12-pdr; J. Lewis & Sons, Aberdeen, 1942; b/up Charlestown 1957.

Trooper: T cls submarine; 1090/1575; 273½ x 26½; 15¼/9; 59; eleven 21-in tt, one 4-in; Scotts SB & E Co, Greenock, 1942; missing in Mediterranean, October 1943.

Troubridge: T cls destroyer; 1730; 362¾ x 35¾; 36; 230; four 4.7-in, eight 21-in tt; John Brown & Co, Clydebank, 1943; b/up Newport, 1970.

Trouncer: Smiter cls escort carrier; 11,420; 496 x 69½; 16; 650; 20 aircraft, two 5-in; Seattle-Tacoma SB Corp, Tacoma, 1944; ex-USN *Perdito, BCVE-47,* transferred Lease/Lend to RN 1944, rtnd USN 1946; 1947, Lancashire Shipping Co, Hong Kong, converted to cargo liner, rnd *Greystoke Castle,* rnd *Gallic* 1954; 1957, Ben Line Steamers, Edinburgh, no name change, rnd *Benrinnes,* 1959; b/up Kaohsiung 1973.

Truant: T cls submarine; 1090/1575; 273½ x 26½; 15¼/9; 59; ten 21-in tt, one 4-in; Vickers-Armstrongs, Barrow, 1939; lost aground on rocks near Cherbourg, December 1946, after tow broke on way to shipbreakers at Briton Ferry.

Truculent: T cls submarine; 1090/1575; 273½ x 26½; 15¼/9; 59; eleven 21-in tt, one 4-in; Vickers-Armstrongs, Barrow, 1942; ex-*P-95;* sunk in collision in Thames Estuary, Jan 12, 1950; raised and b/up Grays 1950.

Truelove: Algerine cls minesweeper; 950; 235 x 35½; 16½; 104; one 4-in; Redfern Construction Co, Toronto, 1943; b/up Blyth 1957.

Trump: T cls submarine; 1090/1575; 273½ x 26½; 15¼/9; 59; eleven 21-in tt, one 4-in; Vickers-Armstrongs, Barrow, 1944; b/up Newport 1971.

Trumpeter: Smiter cls escort carrier; 11,420; 496 x 69½; 16; 650; 20 aircraft, two 5-in; Seattle-Tacoma SB Corp, Tacoma, 1943; ex-USN *Bastian, BCVE-37,* transferred Lease/Lend to RN rnd *Lucifer,* rnd *Trumpeter* 1943, rtnd USN 1946, rnd *Bastian;* 1949, Holland America Line, Holland, converted to cargo liner, rnd *Alblasserdyk;* 1966, Cia Naviera

Rinoula SA, Greece, rnd *Irene Valmas;* b/up Castellon 1971.

Truncheon: T cls submarine; 1090/1575; 273½ x 26½; 15¼/9; 59; eleven 21-in tt, one 4-in; HM Dockyard, Devonport, 1944; transferred 1968 to Israel, rnd *Dolphin;*

Trusty: T cls submarine; 1090/1575; 273½ x 26½; 15¼/9; 59; eleven 21-in tt, one 4-in; Vickers-Armstrongs, Barrow, 1941; b/up Milford Haven 1947.

Tudor: T cls submarine; 1090/1575; 273½ x 26½; 15¼/9; 59; eleven 21-in tt, one 4-in; HM Dockyard, Devonport, 1943; b/up Faslane 1963.

Tulip: Flower cls corvette; 925; 205 x 33; 16; 85; one 4-in; Smith's Dock Co, Middlesbrough, 1940; 1950, Balleneros Ltd SA, Uruguay, converted to whale catcher, rnd *Olympic Conqueror;* 1956, Kyokuyo Hogei KK, Japan, rnd *Otori Maru No 8;* 1957, A/S Thor Dahl, Norway, rnd *Thorlyn;* b/up West Germany 1965.

Tumult: T cls destroyer; 1710; 362¾ x 35¾; 36; 180; four 4.7-in, eight 21-in tt; John Brown & Co, Clydebank, 1943; b/up Dalmuir 1965.

Tuna: T cls submarine; 1090/1575; 273½ x 26½; 15¼/9; 59; ten 21-in tt, one 4-in; Scotts SB & E Co, Greenock, 1940; b/up Briton Ferry 1946.

Turbulent: T cls submarine, 1090/1575; 273½ x 26½; 15¼/9; 59; eleven 21-in tt, one 4-in; Vickers-Armstrongs, Barrow, 1941; missing off Sardinia, March 1943.

Turmoil: Bustler cls tug; 1800; 205 x 38½; 15; 42; one 3-in; H. Robb, Leith, 1944; 1965, Tsavliris (Salvage & Towage) Greece, rnd *Nisos Kerkyra;* 1971, L. Matsas & Sons, Greece, rnd *Matsas;*

Turpin: T cls submarine; 1090/1575; 273½ x 26½; 15¼/9; 59; eleven 21-in tt, one 4-in; HM Dockyard, Chatham, 1944; transferred 1965 to Israel, rnd *Leviathan;*

Turquoise: Gem cls trawler; 641; 160¼ x 26¾; 12; 18; one 4-in; Smith's Dock Co, Middlesbrough, 1935; ex-*Warwickshire* (Warwickshire Fishing Co, Grimsby) bought RN 1935; 1946, Grimsby Merchants Amalgamated Trawling Co, Grimsby, rnd *St Oswald,* rnd *Woolton,* 1950; 1954, Wyre Trawlers, Fleetwood, rnd *Wyre Woolton;* b/up UK 1957.

Tuscan: T cls destroyer; 1710; 362¾ x 35¾; 36; 180; four 4.7-in, eight 21-in tt; Swan Hunter & Wigham Richardson, Wallsend, 1943; b/up Bo'ness, 1966.

Tweed: River cls frigate; 1370; 301½ x 36½; 19; 140; two 4-in; A. & J. Inglis, Glasgow, 1943; torpedoed and sunk by *U-305* in Atlantic, Jan 7, 1944.

Tyler: Captain cls frigate; 1400; 306 x 36⅚; 23½; 220; three 3-in; Bethlehem-Hingham Shipyard, 1944; ex-USN Buckley cls destroyer-escort *DE-567,* transferred Lease/Lend to RN 1944, rtnd USN 1945, b/up.

Tyne: destroyer depot ship; 11,000; 623 x 66; 17; 1000; eight 4.5-in; Scotts SB & E Co, Greenock, 1941; b/up Barrow 1972.

Tynedale: Hunt cls destroyer — Atherstone type; 1000; 280 x 29; 27½; 146; four 4-in; Alex Stephen & Sons, Linthouse, 1940; torpedoed and sunk by *U-593* off Bougie, Dec 12, 1943.

Tynwald: A-A ship; 2376 grt; 328¾ x 46; 21; --; six 4-in; Vickers-Armstrongs, Barrow, 1937; ex-ferry (Isle of Man Steam Packet Co, Douglas) bought RN 1940, converted; sunk by Italian submarine off Bougie, Nov 12, 1942.

Tyrian: T cls destroyer; 1710; 362¾ x 35¾; 36; 180; four 4.7-in, eight 21-in tt; Swan Hunter & Wigham Richardson, Wallsend, 1943; b/up Troon 1965.

Uganda: Uganda cls cruiser; 8875; 555½ x 62; 31½; 950; nine 6-in, eight 4-in, six 21-in tt; Vickers-Armstrongs, Tyne, 1943; transferred 1944 to Royal Canadian Navy, rnd *Quebec;* b/up Osaka 1961.

Ullswater: Lake cls trawler; 560; 147½ x 26½; 12½; 36; one 12-pdr; Smith's Dock Co, Middlesbrough, 1939; ex-whale catcher *Kos XXIX* (A. Jahre, Norway) bought RN 1939; sunk by E-boats in English Channel, Nov 19, 1942.

Ulster: U cls destroyer; 1710; 362¾ x 35¾; 36; 180; four 4.7-in, eight 21-in tt; Swan Hunter & Wigham Richardson,

Wallsend, 1943;

Ultimatum: U cls submarine; 545/735; 196¾ x 16; 11/9; 31; four 21-in tt, one 3-in; Vickers-Armstrongs, Barrow, 1941; ex-*P-34;* b/up Port Glasgow 1950.

Ultor: U cls submarine; 545/735; 196¾ x 16; 11/9; 31; four 21-in tt, one 3-in; Vickers-Armstrongs, Barrow, 1943; ex-*P-53;* b/up Briton Ferry 1946.

Ulva: Isles cls trawler; 560; 164 x 27½; 12; 40; one 12-pdr; Cook Welton & Gemmell, Beverley, 1942; 1946, Rederi A/S Salvesen, Norway, rnd *Salvo;* 1948, A/S D/S Erling Lindoe; Norway, converted to cargo ship, rnd *Plico;* 1950, Alva A. Reid, Jamaica, rnd *Suriname,* rnd *Anne T. William, 1951;*

Ulysses: U cls destroyer; 1710; 362¾ x 35¾; 36; 180; four 4.7-in, eight 21-in tt; Cammell Laird, Birkenhead, 1943; b/up Plymouth 1970.

Umbra: U cls submarine; 545/735; 196¾ x 16; 11/9; 31; four 21-in tt, one 3-in; Vickers-Armstrongs, Barrow, 1941; ex-*P-35;* b/up Blyth 1947.

Umpire: U cls submarine; 540/730; 192¼ x 16; 11/9; 31; four 21-in tt, one 3-in; HM Dockyard, Chatham, 1941; ex-*P-31;* lost in collision in North Sea, July 19, 1941.

Una: U cls submarine; 540/730; 192¼ x 16; 11/9; 31; four 21-in tt, one 3-in; HM Dockyard, Chatham, 1941; ex-*P-32;* b/up Llanelly 1949.

Unbeaten: U cls submarine; 540/730; 192¼ x 16; 11/9; 31; four 21-in tt, one 3-in; Vickers-Armstrongs, Barrow, 1940; ex-*P-33;* sunk in error by British aircraft in Bay of Biscay, Nov 11, 1942.

Unbending: U cls submarine; 545/735; 196¾ x 16; 11/9; 31; four 21-in tt, one 3-in; Vickers-Armstrongs, Barrow, 1941; ex-*P-37;* b/up Gateshead 1950.

Unbroken: U cls submarine; 545/735; 196¾ x 16; 11/9; 31; four 21-in tt, one 3-in; Vickers-Armstrongs, Barrow, 1942; ex-*P-42;* transferred 1944 to Russia, rnd *B-2* rtnd RN 1949; b/up Gateshead 1950.

Undaunted: U cls submarine; 540/730; 192¼ x 16; 11/9; 31; four 21-in tt, one 3-in; Vickers-Armstrongs, Barrow, 1940; ex-*P-34;* lost off Tripoli, May 13, 1941.

Undaunted: U cls destroyer; 1710;

362¾ x 35¾; 36; 180; four 4.7-in, eight 21-in tt; Cammell Laird, Birkenhead, 1943;

Undine: U cls submarine; 540/730; 192¼ x 16; 11/9; 27; six 21-in tt, one 3-in; Vickers-Armstrongs, Barrow, 1938; sunk by German surface forces in North Sea, Jan 6, 1940.

Undine: U cls destroyer; 1710; 362¾ x 35¾; 36; 180; four 4.7-in, eight 21-in tt; J. I. Thornycroft & Co, Southampton, 1943; b/up Newport, 1965.

Unicorn: aircraft maintenance ship; 14,750; 646 x 90; 22; 650; 35 aircraft, eight 4.5-in; Harland & Wolff, Belfast, 1943; b/up Dalmuir 1959.

Union: U cls submarine; 540/730; 192¼ x 16; 11/9; 31; four 21-in tt, one 3-in; Vickers-Armstrongs, Barrow, 1941; ex-*P-35;* sunk by Italian torpedo boat off Cap Bon, July 22, 1941.

Unique: U cls submarine; 540/730; 192¼ x 16; 11/9; 31; six 21-in tt, one 3-in; Vickers-Armstrongs, Barrow, 1940; ex-*P-36;* missing in Atlantic, November 1942.

Unison: U cls submarine; 545/735; 196¾ x 16; 11/9; 31; four 21-in tt, one 3-in; Vickers-Armstrongs, Barrow, 1942; ex-*P-43;* transferred 1944 to Russia, rnd *B-3,* rtnd RN 1949; b/up Stockton-on-Tees 1950.

United: U cls submarine; 545/735; 196¾ x 16; 11/9; 31; four 21-in tt, one 3-in; Vickers-Armstrongs, Barrow, 1942; ex-*P-44;* b/up Troon 1946.

Unity: U cls submarine; 540/730; 192¼ x 16; 11/9; 27; six 21-in tt, one 3-in; Vickers-Armstrongs, Barrow, 1938; lost in collision off River Tyne, Apr 29 1940.

Universal: U cls submarine; 545/735; 196¾ x 16; 11/9; 31; four 21-in tt, one 3-in; Vickers-Armstrongs, Tyne, 1943; ex-*P-57;* b/up Milford Haven 1946.

Unrivalled: U cls submarine; 545/735; 196¾ x 16; 11/9; 31; four 21-in tt, one 3-in; Vickers-Armstrongs, Barrow, 1942; ex-*P-45;* b/up Briton Ferry 1946.

Unruffled: U cls submarine; 545/735; 196¾ x 16; 11/9; 31; four 21-in tt, one 3-in; Vickers-Armstrongs, Barrow, 1942; ex-*P-46;* b/up Troon 1946.

Unruly: U cls submarine; 545/735; 196¾ x 16; 11/9; 31; four 21-in tt, one 3-in; Vickers-Armstrongs, Barrow,

1942; ex-*P-49;* b/up Inverkeithing 1946.

Unseen: U cls submarine; 545/735; 196¾ x 16; 11/9; 31; four 21-in tt, one 3-in; Vickers-Armstrongs, Barrow, 1942; ex-*P-51;* b/up Hayle 1949.

Unshaken: U cls submarine; 545/735; 196¾ x 16; 11/9; 31; four 21-in tt, one 3-in; Vickers-Armstrongs, Barrow, 1942; ex-*P-54;* b/up Troon 1946.

Unsparing: U cls submarine; 545/735; 196¾ x 16; 11/9; 31; four 21-in tt, one 3-in; Vickers-Armstrongs, Tyne, 1942; ex-*P-55;* b/up Inverkeithing 1946.

Unst: Isles cls trawler; 560; 164 x 27½; 12; 40; one 12-pdr; Ferguson Bros, Port Glasgow, 1942; transferred 1946 to Italian Navy, rnd *RD-303;* used as target mid-1960s.

Unswerving: U cls submarine; 545/735; 196¾ x 16; 11/9; 31; four 21-in tt, one 3-in; Vickers-Armstrongs, Tyne, 1943; ex-*P-63;* b/up Newport 1949.

Untamed: U cls submarine; 545/735; 196¾ x 16; 11/9; 31; four 21-in tt, one 3-in; Vickers-Armstrongs, Tyne, 1943; ex-*P-58;* sunk in Firth of Clyde, May 1943, salvaged, refitted and rnd *Vitality;* b/up Troon 1946.

Untiring: U cls submarine; 545/735; 196¾ x 16; 11/9; 31; four 21-in tt, one 3-in; Vickers-Armstrongs, Tyne, 1943; ex-*P-59;* transferred 1944 to Greek Navy, rnd *Amphitriti,.* rtnd RN 1952; sunk as target off Start Point, July 25, 1957.

Upholder: U cls submarine; 540/730; 192¼ x 16; 11/9; 31; six 21-in tt, one 3-in; Vickers-Armstrongs, Barrow, 1940; ex-*P-37;* sunk by Italian surface craft off Tripoli, Apr 14, 1942.

Uplifter: Kin cls coastal salvage vessel; 950; 179½ x 35¾; 9; 34; two 20-mm; Smith's Dock Co, Middlesbrough, 1944;

Upright: U cls submarine; 540/730; 192¼ x 16; 11/9; 31; six 21-in tt, one 3-in; Vickers-Armstrongs, Barrow, 1940; ex-*P-38;* b/up Troon 1946.

Uproar: U cls submarine; 545/735; 196¾ x 16; 11/9; 31; four 21-in tt, one 3-in; Vickers-Armstrongs, Barrow, 1941; ex-*P-31,* ex-*Ullswater,* 1943; b/up Inverkeithing 1946.

Upshot: V cls submarine; 545/740;

204½ x 16; 12¾/9; 31; four 21-in tt, one 3-in; Vickers-Armstrongs, Barrow, 1944; b/up Preston 1949.

Upstart: U cls submarine; 545/735; 196¾ x 16; 11/9; 31; four 21-in tt, one 3-in; Vickers-Armstrongs, Barrow, 1943; ex-*P-65;* transferred 1944 to Greek Navy, rnd *Xifias,* rtnd RN 1952; sunk as target off Isle of Wight, Aug 29, 1957.

Urania: U cls destroyer; 1710; 362¾ x 35¾; 36; 180; four 4.7-in, eight 21-in tt; Vickers-Armstrongs, Barrow, 1944; b/up Faslane 1971.

Urchin: U cls submarine; 540/730; 192¼ x 16; 11/9; 31; four 21-in tt, one 3-in; Vickers-Armstrongs, Barrow, 1941; ex-*P-39;* transferred 1941 to Poland, rnd *Sokol,* rtnd RN 1946; b/up UK 1949.

Urchin: U cls destroyer; 1710; 362¾ x 35¾; 36; 180; four 4.7-in, eight 21-in tt; Vickers-Armstrongs, Barrow, 1943; b/up Troon 1967.

Uredd: U cls submarine; 545/735; 196¾ x 16; 11/9; 31; four 21-in tt, one 3-in; Vickers-Armstrongs, Barrow, 1941; ex-*P-41;* lost off Norway, February 1943.

Urge: U cls submarine; 540/730; 192¼ x 16; 11/9; 31; four 21-in tt, one 3-in; Vickers-Armstrongs, Barrow, 1940; ex-*P-40;* sunk by Italian surface craft in eastern Mediterranean, Apr 28, 1942.

Ursa: U cls destroyer; 1710; 362¾ x 35¾; 36; 180; four 4.7-in, eight 21-in tt; J. I. Thornycroft & Co, Southampton, 1944; b/up Newport 1967.

Ursula: U cls submarine; 540/730; 192¼ x 16; 11/9; 31; six 21-in tt, one 3-in; Vickers-Armstrongs, Barrow, 1938; transferred 1944 to Russia, rnd *B-4,* rtnd RN 1949; b/up Grangemouth 1950.

Urtica: V cls submarine; 545/740; 204½ x 16; 12¾/9; 31; four 21-in tt, one 3-in; Vickers-Armstrongs, Barrow, 1944; b/up Milford Haven, 1950.

Usk: U cls submarine; 540/730; 192¼ x 16; 11/9; 31; four 21-in tt, one 3-in; Vickers-Armstrongs, Barrow, 1940; ex-*P-41;* missing Cap Bon area, May 1941.

Usk: River cls frigate; 1370; 301½ x 36½; 19; 140; two 4-in; Smith's Dock

Co, Middlesbrough, 1943; transferred 1950 to Egyptian Navy, rnd *Abikir;* sunk as blockship in Suez Canal, November, 1956, raised April 1957 and beached; b/up Bitter Lakes 1957.

Usurper: U cls submarine; 545/735; 196¾ x 16; 11/9; 31; four 21-in tt, one 3-in; Vickers-Armstrongs, Tyne, 1943; ex-*P-56;* missing, Gulf of Genoa area, October 1943.

Uther: U cls submarine; 545/735; 196¾ x 16; 11/9; 31; four 21-in tt, one 3-in; Vickers-Armstrongs, Tyne, 1943; ex-*P-62;* b/up Hayle 1950.

Utmost: U cls submarine; 540/730; 192¼ x 16; 11/9; 31; six 21-in tt, one 3-in; Vickers-Armstrongs, Barrow, 1940; ex-*P-42;* sunk by Italian surface craft west of Sicily, Nov 24, 1942.

Vaceasay: Isles cls trawler; 560; 164 x 27½; 12; 40; three 20-mm; Cook Welton & Gemmell, Beverley, 1945; sold Portsmouth shipbreakers, 1967.

Vagabond: V cls submarine; 545/730; 204½ x 16; 12¾/9; 31; four 21-in tt, one 3-in; Vickers-Armstrongs, Tyne, 1945; b/up Newport 1950.

Vagrant: BAT cls tug; 783; 143 x 33; 14; 34; one 3-in; Levingston SB, Orange, 1943; ex-USN, transferred Lease/Lend to RN 1943, rtnd USN 1946, rnd *ATR-49;* 1946 Tug Catherine Moran Inc, US, rnd *Marion Moran;* 1964, Little John Corp, US, rnd *Mary Elizabeth;*

Valentine: V cls destroyer; 1090; 312 x 29½; 24½; 134; four 4-in; Cammell Laird, Birkenhead, 1917; sunk by German aircraft near Terneuzen, May 15, 1940; refloated January 1953, beached, and b/up.

Valentine: V cls destroyer; 1710; 362¾ x 35¾; 36; 180; four 4.7-in, eight 21-in tt; John Brown & Co, Clydebank, 1944; ex-*Kempenfelt,* 1942; transferred 1944 to Royal Canadian Navy, rnd *Algonquin;* b/up Halifax, NS, 1952.

Valiant: Queen Elizabeth cls battleship; 31,520; 639¾ x 104; 24; 1184; eight 15-in, twenty 4.5-in; Fairfield SB & E Co, Govan, 1916; b/up Cairnryan 1948.

Vallay: Isles cls trawler; 560; 164 x 27½; 12; 40; three 20-mm; Cook Welton & Gemmell, Beverley, 1945; 1959,

John S. Latsis (London) Ltd, and b/up.

Valorous: V cls destroyer; 1090; 312 x 29½; 24½; 134; four 4-in; Wm Denny & Bros, Dumbarton, 1917; b/up Thornaby-on-Tees 1948.

Valse: Dance cls trawler; 530; 160½ x 27½; 11½; 35; one 4-in; Smith's Dock Co, Middlesbrough 1941; b/up Port Glasgow, 1951.

Vampire: V cls submarine; 545/740; 204½ x 16; 12¾/9; 31; four 21-in tt, one 3-in; Vickers-Armstrongs, Barrow, 1943; b/up Gateshead 1950.

Vandal: U cls submarine; 545/735; 196¾ x 16; 11/9; 31; four 21-in tt, one 3-in; Vickers-Armstrongs, Barrow, 1943; ex-*P-64;* wrecked Firth of Clyde, Feb 24, 1943.

Vanessa: V cls destroyer; 1090; 312 x 29½; 24½; 134; two 4-in; Wm Beardmore & Co, Dalmuir, 1918; b/up Charlestown 1949.

Vanity: V cls destroyer; 1090; 312 x 29½; 24½; 134; four 4-in; Wm Beardmore & Co, Dalmuir, 1918; b/up Grangemouth 1947.

Vanoc: V cls destroyer; 1090; 312 x 29½; 24½; 134; two 4-in; John Brown & Co, Clydebank, 1917; b/up Falmouth 1946.

Vanquisher: V cls destroyer; 1090; 312 x 29½; 24½; 134; two 4-in; John Brown & Co, Clydebank, 1917; b/up Charlestown 1948.

Vansittart: Modified W cls destroyer; 1120; 312 x 29½; 24½; 134; three 4.7-in; Wm Beardmore & Co, Dalmuir, 1919; b/up Newport 1946.

Varangian: U cls submarine; 545/735; 196¾ x 16; 11/9; 31; four 21-in tt, one 3-in; Vickers-Armstrongs, Tyne, 1943; ex-*P-61;* b/up Gateshead 1949.

Variance: V cls submarine; 545/740; 204½ x 16; 12¾/9; 31; four 21-in tt, one 3-in; Vickers-Armstrongs, Barrow, 1944; transferred to Norwegian Navy, rnd *Utsira;* b/up Hamburg 1965.

Varne: U cls submarine; 545/735; 196¾ x 16; 11/9; 31; four 21-in tt, one 3-in; Vickers-Armstrongs, Barrow, 1944; ex-*P-66;* transferred 1944 to Norwegian Navy, rnd *Ula;* b/up Hamburg 1965.

Varne: V cls submarine; 545/740; 204½ x 16; 12¾/9; 31; four 21-in tt, one 3-in; Vickers-Armstrongs, Tyne, 1944; b/up Troon 1958.

Vatersay: Isles cls trawler; 560; 164 x 27½; 12; 40; one 12-pdr; Cochrane & Sons, Selby, 1944; 1946, Soc Nav de L'Ouest Africain, Senegal, rnd *Vouri;* 1954, Huynh-Van-Gia, Vietnam, rnd *Nam-Viet;* 1971, Ho Van Tu, South Vietnam, no name change;

Vega: V cls destroyer; 1090; 312 x 29½; 24½; 134; four 4-in; Wm Doxford & Sons, Sunderland, 1917; b/up Dunston 1948.

Veldt: V cls submarine; 545/740; 204½ x 16; 12¾/9; 31; four 21-in tt, one 3-in; Vickers-Armstrongs, Barrow, 1943; transferred 1943 to Greek Navy, rnd *Pipinos,* rtnd RN 1957; b/up Dunston 1958.

Veleta: Dance cls trawler; 530; 160½ x 27½; 11½; 35; one 4-in; Smith's Dock Co, Middlesbrough, 1941; sold 1946.

Velox: V cls destroyer; 1090; 312 x 29½; 24½; 134; two 4-in; Wm Doxford & Sons, Sunderland, 1918; b/up Charlestown 1947.

Venerable: Colossus cls aircraft carrier; 13,190; 694½ x 112½; 25; 1350; 39-44 aircraft; Cammell Laird, Birkenhead, 1945; transferred 1948 to Netherlands Navy, rnd *Karel Doorman;* transferred 1968 to Argentine Navy, rnd *25 de Mayo;*

Venetia: V cls destroyer; 1090; 312 x 29½: 24½: 134: four 4-in, six 21-in tt; Fairfield SB & E Co, Govan, 1917; mined in Thames Estuary, Oct 19, 1940.

Vengeance: Colossus cls aircraft carrier; 13,190; 694½ x 112½; 25; 1350; 39-44 aircraft; Swan Hunter & Wigham Richardson, Wallsend 1945; transferred 1956 to Brazilian Navy, rnd *Minas Gerais;*

Vengeful: V cls submarine; 545/740; 204½ x 16; 12¾/9; 31; four 21-in tt, cne 3-in; Vickers-Armstrongs, Barrow, 1944; transferred 1944 to Greek Navy, rnd *Delphin,* rtnd RN 1957; b/up Gateshead 1958.

Venomous: Modified W cls destroyer; 1120; 312 x 29½; 24½; 134; two 4.7-in; John Brown & Co, Clydebank, 1919: ex-*Venom,* 1919; b/up Charlestown 1948.

Venturer: V cls submarine; 545/740; 204½ x 16; 12¾/9; 31; four 21-in tt, one 3-in; Vickers-Armstrongs, Barrow,

1943; transferred 1946 to Norwegian Navy, rnd *Utstein;* sold Sarpsborg shipbreakers 1965.

Venus: V cls destroyer; 1710; 362¾ x 35¾; 36; 220; four 4.7-in, eight 21-in tt; Fairfield SB & E Co, Govan, 1943; b/up Briton Ferry 1972.

Verbena: Flower cls corvette; 925; 205 x 33; 16; 85; one 4-in; Smith's Dock Co, Middlesbrough, 1940; 1948, AB Tore Holms, Gamleby, for conversion, not carried out; b/up Blyth 1951.

Verdun: V cls destroyer; 1090; 312 x 29½; 24½; 134; four 4-in; Hawthorn Leslie, Hebburn, 1917; b/up Inverkeithing 1946.

Verity: Modified W cls destroyer; 1120; 312 x 29½; 24½; 134; two 4.7-in; John Brown & Co, Clydebank, 1919; b/up Newport, 1947.

Veronica: Flower cls corvette; 925; 205 x 33; 16; 85; one 4-in; Smith's Dock Co, Middlesbrough, 1941; transferred 1942 to USN, rnd *Temptress,* rtnd RN 1945; 1947, Wheelock Marden, Hong Kong, converted to cargo ship, rnd *Verolock;* ashore L'Abervrac'h, Jan 12, 1947, after tow broke; salved and b/up Blyth 1951.

Versatile: V cls destroyer; 1090; 312 x 29½; 24½; 134; two 4-in; Hawthorn Leslie, Hebburn, 1918; b/up Granton 1949.

Verulam: V cls destroyer; 1710; 362¾ x 35¾; 36; 180; four 4.7-in, eight 21-in tt; Fairfield SB & E Co, Govan, 1943; b/up Newport 1972.

Vervain: Flower cls corvette; 925; 205 x 33; 16; 85; one 4-in; Harland & Wolff, Belfast, 1941; ex-*Broom,* 1941; torpedoed and sunk by *U-1208,* south of Iceland, Feb 20, 1945.

Veryan Bay: Bay cls frigate; 1580; 307½ x 28½; 19½; 157; four 4-in; C. Hill & Sons, Bristol, 1945; ex-*Loch Swannay,* 1944; b/up Charlestown 1959.

Vesper: V cls destroyer; 1090; 312 x 29½; 24½; 134; two 4-in; Alex Stephen & Sons, Linthouse, 1918; b/up Inverkeithing 1949.

Vestal: Algerine cls minesweeper; 950; 235 x 35½; 16½; 104; one 4-in; Harland & Wolff, Belfast, 1943; sunk by Japanese aircraft off Puket, Siam, July 26, 1945.

Vetch: Flower cls corvette; 925; 205 x 33; 16; 85; one 4-in; Smith's Dock Co,

Middlesbrough, 1941; 1948, Greek government, rnd *Patrai;* 1951, Balleneros Ltd SA, Uruguay, converted to whale catcher, rnd *Olympic Hunter;* 1956, Kyokuyo Hogei KK, Japan, rnd *Otori Maru No 18;*
Veteran: Modified W cls destroyer; 1500; 312 x 29½; 24½; 134; two 4.7-in; three 21-in tt; John Brown & Co, Clydebank, 1919; torpedoed and sunk by *U-404* in North Atlantic, Sept 26, 1942.
Viceroy: Thornycroft V cls destroyer; 1120; 312 x 30½; 24½; 134; four 4-in; J. I. Thornycroft & Co, Southampton, 1918; b/up Grangemouth 1948.
Victoria and Albert: Royal yacht; 4700; 439½ x 40; 20; 363; two 2-pdr; HM Dockyard, Pembroke, 1901; used for gunnery training; b/up Faslane 1954.
Victorious: Illustrious cls aircraft carrier; 23,000; 753 x 95; 31; 1600; 54 aircraft, sixteen 4.5-in; Vickers-Armstrongs, Tyne, 1941; b/up Faslane 1969.
Vidette: V cls destroyer; 1090; 312 x 29½; 24½; 134; two 4-in; Alex Stephen & Sons, Linthouse, 1918; b/up Grangemouth 1947.
Vigilant: V cls destroyer; 1710; 362¾ x 35¾; 36; 180; four 4.7-in, eight 21-in tt; Swan Hunter & Wigham Richardson, Wallsend, 1944; b/up Faslane 1965.
Vigorous: V cls submarine; 545/740; 204½ x 16; 12¾/9; 31; four 21-in tt, one 3-in; Vickers-Armstrongs, Barrow, 1944; b/up Thornaby-on-Tees 1950.
Viking: V cls submarine; 545/740; 204½ x 16; 12¾/9; 31; four 21-in tt, one 3-in; Vickers-Armstrongs, Barrow, 1943; transferred 1946 to Norwegian Navy, rnd *Utvaer;* sold Sarpsborg shipbreakers 1965.
Vimiera: V cls destroyer; 1090; 312 x 29½; 24½; 134; four 4-in; Swan Hunter & Wigham Richardson, Wallsend, 1917; mined in Thames Estuary, Jan 9, 1942, reported raised and b/up UK 1945-47.
Vimy: V cls destroyer; 1090; 312 x 29½; 24½; 134; two 4-in; Wm Beardmore & Co, Dalmuir, 1918; ex-*Vancouver,* 1928; b/up Charlestown 1948.
Vindex: escort carrier; 13,455; 524 x 68; 17; 700; 20 aircraft, two 4-in; Swan Hunter & Wigham Richardson, Wallsend, 1943; bought RN on stocks;

1947, Port Line, London, converted 1947-49 to cargo liner, rnd *Port Vindex;* b/up Kaohsiung 1971.
Vindictive: fleet repair ship; 9750; 605 x 65; 23; 750; two 4.7-in; Harland & Wolff, Belfast, 1918; ordered as cruiser *Cavendish,* completed as aircraft carrier, converted to cruiser 1923-1925, converted to training ship 1937; converted to repair ship 1940; b/up Blyth 1946.
Vineyard: V cls submarine; 545/740; 204½ x 16; 12¾/9; 31; four 21-in tt, one 3-in; Vickers-Armstrongs, Barrow, 1944; transferred 1944 to France, rnd *Doris,* rtnd RN 1947; b/up Charlestown 1950.
Violet: Flower cls corvette; 925; 205 x 33; 16; 85; one 4-in; Wm Simons & Co, Renfrew, 1941; 1947, Zubi Shipping Co, London, rnd *La Aguera;* 1949, Industrias Pesqueras Africanas SA, Spain, rnd *La Guera;* 1958, Fletamentos Maritimos SA, Spain, rnd *Claudio Sabadell;* b/up Spain 1970.
Virago: V cls destroyer; 1710; 362¾ x 35¾; 36; 180; four 4.7-in, eight 21-in tt; Swan Hunter & Wigham Richardson, Wallsend, 1943; b/up Faslane 1965.
Virtue: V cls submarine; 545/740; 204½ x 16; 12¾/9; 31; four 21-in tt, one 3-in; Vickers-Armstrongs, Barrow, 1944; b/up Cochin 1946.
Virulent: V cls submarine; 545/740; 204½ x 16; 12¾/9; 31; four 21-in tt, one 3-in; Vickers-Armstrongs, Tyne, 1944; transferred 1946 to Greek Navy, rnd *Argonaftis,* rtnd RN 1958; broke adrift in tow from Malta to Tyne for b/up, Dec 15, 1958, towed into Pasajes by fishing craft, Jan 6, 1959, sold 1961 at Pasajes to Spanish shipbreakers.
Viscol: Elmo l cls oiler; 2410; 220 x 34⅔; 9½; 19; --; Craig Taylor & Co, Stockton-on-Tees, 1916; 1948, Risdon Beazley & Co, Southampton, no name change; 1950, Ottavio Novella, Italy, rnd *Frecciamare;*
Viscount: Thornycroft V cls destroyer; 1120; 312 x 30½; 24½; 134; two 4-in; three 21-in tt; J. I. Thornycroft & Co, Southampton, 1918; b/up Dunston 1947.
Visigoth: V cls submarine; 545/740; 204½ x 16; 12¾/9; 31; four 21-in tt, one 3-in; Vickers-Armstrongs, Barrow,

1944; b/up Hayle 1950.

Vivacious: V cls destroyer; 1090; 312 x 29½; 24½; 134; two 4-in; Yarrow & Co, Scotstoun, 1917; b/up Charlestown 1948.

Vivid: V cls submarine; 545/740; 204½ x 16; 12¾/9; 31; four 21-in tt, one 3-in; Vickers-Armstrongs, Tyne, 1944; b/up Faslane 1950.

Vivien: V cls destroyer; 1090; 312 x 29½; 24½; 134; four 4-in; Yarrow & Co, Scotstoun, 1918; b/up Charlestown 1948.

Vixen: V cls destroyer; 1710; 362¾ x 35¾; 36; 180; four 4.7-in, eight 21-in tt; J. S. White & Co, Cowes, 1944; transferred 1944 to Royal Canadian Navy, rnd *Sioux;* b/up Spezia 1965.

Volage: V cls destroyer; 1710; 362¾ x 35¾; 36; 180; four 4.7-in, eight 21-in tt; J. S. White & Co, Cowes, 1944; sold Portsmouth shipbreakers 1972.

Volatile: V cls submarine; 545/730; 204½ x 16; 12¾/9; 31; four 21-in tt, one 3-in; Vickers-Armstrongs, Tyne, 1944; transferred 1944 to Greek Navy, rnd *Triana,* rtnd RN 1958; b/up Dunston 1958.

Volunteer: Modified W cls destroyer; 1120; 312 x 29½; 24½; 134; two 4.7-in; Wm Denny & Bros, Dumbarton 1919; b/up Granton 1948.

Voracious: V cls submarine; 545/740; 204½ x 16; 12¾/9; 31; four 21-in tt, one 3-in; Vickers-Armstrongs, Tyne, 1944; b/up Cochin 1946.

Vortex: V cls submarine; 545/740; 204½ x 16; 12¾/9; 31; four 21-in tt, one 3-in; Vickers-Armstrongs, Barrow, 1944; transferred 1944 to French Navy, rnd *Morse,* rtnd RN 1947; transferred 1947 to Danish Navy, rnd *Saelen,* rtnd RN 1958; b/up Faslane 1958.

Vortigern: V cls destroyer; 1090; 312 x 29½; 24½; 134; three 4-in, three 21-in tt; J. S. White & Co, Cowes, 1918; sunk by E-boat off Cromer, Mar 15, 1942.

Votary: V cls submarine; 545/730; 204½ x 16; 12¾/9; 31; four 21-in tt, one 3-in; Vickers-Armstrongs, Tyne, 1944; transferred 1946 to Norwegian Navy, rnd *Uthaug;* b/up Grimstad 1966.

Vox: U cls submarine; 545/735; 196¾ x 16; 11/9; 31; four 21-in tt, one 3-in; Vickers-Armstrongs, Barrow, 1943; ex-*P-67;* transferred 1943 to French

Navy, rnd *Curie,* rtnd RN, rnd *P-67,* 1946; b/up Milford Haven 1949.

Vox: V cls submarine; 545/740; 204½ x 16; 12¾/9; 31; four 21-in tt, one 3-in; Vickers-Armstrongs, Barrow, 1944; b/up Cochin 1946.

Vulcan: coastal forces depot ship; 623; 155 x 26¼; 11½; --; --; Smith's Dock Co, Middlesbrough, 1933; ex-trawler *Aston Villa* (Consolidated Fisheries, Grimsby) bought RN 1936; 1947, Boston Deep Sea Fishing & Ice Co, Fleetwood, converted to trawler, rnd *Fotherby;* 1951, Ezrah Deep Sea Fishing Co, Israel, rnd *Miriam;* 1953, Polish government, rnd *Pollux;* b/up Poland circa 1970.

Vulpine: V cls submarine; 545/740; 204½ x 16; 12¾/9; 31; four 21-in tt, one 3-in; Vickers-Armstrongs, Tyne, 1944; transferred 1947 to Danish Navy, rnd *Storen,* rtnd RN 1958; b/up Faslane 1959.

Wager: W cls destroyer; 1710; 362¾ x 35¾; 36; 180; four 4.7-in, eight 21-in tt; John Brown & Co, Clydebank, 1944; transferred 1956 to Yugoslavia, rnd *Pula;* b/up Split 1971.

Wakeful: W cls destroyer; 1100; 312 x 29½; 24½; 134; four 4-in; six 21-in tt; John Brown & Co, Clydebank, 1917; sunk by E-boat off Nieuport, May 29, 1940.

Wakeful: W cls destroyer; 1710; 362¾ x 35¾; 36; 220; four 4.7-in, eight 21-in tt; Fairfield SB & E Co, Govan, 1944; ex-*Zebra,* 1943; b/up Inverkeithing 1971.

Waldegrave: Captain cls frigate; 1400; 306 x 36⅝; 23½; 220; three 3-in; Bethlehem-Hingham Shipyard, 1944; ex-USN Buckley cls destroyer-escort *DE-570,* transferred Lease/Lend to RN 1944, rtnd USN 1945, b/up.

Walker: W cls destroyer; 1100; 312 x 29½; 24½; 134; two 4-in; Wm Denny & Bros, Dumbarton, 1918; b/up Troon 1946.

Wallace: Shakespeare cls destroyer; 1480; 329 x 31¾; 31; 183; four 4-in; J. I. Thornycroft & Co, Southampton/HM Dockyard, Pembroke, 1919; b/up Dunston 1945.

Wallasea: Isles cls trawler; 560; 164 x 27½; 12; 40; one 12-pdr; H. Robb, Leith, 1943; sunk by E-boat off Mounts Bay, Jan 6, 1944.

Wallflower: Flower cls corvette; 925; 205 x 33; 16; 85; one 4-in; Smith's Dock Co, Middlesbrough 1941; 1949, A/S Kosmos, Norway, converted to whale catcher, rnd *Asbjorn Larsen;* b/up Grimstad 1966.

Walney: Lulworth cls escort; 1546; 250 x 42; 16; 200; one 5-in, three 3-in; Gen Eng & DD Co, Quincy, 1930; ex-US Coast Guard cutter *Sebago,* transferred Lease/Lend to RN 1941; sunk in forcing entry into Oran harbour, Nov 8, 1942.

Walnut: Tree cls trawler; 530; 164 x 27½; 11½; 35; one 12-pdr; Smith's Dock Co, Middlesbrough, 1940; sold Swedish owners 1948.

Walpole: W cls destroyer; 1100; 312 x 29½; 24½; 134; two 4-in, three 21-in tt; Wm Doxford & Sons, Sunderland, 1918; irreparably damaged by mine in North Sea, Jan 6, 1945; b/up Grays 1945.

Wanderer: Modified W cls destroyer; 1120; 312 x 29½; 24½; 134; two 4.7-in; Fairfield SB & E Co, Govan, 1919; b/up Blyth 1946.

War Afridi: War cls oiler; 11,681; 415 x 52¼; 10; --; --; R. Duncan & Co, Port Glasgow, 1920; b/up Hong Kong 1958.

War Bahadur: War cls oiler; 11,660; 415 x 52¼; 10; --; --; Armstrong Whitworth, Newcastle, 1919; b/up Blyth 1946.

War Bharata: War cls oiler; 11,660; 415 x 52¼; 10; --; --; Palmers SB & Iron Co, Jarrow, 1920; 1948, Verano SS Co, Gibraltar, rnd *Wolf Rock;* b/up Troon 1953.

War Brahmin: War cls oiler; 11,660; 415 x 52¼; 10; --; --; Lithgows Ltd, Port Glasgow, 1920; rnd *Olterra* for film role, 1959; b/up Spezia 1960.

Warden: Bustler cls tug; 1800; 205 x 38½; 15; 42; one 3-in; H. Robb, Leith, 1945; rnd *Twyford,* 1946, rnd *Warden* 1951; 1969, Tsavliris (Salvage & Towage) Greece, rnd *Nisos Delos;* 1971, N. E. Vernicos Shipping Co, Greece, rnd *Vernicos Dimitros;*

War Diwan: War cls oiler; 11,660; 415 x 52¼; 10; --; --; Lithgows Ltd, Port Glasgow, 1919; mined in River Scheldé, Dec 16, 1944.

War Hindoo: War cls oiler; 11,660; 415 x

52¼; 10; --; --; Wm Hamilton & Co, Port Glasgow, 1920; b/up Blyth 1958.

War Krishna: War cls oiler; 11,660; 415 x 52¼; 10; --; --; Swan Hunter & Wigham Richardson, Wallsend, 1919; 1947, Bulk Storage Co, UK, as hulk; b/up Karachi 1949.

War Mehtar: War cls oiler; 11,660; 415 x 52¼; 10; --; --; Armstrong Whitworth, Newcastle, 1920; sunk by E-boats off Gt Yarmouth, Nov 20, 1941.

War Nawab: War cls oiler; 11,660; 415 x 52¼; 10; --; --; Palmers SB & Iron Co, Jarrow, 1919; b/up Troon 1958.

War Nizam: War cls oiler; 11,660; 415 x 52¼; 10; --; --; Palmers SB & Iron Co, Jarrow, 1918; 1947, Basinghall Shipping Co, London, rnd *Basinghall;* b/up Belgium 1949.

War Pathan: War cls oiler; 11,660; 415 x 52¼; 10; --; --; Sir James Laing & Sons, Sunderland, 1919; 1947, Basinghall Shipping Co, London, rnd *Basingbank;* b/up Antwerp 1950.

War Pindari: War cls oiler; 11,660; 415 x 52¼; 10; --; --; Lithgows Ltd, Port Glasgow, 1920; 1948, J. Harker, London, rnd *Deepdale H;* 1952, Soc di Nav Ligure Toscana, Italy, rnd *Carignano;* b/up Blyth 1954.

War Sepoy: War cls oiler; 11,660; 415 x 52¼; 10; --; --; Wm Gray & Co, West Hartlepool, 1919; wrecked in bombing raid in Dover Harbour, July 27, 1940, and sunk as blockship; wreck removal work carried out 1950-51 and again in 1960-62 when after end dispersed, part of for'd end also removed but fore-part section still remains.

War Sirdar: War cls oiler; 11,660; 415 x 52¼; 10; --; --; Sir J. Laing & Sons, Sunderland, 1920; bombed by Japanese aircraft and stranded Sunda Straits, Mar 1, 1942; salved by Japanese, refitted, rnd *Honan Maru;* sunk by US submarine, Mar 28, 1945.

Warspite: Queen Elizabeth cls battleship; 30,600; 643¾ x 104; 24; 1184; eight 15-in, eight 6-in, eight 4-in; HM Dockyard, Devonport, 1915; stranded in Prussia Cove Apr 23, 1947 on way to Faslane for b/up, scrapped as she lay.

War Sudra: War cls oiler; 11,660; 415 x 52¼; 10; --; --; Palmers SB & Iron Co, Jarrow, 1920; 1948, Oak Shipping Co,

London, no name change; 1950, Cia Maritima Iguana SA, Panama, rnd *Germaine;* b/up Hendrik Ido Ambacht 1954.

Warwick: W cls destroyer; 1100; 312 x 29½; 24½; 134; two 4-in; Hawthorn Leslie, Hebburn, 1918; torpedoed and sunk by *U-413* off Trevose Head, Feb 20, 1944.

Wastwater: Lake cls trawler; 560; 147½ x 26½; 12½; 36; one 12-pdr; Smith's Dock Co, Middlesbrough, 1939; ex-whale catcher *Kos XXVIII* (A. Jahre, Norway) bought RN 1939, ex-*Grassmere* 1940; sold Norwegian owners 1946.

Watchman: W cls destroyer; 1100; 312 x 29½; 24½; 134; two 4-in; John Brown & Co, Clydebank, 1918; b/up Inverkeithing 1945.

Waterwitch: Algerine cls minesweeper; 950; 235 x 35½; 16½; 104; one 4-in; Lobnitz & Co, Renfrew, 1943; b/up Antwerp 1970.

Wave: Algerine cls minesweeper; 950; 235 x 35½; 16½; 104; one 4-in; Lobnitz & Co, Renfrew, 1944; b/up Gateshead 1962.

Waveney: River cls frigate; 1370; 301½ x 36½; 19; 140; two 4-in; Smith's Dock Co, Middlesbrough, 1942; b/up Troon 1957.

Wayland: depot ship; 13,887 grt; 538 x 65; 15½; 596; four 4-in; Vickers-Armstrongs, Barrow, 1922; ex-passenger liner *Antonia* (Cunard SS Co, Liverpool) bought RN 1942, converted and rnd; b/up Troon 1948.

Wear: River cls frigate; 1370; 301½ x 36½; 19; 140; two 4-in; Smith's Dock Co, Middlesbrough, 1942; b/up Sunderland 1957.

Weazel: BAT cls tug; 783; 143 x 33; 14; 34; one 3-in; Gulfport Co 1943; ex-USN, transferred Lease/Lend to RN 1943, rtnd USN 1946; 1946, China Merchants SN Co, Shanghai rnd *Ming 106,* rnd *Ming 306;*

Wedgeport: Bangor cls minesweeper; 672; 180 x 28½; 16; 60; one 4-in; Dufferin SB & Co, Toronto, 1941; transferred 1946 to Egyptian Navy, rnd *Sollum;* sank in bad weather off Alexandria, Mar 7, 1953.

Welcome: Algerine cls minesweeper; 950; 235 x 35½; 16½; 104; one 4-in;

Lobnitz & Co, Renfrew, 1945; b/up Gateshead 1962.

Welfare: Algerine cls minesweeper; 950; 235 x 35½; 16½; 104; one 4-in; Redfern Construction Co, Toronto, 1943; b/up Grays 1957.

Wellington: Grimsby cls sloop; 990; 266 x 36; 16½; 100; two 4.7-in, one 3-in; HM Dockyard, Devonport, 1934; 1947, Honourable Company of Master Mariners, and moored Kings Reach, River Thames;

Wells: Town cls destroyer; 1090; 314⅓ x 30½; 30; 122; one 4-in, three 21-in tt; Navy Yard, Charleston, 1921; ex-USN *Tillman,* transferred 1940 to RN; b/up Troon 1945.

Welshman: Manxman cls minelayer; 4000; 418 x 39; 40; 246; 160 mines, six 4.7-in; Hawthorn Leslie, Hebburn, 1941; torpedoed and sunk by *U-617* in Mediterranean, Feb 1, 1943.

Wensleydale: Hunt cls destroyer — Albrighton type; 1050; 280 x 31½; 27; 168; four 4-in, two 21-in tt; Yarrow & Co, Scotstoun, 1942; b/up Blyth 1946.

Wessex: W cls destroyer; 1100; 312 x 29½; 24½; 134; four 4-in, six 21-in tt; Hawthorn Leslie, Hebburn, 1918; sunk by German aircraft near Calais, May 24, 1940.

Wessex: W cls destroyer; 1710; 362¾ x 35¾; 36; 180; four 4.7-in, eight 21-in tt; Fairfield SB & E Co, Govan, 1944; ex-*Zenith,* 1943; transferred 1950 to South African Navy, rnd *Jan Van Riebeeck;*

Westcott: W cls destroyer; 1100; 312 x 29½; 24½; 134; two 4-in; Wm Denny & Bros, Dumbarton, 1918; b/up Troon 1946.

Westernland: depot ship; 16,500; 600 x 68; 17; --; --; Harland & Wolff, Govan, 1918; ex-passenger liner *Regina* (Red Star Line, Liverpool) rnd 1929, 1934, Arnold Bernstein, Germany, no name change; 1939, Holland America Line, Holland, no name change; bought RN 1943; 1947, C. Salvesen & Co, Leith, for conversion for whaling service, but not proceeded with; b/up Belgium 1947.

Westminster: W cls destroyer; 1100; 312 x 29½; 24½; 134; four 4-in; Scotts SB & E Co, Greenock, 1918; b/up Rosyth 1948.

Weston: Falmouth cls sloop; 1060; 266

x 34; 16; 100; two 4-in; HM Dockyard, Devonport, 1932; ex-*Weston-Super-Mare,* 1932; b/up Milford Haven 1947.

Westray: Isles cls trawler; 560; 164 x 27½; 12; 40; one 12-pdr; J. Lewis & Sons, Aberdeen, 1942; 1946, Skibs A/S Westray, Norway, no name change; 1961, Anders Stokka, Norway, rnd *Westbay;* 1964, A/S Vestfar, Norway, no name change; 1968, A/S Westbay, Norway, no name change; 1970, P. Borgen, Norway, no name change;

Whaddon: Hunt cls destroyer — Atherstone type; 1000; 280 x 29; 27½; 146; four 4-in; Alex Stephen & Sons, Linthouse, 1941; b/up Faslane 1959.

Whalsay: Isles cls trawler; 560; 164 x 27½; 12; 40; one 12-pdr; Cook Welton & Gemmell, Beverley, 1942; transferred 1943 to Portuguese Navy, rnd *P-4,* rnd *Santa Maria* 1946; for disposal and breaking up 1971.

Wheatland: Hunt cls destroyer — Blankney type; 1050; 280 x 31½; 27; 168; six 4-in; Yarrow & Co, Scotstoun, 1941; b/up Bo'ness 1959.

Whelp: W cls destroyer; 1710; 362¾ x 35¾; 36; 220; four 4.7-in, eight 21-in tt; Hawthorn Leslie, Hebburn, 1944; transferred 1952 to South African Navy, rnd *Simon van der Stel;*

Whimbrel: Black Swan cls sloop; 1350; 299½ x 38; 19¼; 180; six 4-in; Yarrow & Co, Scotstoun, 1943; transferred 1949 to Egyptian Navy, rnd *El Malek Farouq,* rnd *Tarik;*

Whirlwind: W cls destroyer; 1100; 312 x 29½; 24½; 134; four 4-in; six 21-in tt; Swan Hunter & Wigham Richardson, Wallsend, 1918; torpedoed and sunk by *U-34* in Western Approaches, July 5, 1940.

Whirlwind: W cls destroyer; 1710; 362¾ x 35¾; 36; 220; four 4.7-in, eight 21-in tt; Hawthorn Leslie, Hebburn, 1944; in use as target ship;

Whitaker: Captain cls frigate; 1400; 306 x 36⅝; 23½; 220; three 3-in; Bethlehem-Hingham Shipyard, 1944; ex-USN Buckley cls destroyer-escort *DE-571,* transferred Lease/Lend to RN 1944; irreparably damaged by U-boat off Malin Head, Nov 1, 1944; rtnd USN 1945; b/up Whitchurch 1948.

Whitehall: Modified W cls destroyer;

1120; 312 x 29½; 24½; 134; two 4.7-in; Swan Hunter & Wigham Richardson, Wallsend/HM Dockyard, Chatham, 1924; b/up Barrow 1945.

Whitehaven: Bangor cls minesweeper; 656; 174 x 28½; 16; 60; one 3-in; Philip & Son, Dartmouth, 1941; b/up Briton Ferry 1948.

Whitesand Bay: Bay cls frigate; 1580; 307½ x 38½; 19½; 157; four 4-in; Harland & Wolff, Belfast, 1945; ex-*Loch Lubnaig,* 1944; b/up Charlestown 1956.

Whitethorn: Tree cls trawler; 530; 164 x 27½; 11½; 35; one 12-pdr; Smith's Dock Co, Middlesbrough, 1940; sold 1946.

Whitethroat: Bird cls controlled minelayer; 560; 164 x 27½; 12; 40; one 4-in; Cook Welton & Gemmell, Beverley, 1944; ex-Isles cls trawler; sold Vancouver owners 1967.

Whiting: Fish cls trawler; 670; 162 x 25¼; 11; 35; one 4-in; Cochrane & Sons, Selby, 1942; 1946, Consolidated Fisheries, Grimsby, rnd *Burfell;* b/up Sunderland 1960.

Whitley: W cls destroyer; 1100; 312 x 29½; 24½; 134; four 4-in; Wm Doxford & Sons, Sunderland, 1918; bombed by German aircraft and beached near Nieuport, May 19, 1940.

Whitshed: Modified W cls destroyer; 1500; 312 x 29½; 31; 134; two 4.7-in; three 21-in tt, Swan Hunter & Wigham Richardson, Wallsend, 1919; b/up Tyne 1948.

Wiay: Isles cls trawler; 560; 164 x 27½; 12; 40; three 20-mm; Cook Welton & Gemmell, Beverley, 1944; 1961, Honduras owners (?) rnd *Enrico Carlo;*

Widemouth Bay: Bay cls frigate; 1580; 307½ x 38½; 19½; 157; four 4-in; Harland & Wolff, Belfast, 1945; ex-*Loch Frisa,* 1944; b/up Blyth 1958.

Widgeon: Kingfisher cls sloop; 530; 243⅙ x 26½; 20; 60; one 4-in; Yarrow & Co, Scotstoun, 1938; b/up Gateshead 1947.

Widnes: Hunt cls minesweeper; 800; 231 x 28½; 16; 74; one 4-in, one 3-in; Napier & Miller, Glasgow, 1918; ex-*Withernsea,* 1918; damaged by German aircraft and beached at Suda Bay, May 20, 1941; salved by Germans, rnd *Uj-2109;* sunk by Allied surface force in the Dodecanese, Oct 17, 1943.

Wild Goose: Black Swan cls sloop;

1350; 299½ x 38; 19¼; 180; six 4-in; Yarrow & Co, Scotstoun, 1943; b/up Bo'ness 1956.

Wild Swan: Modified W cls destroyer; 1500; 312 x 29½; 31; 134; three 4.7-in, three 21-in tt; Swan Hunter & Wigham Richardson, Wallsend, 1919; damaged by German aircraft and sunk in collision with Spanish trawler in Bay of Biscay, June 17, 1942.

Willow: Berberis cls trawler; 574; 140¼ x 24½; 11; 18; one 12-pdr; Cochrane & Sons, Selby, 1930; ex-*Cape Spartivento* (Hudson Steam Fishing Co, Hull), bought RN 1935; 1946, P/F Tyril, Denmark, rnd *Trondur-I-Gotu;* b/up Hamburg 1957.

Willowherb: Modified Flower cls corvette; 980; 208¼ x 33; 16; 109; one 4-in; Midland Shipyards, Midland, 1943; ex-USN *Vitality,* transferred Lease/Lend to RN 1943, rtnd USN 1946; 1951, Balleneros Ltd SA, Uruguay, for conversion to whale catcher — not converted, laid-up at Hamburg; b/up Hamburg 1961.

Wilton: Hunt cls destroyer — Blankney type; 1050; 280 x 31½; 27; 168; six 4-in; Yarrow & Co, Scotstoun, 1942; b/up Faslane 1959.

Winchelsea: W cls destroyer; 1100; 312 x 29½; 24½; 134; two 4-in; J. S. White & Co, Cowes, 1918; b/up Rosyth 1945.

Winchester: W cls destroyer; 1100; 312 x 29½; 24½; 134; four 4-in; J. S. White & Co, Cowes, 1918; b/up Inverkeithing 1946.

Windermere: Lake cls trawler; 560; 147½ x 26½; 12½; 36; one 12-pdr; Smith's Dock Co, Middlesbrough, 1939; ex-whale catcher *Kos XXVII* (A. Jahre, Norway) bought RN 1939; 1946, A. Jahre & Co, Norway, converted to whale catcher, rnd *Kos XXVII;* b/up Grimstad 1964.

Windflower: Flower cls corvette; 925; 205 x 33; 16; 85; one 4-in; Davie SB & Repair Co, Lauzon, 1940; transferred 1941 to Royal Canadian Navy; lost in collision in North Atlantic, Dec 12, 1941.

Windrush: River cls frigate; 1370; 301½ x 36½; 19; 140; two 4-in; H. Robb, Leith, 1943; transferred 1943 to French Navy, rnd *La Decouverte;* base ship, 1960; 1961, condemned, rnd *Q-301.*

Windsor: W cls destroyer; 1100; 312 x

29½; 24½; 134; two 4-in, three 21-in tt; Scotts SB & E Co, Greenock, 1918; b/up Charlestown 1949.

Wishart: Thornycroft Modified W cls destroyer; 1550; 312 x 30½; 32; 134; three 4.7-in, three 21-in tt; J. I. Thornycroft & Co, Southampton, 1920; b/up Inverkeithing 1945.

Wistaria: Tree cls trawler; 530; 164 x 27½; 11½; 35; one 12-pdr; Smith's Dock Co, Middlesbrough, 1940; sold 1946.

Witch: Thornycroft Modified W cls destroyer; 1550; 312 x 30½; 32; 134; three 4.7-in, three 21-in tt; J. I. Thornycroft & Co, Southampton/HM Dockyard, Devonport, 1924; b/up Rosyth 1945.

Witherington: Modified W cls destroyer; 1500; 312 x 29½; 31; 134; three 4.7-in, three 21-in tt; J. S. White & Co, Cowes, 1919; wrecked on way to shipbreakers at Charlestown, Apr 29, 1947.

Wivern: Modified W cls destroyer; 1500; 312 x 29½; 31; 134; three 4.7-in; three 21-in tt, J. S. White & Co, Cowes, 1919; b/up Charlestown 1948.

Wizard: W cls destroyer; 1710; 362¾ x 35¾; 36; 180; four 4.7-in, eight 21-in tt; Vickers-Armstrongs, Barrow, 1944; b/up Inverkeithing 1967.

Wolfe: destroyer depot ship; 16,418 grt; 570 x 70; 16; 480; four 4-in; John Brown & Co, Clydebank, 1921; ex-passenger liner *Montcalm,* 1939, (Canadian Pacific SS Co, Montreal) bought RN 1942, converted; b/up Faslane 1952.

Wolfhound: W cls destroyer; 1100; 312 x 29½; 24½; 134; four 4-in; Fairfield SB & E Co, Govan, 1918; b/up Granton 1948.

Wolsey: Thornycroft W cls destroyer; 1120; 312 x 30½; 24½; 134; four 4-in; J. I. Thornycroft & Co, Southampton, 1918; b/up Sunderland 1948.

Wolverine: Modified W cls destroyer; 1500; 312 x 29½; 31; 134; two 4.7-in, three 21-in tt; J. S. White & Co, Cowes, 1920; b/up Troon 1946.

Woodcock: Black Swan cls sloop; 1350; 299½ x 38; 19¼; 180; six 4-in; Fairfield SB & E Co, Govan, 1943; b/up Rosyth 1955.

Woodpecker: Black Swan cls sloop; 1350; 299½ x 38; 19¼; 180; six 4-in; Wm Denny & Bros, Dumbarton, 1942; torpedoed by U-boat in North Atlantic

and foundered in tow, Feb 27, 1944.
Woodruff: Flower cls corvette; 925; 205 x 33; 16; 85; one 4-in; Wm Simons & Co, Renfrew, 1941; 1948, South Georgia Co (C. Salvesen) Leith, converted to whale catcher, rnd *Southern Lupin;* b/up Odense 1959.
Woolston: Thornycroft W cls destroyer; 1120; 312 x 30½; 24½; 134; four 4-in; J. I. Thornycroft & Co, Southampton, 1918; b/up Grangemouth 1948.
Woolwich: destroyer depot ship; 8750; 610 x 64; 15; 406; four 4-in; Fairfield SB & E Co, Govan, 1935; b/up Dalmuir 1962.
Worcester: Modified W cls destroyer; 1500; 312 x 29½; 31; 134; four 4.7-in, six 21-in tt; J. S. White & Co, Cowes/HM Dockyard, Portsmouth, 1922; irreparably damaged by mine in North Sea, Dec 23, 1943; used as accommodation ship; rnd *Yeoman,* 1945; b/up Grays 1947.
Worthing: Bangor cls minesweeper; 656; 174 x 28½; 16; 60; one 3-in; Philip & Son, Dartmouth, 1941; b/up Dunston 1948.
Wrangler: W cls destroyer; 1710; 362¾ x 35¾; 36; 180; four 4.7-in; eight 21-in tt; Vickers-Armstrongs, Barrow, 1944: transferred 1957 to South African Navy, rnd *Vrystaat;*
Wren: Modified W cls destroyer; 1500; 312 x 29½; 31; 134; four 4.7-in, six 21-in tt; Yarrow & Co, Scotstoun/HM Dockyard, Pembroke, 1923; sunk by German aircraft off Aldeburgh, July 27, 1940.
Wren: Black Swan cls sloop; 1350; 299½ x 38; 19¼; 180; six 4-in; Wm Denny & Bros, Dumbarton, 1942; b/up Rosyth 1956.
Wrestler: W cls destroyer; 1100; 312 x 29½; 24½; 134; two 4-in; Swan Hunter & Wigham Richardson, Wallsend, 1918; irreparably damaged by mine off Normandy, June 6, 1944, b/up Newport 1944.
Wryneck: W cls destroyer; 1100; 312 x 29½; 24½; 134; four 4-in; Palmers SB & Iron Co, Hebburn, 1918; sunk by German aircraft in Gulf of Nauplia, Apr 27, 1941.
Wye: River cls frigate; 1370; 301½ x 36½; 19; 140; two 4-in; H. Robb, Leith, 1944; b/up Troon 1955.

Yes Tor: Hills cls trawler; 750; 181¼ x 28; 11; 35; one 12-pdr; Cook Welton & Gemmell, Beverley, 1942; 1946, Clyde Trawlers, Hull, rnd *Cape Cleveland,* rnd *Stella Carina* 1947; 1949, Great Grimsby & East Coast Steam Fishing Co, Grimsby, rnd *Cape Finisterre,* rnd *Dragoon* 1952; 1961 Wyre Trawlers, Fleetwood, no name change; b/up Troon 1966.
York: cruiser; 8250; 575 x 57; 32¼; 623; six 8-in, four 4-in, six 21-in tt; Palmers SB & Iron Co, Hebburn, 1930; damaged by Italian explosive boats in Suda Bay, Mar 26, 1941, abandoned May 1941; salved and towed to Bari for breaking-up, 1952.

Zambesi: Z cls destroyer; 1710; 362¾ x 35¾; 36; 180; four 4.5-in, eight 21-in tt; Cammell Laird, Birkenhead, 1944; b/up Briton Ferry 1959.
Zanzibar: Colony cls frigate; 1430; 304 x 37½; 18; 120; three 3-in; Walsh-Kaiser Co, Providence, 1944; ex-USN *PF-92,* transferred Lease/Lend to RN rnd *Prowse,* rnd *Zanzibar* 1944, rtnd USN 1946; b/up 1947.
Zealous: Z cls destroyer; 1710; 362¾ x 35¾; 36; 180; four 4.5-in, eight 21-in tt; Cammell Laird, Birkenhead, 1944; transferred 1955 to Israel, rnd *Elath;* sunk by missile from Egyptian patrol boat, Oct 21, 1967.
Zebra: Z cls destroyer; 1710; 362¾ x 35¾; 36; 220; four 4.5-in, eight 21-in tt; Wm Denny & Bros, Dumbarton, 1944; ex-*Wakeful,* 1944; b/up Newport 1959.
Zenith: Z cls destroyer; 1710; 362¾ x 35¾; 36; 220; four 4.5-in, eight 21-in tt; Wm Denny & Bros, Dumbarton, 1944; ex-*Wessex,* 1944; transferred 1955 to Egyptian Navy, rnd *El Fateh;*
Zephyr: Z cls destroyer; 1710; 362¾ x 35¾; 36; 220; four 4.5-in, eight 21-in tt; Vickers-Armstrongs, Tyne 1944; b/up Dunston 1958.
Zest: Z cls destroyer; 1710; 362¾ x 35¾; 36; 180; four 4.5-in, eight 21-in tt; J. I. Thornycroft & Co, Southampton, 1944; b/up Dalmuir 1970.
Zetland: Hunt cls destroyer — Blankney type; 1050; 280 x 31½; 27; 168; six 4-in; Yarrow & Co, Scotstoun, 1942;

transferred 1954 to Norwegian Navy,
rnd *Tromso;* sold Sarpsborg
shipbreakers 1966.
Zinnia: Flower cls corvette; 925; 205 x
33; 16; 85; one 4-in; Smith's Dock Co,
Middlesbrough, 1941; torpedoed and
sunk by *U-564* in eastern Atlantic, Aug
23, 1941.
Zodiac: Z cls destroyer; 1710; 362¾ x
35¾; 36; 180; four 4.5-in, eight 21-in tt; J.
I. Thornycroft & Co, Southampton,
1944; transferred 1955 to Israel, rnd
Yaffo; withdrawn from service 1972.
Zulu: Tribal cls destroyer; 1870; 377 x
36½; 36½; 190; eight 4.7-in, four 21-in tt;
Alex Stephen & Sons, Linthouse, 1938;
sunk by Italian aircraft off Tobruk, Sept
14, 1942.

Addenda

Beachy Head: reduced to hulk 1972.
Bellwort: b/up Passage West 1971.
Borage: b/up Passage West 1971.
Burnet: withdrawn from service 1973.
Charlock: believed wrecked 1947.
Flamborough Head: reduced to hulk.
1972.
Pique: withdrawn from service 1973.
Pirouette: b/up 1974.
Product: withdrawn from service 1973.
Rousay: 1974 A/S Iversen & Bolle,
Norway, rnd *Mizar;*
Tocogay: *Rino,* 1974, same owners;
Undaunted: used as Exocet missile
target, 1974, severely damaged.
Vagrant: 1972, Inter-Ocean Towing
(Pte) Ltd, Singapore, rnd *Wilbie;*

Other names

Aagtekerk	Chaser	Almirante	
Aalesund	Liscomb	Lacerda	Caraquet
Aaron Ward	Castleton	Almkerk	Patroller
Abbot	Charlestown	Alp Arslan	Milne
Abel P. Upshur	Clare	Al Sudan	Cicero
Abikir	Usk	Altamaha	Battler
Acheloos	LST-3503	Alysse	Alyssum
Achilles	Blenheim	Amalthee	Plantagenet
Aconit	Aconite	Amaryllis	Allington Castle
Action	Comfrey	Ambrose	Cochrane
Adele Bartoli	Kintyre	Ammiraglio	
Adherent	Tenacity	Magnaghi	Larne
Admetus	Sapper	Amphitriti	Untiring
Adrias	Border	Anchorite	Amphion
Adrias	Tanatside	Andenes	Acanthus
Adriatiki	Lossie	Andrew Jewer	Excellent
Adrien de		Andrew King	Ouse
Gerlache	Liberty	Andria	Fritillary
A. F. Dufour	Fancy	Angelis-S	Prospect
AG-1	Barbarian	Anita 1	Pegasus
AG-2	Barbette	Anna	Tocogay
AG-3	Barfair	Anna Gemma	Inchcolm
Agerochos	Lincoln Salvor	Anna Salen	Archer
Aghia Marina	Shapinsay	Anne T. William	Ulva
Aghios Spyridon	Kilmelford	Annlock	Crocus
Agios		Anson	Centurion
Gerassimos	Kilmington	Anson	Duke of York
Agricola	Minalto	Ant	Antic
AGW-VII	Elmol	Anthony G.	Reliant
Aida	Florizel	Antonia	Wayland
Aigaion	Lauderdale	Antonio Maceo	Highway
Akamas	Beauly Firth	AO-1	Oxley
Akhawi	Distol	AO-2	Otway
Alabarda	Larne	Apostolis	Hyacinth
Alacrity	Cornel	Aptotos	American Salvor
Alan Clore	Cherryleaf	Arab	Cedar
Albert W. Vinke	Eyebright	Archangelsk	Royal Sovereign
Alblasserdyk	Trumpeter	Arctic Crusader	Amber
Aldebaran	Promise	Arctic	
Alert	Acute	Endeavour	Pretext
Alexander Hills	Moy	Arctic Prowler	Prefect
Alexandra	Coltsfoot	Arctic Trapper	Moy
Alexandre	Tadoussac	Ardenza	Hickorol
Al Fayez	Shapinsay	Ardpatrick	Lamont
Alfios	LST-3020	Arendal	Badsworth
Algenib	Professor	Argo	Gillstone
Algonquin	Valentine	Argonaftis	Virulent
Alkimos	Southampton	Ariana	Flax
	Salvor	Arion	Kilmarnock
Aliegiance 2	Allegiance	Aris	Fiaray
Alligator	Charon	Ark Royal	Pegasus
Al Maouna	Torridge	Armatolos	Aries
Almdyk	Hunter	Arnarnes	Moy
Almirante	Gillstone	Arne Presthus	Comfrey
Almirante		Arne Skontorp	Abelia
Cochrane	Eagle	Arnfinn Bergan	Aubrietia
Almirante Grau	Newfoundland	Arnprior	Courier

Arrabida	Proctor	BAM-28	Frolic
Arromanches	Colossus	BAM-29	Jasper
Artemis	Shiant	BAM-31	Steadfast
Artillero	Smiter	BAM-32	Tattoo
Arvida Bay	Flax	Banckert	Quilliam
Asbjorn Larsen	Wallflower	Bancroft	St Francis
Assam	Bugloss	Banff	Hythe
Assan Reis	Arran	Bangpakong	Burnet
Astiluzu	Begonia	Barbro	Anticosti
Aston Villa	Vulcan	Bardic	Puncher
Athelglen	Petronel	Bargate	Barrier
Athina	Pentstemon	Barnehurst	Bayonet
Athinai	Kilmington	Barnes	Attacker
Atlas	Destiny	Barnham	Falconet
Atlas	Fiaray	Barnsley	Magnet
ATR-48	Mindful	Barnstone	Martinet
ATR-49	Vagrant	Barnwell	Planet
ATR-91	Patroclus	Barry Castle	Grayling
ATR-96	Emphatic	Barwick	Barcliff
Attacker	LST-3010	Barwood	Plantagenet
Aulick	Burnham	Basingbank	War Pathan
Aurania	Artifex	Basinghall	War Nizam
Avenger	LST-3011	Bastian	Trumpeter
Avisbay	Holm Sound	BAT-1	Oriana
Axios	LST-3007	Battleaxe	Dee
Axum	Crowlin	Battleaxe	Eastway
		BAVG-1	Archer
B-1	Sunfish	BAVG-2	Avenger
B-2	Unbroken	BAVG-3	Biter
B-3	Unison	BAVG-5	Dasher
B-4	Ursula	BAVG-6	Battler
Babr	Derby Haven	BAVG-6	Tracker
Babur	Diadem	BAVG-7	Attacker
Baffins Bay	Ameer	BAVG-8	Hunter
Bagley	St Mary's	BAVG-10	Chaser
Bailey	Reading	BAVG-14	Fencer
Baldaque Da Silva	Ruskholm	BAVG-15	Stalker
Balinas	Begum	BAVG-17	Pursuer
Balthasar	Jasper	BAVG-19	Striker
Balthazar	Butser	BAVG-22	Searcher
Baiuchistan	Greenock	BAVG-24	Ravager
BAM-9	Catherine	BCVE-32	Slinger
BAM-10	Cato	BCVE-33	Atheling
BAM-11	Pique	BCVE-34	Emperor
BAM-12	Chamois	BCVE-35	Ameer
BAM-13	Chance	BCVE-36	Begum
BAM-14	Combatant	BCVE-37	Trumpeter
BAM-15	Cynthia	BCVE-38	Empress
BAM-16	Elfreda	BCVE-39	Khedive
BAM-17	Gazelle	BCVE-40	Speaker
BAM-18	Gorgon	BCVE-41	Nabob
BAM-19	Grecian	BCVE-42	Premier
BAM-20	Magic	BCVE-43	Shah
BAM-21	Pylades	BCVE-44	Patroller
BAM-25	Fairy	BCVE-45	Rajah
BAM-26	Florizel	BCVE-46	Ranee
BAM-27	Foam	BCVE-47	Trouncer

BCVE-48	Thane	Broom	Vervain
BCVE-49	Queen	Broreray	Gweal
BCVE-50	Ruler	Bruizer	LST-3025
BCVE-51	Arbiter	Buchanan	Campbeltown
BCVE-52	Smiter	Buffalo Park	Fort Charlotte
BCVE-53	Puncher	Buk Hae	Rumba
BCVE-54	Reaper	Buk Hae Ho	Rumba
BDE-1	Bayntun	Bull	Bentinck
BDE-2	Bazely	Bunsen	Jennet
BDE-3	Berry	Burak Reis	P-614
BDE-4	Blackwood	Burfell	Whiting
BDE-12	Burges	Burton	Exmoor
BDE-46	Drury	Byron	Leith
Beachflower	Lilac		
Beatty	Howe	C-23	Minerva
Begonlock	Begonia	Cable Guardian	Bullhead
Benjamin Gelcer	Bonito	Cable Restorer	Bullfrog
Benjamin		Cacheu	Fort York
Hawkins	Fastnet	Calliope	Falmouth
Benmark	Rosebay	Cambria	Derg
Ben Nevis	LST-3012	Camelia	Mincarlo
Bennevis	Puncher	Campenia	Miscou
Benrinnes	Trouncer	Canastel	Armeria
Bergen	Berberis	Candarli	Frolic
Berkshire	Tourmaline	Cania	Nasturtium
Berta Kienass	Arran	Cape Argus	Rocksand
Betty	Sarabande	Cape Barfleur	Amber
Bismarck	Caledonia	Cape Bathurst	Ruby
Bittern	Enchantress	Cape Berkeley	Donovan
Blaefell	Bonito	Cape Breton	Flamborough
Block Island	Hunter		Head
Blue Bay	Manitoulin	Cape Cleveland	Yes Tor
Blue Peter II	Manitoulin	Cape Comorin	Sefton
Bonita	Kittern	Cape Compass	Sansovino
Borgenes	Cailiff	Cape Duner	Coral
Bornol	Orangeleaf	Cape Finisterre	Cypress
Bowell	Miscou	Cape Finisterre	Yes Tor
Bowmanville	Coquette	Cape Girardeau	Empire Spearhead
Bracon	Sir Lamorack	Cape Gloucester	Sapper
Braconbank	Sir Lamorack	Cape Gregory	Silvio
Branch	Beverley	Cape Guardafui	Hawthorn
Breconshire	Activity	Cape Kanin	Syringa
Breton	Chaser	Cape Lobos	Empire Javelin
Brimnes	Foyle	Cape Marshall	Empire
Brine	see Coastal		Broadsword
	Forces-Drifters	Cape Matapan	Punnet
Brisk	Flax	Cape Pine	Sir Hugo
Britannic	Miner V	Cape St Roque	Galtee More
British Beacon	Olcades	Cape St Vincent	Cicero
British Columbia	Guava	Cape Scott	Beachy Head
British Lantern	Oligarch	Cape Spartivento	
British Light	Olwen	Cape Turner	Willow
British Star	Olynthus	Cape Warwick	Empire Rapier
Briton	Bandit	Cape Washington	Cornelian
Brocodale H	Thermol	Capitan	
Brommy	Eggesford	Quinones	Sainfoin
Bronzo	P-714	Caprice	Honesty

Captain Arsene	
Blonde	*St Agnes*
Captain Mikes	*Petrella*
Captain	
Spyromilios	*Prosperous*
Captain Theo	*Searcher*
Cardak	*Tourmaline*
Cardiff Castle	*Grilse*
Carella	*Ruby*
Caribia 2	*Fencer*
Caribische Zee	*Cambrian Salvor*
Carignano	*War Pindari*
Carnatic	*Newhaven*
Carnegie	*Empress*
Carola	*Fuday*
Caroline	*Flint*
Caroline Moller	*Growler*
Carsamba	*Tattoo*
Carvalho Araujo	*Chrysanthemum*
Cascade	*see Coastal*
	Forces-Drifters
Castel Forte	*Attacker*
Castle Peak	*Growler*
Catherine	*Dochet*
Cautious	*Prudent*
Cavendish	*Vindictive*
Cawley	*Bridport*
Cayuga	*Totland*
CC-7	*Mindful*
Celeste Aida	*Inchcolm*
Celtic Ferry	*Northway*
Cesme	*Elfreda*
Champlain	*Sennen*
Charger	*Ravager*
Charger	*LST-3026*
Charles McLeod	*LST-3021*
Chatham	*Slinger*
Chaudiere	*Hero*
Chelan	*Lulworth*
Chelmer	*Balsam*
Chernomorez	*Crowlin*
Ching Hai	*Balta*
Chinthe	*Seaham*
Chittagong	*Hartlepool*
Choran Maru	*Ruthenia*
Christina	*Ironbound*
Christine Moller	*Destiny*
Chungking	*Aurora*
Cikaran	*Moorstone*
Cintra	*Enchanter*
Cinzia	*Magdalen*
City of Havana	*Northway*
Ciudad de Santa	
Fe	*Bruizer*
Claes Compaen	*St Kilda*
Clan Brodie	*Athene*
Clan Buchanan	*Engadine*
Clan Davidson	*Bonaventure*
Clan Lamont	*Lamont*
Clash	*Linaria*
Claudio Sabadell	*Violet*
Claxton	*Salisbury*
Claymore	*Highway*
Cleveland	*Miscou*
Cliona	*Bellwort*
Clipper	*Deodar*
Cloud	*see Coastal*
	Forces-Drifters
Cloverlock	*Clover*
Coast Guard	
Barge No 55	*Totland*
Cochrane	*Duncansby Head*
Cockburn	*Drury*
Coimbra	*Hermetray*
Coldsnap	*see Coastal*
	Forces-Drifters
Colin Frye	*Acanthus*
Collinsea	*Cambrian Salvor*
Colwyn Bay	*Duncton*
Comanche	*Masterful*
Comandante	
Almeida	
Carvalho	*Fort York*
Commandant	
d'Estienne	
d'Orves	*Lotus*
Commandant	
Detroyat	*Coriander*
Commandant	
Drogou	*Chrysanthemum*
Comodoro	
Augusto	
Lassere	*Caicos*
Conner	*Leeds*
Conrad	*Danae*
Constantinos S.	*Alisma*
Conte Rosso	*Argus*
Conway	*Lewes*
Coppercliff	*Felicity*
Coracero	*Arbiter*
Coral	*LST-3022*
Coral Island	*Moy*
Cordova	*Khedive*
Coronel	
Bolognesi	*Ceylon*
Corrientes	*Tracker*
Courage	*Heartsease*
Cowell	*Brighton*
Cramond Island	*Foyle*
Craven	*Lewes*
Crescent Moon	*see Coastal*
	Forces-Drifters
Croatan	*Fencer*
Croix de Lorraine	*Strule*

Crowninshield	Chelsea	DE-275	Goodall
Curie	Vox	DE-276	Goodson
Cutlass	Northway	DE-277	Gore
Cyclone	Growler	DE-278	Keats
		DE-279	Kempthorne
Daffodil	Dianella	DE-280	Kingsmill
Dagger	Oceanway	DE-516	Lawford
Dah Lai	Ronaldsay	DE-517	Louis
Dairycoates	Quannet	DE-518	Lawson
Dakar	Totem	DE-519	Pasley
Daniel Fearall	Stour	DE-520	Loring
Daphne	Khedive	DE-521	Hoste
Dart	Godetia	DE-522	Moorsom
Davarr Island	Syringa	DE-523	Manners
DE-52	Bentinck	DE-524	Mounsey
DE-55	Byard	DE-525	Inglis
DE-58	Calder	DE-526	Inman
DE-61	Duckworth	DE-563	Spragge
DE-64	Duff	DE-564	Stayner
DE-67	Essington	DE-565	Thornbrough
DE-71	Affleck	DE-566	Trollope
DE-72	Aylmer	DE-567	Tyler
DE-73	Balfour	DE-568	Torrington
DE-74	Bentley	DE-569	Narborough
DE-75	Bickerton	DE-570	Waldegrave
DE-76	Bligh	DE-571	Whitaker
DE-77	Braithwaite	DE-572	Holmes
DE-78	Bullen	DE-573	Hargood
DE-79	Byron	DE-574	Hotham
DE-80	Conn	De Brouwer	Spanker
DE-81	Cotton	Deepdale H	War Pindari
DE-82	Cranstoun	Deepdale Wyke	Rennet
DE-83	Cubitt	Defiance	Forth
DE-84	Curzon	Deiatelnyi	Churchill
DE-85	Dakins	Delfini	Bergamot
DE-86	Deane	Delgada	Speaker
DE-87	Ekins	Delhi	Achilles
DE-88	Fitzroy	Delphin	Vengeful
DE-89	Redmill	Delphini	Bergamot
DE-90	Retalick	De Moor	Rosario
DE-91	Halsted	Dempsey	Cooke
DE-92	Riou	Denak 1	Barcock
DE-93	Rutherford	Deppie	Armeria
DE-94	Cosby	Dervish	Pearl
DE-95	Rowley	Derzki	Chelsea
DE-96	Rupert	Despina	Kilmore
DE-97	Stockham	Dhanush	Deveron
DE-98	Seymour	Dieppe	LST-3016
DE-266	Capel	Diligent	Tenacity
DE-267	Cooke	Diogo Gomez	Awe
DE-268	Dacres	Dixmude	Biter
DE-269	Domett	Doblestni	Roxburgh
DE-270	Foley	Dolfijn	P-47
DE-271	Garlies	Dolfijn	Taurus
DE-272	Gould	Dolphin	Truncheon
DE-273	Grindall	Domiat	Nith
DE-274	Gardiner	Donaldson	Byard

Donar	St Kilda	Empire Anvil	Rocksand
Donesse	Doon	Empire	
Doran	St Mary's	Arquebus	Cicero
Doris	Vineyard	Empire Audacity	Audacity
Dostoini	St Albans	Empire	
Douglas	Heartsease	Battleaxe	Donovan
Dragaberg	Holly	Empire Celtic	LST-3512
Dragoon	Yes Tor	Empire	
Drattur	Sycamore	Crossbow	Sainfoin
Drente	Rajah	Empire Cutlass	Sansovino
Druzni	Lincoln	Empire Cymric	LST-3010
Duarte	Hotspur	Empire Doric	LST-3041
Duddon	Ribble	Empire Gaelic	LST-3507
Duffy	Dacres	Empire Gannet	LST-3006
Dunay	Hoy	Empire Gauntlet	Sefton
Dunsby	Sapphire	Empire Grebe	LST-3038
D'Vora	Kittern	Empire Halberd	Silvio
Dzik	P-52	Empire Lagan	Archer
		Empire Lance	Sir Hugo
Earl Haig	Barnet	Empire Mace	Galtee More
Eastdale	Springdale	Empire Metal	Eaglesdale
Eastide	Springtide	Empire Nordic	LST-3026
Ebbtide	see Coastal	Empire Oil	Darkdale
	Forces-Drifters	Empire Sentinel	Rampant
Ebert	Bentley	Empire	
Ebgate	Barricade	Shearwater	LST-3033
Eddy	see Coastal	Empire Tern	LST-3504
	Forces-Drifters	Endeavour	Pretext
Edgar	Perseus	Englishman	Enchanter
Edincik	Grecian	Enoshima Maru	Ebonol
Edisto	Nabob	Enrico Carlo	Wiay
Edremit	Chance	Epos	Thyme
Edwards	Buxton	Erato	Cairndale
Eforia	Prosperous	Erdek	Punnet
Eider	Dochet	Erdemli	Catherine
Eifonn	Hamlet	Eregli	Pique
Einar Hund	Rousay	Eritrea	Larne
Eirikur Hin Reidi	Herschell	Esbern Snare	Blackmore
Eisele	Bickerton	Eskimo	Coldstreamer
Eisner	Domett	Este	Narcissus
Ekaterini	Bergamot	Estero	Premier
Elath	Zealous	Etonian	Amber
Elbano	Privet	Ettrick	Tamarisk
Elbano Primo	LST-3028	ETV-7	Miner VII
Electra	Bullhead	Eugene F. Moran	Favourite
Electron	Preventer	Eugene W. Vinke	Lavender
El Fateh	Zenith	Eugenia M.	
El Hascimy	Shapinsay	Moran	Masterful
Elma	Tocogay	Evangelistria	Grassholm
El Malek Farouq	Whimbrel	Evangelistria	Kilmore
Elpis	Hellisay	Evangelistria II	Gruinard
Elpis II	Hellisay	Evan Gibb	LST-3037
El Qaher	Myngs	Evans	Mansfield
Elsa	Quadrille	Evening Star	Strenuous
El Sudan	Mallow	Evertsen	Scourge
Emerson K	Marauder	Evros	Petrella
Empire Activity	Activity	Eyforia	Prosperous

E. Yung	Chaser	Fury	Larkspur
Faial	*Mangrove*	**Gadja Mada**	*Nonpareil*
Fair Barbette	*Barbette*	**Galathea**	*Leith*
Fairfax	*Richmond*	**Galaxidi**	*Pentstemon*
Fairfree	*Felicity*	**Galaxy Queen**	*Fencer*
Fairsky	*Attacker*	**Galilei**	*P-711*
Fairwater	*Scottish*	**Gallic**	*Trouncer*
	American	**Ganga**	*Chiddingfold*
Federal	*Sir Agravaine*	**Gary**	*Duckworth*
Federico Bartoli	*Pirouette*	**Gatineau**	*Express*
Federico Bartoli	*Shillay*	**Gay Corsair**	*MGB/MTB 507*
Fedredge Isabel	*LST-3024*		*(Coastal*
Ferrymar III	*Halladale*		*Forces)*
Fighter	*LST-3038*	**Gay Moran**	*Mindful*
Findus 1	*Sapphire*	**Gayret**	*Ithuriel*
Fiocina	*Kintyre*	**Gayret**	*Oribi*
Firdausa	*Reliant*	**Gay Viking**	*MGB/MTB 506*
Fjellberg	*Eday*		*(Coastal*
Fleming	*Garlies*		*Forces)*
Fleur	*Barbrake*	**Gele Zee**	*Destiny*
Foote	*Roxburgh*	**Generalisimo**	*Fame*
Forbes	*Moy*	**George**	*Goodson*
Forest Hill	*Ceanothus*	**Georges**	
Forest Hill	*Providence*	**Lecointe**	*Cadmus*
Formoe	*Calder*	**Georgios F.**	*Kilkhampton*
Fort Lamalgue	*Hamlet*	**Georgios L.**	
Fort Lavernock	*John Evelyn*	**Matsas**	*Envoy*
Fort		**Germaine**	*War Sudra*
Malbousquet	*Harris*	**Gerrit W. Vinke**	*Meadowsweet*
Fotherby	*Vulcan*	**Ghedem**	*Quadrille*
Foudre	*Oceanway*	**Giffard**	*Buddleia*
Foundation		**Gillette**	*Foley*
Josephine	*Samsonia*	**Gilsay**	*Harris*
Foundation		**Giuseppe**	
Venture	*Dragonet*	**Riccardi**	*Springtide*
Fowlock	*Fowey*	**Giuseppina**	*Anticosti*
Francois C.	*Cambrian Salvor*	**Glacier**	*Atheling*
Frankfurt-Main	*Biggal*	**Glenarm**	*Strule*
Fraser Eaves	*Doon*	**Glenella**	*Amber*
Frecciamare	*Viscol*	**Glenrock**	*Gillstone*
Frederick Clover	*LST-3001*	**Glitter**	*Raleigh (Coastal*
Freedom First	*Gillstone*		*Forces-Drifters)*
Freelock	*Freesia*	**Glomma**	*Bangor*
Frida	*Rosebay*	**Glory**	*Nabob*
Friendship	*Leith*	**Gneisenau**	*Oakley*
Friesland	*Ranee*	**Godavari**	*Bedale*
Friso	*Carnation*	**Goldaxe**	*Garry*
Frobisher	*Fastnet*	**Gold Coast**	*Labuan*
Frosty Moller	*Destiny*	**Golden Cape**	*Aimwell*
Fumarole	*see Coastal*	**Gomati**	*Lamerton*
	Forces-Drifters	**Gondwana**	*Burnet*
Fu Ming	*Rocksand*	**Good Hope**	*Loch Boisdale*
Fundiciones		**Goodmar**	*Blackbird*
Molinas	*Begonia*	**Gorey Castle**	*Hedingham*
Fu Po	*Petunia*		*Castle*
Furka	*Hermetray*	**Gossamer**	*Miner II*

Governor Wright	Kilkenzie
Graf Spee	Flamingo
Grammos	Hickorol
Granny Marigo	Springtide
Grassmere	Wastwater
Grey Fox	SGB-4 (Coastal Forces)
Grey Goose	SGB-9 (Coastal Forces)
Grey Owl	SGB-5 (Coastal Forces)
Grey Seal	SGB-3 (Coastal Forces)
Grey Shark	SGB-6 (Coastal Forces)
Greystoke Castle	Trouncer
Grey Wolf	SGB-8 (Coastal Forces)
Grigorousa	Skokholm
Gruna	Earraid
Grunningur	Myosotis
Guardiamarina Zicari	King Salvor
Guard Mavoline	Romeo
Guloy	Anticosti
Gypol	Pearleaf
Hai Aw	Sansovino
Haifa	Mendip
Hai Ma	Sluna
Hai Mei	Empire Spearhead
Hai Ou	Donovan
Hai Ou	Sansovino
Hair-Ed-Din Barbarosso	Sir Lancelot
Hai Ya	Rocksand
Hale	Caldwell
Hallowell	Anguilla
Halo	see Coastal Forces-Drifters
Halsted	Barbados
Hamlin	Stalker
Hammond	Antigua
Handy	Harvester
Hang Tuah	Loch Insh
Hannam	Caicos
Hannover	Audacity
Hans Hansen	Miscou
Haraden	Columbia
Hargood	Ascension
Hargood	Portsdown
Harland	Cayman
Harman	Dominica
Harmattan	see Coastal Forces-Drifters
Harmon	Aylmer
Harry J. Mosser	Mindful
Harvey	Labuan
Hasan	Frisky
Haste	Mandrake
Hastings	Catterick
Haugesund	Beaufort
Haugesund	Kilbirnie
Havborgin	Hawthorn
Haven Star	Sir Geraint
Hawea	Loch Eck
Hawkeye	Aimwell
Hearty	Hesperus
Heather Island	Colne
Heiyo	Herald
Helen Tola	Kittern
Heliolock	Heliotrope
Hellenic Prince	Albatross
Helm	Elm
Helmsdale	Huntley
Hembury	Greenwich
Hemsley 1	Scotol
Hemsley II	Hickorol
Hermes	Product
Hermes	Tenacity
Hermopolis	Coltsfoot
Herndon	Churchill
Herzog	Gore
Hespeler	Lysander
Hesperides	Chanticleer
Hetty Milne	Foyle
Hetty W. Vinke	Camellia
Hochmeister	Skokholm
Holger Danske	Monnow
Holmes	Tobago
Holstentor	Minalto
Honan Maru	War Sirdar
Hong Kong	Tobago
Hongkong Knight	Premier
Hopewell	Bath
Hopewell	MGB/MTB 504 (Coastal Forces)
Horizon	see Coastal Forces-Drifters
Hornby	Montserrat
Hoste	Nyasaland
Hotham	Bahamas
Howett	Papua
Humberstone	Golden Fleece
Hunt	Broadway
Huntsville	Prompt
Huta Florian	Solway Firth
Hydralock	Hydrangea
Hyperion	Eastway
Iason	Blackbird

Ibraham El Awal	Cottesmore	Juruena	Hesperus
Ibraham El Awal	Mendip	Jutahy	Havelock
Iceaxe	Kennet	Jylland	Kilbride
Ifugao	Emphatic		
Immortelle	Eden	Kai Feng	Clover
Impulse	Begonia	Kairos	Baffin
Imroz	Salvage Duke	Kalk	Hamilton
Indian Summer	see Coastal	Kalk	Sherwood
	Forces-Drifters	Kallsevni	Loosestrife
Indrabarah	Cyclops	Kanaris	Hatherleigh
Intensity	Milfoil	Kaniere	Loch Achray
Investigator	Trent	Karel Doorman	Nairana
Ion	Copinsay	Karel Doorman	Venerable
Irene M	Mixol	Karmoy	Inchmarnock
Irene Valmas	Trumpeter	Kashmir	Javelin
Iris	Coriander	Kathiawar	Hartlepool
Irving Birch	Charon	Katina	Arabis
Irvingdale 1	Derwentdale	Katingo	Mullion Cove
Irving Forty	Charon	Keeweenaw	Patroller
Irving Tamarack	Assiduous	Kefalonia	Dullisk Cove
Isaac Chant	Colne	Kellenhusen	Baffin
Isernia	Grenadier	Kempenfelt	Valentine
Isly	Islay	Kentbrook	Corbrae
Itaca	Hamlet	Kevin Moran	Patroclus
Itasca	Gorleston	Khyber	Harwich
I-Yung	Begum	Kilic Ali Pasa	Matchless
		Kinburn	Corbrae
Jaguaribe	Highlander	Kincardine	Mariner
Jaki	Samsonia	Kingfisher	King Salvor
Jamaica	Shah	Kingsmoor	Dunnet
James Clunies	Cuillin Sound	Kingston Coral	Holly
James Jones	Cherwell	Kingston	
Jan E. Van		Cyanite	Laurel
Haverbeke	Ready	Kinnaird Head	Mull of Galloway
Jannikke	Coverley	Klaas Wyker	Quannet
Jan Ove	Blackthorn	Klan	Blackthorn
Jan Van		Kongsborg	Solway Firth
Riebeeck	Wessex	Kong Sverre	Kilchattan
Japarua	Hurricane	Konkan	Tilbury
Jaslock	Jason	Kootenay	Decoy
Jason	Kerrera	Korso	Ironbound
Jastrzab	P-551	Kortenaer	Scorpion
Javary	Havant	Korytsa	Blue Ranger
Javelin	Kashmir	Kos XXIV	Ellesmere
Jellicoe	Anson	Kos XXV	Buttermere
Jeloy	Shiant	Kos XXVI	Thirlmere
Johan Maurits		Kos XXVII	Windermere
van Nassau	Ribble	Kos XXVIII	Wastwater
John Biscoe	Pretext	Kos XXIX	Ullswater
John Edmund	Foyle	Kotor	Kempenfelt
John Mann	Barnet	Kowloondocks	Allegiance
Jorge F. El Joven	Shoreham	Kraft	Abelia
Jose Marti	Northway	Krakowiak	Silverton
Julia Brierley	Grilse	Kriezis	Coreopsis
Julia C.	Thermol	Kristianborg	Mincarlo
Jupiter	Sycamore	Kriti	Hursley
Jurua	Harvester	Kuala Kangsar	Celia

Kujawiak	Oakley	Lin 1	Heliotrope
Kukri	Trent	Lincoln City	Cornelian
Kumaon	Middlesbrough	Lindsay	Pasley
Kurtaran	Moorstone	Lin Fu	Mendip
Kvitfjell	Ophelia	L. M. Sea Piper	Barsing
Kyo Maru No 12	Musk	Lobito	Stalker
Kyo Maru No 15	Nepeta	Loch Achilty	St Brides Bay
Kyo Maru No 16	Trillium	Loch Assynt	Derby Haven
Kyo Maru No 25	Bulrush	Loch Carloway	Bigbury Bay
Kyriaki	Tocogay	Loch Frisa	Widemouth Bay
		Loch Laxford	Cardigan Bay
La Aguera	Violet	Loch Lubnaig	Whitesand Bay
Labuan	LST-3501	Loch Lydoch	St Austell Bay
La Combattante	Haldon	Loch Swannay	Veryan Bay
La Confiance	Moyola	London Importer	Reliant
Laconia	Alisma	Longbranch	Candytuft
La Decouverte	Plantagenet	Longbranch	Regulus
La Decouverte	Windrush	Lord Bann	Jennet
La Dieppoise	Fleur de Lys	Lord	
Lady Adelaide	Beryl	Beaverbrook	Sycamore
Lady Dina	Fencer	Lord Brentford	Magnolia
Lady		Lord Davidson	Alder
Enchantress	Enchantress	Lord Dawson	Beech
Lady June	Oak	Lord Hewart	Berberis
Lady Lillian	Jade	Lord Trent	Hornbeam
Lady Madeleine	Moonstone	Lotharingen	Empire Salvage
Lae	LST-3035	Louise Moller	Rapidol
La Guera	Violet	Lovering	Gould
L'Ailette	Frome	Loyal	Home Guard
Lake Champlain	Ruthenia	LSD-9	Eastway
Lambourne	Dovey	LSD-10	Highway
Lambros	Rajah	LSD-11	Northway
Lamons	Duff	LSD-12	Oceanway
Lancero	Speaker	Lucia Venturi	Cava
Landfall	see Coastal	Lucifer	Trumpeter
	Forces-Drifters	Lucky One	Queen
Lanka Bahu	Kimmerol	Lucky Two	Arbiter
La Paimpolaise	Nasturtium	Lucky Three	Speaker
Larkslock	Larkspur	Lunar Bow	see Coastal
Larne	Gurkha		Forces-Drifters
Lars Nyvoll	Liscomb	Lung Huan	Falcon
Lasithi	Florizel	Lusitania	Chanticleer
La Surprise	Torridge	Lusitania II	Chanticleer
Laub	Burwell	Lydney	Lydd
Lauro Express	Kilbirnie	Lyngas	Harris
L'Aventure	Braid		
Leaside	Serene	M-29	Medusa
Leeward	see Coastal	M-31	Melpomene
	Forces-Drifters	M-33	Minerva
Leif Welding	Columbine	McAnn	Balfour
Lemnos	Jonquil	McCalla	Stanley
L'Escarmouche	Frome	McClure	Rajah
Leviathan	Turpin	McCook	St Croix
Levuka	Dungeness	Macedonia	Anchusa
Liddle	Bligh	Macha	Borage
Lilian	Armeria	Machitis	Postillion
Lillen	Minalto	Mackenzie	Annapolis

Mackerel	Corncrake	Merry Hampton	Herald
McLanahan	Bradford	Messina	LST-3043
Maddox	Georgetown	Miaoulis	Modbury
Madonna	Hibiscus	Michael	Imersay
Maev	Oxlip	Might	Musk
Magar	LST-3011	Mildenhall	Sapphire
Magnolia	Birch	Milford Star	Sir Gareth
Magsaysay	Mullion Cove	Milliam Kihl	Fennel
Magul	Elm	Mil Venture	Dragonet
Mahratta	Charlock	Mimico	Bulrush
Maiken	Rowan	Mimico	Moon
Majestic	Caledonia	Minas Gerais	Vengeance
Maj Vinke	Rhododendron	Mindful	Miner VIII
Malvern	Excellent	Ming 102	Flaunt
Manipur	Sandhurst	Ming 106	Weazel
Man Soon	Restive	Ming 108	Lariat
Maresal Fevzi		Ming 301	Flare
Cakmak	Marne	Ming 302	Flaunt
Margaree	Diana	Ming 305	Eminent
Margaret		Ming 306	Weazel
Clunies	Mullion Cove	Ming 309	Advantage
Margaret Foss	Mindful	Mingan	Fort York
Margaret Walsh	Mindful	Minor Eagle	Miner VI
Maria Paolina	Rampant	Minotaur	Newcastle
Marigoula	Kilmartin	Minstrel	Miner 1
Marion Moran	Vagrant	Miraflores	Lowestoft
Marksman	Mahratta	Miriam	Vulcan
Marnix	Garland	Misr	Galtee More
Maroy	Magdalen	Mist	see Coastal
Mars	Pioneer		Forces-Drifters
Marteresa	Inchmarnock	Mitchell	Hoste
Mary	Redwood	Mocni	Bustler
Mary Elizabeth	Vagrant	Mocoma	Totland
Marylock	Primula	Mohamed Ali El	
Maryston	John Evelyn	Kebir	Cottesmore
Mary Sven	Palomares	Mohamed Ali El	
Mason	Broadwater	Kebir	Mendip
Master	MGB/MTB 508	Mohawk	Patroclus
Standfast	(Coastal Forces)	Molaglen	Petronel
Matrouh	Stornoway	Mollex VI	Deodar
Matrozos	P-712	Monsanto	Favourite
Matsas	Envoy	Mont Blanc	Shillay
Matsas	Turmoil	Montcalm	Wolfe
Mavis Rose	Agate	Monteponi	Sarabande
Maxwell		Mormacgulf	Chaser
Brander	LST-3024	Mormacland	Archer
Maythorn	Blackthorn	Mormacland	Pursuer
Mayu	Fal	Mormacmail	Battler
Meade	Ramsey	Mormacpenn	Hunter
Medway II	Bagshot	Morning Star	Chamois
Medway II	Medusa	Morse	Vortex
Megalohari	Petrella	Mount Cameron	Rapidol
Mehmet Aksoy	Imersay	Muavenet	Inconstant
Melanie Fair	Stormking	Muncaster	
Melbourne	Topaze	Castle	Puncher
Mendota	Culver	Murat Reis	P-612
Menelaus	Melpomene	Murten	Quadrille

Mushtari	Olwen	Nostra Senora	
Musi	Rowan	De La Luz	Affleck
Mysore	Nigeria	Nullagine	Restive
		Nuno Tristao	Avon
No 101	Barlight	Nypuberg	Boyne
No 101	Thracian	N'Zadi	Fancy
Nada	Mallow		
Nadodd	Kilkenzie	O-1	Oberon
Nador	Inchmarnock	Oborg	Mincarlo
Nafkratoussa	Eastway	Ocean Pride	Oriana
Nam Viet	Vatersay	Oceanus	Destiny
Nan Chiang	Falcon	Octopus	Moorgrieve
Naprijed	Holm Sound	Odin	Gruinard
Narval	P-714	Ofotfjord	Coverley
Narval	Spur	Okeanos	Oceanway
Narvik	Glaisdale	Oksoy	Kerrera
Nasr	Bude	Olofsborg	Solway Firth
Natal	Loch Cree	Olterra	War Brahmin
Nautilo	Saga	Olympic	
Navarinon	Echo	Conqueror	Tulip
Navem Hembury	Greenwich	Olympic Cruiser	Dittany
Naver	Loch Achanalt	Olympic	
Navmachos	Lightfoot	Explorer	Musk
Neath Castle	Mullet	Olympic Hunter	Vetch
Nenter	Hermetray	Olympic Leader	Nepeta
Neptun	Lark	Olympic	
Neptuno	Spearhead	Promoter	Milfoil
Nettle	Hyderabad	Olympic Rider	Jonquil
Neza	Test	Olympic Runner	Trillium
Niantic	Ranee	Olympic Victor	Bulrush
Niedermehnen	Baffin	Onslaught	Pathfinder
Niels Ebbesen	Annan	Onslow	Pakenham
Nigelock	Nigella	Onyx	see Coastal
Nigeria	Hare		Forces-Drifters
Nilla	Bruizer	Orangeville	Marmion
Nisos Chios	Saucy	Oranjezicht	Magnolia
Nisos Crete	Hengist	Oriental Banker	Searcher
Nisos Delos	Warden	Orion	Loch Gorm
Nisos Ikaria	Dexterous	Orion 1	Fuday
Nisos Kerkyra	Turmoil	Orissa	Clydebank
Nisos Rodos	Earner	Orkan	Myrmidon
Nisos Skiathos	Enchanter	Oruc Reis	P-611
Nisos Zakynthos	Mediator	Ostfold	Anemone
Nith	Excellent	Oswald	Affleck
Noble	Nerissa	O'Toole	Gardiner
Nonsuch	MGB/MTB 505	Otori Maru No 1	Nepeta
	(Coastal	Otori Maru No 2	Dittany
	Forces)	Otori Maru No 3	Musk
Noontide	see Coastal	Otori Maru No 5	Milfoil
	Forces-Drifters	Otori Maru No 8	Tulip
Norden	Halladale	Otori Maru No 10	Trillium
Nordkyn	Buttercup	Otori Maru No 12	Bulrush
Norfinn	Primrose	Otori Maru No 18	Vetch
Norman	Bombardier	Ottawa	Griffin
Norseman	Nepal		
Norte	Azalea	P-1	Bruray
North Star VI	Prefect	P-2	Mangrove

P-3	Hayling	P-77	Spiteful
P-4	Whalsay	P-78	Splendid
P-7	Gruinard	P-79	Sportsman
P-8	Eriskay	P-91	P-311
P-31	Umpire	P-92	Trespasser
P-31	Uproar	P-93	Taurus
P-32	Una	P-94	Tactician
P-33	Unbeaten	P-95	Truculent
P-34	Ultimatum	P-96	Templar
P-34	Undaunted	P-97	Tally-Ho
P-35	Umbra	P-247	Saracen
P-35	Union	Pacheo Pereira	Bigbury Bay
P-36	Unique	Pacific Alliance	Patroller
P-37	Unbending	Pacific Breeze	Ranee
P-37	Upholder	Pacific Pioneer	LST-3001
P-38	Upright	Padstow	Pangbourne
P-39	Urchin	Pakenham	Onslow
P-40	Urge	Palang	Fly
P-41	Uredd	Panama	Maine
P-41	Usk	Pan America	Oriana
P-42	Unbroken	Pandelis	Jasper
P-42	Utmost	Pannesi	Hickorol
P-43	Unison	Pansy	Heartsease
P-44	United	Papendrecht	Empire Salvage
P-45	Unrivalled	Parakrama	Pickle
P-46	Unruffled	Parnon	Alisma
P-49	Unruly	Partizanska	Mallow
P-51	Unseen	Pasley	St Helena
P-53	Ultor	Pass of Glencoe	Petronel
P-54	Unshaken	Pathfinder	Onslaught
P-55	Unsparing	Patrai	Vetch
P-56	Usurper	Patricia Hague	Laurel
P-57	Universal	Patricia Moller	Aimwell
P-58	Untamed	Patton	Sarawak
P-59	Untiring	PCE-827	Kilbirnie
P-61	Safari	PCE-828	Kilbride
P-61	Varangian	PCE-829	Kilchattan
P-62	Uther	PCE-830	Kilchrenan
P-62	Sahib	PCE-831	Kildary
P-63	Saracen	PCE-832	Kildwick
P-63	Unswerving	PCE-833	Kilham
P-64	Satyr	PCE-834	Kilkenzie
P-64	Vandal	PCE-835	Kilkhampton
P-65	Sceptre	PCE-836	Kilmalcolm
P-65	Upstart	PCE-837	Kilmarnock
P-66	Seadog	PCE-838	Kilmartin
P-66	Varne	PCE-839	Kilmelford
P-67	Sibyl	PCE-840	Kilmington
P-67	Vox	PCE-841	Kilmore
P-68	Sea Rover	Pearl	Seychelles
P-69	Seraph	Pei Ching	Aurora
P-71	Shakespeare	Pelikaan	Thruster
P-72	P-222	Pelikan	Anemone
P-73	Sea Nymph	Pellew	Cavalier
P-74	Sickle	Pembroke	Stour
P-75	Simoon	Pensilvania	Olynthus
P-76	Sirdar	Penyu	Dabchick

Perdito	Trouncer	Planeta	Narcissus
Perilock	Periwinkle	Plassy	Juliet
Perla	P-712	Plico	Ulva
Perna	Minalto	Polarfront 1	Saxifrage
Persistent	Petard	Polarfront II	Bryony
Persol	Cherryleaf	Polemistis	Gozo
Pert	Nepeta	Pollux	Vulcan
Peterjon	Juliet	Polo Norte	Probe
Petrola XIV	Black Ranger	Polyphemus	Southampton
Petrolia	Lioness	Pontchartrain	Hartland
Peyton	Tortola	Popham	Somaliland
PF-72	Anguilla	Portadown	Proctor
PF-73	Antigua	Portaferry	Probe
PF-74	Ascension	Porthleven	Prodigal
PF-75	Bahamas	Port Jackson	Product
PF-76	Barbados	Portmadoc	Professor
PF-77	Caicos	Portnall	Boxol
PF-78	Cayman	Port Natal	Promise
PF-79	Dominica	Porto Azzuro	Mandrake
PF-80	Labuan	Portobello	Prophet
PF-81	Tobago	Portoferraio	Cornel
PF-82	Montserrat	Porto Grande	Freshwater
PF-83	Nyasaland	Portpatrick	Protest
PF-84	Papua	Port Quebec	Deer Sound
PF-85	Pitcairn	Portreath	Prowess
PF-86	St Helena	Port Royal	Proof
PF-87	Sarawak	Portrush	Property
PF-88	Seychelles	Port Said	Cottesmore
PF-89	Perim	Port Stanley	Prong
PF-90	Somaliland	Port Victor	Nairana
PF-91	Tortola	Port Vindex	Vindex
PF-92	Zanzibar	Prah	Holm Sound
PG-103	Barle	Prase	Betony
PG-104	Cuckmere	Presidente	
PG-105	Evenlode	Alfaro	Quantock
PG-106	Findhorn	Presidente	
PG-107	Inver	Velasco Ibarra	Meynell
PG-108	Lossie	President F. D.	
PG-109	Parret	Roosevelt	Gruinard
PG-110	Shiel	President Garcia	Smiter
Phaedra	Rampant	President	
Philip	Lancaster	Macapagal	Arbiter
Phillimore	Perim	President	
Phlox	Lotus	Magsaysay	Mullion Cove
Phosamton	Minstrel	President	
Phyllis Rosalie	Amethyst	Marcos	Queen
Pietermaritzburg	Pelorus	President	
Piet Hein	Serapis	Osmena	Speaker
Pilford	Pitcairn	Pride of the West	Strenuous
Pindos	Bolebroke	Pride of Torquay	Albatross
Pinios	LST-3506	Prince	Rajah
Pinner	Fitzroy	Prince William	Striker
Piorun	Nerissa	Procher	Porcher
Pipinos	Veldt	Prof Heincke	Fuday
Pique	Carysfort	Prof Henking	Arran
Pirpolitis	Arcturus	Prof Hensen	St Kilda
Piyale Pasa	Meteor	Protea	Rockrose

Provost	Prowess	RD-312	Gavotte
Prowse	Zanzibar	RD-313	Foula
Prudent	Privet	RD-314	Ensay
Pukaki	Loch Achanalt	RD-315	Stroma
Pula	Wager	RD-316	Hornpipe
Pulau Bali	Bacchus	Ready	Calendula
Puncher	LST-3036	Recepto	Oak
Pursuer	LST-3504	Red Archer	Rennet
Pybus	Emperor	Red Gauntlet	Cedar
		Red Knight	Beryl
Q-301	Windrush	Red Lancer	Moonstone
Q-306	Strule	Red Sabre	Portsdown
Q-307	Frome	Reeves	Cosby
Q-308	Moyola	Regina	Westernland
Qu'Appelle	Foxhound	Reginald Kerr	LST-3009
Quebec	Uganda	Remex	Quadrille
Queen Patricia	Manitoulin	Rempang	Khedive
		Renoncule	Ranunculus
R-3	P-511	Renown	Revenge
R-17	P-512	Republica	Smilax
R-19	P-514	Restless	Periwinkle
Raasay	Sheppey	Retriever	Bullfrog
Radbourne	Blyth	Retriever III	Bullfrog
Radford	Basset	Rexton Kent	Candytuft
Radley	Flinders	Rexton Kent II	Candytuft
Radni	Herschell	Reybold	Goodall
Rahav	Sanguine	Reynolds	Halsted
Rajput	Rotherham	Rhodesia Star	Premier
Rajputana	Lyme Regis	Ringgold	Newark
Raki	Begum	Rio Agueda	Kilmalcolm
Raleigh	see Coastal	Rio Blanco	Armeria
	Forces-Drifters	Rio de Janeiro	Dasher
Rami	Poppy	Rio Hudson	Avenger
Ramsey	Ross	Rio Marina	Cornel
Ran	Manitoulin	Rio Mero	Begonia
Rana	Raider	Rio Parana	Biter
Ran B	Manitoulin	Riouw	Stalker
Ranger	Caesar	Rio Vouga	Kildary
Ranjit	Redoubt	Rivtow Lion	Prudent
Rankin	Hornbeam	Rivtow Viking	Tenacity
Ras Adar	Oriana	Robert	
Rashid	Spey	Cloughton	Coronet
Rask	Kilmun	Robert Croan	Sir Kay
Rattler	Loyalty	Robert Hewett	Lilac
Raule	Albrighton	Robert Limbrick	Sir Galahad
Raymond Olivier	Rampant	Robert Moore	Buttermere
RD-301	Burra	Robin Kirk	Ameer
RD-302	Cumbrae	Robin Mowbray	Slinger
RD-303	Unst	Robinson	Newmarket
RD-304	Staffa	Robin Trent	Ravager
RD-305	Filla	Rodgers	Hamilton
RD-306	Egilsay	Rodgers	Sherwood
RD-307	Minuet	Roebiah	Queen
RD-308	Tarantella	Rohilkhand	Padstow
RD-309	Grain	Rolf Krake	Calpe
RD-310	Othello	Roma	Atheling
RD-311	Mousa	Roma	Fencer

Rooke	Broke	Saranac	Banff
Rorvik	Llandudno	Saskatchewan	Fortune
Rosa Vlassis	Pentstemon	Satellite	Brave
Roselys	Sundew	Satellite	Melita
Roskva	Heartsease	Satterlee	Belmont
Rotoiti	Loch Katrine	Saucy	Arabis
Royal Marine	Butser	Saudanes	Colne
Royaumont	Dingledale	Scarba	Fluellen
Rubis	Kingcup	Scharnhorst	Mermaid
Rudlias	Sir Gareth	Scheer	Hart
Rumol	Brambleleaf	Scotia	Fluellen
		Seabird	Heartsease
S-1	P-552	Seabreeze	see Coastal
S-21	P-553		Forces-Drifters
S-22	P-554	Sea Enterprise	Gillstone
S-24	P-555	Sea Lion	Mindful
S-25	P-551	Searcher	LST-3508
S-29	P-556	Sebago	Walney
Sabina	Magdalen	Sebec	Banff
Saelen	Vortex	Seislim	Kingcup
Safir	Dee	Selat Surabaja	Griper
St Alexandria	Larch	Sempach	Eday
St Andrews	Queen	Serron	Fusilier
St Anne	Islay	Servannaise	Inchmarnock
St Christopher	Justice	Shackleton	Sharpshooter
St Gatien	Tamarisk	Shamsher	Nadder
St George	Pursuer	Sheen	see Coastal
St Gerontius	Maple		Forces-Drifters
St Irene	Myrtle	Sheila Margaret	Harris
St Joseph	Ruler	Sheppey	Blackbird
St Lykoudis	Nasturtium	Shipway	Swin
Saint Matthew	Kilmelford	Shoshone	Landguard
St Oswald	Turquoise	Shower	see Coastal
St Romanus	Oak		Forces-Drifters
St Rose	Redwood	Shubrick	Ripley
St Simon	Arbiter	Shun Wa	Sluna
St Stephen	Oak	Sibyl	Cavendish
St Thomas	Seabear	Sibylle	Sportsman
Sakhtouris	Peony	Sierra Leone	Perim
Salamis	Boreas	Sigourney	Newport
Salcombe	Sutton	Sigurd Hund	Miscou
Salta	Shah	Silvana Otto	Kintyre
Salvador Correia	Saltarelo	Silverlord	Anchusa
Salvager	Barsing	Silver Star	Bruizer
Salvaliant	Encore	Simon de Danser	Fuday
Salvo	Ulva	Simon van der	
Samba	Olive	Stel	Whelp
Samfrost	Fandango	Sinai	Lucia
Sanchez	Fame	Sind	Betony
San Ciriaco	St Day	Sioux	Vixen
Sanders	Grindall	Sir Edgar	Anchusa
San Miguel	Bruray	Sirene	Spiteful
Santa Maria	Whalsay	Sisapon	Royal Marine
Santissima		Sjosterk	Prong
Trinidad	Caicos	Skaidi	Sapphire
Saphir	Satyr	Skepsis	Beauly Firth
Sarabande	Palomares	Skogholm	Skokholm

Slazak	Bedale	Straub	Braithwaite
Sledway	Kingarth	Strenuous	Carron
Smiter	LST-3514	Striker	LST-3516
Snapdragon	Arabis	Strymon	LST-3502
Snowden Smith	LST-3028	Sudbury II	Caledonian
Sognefjord	Kilham		Salvor
Sokol	Urchin	Sullberg	Springtide
Solebay	Skipjack	Sultane	Statesman
Sollum	Portsdown	Suma	Moth
Sollum	Wedgeport	Sumatra	Maple
Somerset	Barcross	Sunderland	Lyme Regis
Sonneblom	Foyle	Sung Hwei	Hoxa
Sophia G.	Moorfly	Sunnfjord	Kildwick
Soroy	Eglantine	Sunnhordland	Kilchrenan
Sotir	Salventure	Sunset	Thane
South Africa Star	Reaper	Sunset	see Coastal
Southern Briar	Cyclamen		Forces-Drifters
Southern Broom	Starwort	Surabajah	Griper
Southern		Suriname	Ulva
Larkspur	Arrowhead	Surprise	Heliotrope
Southern Laurel	Carnation	Susan A. Moran	Favourite
Southern Lily	Ranunculus	Svenner	Shark
Southern Lotus	Lotus	Sverre Hund	Mincarlo
Southern Lupin	Woodruff	Swallow	Caprice
Southern Terrier	Aconite	Swansea Castle	Pollack
Speedon	Speedy	Swasey	Rockingham
Spitfire	Cambrian	Sweet Sail	Kilkenzie
Spleis	Blackwater	Sydney	Fencer
Splendor	Rosebay	Syros	Bergamot
Spray	Hibiscus		
Spreewald	Lucia	T-13	Garry
Springeren	P-52	T-14	Liffey
Staffetta	Privet	T-16	Dee
Stalker	LST-3515	T-17	Kennet
Stanfirth	Beauly Firth	Tabarchin	Pirouette
Star IX	Sweetbriar	Tact	Smilax
Star of Beirut	Comfrey	Tahoe	Fishguard
Star of Freedom	Sir Galahad	Tai Hing	Cornflower
Star of Mariam	Comfrey	Talas	Barcock
Star of Riwiah	Comfrey	Talbot	Medusa
Star of the East	Sir Gareth	Talis	Rowan
Star of the North	Sir Kay	Tampa	Banff
Star of the South	Sir Geraint	Tana	Blackpool
Stat	Kittern	Tangvik	Rousay
Stavanger	Kilchattan	Tanin	Springer
Steady	Miner VII	Tarakan	LST-3017
Steel Artisan	Attacker	Tarik	Whimbrel
Stelios	Skokholm	Tariq	Offa
Stella Capella	Dunkery	Tasman	Talent
Stella Carina	Yes Tor	Tasmania	Archer
Stella Orion	Lancer	Taupo	Loch Shin
Stockton	Ludlow	Tehuelche	King Salvor
Stoneaxe	Liffey	Telemachus	Activity
Stord	Success	Temptress	Veronica
Storen	Vulpine	Tenacity	Candytuft
Storesse	Stour	Tenena	Kimmerol
Strathyre	Laurel	Terceira	Hayling

Terje 10	Chrysanthemum	Trias	Kilmington
Terje 11	Aconite	Tridente	Pirouette
Teti	Lossie	Trinol	Plumleaf
Tewfik	Arabis	Tris Ierarchal II	Prospect
Texol	Appleleaf	Tristania	Bay
Thatcher	Niagara	Tromoy	Eday
Themistoklis	Bramham	Tromoy	Mincarlo
Theoxenia	Baffin	Tromso	LST-3006
Thermo	Crowlin	Tromso	Zetland
Thessaloniki	Spiraea	Trondur-I-Gotu	Willow
Thetis	Geranium	Trujillo	Hotspur
Thetis	Thunderbolt	Trumpeter	Kempthorne
T'Ho	Hermetray	Tughril	Onslaught
Thomas	St Albans	Tulipbank	Neave
Thomas Johns	Eden	Tulipdale	Lingay
Thor	St Agnes	Tulipglen	Porcher
Thorgeir	Lobelia	Tunsberg Castle	Shrewsbury
Thorglimt	Eglantine		Castle
Thoris	Buttercup	Turbot	Redshank
Thorlyn	Tulip	Turist Expressen	Halladale
Thororn	Myosotis	Turoy	Ironbound
Thorslep	Dianthus	Tutankhamen	P-311
Thuringia	Guardsman	Tutira	Loch Morlich
Tickham	Oakley	25 de Mayo	Venerable
Tiern	Buttermere	Twiggs	Leamington
Tijgerhaai	Tarn	Two Step	Tarantella
Tillman	Wells	Twyford	Warden
Tillsonburg	Flying Fish	Tyalla	Dullisk Cove
Tilthorn	Inchmarnock		
Tippu Sultan	Onslow	U-1	P-52
Tir	Bann	U-570	Graph
Tisdale	Keats	UB	Seal
Tjerk Hiddes	Nonpareil	Uj-2109	Widnes
TMT Florida		Ula	Varne
Queen	Highway	Ulisse	Rajah
Tompazis	Tamarisk	Ullswater	Uproar
Tonkinois	Moyola	Uluc Ali Reis	P-615
Topaze	Speedwell	Ulva	Annet
Topmast 19	Barmouth	Union	Hamlet
Toran	Ailsa Craig	Union Reliance	Archer
Toro	Stormking	Uppingham	Kellett
Toronto	Mary Rose	Ursus	St Day
Toshi Maru	Monkshood	Usage	Tourmaline
Toshi Maru No 1	Monkshood	Uthaug	Votary
Toshi Maru No 2	Acanthus	Utheim	Sir Agravaine
Tottan	Ophelia	Utsira	Variance
Tourmaline	Cassandra	Utstein	Venturer
Tova	Rousay	Utvaer	Viking
Trailer	Hunter		
Tran	Dee	Vaagnes	Property
Tranoy	Dee	Vaagso	LST-3019
Transvaal	Loch Ard	Vaila	Acacia
Trave	Flint	Valafell	Bream
Trave	Minalto	Valdemar Sejr	Exmoor
Trent	Ravager	Valentine	Kempenfelt
Triadic	Dungeness	Vancouver	Vimy
Triana	Volatile	Vanda	Celia

Van Galen	Noble	Westella	Pearl
Vardberg	Cypress	Westheron	Jennet
Velox	Gweal	Westhill	Larch
Venom	Venomous	Weston-Super-	
Ventura	Restive	Mare	Weston
Vermillion	Smiter	Whirlpool	see Coastal
Vernicos	Enigma		Forces-Drifters
Vernicos Dimitros	Warden	Whitebrook	Mixol
Vernicos Marina	Frisky	Whitfleet	Corbrae
Vernon	Strathcoe	Wickes	Montgomery
Verolock	Veronica	Willapa	Puncher
Veslemoy	Ailsa Craig	Wm Fenton	Calvay
Vestfar	Miscou	William Inwood	Blackwater
Victory	Aurora	William Jones	Boyne
Vigilant	Benbecula	William S.	Manitoulin
Vijaya	Flying Fish	Williams	St Clair
Vilfjell	Dee	Winjah	Reaper
Villa Bens	Calendula	Winston Spencer	
Villa Cisneros	Calendula	Churchill	Biggal
Vim	Statice	Wintle	Capel
Vital	Strenuous	Withernsea	Widnes
Vitality	Untamed	Wodan	Hannaray
Vitality	Willowherb	Wolf Rock	War Bharata
Vivi	Aspirant	Woolton	Turquoise
V. O.		W. R. Strang	Monkshood
Chidambaram	Fritillary	WS-1	Northway
Vollen	Sarabande	Wyre Woolton	Turquoise
Vouri	Vatersay		
Vrystaat	Wrangler	X-2	P-711
Vulkaan	Beachy Head	Xifias	Upstart
Wakeful	Zebra	Yaffo	Zodiac
Warwick Castle	Pretoria Castle	Yan Myo Aung	Mariner
Warwickshire	Turquoise	Yarnall	Lincoln
Waynegate	Mullion Cove	Yeoman	Worcester
Wear Breeze	Dullisk Cove	Yiaghos	Rampant
Weather Adviser	Amberley Castle	Ying Hao	Sandpiper
Weather Explorer	Thyme	Ying Shan	Gannet
Weather Monitor	Pevensey Castle	Ying Teh	Falcon
Weather		Ypapandi	Hascosay
Observer	Marguerite		
Weather		Zaida	Flax
Recorder	Genista	Zebra	Wakeful
Weather Reporter	Oakham Castle	Zeehond	Sturgeon
Weather Reporter	Thyme	Zeehond	Tapir
Weather		Zeeland	Oriana
Surveyor	Rushen Castle	Zenith	Wessex
Weather Watcher	Snowflake	Zenobia	Snowflake
Welborn C.		Zero	Coldstreamer
Wood	Chesterfield	Zharki	Brighton
Welles	Cameron	Zhguchi	Leamington
Welshman	Growler	Zhivuchi	Richmond
Werner Felter	Deodar	Zhostki	Georgetown
Wessex	Derg	Ziang Teh	Heliotrope
Wessex	Erne	Zulfiquar	Deveron
Wessex	Zenith	Zurmand	Dexterous
Westbay	Westray	Zwaardvis	Talent

Coastal and small craft

Coastal forces craft, midget
submarines, motor fishing
vessels, drifters, landing craft.
MTB = Motor Torpedo Boat
MGB = Motor Gunboat
SGB = Steam Gunboat
MA/SB = Motor Anti/Submarine
Boat
ML = Motor Launch
ASRL = Air-Sea Rescue Launch
MMS = Motor Minesweeper
BYMS = Motor Minesweeper

Coastal Forces Craft

1-5(MA/SB): 19; 60¼ x 13¼; 25; 9; light armament; British Power Boat Co, Hythe.

1-12(MTB): 22; 63¼ x 13¼; 33; 9; two 18-in torpedoes; British Power Boat Co, Hythe, 1936-39.

1-118(MMS): 240; 119 x 23; 11; 20; two 20-mm; various builders, wood construction; gaps in RN number sequence. 1500 added to each number in 1951;

1-284(BYMS): 207-215; 135½ x 24½; 14; 30; one 3-in; US yards, 1942 onwards; transferred Lease/Lend to RN, rtnd; gaps in RN number sequence; 2000 added to each number in 1944.

3-9(SGB): 250; 145 x 20; 30; 34; one 3-in; builders: 3,4, Yarrow 1942; 5,6, Hawthorn Leslie 1942; 7,8, Wm Denny & Bros, 1942; 9, J. S. White & Co, 1941; 1943, *SGB-3* rnd *Grey Seal, SGB-4* rnd *Grey Fox, SGB-5* rnd *Grey Owl, SGB-6* rnd *Grey Shark, SGB-8* rnd *Grey Wolf, SGB-9* rnd *Grey Goose; SGB-7* lost in action in Channel, June 19, 1942.

6-21(MGB): 31-34; 70 x 20; 23-42; 9-12; light armament; British Power Boat Co, Hythe.

14-19(MTB): 22; 63¼ x 13¼; 33; 9; two 18-in torpedoes; British Power Boat Co, Hythe, 1936-39.

20-23(MTB): 37; 70 x 15; 42; 10; two 21-in tt; Vosper, Portsmouth.

22-39(MA/SB): 20; 63 x 15; 25; 10; light armament; British Power Boat Co, Hythe.

24-25(MTB): 37; 72 x 16½; 40; 10; two 21-in tt; J. I. Thornycroft, Hampton, 1939-40.

26-27(MTB): 17; 55 x 11; 40; 5; two 18-in torpedoes; J. I. Thornycroft, Hampton, 1938-40.

28(MTB): 72 x 16½; 40; 10; two 21-in tt; J. I. Thornycroft, Hampton, 1940.

29-30(MTB): 37; 70 x 15; 42; 10; two 21-in tt; Camper & Nicholson, Gosport.

31-34(MTB): 40; 70 x 15; 40; 12; two 21-in tt; Vosper, Portsmouth, 1940.

35-40(MTB): 40; 70 x 15; 25; 12; two 21-in tt; Vosper, Portsmouth.

40-45(MGB): 24; 63 x 15; 40; 10; one 2-pdr; British Power Boat Co, Hythe.

41-48(MTB): 33-46½; 73 x 18; 39½; 17; two 21-in tt; J. S. White, Cowes.

46(MGB): 32; 70 x 20; 23-42; 9-12; light armament; British Power Boat Co, Hythe.

47-48(MGB): 39; 70 x 16½; 38; 12; light armament; J. S. White, Cowes.

49(MA/SB): 20; 63 x 15; 25; 10; light armament; British Power Boat Co, Hythe.

49-56(MTB): 52; 75½ x 16¾; 29; 12; two 21-in tt; J. I. Thornycroft, Hampton, 1941.

50-67(MGB): 31-34; 70 x 20; 23-42; 9-12; light armament; British Power Boat Co, Hythe.

57-66(MTB): 40; 70 x 15; 25; 12; two 21-in tt; Vosper, Portsmouth.

67-68(MTB): 17; 55 x 11; 40; 5; two 18-in torpedoes; J. I. Thornycroft, Hampton.

68(MGB): 34; 81 x 20; 35; 14; light armament; Higgins built, transferred Lease/Lend to RN, rtnd.

69-70(MTB): 32; 70 x 15; 25-27; 10; two 21-in tt; Vosper, Portsmouth.

69-73(MGB): 30; 69¼ x 19; 27; 12; light armament; Higgins built, transferred Lease/Lend to RN, rtnd.

71-72(MTB): 25; 60 x 15; 35; 10; two 18-in tt; Vosper, Portsmouth.

73-98(MTB): 52; 72½ x 19¼; 38; 13; two 21-in tt; various yards.

74-81(MGB): 47; 71¾ x 20¾; 42; 12; one 2-pdr; British Power Boat Co, Hythe, 1942-45.

82-93(MGB): 45; 77 x 20; 40; 12; light armament; Electric Boat, Bayonne, NJ, ex-USN Elco boats PTC 1-12, transferred Lease/Lend to RN, rtnd.

98-99(MGB): --; -- x --; --; --; --; ex-French motor anti-submarine boats, seized 1940.

100-106(MGB): 30; 69¼ x 19; 27; 12; light armament; Higgins built, ex-USN transferred Lease/Lend to RN.

100-111(ML Fairmile Type A): 60; 110 x 17½; 25; 16; one 3-pdr, machine guns, some fitted as minelayers; built by 10 firms.

101(Experimental Hydrofoil MTB): 22; 67½ x 14½; 40; 10; two 21-in tt; J. S. White, Cowes, 1937.

102-103(Experimental MTB): 32; 68 x 14¾; 45; 10; two 21-in tt; Vosper, Portsmouth, 1937 (102), 1939 (103).

104(Experimental MTB): 10; 50ft.

105-106(Experimental) MTB: 9; 45¾ ft.

107(Experimental MTB): --; 44¼ ft.

107-176(MGB): 47; 71¾ x 20¾; 42; 12; one 2-pdr; British Power Boat Co, Hythe, 1942-45.

109(Experimental MTB): 17; 41 x 11; Wm Denny, Dumbarton.

112-311(ML Fairmile Type B): 63; 112 x 18¼; 20; 16; one 3-pdr, machine guns, some fitted as minelayers; type built by over 80 firms; gaps in RN number sequence.

123-313(MMS): 240; 119 x 23; 11; 20; two 20-mm; various builders, wood construction; gaps in RN number sequence; 1500 added to each number in 1951.

177-192(MGB): 46; 81¼ x 20; 36; 12; two 20-mm; Higgins built; transferred Lease/Lend to RN.

201-212(MTB): 33-46½; 73 x 18; 39; 17; two 21-in tt; J. S. White, Cowes.

213-217(MTB): 17: 55 x 11; 40; 5; two 18-in torpedoes; J. I. Thornycroft, Hampton.

218-221(MTB): 35; 70 x 15; 25-27; 10; two 21-in tt; Vosper, Portsmouth.

222-245(MTB): 52; 75½ x 19¼; 39; 13; two 21-in tt; various yards; gaps in RN number sequence.

246-257(MTB): 33-46½; 73 x 18; 39; 17; two 21-in tt; J. S. White, Cowes.

258-268(MTB): 35; 70 x 20; 40; 11; two 21-in tt; Electric Boat, Bayonne, NJ; ex-USN PT boats, transferred Lease/Lend to RN.

275-306(MTB): 52; 72½ x 19¼; 39; 13; two 21-in tt; various yards; gaps in RN number sequence.

307-316(MTB): 45; 77 x 20; 45; 12; two 21-in tt; Electric Boat, Bayonne, NJ; ex-USN PT boats, transferred Lease/Lend to RN.

312-335(MGB Fairmile Type C): 72; 110 x 17½; 26½; 16; light armament; type built by 13 firms; ex-motor launches, 1941.

327-331(MTB): 17; 55 x 11; 40; 5; two 18-in; torpedoes; J. I. Thornycroft, Hampton.

332-343(MTB): 32; 70 x 20; 40; 12; four 18-in tt; Canadian Power Boat.

336-491(ML Fairmile Type B): 73; 112 x 18¼; 20; 16; one 3-pdr, machine guns, some fitted as minelayers; type built by over 80 firms; gaps in RN number sequence.

347-378(MTB): 52; 72½ x 19¼; 39; 13;

two 21-in tt; various yards.

379-395(MTB): 46¾; 73 x 19½; 39½; 13; four 18-in tt; Vosper, Portsmouth.

396-411(MTB): 52; 72½ x 19¼; 39; 13; two 21-in tt; various yards.

412-418(MTB): 51½; 71¾ x 20¾; 39; 17; two 18-in tt; British Power Boat Co, Hythe, 1942-45.

419-423(MGB): 35; 81 x 20; 40; 12; two 21-in tt; transferred Lease/Lend to RN.

430-432(MTB): 51½; 71¾ x 20¾; 39; 17; two 18-in tt; British Power Boat Co, Hythe.

434-500(MTB): 51½; 71¾ x 20¾; 39; 17; two 18-in tt; British Power Boat Co, Hythe; gaps in RN number sequence.

492-500(ASRL): 73; 112 x 18¼; 20; 16; Fairmile Type B motor launch, completed as A/S rescue.

501-509(MGB/MTB): 95; 117 x 20¼; 28; 21; two 21-in tt, light armament; Camper & Nicholson, Gosport, 1941; *504-508* completed as blockade runners, carrying 45 tons of cargo, *504* rnd *Hopewell*, *505* rnd *Nonsuch*, *506* rnd *Gay Viking*, *507* rnd *Gay Corsair*, *508* rnd *Master Standfast*.

502-509(MTB): 51½; 71¾ x 20¾; 39; 17; two 18-in tt; British Power Boat Co, Hythe; gaps in RN number sequence.

511-518(MGB/MTB): 115; 117 x 22¼; 31; 30; four 18-in tt, two 6-pdr, light armament; Camper & Nicholson, Gosport, 1944 (5000 added to numbers in 1947).

511-553(ASRL): 73; 112 x 18¼; 20; 16; Fairmile Type B motor launch, completed as A/S rescue.

519-522(MTB): 51½; 71¾ x 20¾; 39; 17; two 18-in tt; British Power Boat Co, Hythe; gaps in RN number sequence.

523-530(MTB): 49; 72½ x 19½; 40; 13; two 18-in tt; Vosper, Portsmouth.

532-533(MTB): 49; 72½ x 19½; 40; 13; two 18-in tt; Vosper, Portsmouth.

534-600(ML Fairmile Type B): 73; 112 x 18¼; 20; 16; one 3-pdr, machine guns, some fitted as minelayers; type built by over 80 firms; gaps in RN number sequence.

601-800(MGB/MTB Fairmile Type D): 105; 115 x 21¼; 31; 30; four 18-in tt, heavily armed; Admiralty design, built by many firms; gaps in RN number sequence.

801-933(ML Fairmile Type B): 73; 112 x 18¼; 20; 16; one 3-pdr, machine guns, some fitted as minelayers; type built by over 80 firms; gaps in RN number sequence.

1001-1090(MMS): 360; 139 x 26;10; 21; two 20-mm; various yards, 1943-45, wood construction; gaps in RN number sequence.

1001-1600(ML): 46; 72 x 15; 11-12; 10; machine guns, depth charges, sweeping gear; type built by over 40 firms; rnd *Harbour Defence Motor Launch (HDML)* 1944, rnd *Seaward Defence Motor Launch (SDML)* 1949, except 1001, 1053, 1081, 1085, 1091, 1393, 1411, rnd *Survey Motor Launch (SML) 1946;* gaps in RN number sequence.

2001-2284(BYMS): see 1-284.

2001(Experimental ML Fairmile Type F):

4001-4004(ML Fairmile Type B): 73; 112 x 18¼; 20; 16; one 3-pdr, machine guns, some fitted as minelayers; type built by over 80 firms.

5001-5015(MGB/MTB Fairmile Type D): 120; 115 x 21¼; 30; 30; four 21-in tt, heavily armed; Admiralty design, built by many firms; gaps in RN number sequence.

Midget Submarines

X-3-10, X-20-25, XT-1-6: 27 tons; 51 x 5½; two explosive charges.

XE-1-9, 11-12: 30 tons; 53 x 6; two explosive charges.

War losses: X-5, X-6, X-7, scuttled in Alten Fjord, Sept 22, 1943; *X-8,* scuttled in North Sea, Sept 17, 1943; *X-9,* foundered in tow, North Sea, Oct 15, 1943; *X-10,* scuttled North Sea, Oct 3, 1943; *X-22,* lost in collision, Pentland Firth, Feb 7, 1944; *XE-11,* lost in collision, Mar 6, 1945, salved and scrapped.

Drifters

Brine, Cascade, Cloud, Coldsnap, Crescent Moon, Ebbtide, Eddy, Fumarole, Halo, Harmattan, Horizon, Indian Summer, Landfall, Leeward, Lunar Bow, Mist, Noontide, Onyx, Raleigh (ex-*Glitter*), **Seabreeze, Sheen, Shower, Sunset, Whirlpool:** 199; 93 x 19¾; 9; --; one 6 or 3-pdr. *War loss: Eddy,* May 26, 1942;

Motor Fishing Vessels (MFV)

1-442: 50 tons; 64½ ft long.
601-995: 28 tons, 50 ft long.
1001-1258: 114 tons; 75½ ft long.
1501-1610: 200 tons; 97¼ ft long.

Landing Craft

1-99(LCT(1)): tank landing craft; 226; 151 x 29; two 2-pdr.

2-1021(LST(2)): tank landing ship; 1625; 327¾ x 50; one 12-pdr; transferred from US under Lease/Lend to RN.

3-537(LCI(L)): infantry landing craft (large); 234; 158½ x 23; four 20-mm; built in US, transferred Lease/Lend to RN.

100-299(LCT(2)): tank landing craft; 296; 160 x 31; two 2-pdr.

300-499(LCT(3)): tank landing craft; 350; 190¾ x 31; two 2-pdr.

500-upwards(LCT(4)): tank landing craft; 200; 187¼ x 39; two 20-mm.

501-upwards (LCI(S)): infantry landing craft (small); 63; 105 x 21½; two 20-mm; 2000 added to each number in 1944.

2001-upwards(LCT(5) and LCT(6)): tank landing craft; 143; 120 x 33; two 20-mm.

3001-upwards(LST(3)): tank landing ship; see Fleet List & Alphabetical Sections.

4001-upwards(LCT(8)): tank landing craft; 657; 231½ x 39; four 40-mm.

7001-7050(LCT(3)): tank landing craft; 350; 190¾ x 31; two 2-pdr.

Other landing craft: landing craft, assault (LCA); landing craft, mechanised (LCM); landing craft, personnel (LCP); landing craft, vehicle (LCV); landing craft, support (LCS); landing craft gun (LCG); landing craft, rocket (LCT **(R)**); landing barges and Z-lighters.

War losses: over 1300 landing craft were lost during the war.